EUROPEAN INTERNAL SECURITY

MANCHESTER
1824

Manchester University Press

EUROPE IN CHANGE GENERAL EDITORS: THOMAS CHRISTIANSEN AND EMIL KIRCHNER

The formation of Croatian national identity
ALEX J. BELLAMY
The European Union and the accommodation of Basque difference in Spain
ANGELA K. BOURNE
Theory and reform in the European Union, 2nd edn
DIMITRIS N. CHRYSSOCHOOU, MICHAEL J. TSINISIZELIS, STELIOS STAVRIDIS AND KOSTAS IFANTIS
From integration to integrity: Administrative ethics and reform in the European Commission
MICHELLE CINI
The transatlantic divide
OSVALDO CROCI AND AMY VERDUN
Germany, pacifism and peace enforcement
ANJA DALGAARD-NIELSEN
The changing European Commission
ED. DIONYSSIS DIMITRAKOPOULOS
Supranational citizenship
LYNN DOBSON
Reshaping Economic and Monetary Union
SHAWN DONNELLY
The time of European governance
MAGNUS EKENGREN
Adapting to European integration? Kaliningrad, Russia and the European Union
ED STEFAN GÄNZLE, GUIDO MÜNTEL AND EVGENY VINOKUROV
An introduction to post-Communist Bulgaria
EMIL GIATZIDIS
Mothering the Union
ROBERTA GUERRINA
Non-state actors in international relations: the case of Germany
ANNE-MARIE LE GLOANNEC
Turkey: facing a new millennium
AMIKAM NACHMANI
Europolis: constitutional patriotism beyond the nation state
PATRIZIA NANZ
The changing faces of federalism
ED. SERGIO ORTINO, MITJA ŽAGAR AND VOJTECH MASTNY
The road to the European Union
Vol. I The Czech and Slovak Republics ED. JACQUES RUPNIK AND JAN ZIELONKA
Vol. II Estonia, Latvia and Lithuania ED. VELLO PETTAI AND JAN ZIELONKA
A political sociology of the European Union: reassessing constructivism
ED. MICHEL MANGENOT AND JAY ROWELL
Democratising capitalism? The political economy of post-Communist transformations in Romania, 1989–2001
LILIANA POP
Europe and civil society: movement coalitions and European governance
CARLO RUZZA
Constructing the path to eastern enlargement
ULRICH SEDELMEIER
Governing Europe's new neighbourhood: partners or periphery?
ED. MICHAEL SMITH, KATJA WEBER AND MICHAEL BAUN
Two tiers or two speeds? The European security order and the enlargement of the European Union and NATO
ED. JAMES SPERLING
Recasting the European order
JAMES SPERLING AND EMIL KIRCHNER
Political symbolism and European integration
TOBIAS THEILER
Rethinking European Union foreign policy
ED. BEN TONRA AND THOMAS CHRISTIANSEN
The European Union in the wake of eastern enlargement
ED. AMY VERDUN AND OSVALDO CROCI
Democratic citizenship and the European Union
ALBERT WEALE
Inclusion, exclusion and the governance of European security
MARK WEBBER

Christian Kaunert

EUROPEAN INTERNAL SECURITY

Towards supranational governance in the Area of Freedom, Security and Justice

MANCHESTER UNIVERSITY PRESS
Manchester and New York

distributed in the United States exclusively by Palgrave Macmillan

Published by Manchester University Press
Oxford Road, Manchester M13 9NR, UK
and Room 400, 175 Fifth Avenue, New York, NY 10010, USA

www.manchesteruniversitypress.co.uk

Distributed in the United States exclusively by
Palgrave Macmillan, 175 Fifth Avenue, New York,
NY 10010, USA

Distributed in Canada exclusively by
UBC Press, University of British Columbia, 2029 West Mall,
Vancouver, BC, Canada V6T 1Z2

British Library Cataloguing-in-Publication Data
A catalogue record for this book is available from the British Library

Library of Congress Cataloging-in-Publication Data applied for

ISBN 978 0 7190 7941 2 hardback

First published 2010

Typeset in Minion with Lithos
by Action Publishing Technology Ltd, Gloucester
Printed in Great Britain
by CPI Antony Rowe Ltd, Chippenham, Wiltshire

Contents

LIST OF TABLES AND ILLUSTRATIONS

Tables

Figures

Preface

The idea for this book originated in my PhD project at the University of Wales Aberystwyth, where I spent some excellent years until 2006. My most heartfelt thanks go to Mike Foley, an exceptional supervisor and great friend. Without his assistance, expertise and kind patience the book would not have been possible. My thanks also go to Alistair Shepherd. His assistance, expertise and endurance have been phenomenal. In addition I am very grateful to Thomas Christiansen and Charlie Burns, who shaped my project from the earlier stages with their ability to comprehend and to criticise at the right moment. This truly made it a much better book. Thanks very much also for the personal support. Furthermore, I am grateful to my former colleagues Roger Scully, Hidemi Suganami, Elena Korosteleva, Martin Alexander, Ken Booth, Richard Wyn Jones, Colin McInnes, Marie Breen Smyth, Jeroen Gunning, Jan Selby and Anwen Elias. They were wonderful colleagues in the Department of International Politics at Aberystwyth during my first year as a young lecturer from 2005 until 2006. In this regard I am also grateful to the Department of International Politics and the University of Wales Aberystwyth for their academic and financial assistance in facilitating this research, as well as the University Association for Contemporary European Studies (UACES) for financing my field research in Brussels. I would also like to thank the Commission officials, Council Secretariat officials and MEPs, as well as the JHA councillors in twenty-six Member States of the European Union and NGO representatives who gave so freely of their time in order to answer questions. In this context I am also grateful to the two external examiners of my PhD, Andrew Geddes and Brigid Laffan.

During work on the book I changed institutions a number of times. After being a young lecturer at the University of Wales Aberystwyth I took a position at the University of Maastricht, and at the University of Salford subsequently. I am most grateful to all these institutions for the support that enabled me to work on the project. I am also particularly grateful to a number of colleagues at the University of Salford. First, John Keiger has been an exceptional source of support, good words, encouragement and guidance. I would like to also mention Gaynor Johnson, Chris Murphy, Jonathan Colman, Lars Berger, Jim Newell, John Callaghan, Eric Grove, Jim Beach, Alaric Searle, Chris Birkbeck, Andrew Cooper, Gaynor Bagnall and Joanne Milner. Finally, I am also grateful for the constant support and the critical questioning of my ideas by my doctoral students, in particular Kamil Zwolski,

Alex MacKenzie, Sergei Mudrov, Viviana Merendino, Briony Callander, Stephen Rozee and Ulrike Hoffmann. In addition, I would also like to thank the Institut Barcelona d'Etudis Internacionals (IBEI), Barcelona, for its support during my research fellowship while I had the privilege of a sabbatical from the University of Salford, as well as the Université Libre de Bruxelles, which hosted me during my research stay in Brussels. I am also grateful to my colleagues from the Jean Monnet Centre of Excellence, Manchester, which embraces the University of Salford, the University of Manchester and Manchester Metropolitan University. I am especially grateful to Neil Nugent, Clive Archer, Stefan Berger and Dimitris Papadimitriou.

While writing the book I also benefited enormously from the criticism and insights of numerous experts in the field. I would like to thank in particular John Occhipinti, Mark Rhinard, Thierry Balzacq, Juliet Lodge, Maria O'Neil, Oldrich Bures, Paul Wilkinson, Paul Rogers, Christina Boswell, Javier Argomaniz, Adrienne Héritier, Katy Hayward, Jane O'Mahony, Ben Tonra, Christopher Kinsey, Emmanuel-Pierre Guittet, John Tonge, Wyn Rees, Claudia Hillebrand, Björn Müller-Wille, Adam Svensden, Giselle Bosse, Karolina Pomorska, Sophie Vanhoonacker and Amandine Scherrer. The support and expertise of the University Association for Contemporary European Studies has also been outstanding. I am particularly grateful to Sue Davis and Luke Foster, as well as Alex Warleigh-Lack, Richard Whitman, Amelia Hadfield, Jenny Fairbrass, David Galbreath and Kenneth Armstrong, as well as Eamonn Butler for his support in taking over the *Journal of Contemporary European Research* in September 2009.

Throughout the entire publication process the series editors, Thomas Christiansen and Emil Kirchner, provided very useful comments and suggestions during the main stages. The support by Tony Mason from Manchester University Press was also exceptional. Completing this book took place over a long period of time during which my private life had to make sacrifices at times. The work could not have been possible without the help and support of a number of people: first, my parents encouraged and supported me throughout my studies and helped me realise my ambition with their support emotionally, financially and intellectually. Moreover, friends in all parts of the world supported me throughout the duration of the project: special thanks to Scott Bryan, Florian Böck, Jarlath Boylan, Joan O'Donoghue, Jörg Schnermann, Marc Weegen, Christian Hofer, Mladen Karalic, Luis Felipe Caicedo, Derya Arslanbuga, Dorothee Fischer, Miles Vrahimis, Euros Jones Evans and Alex Platt. Finally, I would like to thank my wife, Sarah Leonard. Her support has been too great over the years to even mention the endless times of encouragement, support and patience.

C.K.

List of abbreviations

AFSJ	Area of Freedom, Security and Justice
CEAS	Common European Asylum System
CFE	Convention on the Future of Europe
CFI	Court of First Instance
CFSP	Common Foreign and Security Policy
COREPER	Committee of Permanent Representatives
CT	Constitutional Treaty
EAW	European Arrest Warrant
EAP	European Asylum Policy
EC	European Community
ECHR	European Convention on Human Rights
ECJ	European Court of Justice
EEA	European Economic Area, now composed of Norway, Iceland and Liechtenstein plus the EU
EEC	European Economic Community
EP	European Parliament
EPC	European Political Co-operation
EMU	Economic and Monetary Union
EU	European Union, established by the Maastricht Treaty (TEU) and consisting of three pillars: EC, CFSP, JHA
EUROPOL	European Police Office, based in The Hague
IGC	Intergovernmental Conference
IGO	Intergovernmental organisation
IR	International relations
JHA	Justice and home affairs
LT	Lisbon Treaty
NATO	North Atlantic Treaty Organisation
NGO	Non-governmental organisation
PE	Policy entrepreneur
QMV	Qualified majority voting in the Council
SEA	Single European Act, signed February 1986
SPE	Supranational policy entrepreneur
TEC	Treaty establishing the European Communities
TEU	Treaty of European Union, signed at Maastricht, 7 February 1992
TFEU	Treaty on the Functioning of the Union

TOR	Treaty of Rome
UK	United Kingdom
UN	United Nations Organisation
UNHCR	United Nations High Commissioner for Refugees
US	United States of America

1

Introduction

'Thank you, Ireland! It's a great day for Ireland; it's a great day for Europe' (*EUobserver*, 3 October 2009). The words of European Commission President Jose Manuel Barroso expressed the feelings of many decision-makers in Brussels. Ireland's strong 'Yes' to the Lisbon treaty on 2 October 2009 was greeted with widespread relief in Brussels. 'The Irish people have spoken with a clear and resounding voice', a result much welcomed by the Irish Taoiseach, Brian Cowen. He called the Irish vote a 'declaration of intent to remain at the heart of Europe'; 67.1 per cent of the Irish electorate voted in favour of the Lisbon Treaty, while 32.9 per cent voted against. This represents a 20 per cent swing to the 'yes' side when compared with Ireland's rejection of the Lisbon treaty in June 2008 (*EUobserver*, 3 October 2009).

Less obvious to the general European public, the European Commission had become one of the more contentious actors during both Irish referenda on the Lisbon Treaty. Firstly, during the first Irish referendum on the Lisbon Treaty in June 2008, Irish government officials perceived that the fear of losing the 'Irish commissioner' contributed to the success of the 'no' vote. Consequently, Ireland was promised that it would keep its commissioner as part of guarantees EU leaders gave the Irish government in return for holding a second referendum (Euractiv, 15 October 2009). It was agreed to maintain the level of one commissioner per member state if the Lisbon Treaty was ratified in Ireland. As a result of these new promises, the right to an 'Irish commissioner' became one of the selling points for the Lisbon Treaty by the Yes side during the second referendum in October 2009. Secondly, the Commission entered the Irish Lisbon debate by coming under fire for 'gross interference' (*Telegraph*, 29 September 2009) by Patricia McKenna, a former Green MEP who opposed the Lisbon Treaty. Finally, even after the massive success of the 'yes' side, the European Commission stayed at the forefront of the political debate on the role of Ireland in the European Union (EU). In addition to Ireland formally proposing an Irish commissioner candidate early, the Irish government was urged to review its position on key EU portfolios, particularly in the justice and home affairs field, where in recent years Ireland has tended to follow the British line. Both these issues are at the heart of this book: (1) the role of the European Commission and institutions more generally, as well as (2) the policy area of justice and home affairs.

Yet is the Commission so important, actually? If it is not important, why is the right to an Irish commissioner a 'selling point' in the political debate on ratification? These questions link to the subject of debates of long-gone time periods. The question of how important the European Commission is in EU policy-making is even the object of legendary fiction from the early 1980s. In the famous BBC comedy series *Yes, Minister*, the episode 'The devil you know', first broadcast 23 March 1981, deals extensively with the alleged powers of the EU. The fictional character, UK Minister Jim Hacker, becomes upset about the (then) European Economic Community (EEC). A supposed EEC directive 'from Brussels' creates difficulty for his idea of placing a single British order for word processors, thus creating obstacles to 'British' investment in technology. His head of the civil service, Sir Humphrey Appleby, debates with him the pros and cons of the EU, Hacker criticising the Brussels 'gravy train' and his civil servants defending it. Subsequently, as a twist in this episode, Minister Hacker is suggested to become one of the new EU commissioners himself. In the evening, at home with his wife, Hacker laments that if he left Westminster his political career would be a failure. Needless to say, during the course of the next day the argument reverses: the Minister can see the personal benefits that go with a commissioner's position, while his civil servant, Sir Humphrey, can now suddenly appreciate all the disadvantages. In the end, while the Minister is confused, Sir Humphrey manages to convince him to stay in London. Hacker decides to defy the EU directive and to go ahead with his original plan for the word processors: that would be politically popular.

This episode in *Yes, Minister* exposes very clearly ambivalence towards the European Commission. Popular discourse often depicts the EU as an 'undemocratic and bureaucratic monster' imposing its will upon the unwilling and 'sovereignty-less' member states, as indicated by the examples above. The political debate across European countries during the ratification process of the Lisbon Treaty (signed in December 2007), especially Ireland during its two referenda in June 2008 and October 2009, revealed these old stereotypes. The media focus is upon all the negative attributes accorded to the EU – undemocratic, bureaucratic and, ultimately, not 'sexy'. Yet, of course, there is an inherent contradiction in this depiction: either the European Commission (which is often taken as the only representative of the EU) is extraordinarily powerful, and can impose its will upon the member states, or, rather, it is of little importance. Why else would Hacker want to stay in Britain if all power were delegated to the EU? This book will shed new light on such issues by examining the powers of the EU institutions in the policy-making process.

What is this book about?
EU institutions in the Area of Freedom, Security and Justice

This book argues that it is important to evaluate the role of EU institutions for the process of European integration. This debate falls within the dispute between intergovernmentalists (Hoffmann, 1966, 1982; Moravcsik, 1993), supranationalists (Haas, 1958, 1964, 1967; Lindberg, 1963; Lindberg and Scheingold, 1970, 1971; Stone Sweet and Sandholtz, 1997, 1998; Stone Sweet et al., 2001), and institutionalists 'somewhere in between' (Pollack, 1997a, b, 2003; Hix, 1994, 1998; Tallberg, 2002, 2003, 2006, 2008; Beach, 2004a, 2005a; Kaunert, 2005, 2007, 2009) concerning the role of EU institutions in the process of European integration.

Neofunctionalism (the early form of supranationalism), the 'mainstream approach' in the early years of European integration with Haas (1958, 1967) and Lindberg (1963) as the main scholars, used to portray integration as an incremental process where integration in one policy area triggers more integration in other areas due to 'spill-over effects'. This was later countered by intergovernmentalists, such as Moravcsik (1991, 1993, 1998, 1999a, b), who suggested that European integration can best be explained as a series of rational choices made by national leaders (Moravcsik, 1998, p. 18). Nowadays 'institutions matter', especially the Council of Ministers. Some scholars have addressed the question of the sources of bargaining power (Bailer, 2004), the modes of negotiation (Elgström and Jönsson, 2000, 2005), the patterns of coalition formation, the scope for leadership (Tallberg, 2002, 2003, 2006, 2008) and the impact of norms on negotiation behaviour (Lewis, 2005).

This book suggests a reconceptualisation of the framework of supranational policy entrepreneurs (SPEs), which is often referred to by the academic literature that discusses the role of agency in European integration (Moravcsik, 1999a; Hix, 1994, 1998; Pollack, 1997a, b, 2003; Tallberg, 2002, 2003, 2006, 2008; Beach, 2004a, 2005a; Stone Sweet and Sandholtz, 1997, 1998; Stone Sweet et al., 2001; Kaunert, 2005, 2007, 2009). The concept of a political entrepreneur is grounded in the work of Kingdon within the context of US politics. Kingdon (1984, p. 173) suggests a policy-making model starting with the identification of a problem (first stream), which is then followed by a search for alternative solutions (second stream) and a decision among these alternatives (third stream). On some occasions, a 'policy window' opens for the adoption of certain policies. Policy entrepreneurs, 'advocates … willing to invest their resources – time, reputation, money' (ibid., p. 188), stand at this window in order to propose, lobby for and sell a policy proposal. However, as will be demonstrated in Chapter 2, this conceptualisation needs to be extended by using constructivist insights of norm construction and entrepreneurship (Kaunert, 2007, 2009).

Why is it important to reconceptualise policy entrepreneurship? At the political bargaining stage (the politics stream), where decisions amongst different alternatives are taken, the EU is dominated by member states preferences and interests. This is especially the case for the third pillar decision-making through the Council of Ministers. In principle, this would indicate the benefits of a liberal intergovernmental analysis for this policy area. In this view, European integration can best be explained as a series of rational choices made by national leaders and dominated by national interests (Moravcsik 1991, 1993, 1998, 1999a, b). Thus EU integration occurs due to (1) a change in interests within the member states, or (2) the result of a grand political bargain. The role of international institutions is merely to bolster the credibility of interstate commitments (Moravcsik, 1998, p. 18) by ensuring that member states keep their promises and thus dare to agree to a mutually favourable solution without the fear of 'free-riders'.

But where do member states' national interests and preferences come from? Moravcsik (1998) assumes national interests to be exogenous from the EU process. The interests of the member states are stable before they come to the bargaining table. However, it does not seem reasonable to assert that preferences are exogenous. The EU has created a system whereby member states continuously interact at different levels. The claim that this would not alter preferences over time appears doubtful. Even within the context of the international system with less social interaction amongst states, Katzenstein (1996) has convincingly demonstrated how norms and values shape national interests. Constructivist literature clearly shows how these norms change over time (Finnemore, 1996a, b; Finnemore and Sikkink, 1998).

Yet, if national interests and preferences are shaped by different norms and values, as argued later in this book, this implies that a fourth stream – the norm stream – is underpinning the three other streams. Norms consequently influence the definition of political problems, the search for policy alternatives and finally the national preferences in the politics stream where decisions are taken. How can norms be constructed and how can they be observed? Firstly, actors provide reasons for action. The SPE constantly pushes for his reasons for action to become accepted as a norm, albeit in competition with other actors. This is the first stage of norm creation in the norm life cycle as described by Finnemore and Sikkink (1998), and is followed by the norm socialisation stage. Eventually a norm becomes the dominant norm. Consequently, SPEs are important in the social construction and reconstruction of norms that steer the political movement of the other streams.

This book suggests different ways in which political entrepreneurs can achieve this:

- *First-mover advantage.* SPEs need to come in faster with their proposals than their rivals.
- *Persuasion strategy.* As suggested above, in order to achieve acceptance, the SPE need to convince other actors of the reasons for the action suggested.

- *Alliances.* It is vital for the SPE to form initial alliances with other powerful actors to create a bandwagon effect, whereby more actors will want to join the 'winning team'.

Furthermore, this book argues that it is important to conceptualise the EU institutions' political role in the integration process on two levels: (1) the constitutional level of the Treaties of the EU (the Lisbon Treaty), and (2) on the policy-making level (AFSJ). In agreement with Christiansen (2002), treaty-making in the EU is a process dependent on the policy level, and not separate from it. The treaty level provides the legal tools required at the policy level. Yet, without policy change, there is no need to alter the existing tools or to provide new ones. Thus, given that one level depends on the other, it is crucial to analyse and evaluate the role of the European institutions on both levels.

This book connects with the broader literature, where a number of scholars have identified a prominent role for the European Commission (Haas, 1958, 1964, 1967; Lindberg, 1963; Lindberg and Scheingold, 1970, 1971; Puchala, 1971, 1984; Stone Sweet and Sandholtz, 1997, 1998; Stone Sweet et al., 2001; Pollack, 1997a, b, 2003; Hix, 1994, 1998; Tallberg, 2002, 2003, 2006, 2008; Beach, 2004a, 2005a; Kaunert, 2005, 2007, 2009), and increasingly the Council Secretariat, in a number of policy areas, such as telecommunications (Fuchs, 1994, 1995), equal opportunities (Mazey, 1995) and research (Peterson, 1995b).

This book focuses on the Area of Freedom, Security and Justice (AFSJ) at the policy and treaty levels; primarily on four grounds. Firstly, the academic literature has virtually neglected the topic, with the notable exception of Uçarer (2001a), who provided a formal analysis of the institutional powers of the Commission in the Area of Freedom, Security and Justice, but not of its political role. Areas of 'high politics', or 'security', are generally perceived to be the prerogative of the nation-state. The theoretical assumptions regarding the primacy of states therefore blind the academic examination of the question of the importance of the Commission.

Secondly, it is amongst the most extreme, historically deviant and hardest cases for examining SPE behaviour. It represents an area of 'high politics' and security concerns, as well as providing the weakest institutional arrangements, both in the policy area and in the treaty negotiations. Hence, this selection of a 'hard case' ensures that it is possible to generalise the conclusions of the present study to the widest possible range of EU policy-making areas. Thirdly, the AFSJ has experienced significant policy developments since the late 1990s. Jörg Monar (1999b) emphasises the fact that there has been no other example of a policy-making area which made its way so quickly and comprehensively to the centre of the treaties and to the top of the EU's policy-making agenda. After major treaty revisions in Amsterdam (1997), Nice (2001) and an increased political impetus at Tampere (1999) and the Hague

(2004), the area appears as one of the most promising policy fields for integration in the EU in the foreseeable future. This process has deepened even more significantly after the terrorist attacks in the US on 11 September 2001, in Madrid on 11 March 2004 and in London on 7 July 2005.

Fourthly, there are also important reasons to examine the interplay between treaty negotiations and policy-making. Moravcsik (1999a) attempts to disprove the concept of supranational policy entrepreneurship (SPE) mainly by focusing on the 'five major decisions' – the grand bargains – and therefore the process of treaty reform. Wincott (1995, p. 602) rightly criticised him for making a one-sided analysis. A concern with negotiations between states over major constitutional innovations is too narrow a focus to yield conclusive results. Wincott finds it hardly surprising that Moravcsik came to the view that the European Community is primarily motivated by the aggregation and conciliation of national interest, given his research attention. It is difficult to separate the policy-making from the architecture that creates the policy-making structures in the first place. Christiansen (2002, p. 5) suggests that the significance of the European Commission in the EU's policy process is well documented and widely recognised, which is rather different from treaty reform, with some exceptions (Ross, 1995; Dinan, 2000; Christiansen and Jorgensen, 1998; Gray, 2001; Budden, 2002; Falkner, 2002). Therefore, in order to analyse the role of the European institutions, this book combines an analysis of the Lisbon Treaty in relation to the Area of Freedom, Security and Justice with an analysis of the policy-making in the same area.

Why is this book relevant?
The growth of the Area of Freedom, Security and Justice

Since the events of 9/11 it has been argued by some scholars that security has become the dominant force in the Area of Freedom, Security and Justice (Huysmans, 2000, 2004; Bigo, 1996, 1998a, b, c, d, 2001, 2002; Guild, 1999, 2002, 2003a, b, c, 2004, 2006; Guiraudon, 2000, 2003). In this context, 'securitisation' refers to the theoretical suggestion that policy objects are presented as security threats, based on the framework by the so-called 'Copenhagen school' (Buzan, 1991; Buzan et al., 1998; Waever et al., 1993, 1995). Levy (2005: 35) suggests that 9/11 represents a turning point because 'the trend towards liberalisation seemed to be stopped dead in its tracks by the events of 9/11'. Some non-governmental organisations (Human Rights Watch, Amnesty International and Statewatch) have also expressed their fear that security concerns could affect the EU policy.

However, this fear should be counter-intuitive. Especially the EU is well known for its legalistic approach to policy problems, which aims to appear to always follow the letter of the law; in fact the Commission is often derided for being technocratic. It seems thus counter-intuitive that the EU would 'securitise'.

Moreover, this goes against several academic arguments that were often made about the Area of Freedom, Security and Justice. Amongst academic scholars, the argument has been advanced that EU governments decided to 'venue shop'; they decided to circumvent domestic pressures and obstacles, and therefore 'escaped' to legislate at the EU level, where they were protected from these issues (Joppke, 1998, 2001; Freeman, 1998; Guiraudon, 2000, 2001, 2003; Boswell, 2003a, b, 2008; Ellermann, 2008; Geddes, 2000, 2001; Stetter, 2000, 2007; Thielemann, 2001a, b, 2004, 2005, 2006; Thielemann and Dewan, 2006; Lavenex, 1998, 1999, 2001a, b, 2004, 2006; Occhipinti, 2003). EU member states, in this argument, have thus decided to enhance their co-operation in a process driven by national bureaucracies. These state-centred accounts (especially Joppke, 1998; Freeman, 1998) stress the resilience of nation-states, which make use of the EU as a device for attaining policy objectives unlikely to be achieved at the domestic level alone.

This book intends to fill a distinct gap in the scholarship on European internal security and EU policy-making. Although a growing body of literature has emerged that provides regional and thematic explorations of the EU justice and home affairs policies (see Balzacq and Carrera, 2005, 2006; Bures, 2006; Bossong, 2008; Boswell, 2003b, 2008; Friedrichs, 2005; Guild, 2002; Geddes, 2000; Guiraudon, 2000; Kaunert, 2007, 2009; Mitsilegas, Monar and Rees, 2003; Occhipinti, 2003), crucially, there is no book that addresses the entire Area of Freedom, Security and Justice).

Furthermore, the existing literature on policies that we might classify as components of the AFSJ discusses them in isolation from one another. There are some excellent individual studies of asylum, migration and police co-operation (Joppke, 1998, 2001; Freeman, 1998; Guiraudon, 2000, 2001, 2003; Boswell, 2003a, b, 2008; Ellermann, 2008; Geddes, 2000, 2001; Stetter, 2000, 2007; Thielemann, 2001a, b, 2004, 2005, 2006; Thielemann and Dewan, 2006; Lavenex, 1998, 1999, 2001a, b, 2004, 2006; Occhipinti, 2003), but not of the entire Area of Freedom, Security and Justice.

The critical value of the present study is thus twofold. Not only does it provide a comprehensive picture of EU activities in this policy area, but it also seeks to explore the role of EU institutions from a theoretically informed perspective. This further allows considerable policy relevance. As such, this book constitutes an important and original input in the debate on European internal security.

Methodological issues

The methodology selected for this book is the so-called 'triangulation of methods' (Neuman, 1999, p. 124; Blaikie, 2000, p. 262), which has been endorsed by several scholars, including Checkel (1999a, b). In practice, this means that empirical observations have been analysed from three different angles: (1) the academic literature on the AFSJ (2) the most crucial policy documents, and (3) elite interviews with actors and decision-makers in the area.

How was this research process organised? The initial findings of the documentary analysis were the starting points of the triangulation process. It was therefore of crucial importance to corroborate and substantiate the initial findings from the documentary analysis with evidence from in-depth semi-structured interviews. This is the principal reason why the researcher conducted elite interviews with 102 actors and decision-makers. The 102 interviewees could be subdivided as follows: (1) twenty-eight officials and senior officials in the European Commission, (2) forty-four JHA counsellors in twenty-four out of twenty-seven Permanent Representations of the member states and the candidate country Turkey (3) nine officials from the Council Secretariat, (4) five Members of the European Parliament (Committee on Civil Liberties, Justice and Home Affairs, LIBE) (5) twelve non-governmental organisation (NGO) representatives, (6) two officials from the intergovernmental organisations (IGOs) UN High Commissioner for Refugees (UNHCR) and the International Organisation for Migration (IOM), and (7) two academic experts in the field.

Which documents were analysed in this research project? This book entails a systematic analysis of the EU official documents relating to the AFSJ, which include Green Papers, White Papers and communications from the Commission, as well as decisions, framework decisions, directives and action plans which were adopted by the Council. It also analyses press releases, speeches and official statements, as well as documentation for the public at large, and the content of the Europa website (http://www.europa.eu.int).

With regard to documents, one must note that the area has undergone significant changes over the last few years. In the early years of the Schengen co-operation, before 1997, not even the European Parliament had access to some crucial documents pertaining to this policy area. Nowadays, significant amounts of documents are legally available from the sources cited above. Nevertheless, this was achieved only after intense public shaming of the EU institutions by the non-governmental organisation Statewatch. Its founder, Tony Bunyan, made frequent complaints to the European Ombudsman, who then decided to ask the European Council to disclose a significant number of previously undisclosed documents (European Ombudsman, 1056/25 November 96/STATEWATCH/UK/IJH). This increased the transparency of the EU decision-making process. Nonetheless, there are still some internal documents which are not available to the public. Those predominantly concern the negotiation stage of policies. However, Statewatch (www.statewatch.org) occasionally manages to acquire important documents that are not officially in the public domain. This facility has contributed to significantly increase the research opportunities open to academics interested in analysing traditionally secretive policy areas. Thanks are due to Tony Bunyan for achieving greater transparency regarding the AFSJ policy-making process.

With regard to the Lisbon Treaty (LT) and its predecessor, the Constitutional Treaty (CT), significant documents were published on the Convention website (http://european-convention.eu.int). This website contained all the meeting schedules of the different working groups, including the minutes of the different meetings, a list of attendance of working group members, and the contributions by all Convention members to both the working groups and the plenary sessions. All in all, this was more than enough information for this treaty stage. However, once the Intergovernmental Conference (IGC) started (for both the CT and the LT), the internal documents became classified under diplomatic secrecy and were consequently not available to the general public. It was therefore necessary to rely on triangulating the process at this stage from the document output before the IGC, the final results of the IGC, and interviews during the IGC with officials present at the discussion table.

Structure of the book

The book is divided into seven chapters. **Chapter 1** conceptualises the role of the different EU institutions, especially the European Commission, in the European integration process, with particular reference to the concepts of supranational policy entrepreneurship. Despite the continued importance of member states in the EU, increasingly, institutional actors such as the European Commission or the Council Secretariat are gaining in importance. Thus an examination of the role of EU institutions, in particular the European Commission, is crucial in order to have a comprehensive understanding of European governance. This chapter has two main aims: to provide a framework for analysis of the potential role of and powers of EU institutions, and to situate this framework within the existing EU integration literature and its conceptualisation of the role and powers of the EU institutions.

The chapter demonstrates that the literature on European integration is well equipped to deal with questions of agency. The academic literature (Moravcsik, 1999a; Pollack, 2003; Beach, 2005a; Stone Sweet and Sandholtz, 1997, 1998; Stone Sweet et al., 2001) often utilises the concept of supranational policy entrepreneurship (SPE) when discussing and evaluating the political role of the European institutions. This concept builds on the works of Kingdon within the context of US politics, who in turn builds on March and Olsen (Kingdon, 1984, p. 173). This research project engages with Kingdon (1984) and further refines his concepts in order to create an adequate conception of the role of European institutions in the Area of Freedom, Security and Justice. The chapter outlines and synthesises the public policy model by John Kingdon with constructivist international relations literature.

Chapter 2 analyses the institutional and normative changes in the Area of Freedom, Security and Justice up to the Tampere Council Summit in 1999, which was the first European Council to be entirely dedicated to this policy area. Firstly, an analysis of the legal norms in the policy area is used in order to demonstrate the changing nature of the 'constitutional' arrangements. Secondly, this chapter argues that these legal and normative changes are indicative of a political process that is aimed at constructing a step towards supranational governance in the Area of Freedom, Security and Justice. The aim of this chapter is to map the historical development of the political norms of decision-makers in order to understand the contextual environment in which the political entrepreneurs operate. Political agency in the AFSJ needs to build on this environment in order to facilitate policy change; thus a comprehension of the normative environment is indispensable in order to analyse agency.

Chapter 3 investigates the construction of an Area of Freedom, Security and Justice in response to terrorism. Since the terrorist attacks on 11 September 2001, the first and foremost security threat to enable the construction of the AFSJ is terrorism. Some authors have argued that it has become the 'greatest security threat of our times' (Hoffmann, 2006; Wilkinson, 2006). This chapter will argue that EU institutions have capitalised on the presence of this 'security threat' in order to drive forward the process of European integration, despite some diverging as to which extent EU competences matter in the fight against terrorism (Bures, 2006; Zimmermann, 2006; Gregory, 2005; Kaunert, 2007).

Chapter 4 analyses the external dimension of counter-terrorism in the EU. Following the 11 March 2004 attacks on Madrid, the EU stepped up its efforts against terrorism (Wilkinson, 2006, p. 172), with particular emphasis on the external dimension. The latter represents an important element in the possible construction of an Area of Freedom, Security and Justice, as making the EU secure depends at least to some extent on successful co-operation with countries outside the EU. This chapter examines different cases of this recent and comparatively less developed policy area. The chapter will demonstrate that the EU institutions, in particular the Commission and the Council Secretariat, have played an active and significant role in these policy developments – the role of a SPEs – albeit to different degrees across policy areas.

Chapter 5 examines the second step in the construction of an Area of Freedom, Security and Justice. The first major security threat has been terrorism as analysed in the two preceding chapters. However, more quietly, asylum and migration have also come to be seen as a significant security threat (Huysmans, 2000; Guild, 1999, 2002; Guiraudon, 2000, 2001). Policy developments after 9/11 have prompted a series of scholars (Faist, 2004; Karyotis, 2003; Huysmans, 2000; Ceyhan and Tsoukala, 2002; Kostakopolou, 2000) to argue that migration has been constructed as a security threat in Europe. This chapter analyses the role of the EU institutions in the construction of this 'Area of Freedom, Security and Justice'. This chapter will make two significant points. Firstly, the role of the EU institutions in EU asylum and migration has been significantly underestimated. Contrary to expectations, EU institutions, and especially the European Commission, played the significant role of a Supranational policy entrepreneur for the Common European Asylum System (CEAS). However, the strategy of the Commission in asylum policy was significantly different from its counter-terrorism strategy. While the Commission actively constructed terrorism politically as a 'European threat' rather than providing space for national threat constructions, it never attempted to construct asylum as a threat. Thus, its policy strategy was more difficult to achieve than in counter-terrorism, successful though it was.

Chapter 6 analyses the external dimension of asylum and migration, including border management. The external dimension of asylum and migration, part of the foreign policy dimension of the AFSJ, represents an increasingly important element of EU policy activity. With the establishment of internal competences in the area of asylum and border management, it represents the acceptance of third countries of EU actorness, notably in the external dimension of the policies on asylum and borders. This chapter argues that mainly the European Commission played the role of a supranational policy entrepreneur in the external dimension of asylum and border management. In this area, the Commission achieved two main successes: (1) it pushed for, and succeeded partially, with its 'root causes' approach to refugee matters, while at the same time (2) managing to divert the attention from the extraterritorial control approach advocated particularly by the UK. It is important to note that the role of an SPE in this particular case involves the shaping of the agenda through the pushing of its policies, as well as through the diversion of the actions of rival policy entrepreneurs, such as the UK government.

Finally, **Chapter 7** investigates the role of EU institutional actors at the treaty level in the process of constructing an 'Area of Freedom, Security and Justice'. It also analyses the role of the EU institutions in the communitarisation of the Area of Freedom, Security and Justice, in the Treaty establishing a Constitution for Europe, and thus subsequently in the Lisbon Treaty (2007). But what is the role of the European institutions, in particular the Commission, in this treaty-building process? This chapter argues that the Commission in particular (through alliances with other institutional actors during the Convention phase) managed to contribute to a shift in norms incrementally over a decade, but substantially and specifically during the negotiations of the Constitutional Treaty and subsequently the Lisbon Treaty. The Commission acted with the support and the use of other supranational actors during the Convention, without which this result would have been difficult, if not impossible, to obtain. Thus the role of EU institutional actors is significant for as long as they act in unison.

2

Supranational policy entrepreneurship and EU institutions

> Let us remember what we are talking about here. We are talking about a European Commission and a President of the European Commission. I would suggest that the super-bureaucrat, Jean Monnet, is resting very easily in his grave because the Commission model that he wanted is here. . . . What we have today is a European Union that is effectively ruled by unelected bureaucrats based in Brussels, issuing directives and regulations with which this House can do nothing other than tamper. (Farage, 11 October 2004)

EU institutions have become very controversial, either for their absolute power, or, alternatively and conversely, for their impotence. The UK Independence Party leader in the European Parliament, Neil Farage, especially mocks the European Commission as the epitome of all that 'is wrong' with the EU. At the election in 2004 of the outgoing (and re-'elected' in 2009) Commission President José Manuel Barrosso, Farage presented the Commission as the traditional stereotype of 'unelected bureaucrats'. More important, it was presented as an institution that could issue 'directives and regulations with which this House [the European Parliament] can do nothing other than tamper' (Farage, 11 October 2004). This quote underlines ambivalent mixture of fear and admiration with regards to the role of the European Commission, notably by Eurosceptics in Britain and beyond. It is perceived as a strange mix of being bureaucratic yet politically successful. To Jean Monnet, the first President of the High Authority, the predecessor of the Commission, it was to be an independent arbiter of the European interest (Monnet, 1978), whereas to Walter Hallstein it was a body committed to economic and political integration (Hallstein, 1972). The 'heyday' of success for the Commission is supposed to have been the days of Delors, during which the single market and the economic and monetary union were designed. More recently, scholars (Kurpas et al., 2008) have suggested that the 'heyday' of the Commission in the Delors era is in decline, to which the 2004 'Bing Bang enlargement' was expected to contribute to. 'More would add up to less': a larger Union would come at the expense of a weaker Commission. Thus, several authors (see Settembri, 2007; Kurpas et al., 2008; Peterson and Birdsall, 2008) have suggested multiple sources of pressure which explain how and why the role, work and status of the European Commission have changed: (1) the rise of new modes of EU governance and (2) administrative reforms in the Commission and changed leadership under President José Manuel Barroso.

This presents an immediate puzzle. On the one hand, the Commission has the reputation of being politically successful, especially by those who dislike it. On the other hand, it is curiously bureaucratic, independent, the 'guardian of the treaties' (Nugent, 2001). This implies a neutral institution which does not get involved politically on either side of the debate. However, Matláry (1997, p. 140) suggests differently: 'the Commission is no neutral arbiter or technocracy, but a player with vested interests of its own to promote'. Its main interests are to establish itself as a crucial actor in different policy areas and thus to drive forward the process of European integration. Peterson and Birdsall (2008, p. 69) therefore make the argument that, in fact, it is not just a supranational actor defending the 'composite, supranational, general European interest' but also pursues its own institutional interests. Furthermore, it can also act as an intergovernmental organisation due to the fact that members of the College of Commissioners or civil servants from the administrative structures cannot fully independent from external pressure. This confirms the depiction of the Commission as a politico-administrative hybrid, which is due to the dual nature of its internal organisation, consisting of a highly political College of Commissioners, as well as the services of the Commission, or Directorates General (DGs) (Nugent, 2001). Clearly, these are positions which are not easily reconciled, which is reflected in the academic debate (for examples, see Haas, 1958, 1964, 1967; Lindberg, 1963; Lindberg and Scheingold, 1970, 1971; Puchala, 1971, 1984; Stone Sweet and Sandholtz, 1997, 1998; Stone Sweet et al., 2001; Pollack, 1997a, b, 2003; Hix, 1994, 1998; Tallberg, 2002, 2003, 2006, 2008; Beach, 2004a, 2005a; Kaunert, 2005, 2007, 2009).

So what is the role of the Commission in the EU? This book argues, despite the continued importance of member states in the EU, increasingly, institutional actors such as the European Commission or the Council Secretariat are gaining in importance politically. Yet, 'can faceless bureaucrats, unelected and without power of purse or sword really influence the decisions of powerful nation-states? Are we seeing the emergence of a 'new statecraft' grounded in international networks managed by supranational political entrepreneurs?' (Moravcsik, 1999a).

In the article, 'A New Statecraft? Supranational Entrepreneurs and International Co-operation', Andrew Moravcsik (1999a) questions whether unelected bureaucrats without financial and legal enforcement powers would actually be able to influence political decisions made by national governments. Consequently, he disputes the emerging power of international networks of supranational policy entrepreneurs. However, this leads to the immediate puzzle of why Moravcsik would feel the need to answer this question if not for there is significant amount of evidence underlining the importance of SPEs.

Various scholars (Haas, 1958, 1964, 1967; Lindberg, 1963; Lindberg and Scheingold, 1970, 1971; Puchala, 1971, 1984; Moravcsik, 1999a; Hix, 1994, 1998; Pollack, 1997a, b, 2003; Tallberg, 2002, 2003, 2006, 2008; Beach, 2004a, 2005a; Stone Sweet and Sandholtz, 1997, 1998; Stone Sweet et al., 2001; Kaunert, 2005, 2007, 2009) examine the role of European institutions in detail, notably through the prism of Supranational Political Entrepreneurship (SPE), a concept derived from John Kingdon (1984). This book suggests it is beneficial to use Kingdon's (1984) original concept rather than the more recent interpretations and references.

Thus, an examination of the role of EU institutions, in particular the European Commission, is crucial in order to have a comprehensive understanding of European governance. This chapter conceptualises the institutions' role in the integration process on two levels: (1) the treaty level of the EU and (2) the policy-making level. In agreement with Christiansen (2002), treaty-making in the EU is a process entirely dependent on the policy level, and not separate from it. This chapter has three aims: to provide an introduction to the concept of supranational policy entrepreneurship in order to provide avenues for further development; to review the existing EU integration literature and its conceptualisation of the role and powers of the EU institutions as supranational policy entrepreneurs; and finally to provide a framework for analysis for this book.

Theorising policy entrepreneurship in the European Union

Objectives for the theoretical framework of supranational policy entrepreneurship

What does the SPE framework need to explain? Firstly and foremost, the theoretical framework needs to explain policy change within the framework of the EU institutions. This book will suggest that qualitative approaches, which are more commonly used by interpretative social science (Burns, 2000), are ideally suited for this endeavour. These approaches allow to a greater extent to investigate people's beliefs, values and actions. The meanings of social activities can be put into a proper social context. This can be traced to German sociologist Max Weber (1864–1920) and German philosopher Wilhelm Dilthey (1833–1911). Weber argued that social science needed to study meaningful social actions. These actions can be analysed as more non-linear and cyclical.

Kingdon (1984) provides an excellent starting point for such a framework. He incorporates many important aspects of public policy in his model which is a very good representation of EU policy-making, notwithstanding the fact that his model was developed in the context of US politics.

Given the federal and confederal elements of EU politics, such a public policy model invariably comes very close to the defining features of EU governance. In the foreword of the second edition of his book, Thurber (Kingdon, 2003, p. vii) argues that Kingdon provides an interactive model of identifiable forces that drive the policy process and an outstanding tool for students and teachers for understanding the policy process. In short, one can agree with John (1998) and Richardson (2001, pp. 3–24) that Kingdon provides a useful tool for understanding policy-making in the EU.

Secondly, it is important for the theoretical framework to take account of the fact that agency is needed in the policy-making process and structural forces alone do not determine the policy outcomes. This relates to Alexander Wendt's (1999) suggestion that agents and structures are mutually constitutive – one of the premises of International Relations constructivism. The challenge relates to what determines policy change within the system, or respectively, the EU policy-making system. Neither agents nor structures can define the other but they must exist in a relationship of mutual constitution (Ruggie, 1998a, b; Wendt, 1999). International life is primarily (though not exclusively) about social rather than material life. The latter is given meaning only by the former. This encompasses all of the complex norms, institutions, rules and shared practices that international and European lives involve. Shared knowledge influences state behaviour as well as state interests.

Thirdly, the theoretical framework needs to be beneficial in cases where the object of enquiry is somewhere between a state and an international system, such as the EU. The EU is clearly not a state yet – even though it shares some attributes of one, such as a common currency. It is not a self-proclaimed state by international law, nor does any other state recognise the EU as a state. In fact, it may never become a state. Yet, its attributes are clearly more advanced than generally expected from an international organisation. The EU works according to its own laws (EU laws, not international law), has a legislature (The Council and the European Parliament), and two quasi-executives with the Council and the Commission. It is a union of states and citizens according to the treaties – and thus somewhere between an international organisation (an organisation of states only) or a state (a community of citizens). Christiansen, Jørgensen and Wiener (2001) make a note in the introduction of their book of the paradox that the 'European construction' has not received any systematic attention from constructivist scholars. This is despite the fact that the EU construction is often regarded as advanced enough to use comparative political science tools to analyse it. Hence they argue that in order to analyse the constructive force of European integration, one needs a research context which is not closed towards interpretive tools, i.e. constructivism.

Constructivism is an appropriate approach for understanding the dynamics of areas 'under construction'. The EU is in itself a perfect example of an organisation under 'permanent construction' due to its dynamic and evolutionary nature. However, the case study selected in this book, which will be discussed in greater detail in the following chapters, is even special for the EU. The Area of Freedom, Security and Justice (AFSJ) has been one of the anomalies of EU policy-making over the last few years, as it provides the most complicated decision-making structures of all areas with the Treaties of Amsterdam and Nice. The chapter on the historical developments in the AFSJ will demonstrate how much these decision-making structures have been constructed and reconstructed over and over again during the last fifteen years.

Furthermore, Christiansen et al. (2001) argue that there are a number of particular reasons concerned with a European integration, which make it such a fertile ground for constructivists. As European integration works through the force of law, legal scholars (Weiler 1991, 1999) have argued for decades how important norms are for our understanding of the EU. The disciplines of sociology and law have analysed norms for decades. Constructivist scholars often use norms as analytical concepts as well. In fact, the EU is structured through a saturated regime of legal and institutional norms, i.e. the *acquis communautaire*. Eventually, new norms are often codified in EU law.

Finally, an inclusion of the concept of norms is highly beneficial for the realities of EU policy-making. More often than not, the nature of the EU between a fully fledged state and an international organisation means that different norms are competing with one another. National sovereignty is the prevailing and generally accepted norm within the international system. Of course, there are international developments to the contrary such as humanitarian interventions, but overall this remains true. Yet, within the EU system this norm is constantly competing with the norm to pool national sovereignty at the EU level. A successful SPE needs to reconstruct and align these norms, before any serious policy proposal be pushed. The differences between these approaches are greater than normally found within established systems, such as within states or on the international level. Thus, a successful SPE in the EU has to be able to construct and reconstruct norms as well as pushing for a new substantive policy. Evidently, this point is more important in the EU than in a federal state like the US.

European integration debate and the role of the European Commission

The following section will demonstrate the fact that there has been a lively debate amongst scholars of European integration over the European Commission's importance and power in policy-making and treaty negotiation (Haas, 1958, 1964, 1967; Lindberg, 1963; Lindberg and Scheingold, 1970, 1971; Puchala, 1971, 1984; Stone Sweet and Sandholtz, 1997, 1998; Stone Sweet et al., 2001; Pollack, 1997a, b, 2003; Hix, 1994, 1998; Tallberg, 2002, 2003, 2006, 2008; Beach, 2004a, 2005a; Kaunert, 2005, 2007, 2009). Very often, this has even been one of the central questions within the literature on

European integration. In fact, one of the distinguishing features of the EU compared to other international organisations is the degree of delegation and functions of EU institutions.

There are three policy-making institutions at the EU level, i.e. the Council, the European Parliament and the European Commission. The Council of the European Union forms, along with the European Parliament, the legislative arm of the EU. It contains Ministers of the governments of each of the twenty-seven member states (Wallace, Wallace and Pollack, 2005). The Council is responsible for adopting legislation, and deals with the day-to-day details of EU policy. It is part of a hierarchy with the European Council at the top, followed by the Council of Ministers, the Committees of Permanent Representatives (COREPER), and other senior preparatory groups (ibid., p. 58). COREPER generally prepares the Council agenda, and negotiates minor and non-controversial matters, leaving controversial issues, and other issues for formal agreement, for discussion by the Council. Below COREPER, civil servants from the member states negotiate in Council Working Groups, often reaching de facto agreement which is formalised through COREPER and the Council of Ministers (Peterson and Shackleton, 2002). In the Area of Freedom, Security and Justice (AFSJ), these working groups of national officials often even act as the decision-makers (Wallace et al., 2005, p. 58).

The Council General Secretariat conducts the administrative work of the Council. Officials from the Secretariat have the responsibility for drafting agendas, keeping records, providing legal advice, processing and circulating documentation, and translating and monitoring policy decisions (Nugent, 1999, pp. 152–153). At a basic level the General Secretariat provides consistent policy advice and support for the rotating Presidencies. The Secretary General also serves as the High Representative for the Common Foreign and Security Policy (CFSP). Indeed, and it has been a remarkable development over the last few years, the Secretariat has been particularly 'successful in gaining an executive role in the more intergovernmental policy areas of the Union' which has led to a redefinition of its relations with the European Commission in some policy areas (Christiansen, 2006, p. 165).

The European Parliament (EP) is the parliamentary body of the EU, directly elected by EU citizens (since 1979) once every five years. It meets in two locations: Strasbourg and Brussels (Wallace et al., 2005, p. 65). In the early years of the EU, the EP had only a marginal role in the policy process due to the 'consultation method'. In the Area of Freedom, Security and Justice, the EP was only required to be consulted throughout the Tampere programme from 1999 to 2004, and thus its role here was different from other policy areas. Since 2004, however, its powers have increased to 'co-decision' in many areas, and are further increased by the Lisbon Treaty. The European Parliament, in general, cannot initiate legislation on its own, but it can amend or veto it in many policy areas. The frequent decision-making method is 'co-decision', which implies a co-legislating role with the Council of Ministers. In general, the Parliament also supervises the European Commission, must approve all appointments to it, and can dismiss it with a vote of censure (Wallace et al., 2005).

The Commission is often described as a hybrid institution as it combines the functions of bureaucracy and executive (Nugent, 2001). This 'split personality' is attributed to the fact that it has political and administrative arms. The political arm consists of commissioners, who are appointed ('elected' with the Lisbon Treaty) via a highly politicised process, and are often former senior national politicians. The administrative arm consists of the Commission's services, appointed in the bureaucratic and meritocratic way. This mixed political and administrative character can be seen lucidly in the nature of the roles of the Commission in the system. It is responsible for initiating and implementing EU policy; however, it is also, as the Union's bureaucracy, responsible for the detailed drafting of legislation. The Commission acts as the conscience of the Community, as it is formally the Guardian of the Treaties and responsible for determining whether policy proposals fall within the EU's competence (Wallace et al., 2005). It also plays a crucial mediating role between the institutions and amongst the member states within the Council.

These functions and delegated powers to the EU institutions, have been the subject of fierce academic debate since the beginning of European integration (Haas, 1958, 1964, 1967; Lindberg, 1963; Lindberg and Scheingold, 1970, 1971; Hoffman, 1966, 1982; Moravcsik, 1993; Stone Sweet and Sandholtz, 1997, 1998; Stone Sweet et al., 2001; Pollack, 1997a, b, 2003; Hix, 1994, 1998; Tallberg, 2002, 2003, 2006, 2008; Beach, 2004a, 2005a; Kaunert, 2005, 2007, 2009). Despite minor disagreements, it is accepted that the European institutions play a very significant role in the first quadrant in Figure 2.1, i.e. on the policy level in areas of low politics, predominantly issues related to the single market of the EU. It is less widely accepted that the institutions, in particular the Commission, play a significant role in the second quadrant, i.e. on the treaty level in areas of low politics. Nonetheless, this book will engage especially with quadrants three and four, i.e. the areas of high politics, of security, at both the policy and the treaty level. The academic literature related to these is virtually absent. The areas of quadrants three and four are generally perceived to be the prerogative of the nation-state. This section will examine the different approaches along largely theoretical lines.

Empirical approaches

A seminal anthropological work on the European Commission is David Coombes's (1970) *Politics and Bureaucracy in the European Community*. This book can be seen as an early work in a series of empirically rich research insights on the Commission. In his analysis, he demonstrates rich empirical data on the bureaucratic structure, the civil service and its composition, and its influence. Nonetheless, according to Coombes, the Commission shows

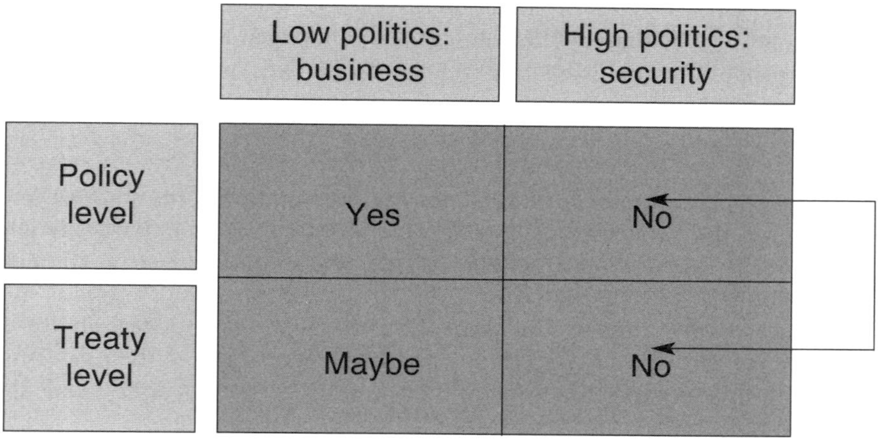

Figure 2.1 The significance of the European Commission: an analytical matrix

deficiencies in not mobilising sources of support for the EU that are truly independent of the national governments. The secretive decision-making is also criticised. His extensive case studies include the Kennedy Round negotiations and the frontier region of Luxembourg–Lorraine. Ultimately, 'the Commission is bound to become a bureaucracy in this functional sense, whatever its constitutional powers may be and whatever the founders of the Community might have envisaged' (ibid., p. 298). Coombes's seminal work strengthened academic interest in the Commission and empirical analyses became increasingly attractive (Cassese, 1987; Louis and Waelbroeck, 1989; Ludlow, 1991; Westlake, 1994).

The second seminal work, Edwards and Spence's (1994) *The European Commission*, brought together a team of commentators, both academics and practitioners, to explain what the Commission is and how it does its business. The work puts the institution into perspective, and provides a detailed and empirically rich description of the College of Commissioners, the Cabinets, the staff and personnel, the structure and functioning of the EC, as well as its execution of Community policy. Again, in the same way as Coombes, it does not provide a comprehensive analysis of the political role of the Commission, and, unfortunately, overlooks this aspect. Nevertheless, it provides important details which can be used for future analyses. In fact, it can be seen as the building block for other significant research (Fuchs, 1994, 1995; Laffan, 1997a; Peterson, 1995a, b, 1999a; Schmidt, 1998; Cram, 2001; Hooghe, 2001).

Nugent's (1997, 2000) *At the Heart of the European Union* provides the third seminal work in this literature. Nugent's book, *The European Commission* (2001), provides further good empirical insights into the working of the organisation, including the different Presidents, the College, the Cabinets, and the Services. In addition, he analyses the leadership function of the Commission, building on his earlier work (Nugent, 1995). In the latter he claims there are several ways in which the Commission can exercise leadership responsibilities structurally, e.g. by shaping the political and policy agendas, bringing forward specific proposals, mobilising support behind initiatives, and guiding proposals through the EU procedures. Nugent groups the factors influencing the EC leadership capacity into two broad categories:

- *The resources:* the constitutional powers, the standing of the commissioners and the President, its knowledge and expertise, its impartiality and neutrality, its duty as an engine of integration, and its central strategic position.
- *The operating context:* the perception of the need and desirability of political activity, the perceptions by the member states of the role of the Commission, and the institutional context. The resources and the operating contexts are interlinked.

Neofunctionalism

While several scholars of European integration have consistently emphasised the importance of European institutions empirically, in particular the European Commission, this has also been at the centre of the debate in the European integration theory. Here, the debate has been markedly controversial. The debate centred on the issue whether strong EU institutions could constitute an explanatory factor in the integration process.

Early neofunctionalist literature addressed supranational institutions and policy entrepreneurship mainly indirectly. As the 'mainstream approach' in the early years of European integration with Haas (1958) and Lindberg (1963) as the main scholars, Neofunctionalism dominated the discussion of the study of European integration for a long time. It portrays integration as an automatic incremental process where integration in one policy area triggers more integration in other areas due to 'spill-over effects'.

Haas (1958) defines European integration as: 'the process whereby political actors in several distinct national settings are persuaded to shift their loyalties, expectations and political activities towards a new centre, whose institutions possess or demand jurisdiction over pre-existing national states' (ibid., p. 16). The work is a systematic study of the process of community formation through international organisations. Furthermore, he explains how the 'loyalty' of the community's citizens can shift towards a new political entity, notably supranational organisations, i.e. the European Commission.

Given the historical setting in which Haas produced his study, he refers to the High Authority, as it was called then, rather than the Commission, as it is called today. He describes it as being anxious to draw on popular support for a policy which would benefit from the so-called 'spill-overs' from other, most notably, economic areas. It relies considerably on groups with long-run positive expectations of this policy, e.g. trade unions, chambers of commerce, various interest groups and, in particular, political elites. He therefore concludes that 'this institutional logic would lead naturally to an increase of supranational responsibilities and thereby to the increasing importance of the ECSC as a focus of loyalty or opposition' (ibid., p. 299). In fact, 'the intergovernmental Council of Ministers would not in fact make any decision without following the studies and recommendations of the Commission' (ibid., p. 312).

Intergovernmentalism

On the other hand, according to Intergovernmentalism, European integration can best be explained as a series of rational choices made by national leaders (Moravcsik, 1998, p. 18). Throughout a large series of works, Moravcsik (1991, 1993, 1995, 1997, 1998, 1999a, b) portrays the EU as largely intergovernmental and dominated by national interests. The national leaders make choices in response to constraints and opportunities derived from economic interests of powerful domestic constituents and the relative power of each state in the international system. International institutions are merely there to bolster the credibility of interstate commitments (Moravcsik, 1998, p. 18). The EU, in this view, strengthens the nation-state as opposed to weakening it.

Moravcsik offers a model of a two-level game consisting of a liberal theory of national preference formation and an intergovernmentalist account of strategic bargaining between states. This model is then tested across the five most salient negotiations in the history of the European Community (as it was then called) in his view: (1) the Treaty of Rome in 1957, (2) the consolidation of the customs union and the common agricultural policy during the 1960s, (3) the establishment of the European monetary system in 1978/79, (4) the negotiations of the single European Act in 1985/86, and (5) the Maastricht treaty on the EU signed in 1991.

The first stage in his model in explaining the outcome of international negotiations is to account for national preferences (ibid., p. 24). They are defined as ordered and weighted sets of values placed on substantive outcomes. These preferences are exogenous to a specific political environment, and thus are not changed in response to any action of any actor (ibid., p. 25). In his model, two categories of motivation account for underlying national preferences for and against European integration (ibid., p. 26), notably geopolitical and economic interests. Moravcsik could be criticised for his assumption of exogenous preferences. While it is necessary for research to isolate some factors over others to improve the clarity of the analysis, it does not seem reasonable to assert that preferences are exogenous. The EU has created a system where the member states continuously interact at different levels. Even in the international system, Katzenstein (1996) has demonstrated convincingly how norms and values shape national interests. Constructivist literature convincingly showed how these norms change over time (Finnemore, 1993, 1996a, b; Finnemore and Sikkink, 1998).

The second stage of his model (Moravcsik, 1998, p. 50) is interstate bargaining. In his book, Moravcsik claims to test whether a supranational or intergovernmental bargaining would account best for empirical developments. Supranational theory (ibid., p. 52), which he derives from neofunctionalism, is thought to stress the decisive role of leading supranational officials, such as Jean Monnet and Jacques Delors, in providing policy entrepreneurship. This, however, is rejected vigorously by Moravcsik. In his only article dedicated entirely to policy entrepreneurship, Moravcsik (1999a) builds on this argument and emphatically rejects claims about the Commission acting as a supranational policy entrepreneur (SPE). The nation-state powerfully holds the 'purse and the power of the sword' (Moravcsik, 1999a).

It is very interesting to note how he attempted to disprove the concept of supranational policy entrepreneurship, mainly by focusing on the 'major decisions', i.e. the grand bargains, and therefore the process of treaty reform. This has been rightly criticised. If one chooses an intergovernmental setting for analysis, it is hardly a surprise to find that the character is intergovernmental. Wincott (1995, p. 602) makes this point lucidly. Moravcsik chooses to isolate treaty reform from day-to-day policy-making. Treaty reform is constructed as an event rather than a process. This seems to be at odds with the fact that the EU has negotiated a significant amount of different treaties, each reforming the predecessor. This in itself is an indicator of the procedural nature of treaty reform.

To his credit, Moravcsik (1999a) recognises the formal powers of the supranational institutions of the EU. Nonetheless, he reduces the concept of an SPE to only informal powers on methodological grounds in order to test how effective the informal powers of the Commission are. In fact, his definition differs significantly from the original concept of an SPE brought forward by Kingdon (1984). In Moravcsik's view, the SPE is 'an effort to wield political powers ... to induce political decisions that would not otherwise occur' (p. 271). This can be explained through the increase of the efficiency of negotiations, or the alteration of the distributional impact. However, supranational institutions lack resources that member states possess, including financial, staff and information-related aspects. Hence, it would seem unreasonable to assume that the Commission could induce political decisions.

Again, this is hardly a surprising finding, as the definition of policy entrepreneurship is constructed in such a way as to eradicate any possibility for the Commission (or any other EU institutional actor) to ever fulfil this role. Thus, Moravcsik's main contribution lies in his emphasis on state actors. It is clear from his analysis that states matter. Neofunctionalism tends to emphasise strongly the Commission, whereas he chooses to emphasise the member states. Nonetheless, in his intergovernmental outlook, this is taken to an extreme. While granting that the supranational institutions possess formal powers, he chooses to isolate the informal powers (ibid.). He therefore measures effectiveness only in terms of informal powers instead of powers in general.

Institutionalist perspectives on the Commission

Institutionalist approaches are built around the claim that 'institutions matter' (see Pierson, 1996; Pollack, 1997a, b, 2003; Armstrong and Bulmer, 1998; Tallberg, 2002, 2003, 2006, 2008; Aspinwall and Schneider, 2000; Tsebelis and Garret, 2001). What are institutions? March and Olsen (1998, p. 948) define them as 'a relatively stable collection of practices and rules defining appropriate behaviour for specific groups of actors in specific situations'. Analytical distinctions can be drawn between 'social' and 'specific' institutions. Here, the former relates to organisations like states or international organisations and the latter to more generalised patterns of activity and practices like rituals, marriage, or principles like sovereignty.

According to Hall and Taylor (1996), there are three different kinds of institutionalism, i.e. rationalist, historical and sociological/constructivist variants. In general, these approaches are incorporated into the study of international relations, comparative politics and European integration, ranging from themes about the dynamics of international co-operation to the governance of the EU (Kohler-Koch, 1996; Armstrong and Bulmer, 1998). On the question of power delegation to EU institutions, institutionalists share the ambition to move beyond the debate of the competing claims made by neofunctionalist and intergovernmentalists. In fact, institutionalists aim to demonstrate the merits of institutionalist theory in explaining EU policy-making.

Principal–agent analysis, developed within a rational choice institutionalism, has become the dominant tool for conceptualising supranational influence, and variations across different forms of delegation (Majone, 1996, 1997, 2005; Kelemen, 2002, 2004, 2005; Coen and Héritier, 2005; Héritier, 2005, 2007; Héritier and Knill, 2008). This theoretical model involves 'principal–agent' relationships, where 'principals' (EU member states) delegate specific powers to 'agents' (institutions) (Kelemen, 2002). Three of the dominant themes in the literature are those of control and autonomy, legitimacy, and co-ordination. Rational institutionalists emphasise the constraining nature of institutions, as agents like the Commission, on EU member states as principals.

Schneider and Aspinwall (2001, p. 7) argue that all actors in all relevant decision-making arenas behave strategically to reach their preferred outcome. In their view, member states as principals delegate powers to agents such as the European Commission, but the latter often exploits its superior knowledge and experience to reach its goals. Furthermore, rationalist scholars also analyse how the latter exploits the uncertainty which results from the imperfect division of power between competing European actors. A further strand of rational choice literature centres on the question of how much power the Commission possesses under different voting mechanisms (Crombez, 2000; Steuneberg, Koboldt and Schmidtchen, 2000).

Hix (1994, 1999) also uses a principal–agent analysis to examine the Commission, with the member states as principals and the Commission as an agent. 'The governments of the EU member states have delegated significant powers of political leadership, policy implementation and regulation to the Commission. The result is a dual executive in the EU, where the Council and the Commission share the responsibilities of government' (Hix, 1999, p. 21). Agents have their own preferences which can cause 'bureaucratic drift' (ibid., p. 23). Derived from Niskanen's public choice theory, Hix assumes that bureaucracies are budget maximisers. Therefore, agents have a desire to move from the principal's original policy intention in order to maximise budgets. This causes the aforementioned bureaucratic drift, i.e. a shift away from the principal's original intention.

This same principal–agent analysis is also used by Pollack (1996, 1997a, b, 2000, 2003). Likewise, he assumes member states to be principals, as well as the Commission being the agent seeking a bureaucratic drift. Yet, member states aim to prevent this drift with the establishment of procedures. Pollack (2003) aims to answer the question as to why member states' governments delegate certain powers to the EU level – such as to the EU institutions like the European Commission, the European Parliament, and the European Court of Justice. Thus, Pollack suggests that an institutional choice can be explained in terms of the functions the given institution is expected to perform (ibid., p. 20). Pollack therefore hypothesises that institutions have four key functions (ibid., p. 21): (1) monitoring compliance with agreements of the delegating principal, (2) solving the problems of 'incomplete contracting' and adjudicating in cases of dispute, (3) adopting credible expert regulation, and (4) setting the parliamentary agenda to avoid endless cycling of policy alternatives.

Pollack (1997a) concedes the possibility of the Commission being a formal agenda-setter. He argues that the Commission enjoys agenda-setting power if the Council adopts a Commission proposal by a qualified majority vote (QMV), but amends only by unanimity. Furthermore, it is claimed that agenda-setting power depends on several key variables, especially the institutional rules governing who may propose an legislative initiative, as well as the institutional voting procedures (i.e. QMV), the rules governing amendments, the actor's preferences, and the impatience of the various actors to reach a decision. Finally, Pollack (2000) concedes that the Commission can exercise supranational policy entrepreneurship under three conditions: (1) in areas where it possesses a significant policy expertise (2) after careful examination of the policy preferences of the member states (3) in constructing transnational coalitions of policy networks. Pollack is one of the most prominent scholars using a principal–agent model to analyse the political role of the European Commission. As demonstrated, he uses a well established literature, which has been used for some time in different areas of political analysis. He has developed a sophisticated model based on simple rational choice assumptions. As such, it is convincing, logical and elucidates issues of great significance.

Nonetheless, Pollack refers to policy entrepreneurship in a loose sense, which means he refers to the term without clearly relating it to the substance of the model or the definitions provided by Kingdon (1984). At the same time, his suggestion of the three conditions under which the Commission could exercise policy entrepreneurship seems sound: (1) policy expertise (2) member states preferences, and (3) transnational coalitions. It is upon these conditions that future models can certainly build.

The most prominent recent contribution has been made by Beach (2005a), *The Dynamics of European Integration: Why and When EU Institutions Matter*. The basic argument of his book is that there is evidence that the EU institutions play a significant role even in the most intergovernmental forums of the EU, i.e. intergovernmental conferences amending the EU treaties. In fact, the EU institutions do matter vis-à-vis governments in the history of making decisions, but their influence varies according to the leadership resources they possess, the negotiating context and their choice of strategy in the negotiations. He conducts a comparative study across six different EU treaties and across the three EU Institutions, i.e. the European Commission, the European Parliament and the Council Secretariat. The treaties examined are: (1) the Single European Act, 1986; (2) the Treaty of Maastricht, 1992; (3) the Treaty of Amsterdam, 1997; (4) the Treaty of Nice, 2000; (5) the Constitutional Treaty, 2004; (6) the Eastern Enlargement accession treaties, 2004.

Beach (2005a) draws on rational choice institutionalism as well as negotiation theory. He hypothesises that the institutions can play a key role when (p. 3): (1) strong leadership resources are available, such as comparative informational advantages, (2) they have privileged institutional positions in the negotiations, (3) the negotiating situation is complex (4) the distribution and governmental preferences open a window of opportunity, (5) the issues are of low salience and technically complex, (6) the institutions choose a low-profile leadership strategy.

Beach merits careful examination. The comparison of six different treaties and three EU actors displays a great breadth of research. In opposing Moravcsik's interpretation, he contributes significantly to our understanding of the earlier treaties. He suggests a sophisticated, rational choice, institutionalist model, which provides a sound tool to analyse the treaties at hand. His methodology is rigorous and sophisticated at the same time. Nonetheless, certain strengths can be weaknesses. The breadth of six different treaties invariably leads to a less detailed treatment of individual issues. Equally, his work focuses only on the treaty level. Christiansen (2002), on the other hand, clearly demonstrates that the policy level and the treaty level influence each other. Without the development of policies in the respective areas, there is no need to change the treaties. Beach's work has its strengths in its insights at the treaty level, but remains limited by this focus without reference to the policy level.

Historical institutionalists perceive the Commission as more important than rational choice scholars do. Armstrong and Bulmer's case study of the single market is a major case in point (Armstrong and Bulmer, 1998). Drawing on March and Olsen (1984), institutions are regarded as 'normative vessels', i.e. carriers of beliefs, knowledge, understandings, values and established ways of doing things. Institutions tend to replicate patterns over time and so create path dependencies. These claims are built on previous works. Bulmer (1994) also demonstrated the importance of the Commission in the area of merger control. In his view, political decisions have unintended integrationist consequences. The reason for this is the assumption that the Commission uses every opportunity presented to advance the integration agenda. Institutions are seen as having resources beyond formal powers, e.g. the setting of procedures, and the norms and regulations which require a study of the institutions over time. Bulmer concludes that the Commission started utilising its capabilities once the merger regulations had been agreed. It then developed procedural arrangements, which did not derive from the agreements, and moved them into new territory, i.e. oligopoly situations.

Cram (1994), in her study on social and IT policy, argues that a vital characteristic of the Commission's ability to influence any policy sector is its ability to respond rapidly to any 'window of opportunity'. It is argued that both the Commission as a whole and its individual Directorates are constantly engaged in a strategy of purposeful opportunism. In this process, the Commission can even facilitate the appearance of these windows. This is particularly remarkable since, as she claims, the areas of both of her case studies were marked by strong opposition on the part of the member states.

In conclusion, the different forms of institutionalism demonstrate the different shades of importance of the European Commission. For rational choice scholars, except Beach, it is an agent acting according to the preferences of the member states. Admittedly, due to bureaucratic drifts, it can achieve further European integration. However, this is highly dependent on the preferences of member states. Historical institutionalists, as well as network scholars, provide a more nuanced picture. The preferences of member states are not fixed. Over time, institutions can change these preferences and thus further the integration process.

Network governance and leadership

The network approach to the policy analysis of the EU provides a different conceptualisation to institutionalism. Group and network approaches stress the importance of interaction between the participants in the policy process. It assumes that groups and interest groups set the agenda, because governments and bureaucracies need them as a source of policy ideas. Mazey (1995) argued along the lines of this approach that the Commission's role has been crucial in creating and using policy networks, and in steering and managing incrementalist policy development with regards to equal opportunities. Mazey and Richardson (2001) further explored the relationship between interest groups and the Commission. The latter is represented as a 'purposeful opportunist' who recognises the importance of interest groups as sources of (1) information (2) support, and (3) legitimacy. It acts as a broker at the centre of a complex and varied network of relationships (ibid., p. 78). Both sides see a vital interest to have close relations with each other. This is reinforced by the fact that EU policies come on to the agenda sometimes even without major treaty changes, such as the environment, agriculture and telecommunication.

This research agenda connects to leadership approaches, which can provide valuable contributions to the study of European institutions. These approaches converge around the fact that personalities and leadership matter. Drake (1995) clearly stresses personality in her account of Jacques Delors. She analyses him, drawing upon his personal background and his rhetoric. He is perceived to possess strong leadership capacity, mixed with a personal vision of a particular model of European society, which should be more peaceful, fair and participative. In her view, he represents the only personality since Monnet that has radically influenced the integration process. Ross (1993, 1995) and Ludlow (1991) also underline the importance of the 'Delors factors' and his leadership skills in their analysis. He is described as having been able to capitalise on both a Community and a national reputation. In this view, it was the perception of Delors as a potential President of France which gave him additional weight as a leader. Ludlow (1991, p. 117) pointed out that this gave him a special relationship with the European Council and, therefore, more political influence. Within the Commission itself, Delors is described as possessing a dominant style, amounting to an almost presidential system and a position beyond the formal primus inter pares as foreseen by the treaties. Ross (1993, p. 26) argues that part of Delors's success was due to relying on Pascal Lamy, 'arguably the single most powerful individual in the Commission after Delors himself.'

Endo (1999) provides a resource-constraint analysis in order to theorise the leadership of the aforementioned Jacques Delors. In fact, he examines the resource-constraint structure surrounding the Commission President, which includes the formal powers, the internal actors and the external allies who may be utilised by the President, and finally, the situational factors, like socio-economic conditions and general public opinion. Moreover, he then considers the leadership capabilities of the Commission President as experienced by Jacques Delors. Consequently, he concludes that the Commission President is sometimes able to modify the structure of resources and constraints, even in the face of an intergovernmental structure.

Thus, there are several advantages in leadership analysis. Firstly, leadership does not just rely on formal resources, despite the suggestions by Pollack (2003) and Moravcsik (1999a) to the contrary. Of course, an increase in the formal resources can lead to an increase in power, even though this is not the only source. Informal power resources are vitally important, such as interpersonal and persuasive mediating skills. Structures, such as formal rules and intergovernmental settings, can also be used by skilful agents. It is unfortunate that this literature does not refer to Kingdon (1984) more explicitly. In Kingdon's definition (ibid., p. 188), policy entrepreneurs are 'advocates who are willing to invest their resources – time, reputation, money – to promote a position in return for anticipated future gain in the form of material, purposive, or solidary benefits'. As will be demonstrated in more detail below, Kingdon's model has many advantages, and could just be improved on.

Supranational governance

As neofunctionalism came out of fashion, especially during the 1970s and 1980s, newer theories started to connect back to it. Stone Sweet and Sandholtz reinterpret neofunctionalism and provide an 'updated' version of neofunctionalism, yet also attempt to incorporate some valid criticisms (Stone Sweet and Sandholtz, 1997; Stone Sweet and Sandholtz, 1998). European integration, according to the model, is encouraged and sustained by the development of causal connections between three factors: transnational exchange borrowed from Deutsch's transactionalist theory, supranational organisation, and EC rule-making. The transition to supranational governance is reached in two ways. Firstly, cross border transactions generate social demand for EU laws, which supranational organisations then supply. In their view, the role of supranational organisations is considerable, their acknowledgement, hence, very important.

But how is the Commission characterised by this theory? Like in neofunctionalist logic, institutions matter (Stone Sweet and Sandholtz, 1997, p. 310). Rules define roles (who is an actor), and norms matter. Actors behave in self-interested, rationalist-materialist ways. Therefore, institutions like the Commission work to enhance their own autonomy and influence within the European polity. Thereby, it acquires legitimacy by promoting the interests of transnational society.

In *The Institutionalization of Europe* (Stone Sweet, Sandholtz and Fligstein, 2001), the authors built upon this theme again. Emphasising that institutions are human artefacts which are made by humans, they also introduce a notion of institutional change, which should counter the static vision of institutionalist path dependence. Reasons for change are (1) exogenous shocks (2) the fact that rule innovations are endogenous to politics (3) diffusion of organisational behaviour and models of action, and (4) policy entrepreneurship.

Institutional entrepreneurs (ibid., p. 11) are conceptualised to construct and revise 'policy frames' (i.e. the collectively held sets of meanings), that (1) engage other actors and define new relationships between them, and (2) chart courses of action. The 'policy entrepreneur generates and attempts to propagate ideas that will define problems and solutions in ways that other actors find convincing and useful' (ibid.). This definition is very close to the one provided by Kingdon (1984). It borrows useful aspects from him in order to locate this within their theory. Nonetheless, they do not engage fully with his suggestion of the three policy streams, whose coupling can open windows of opportunity seized upon by the SPE.

The conceptualisation of institutional entrepreneurs builds on earlier work by Sandholtz. Sandholtz and Zysman (1989) suggest that informal entrepreneurship has been a necessary condition for European integration regarding the single market. They hypothesise that while structural change (e.g. American decline and Japanese ascent in economic power) was a necessary condition for the revitalisation of the European project in the 1980s, it was not in itself sufficient. In particular, it is argued that the Commission played the role of a policy entrepreneur, and the move towards market unification can only be explained if theory takes into account this leadership. They conclude that the Commission took advantage of favourable conditions but exercised policy entrepreneurship, mobilising a transnational coalition in favour of a unified market.

Similarly, Sandholtz (1993a) claims an important role for the Commission in the area of telecommunications. He argues that the latter played a leading role in promoting collective action to liberalise the telecommunication industry. The Commission initiated the proposals for market opening, set the agenda for Community deliberations, and pushed for approval of specific directives. The Commission was ahead of the member states in its objective for EC-level reforms. Drawing upon the regime literature contribution of Oran Young (1991), he cites five different leadership functions: (1) proposing (2) mobilising (3) shaping the agenda (4) building consensus, and (5) brokering compromises. But he concludes that the functions can be provided by national as well as international leaders. He then identifies four conditions under which leadership of international organisations can be exercised most effectively: (1) extent of initial authority of the organisation (2) degree of substantive knowledge and preparation (3) personal characteristics of the leader in terms of charisma, expertise, negotiating ability, achievements, etc. (4) periods of policy adaptation in the wake of national leaders facing policy failure.

Sandholtz has been one of the main scholars making the case for the significant political role of the European Commission. Interestingly, he was also the first scholar to draw on Kingdon's model. In fact, his analysis is most consistent with the model as it is. Indeed, he demonstrates very succinctly how the Commission fulfils the role of a policy entrepreneur. Sandholtz, Stone Sweet and Zysman have all contributed significantly to the conceptualisation of policy entrepreneurship. Yet, since these studies, European integration has moved on into other significant policy areas, for instance the Area of Freedom, Security and Justice. This book will examine these areas further though the prism of supranational policy entrepreneurship.

Kingdon and his impact on European integration literature: moving back to Kingdon

The review above indicates that concept of policy entrepreneurship, often preceded by the term 'supranational' when referring to an EU institution, is often referred to when conceptualising the role of EU institutions in EU policy-making. policy entrepreneurship was originally conceptualised by John Kingdon (1984) in the context of US politics. Sandholtz and Zysman (1989) first suggested that the role played by the Commission in EU policy-making was that of a policy entrepreneur. Their argument about its importance is related to the single market, and was subsequently reaffirmed by Sandholtz (1993a) in the area of telecommunications. Since these studies, European integration scholars increasingly analyse the role played by EU actors by referring to the concept of policy entrepreneurship, whether their empirical claims confirm or reject this notion (Haas, 1958, 1964, 1967; Lindberg, 1963; Lindberg and Scheingold, 1970, 1971; Puchala, 1971, 1984; Moravcsik, 1999a; Hix, 1994, 1998; Pollack, 1997a, b, 2003; Tallberg, 2002, 2003, 2006, 2008; Beach, 2004a, 2005a; Stone Sweet and Sandholtz, 1997, 1998; Stone Sweet et al., 2001; Kaunert, 2005, 2007, 2009).

This book argues that it is beneficial to build on Kingdon's (1984) original concept rather than some of the more recent suggestions. Firstly, the original is often better than the copy. Secondly, a reinterpretation of the concept by rationalist scholars such as Moravcsik has led to easy refutations empirically (Moravcsik, 1999a). The new definition often results in creating impossible conditions for any actor to achieve, and empirically difficult conditions to either prove or falsify. This section will demonstrate the fact that the combination of these 'hurdle' conditions makes the concept too easy to dismiss in theory, but consequently harder to explain as a phenomenon in practice. In addition, the result of this redefinition of an established concept is the refutation of a claim which does not exist in the literature.

Firstly, the reinterpretation of the concept has led to easy refutations empirically. Moravcsik (1999a) attempts to give policy entrepreneurship a different meaning by coining a new definition. In his view, the SPE is 'an effort to wield political powers ... to induce political decisions that would not otherwise occur' (p. 271). Yet, he assumes that supranational institutions lack resources that member states supposedly possess, which, according to this argument, makes it seem unreasonable to assume that the Commission could induce political decisions. Of course, the Commission may have more resources allocated to certain negotiations than member states in practice, despite having less budgetary means in general. But even if the resources of member states were indeed greater than the resources of the Commission, one cannot logically deduce that member states could therefore induce political decisions which would not occur without them. How would any actor do this? And how would the analyst know whether this case has actually occurred? Nonetheless, Moravcsik asserts that supranational intervention, 'far from being a necessary condition for efficient interstate negotiation', is generally 'late, redundant, futile and even counterproductive' (ibid., p. 270). Pollack (2003) and Beach (2005a) both seem to build on Moravcsik's definition of policy entrepreneurship, and their models explain 'political decisions that would not otherwise occur' (Moravcsik, 1999a, p. 271).

However, the model conceptualised by Kingdon is different to its use by the aforementioned scholars. Firstly, he explains that 'policy entrepreneurs lie in wait, in and around the government with their solutions in hand, waiting for problems to float by to which they can attach their solutions, waiting for a development in the politics stream they can use to their advantage' (Kingdon, 1984, p. 165). He defines them as 'advocates willing to invest their resources – time, energy, reputation, money – to promote a position in return for anticipated future gains in the form of material, purposive, or solidary benefits' (ibid., p. 181).

Demonstrably, these definitional points have a significant impact on what one could find empirically. Scholars following Moravcsik's definition will try to establish whether a political decision would have been found without a specific actor, for instance the Commission. Yet, this is not Kingdon's argument. Policy entrepreneurs are necessary in order for political decisions to take place because every idea needs to be pushed forward by some actor, which means that some 'advocate willing to invest their resources' needs to do so in order to convince decision-makers of the political merits of a case. However, this does not prejudge *who* this would be or *whether* it would be successful. It could be a senior politician from member states, a head of state, a senior MEP, or alternatively, the Commission represented by one of its officials or commissioners.

With regards to Moravcsik's definition, it is inconceivable in practice that the Commission or indeed any actor could induce a 'political decision that would not have otherwise occurred', which would be necessary to fulfil his criteria for policy entrepreneurship. Any actor at any given moment will make some limited impact. Therefore, an exact political decision without the same actors involved would never be taken in exactly the same way anymore. Further, it is more likely in practice that one actor may 'promote a position in return for anticipated future gain in the form of material, purposive, or solidary benefits' and will actually succeed in the investment of resources, as suggested by Kingdon. Empirically, it is far easier to establish whether a political decision followed the direction of a political entrepreneur than whether or not it would have otherwise occurred. The latter is purely hypothetical and thus impossible to prove or falsify. Thus, the suggestion by Kingdon offers a more empirically grounded definition.

Secondly, the studies by Moravcsik (1999a), Pollack (1997a, 2000, 2003), and Beach (2005a) are based on a different logic of enquiry compared to Kingdon (1984). This fact may explain why Kingdon's definition is more practically grounded. At the same time, this makes it difficult to compare research results between analysts when different definitions are used combined with different logics of enquiry. Kingdon's work was developed in a research study based on an *inductive* logic of enquiry. The work was drawn from interviews conducted with people in and around the US federal government, and from case studies, government documents, party platforms, press coverage, and public opinion surveys. He tried to engage with the question of why decision-makers attend at any given time to a certain subject, but not to an alternative subject. In this way, his main focus is to understand and analyse how ideas come about on the governmental agenda, how the alternatives, from which the policy was chosen, were generated, and why some issues were never thoroughly discussed. He did not start the research process with hypotheses that he wanted to falsify or demonstrate, but rather he wanted to establish how policy-makers saw their involvement in the policy process. At the end of this research, he was then able to theorise in the abstract.

On the other hand, Moravcsik (1999a), Pollack (2003), and Beach (2005a) do not use an inductive logic, but rather a *deductive* logic. They establish the research question, develop hypotheses, and aim to falsify or demonstrate these. This approach is sound in general and indeed followed by a significant number of research projects. However, the problem arises when one changes the logic of enquiry from one definition across to another in order to compare the two. In short, though referring to policy entrepreneurship by name, Moravcsik, Pollack and Beach really use a different model than John Kingdon (1984). The studies by Sandholtz and Zysman (1989) and Sandholtz (1993a) use the original model and relate their definitions closely to the definitions provided by Kingdon (1984). This book suggests that this is a better starting point for conceptualising policy entrepreneurship.

Supranational policy entrepreneurship: the return to Kingdon

John Kingdon, 1984: agendas, alternatives and public policy

This book will build on John Kingdon (1984) as the original starting point of the debate on policy entrepreneurship. The purpose of the following section is to examine Kingdon's original model and to build on it in the light of more recent theoretical developments in international relations literature. John (1998, pp. 12–21) explains that there are two main phenomena which are explained by public policy, i.e. (1) policy variation between sectors and (2) policy change within sectors. Kingdon's model mainly focuses on the latter phenomenon. Why do policies emerge? Do the origins of change lie in human agency or rather in structures?

Kingdon aims to explain policy change. His approach to the subject is based on an 'evolutionary' (John, 1998, p. 173) model of how ideas affect public policy (ibid., p. 15). Its roots are linked to a constructivist approach to international relations, which will be explained in the next section. At the beginning of his landmark work on agenda setting and policy formulation, Kingdon presents the puzzle that has led his research – 'What makes an idea's time come?' (Kingdon, 1984, p. 1). At the very core of his assumptions is the public policy model, described as a set of processes, including the categories of (1) the setting of the agenda (2) the specification of alternatives from which a choice is made, and (3) an authoritative choice among those alternatives in a legislative vote (ibid, p. 3). The agenda is 'the list of subjects or problems to which governmental officials ... are paying some serious attention at any given time' (ibid, p. 3).

The agenda-setting process narrows the set of alternatives for different policies due to the fact that only a certain number of issues can potentially be considered simultaneously. Thus, it becomes important to understand how and why the agenda changes from one time to another. Kingdon stresses two factors which influence agenda-setting and the specification of alternatives: (1) the participants who are active and (2) the process by which agenda items and alternatives come into prominence. He foresees three potential mechanisms of how issues arrive from the non-governmental, 'systemic' agenda on to the 'formal' agenda. This is described either (1) through the mobilisation of the relevant public by leaders (2) through diffusion of ideas in professional circles and bureaucrats, or (3) from a change in party control (Kingdon, p. 17).

The empirical research led Kingdon (1984, pp. 92, 93) to present his revised garbage can model. In his view, there are three major process streams, i.e. (1) the problem stream (2) the policy stream, and (3) the politics stream. Various issues can grab the attention of decision-makers for different reasons, e.g. indicators, events, etc. Policy communities of specialists, or even epistemic communities, bureaucrats, academics, interest groups and researchers, contribute to the formation of policy proposals. Thus, in his view, the political stream is composed of political moods and campaigns. These three aforementioned streams are thought to operate largely independently from one another. Solutions are developed whether or not they respond to problems, and the political stream may change with changing public opinion.

The problem stream

Kingdon explains the way problems are defined in the problem stream: 'important people in and around the government' (Kingdon, 1984, p. 90) can attend to a long list of problems. However, they attend to certain problems while they ignore others. The problem stream describes in essence how problems capture the attention of decision-makers. Their attention is affected by a variety of indicators (statistical or non-statistical) of a problem, but dramatic events also seize their attention. Are problems self-evident to decision-makers? Kingdon suggests that they are not.

Indicators can lead the attention of decision-makers towards certain problems and therefore define the very essence of them. Kingdon states that these indicators are used in the political world by both governmental and non-governmental agencies to routinely monitor various activities and events. Of course, a critical reader may note that not all activities are regularly monitored, and the selection of monitoring activities already indicates certain assumptions made by the analyst. For instance, it could be construed as a useless exercise to collect information on either the number of immigrants or the public's perception of immigration if the latter was not assumed to be a potential threat.

A crisis or a prominent event may also signal the emergence of a problem. This can be related to a gradual accumulation of knowledge and perspectives among specialists in a policy area (Kingdon, 1984, p. 18), which can contribute to the agenda. Ideas may also sweep through policy communities through a constant process of discussions, speeches, hearings, and Bill introductions. Kingdon thus raises explicitly the importance of ideas for policy communities and implicitly the related importance of norms.

Logically, a crisis is an event with extraordinary consequences. Thus, in order to appreciate the magnitude of these consequences, humans need the guidance of socially constructed and shared knowledge. Take the example of a bomb, which is not perceived as a threat without the socially constructed knowledge of how to work it and of its consequences. Equally, the possibility of repetitions of incidents such as 9/11 is not perceived as a threat without socially constructed knowledge of the first occurrence. On the face of it, two planes crashed into a building. Without the shared knowledge of the further aspirations and motivations of the terrorists, this could have been simply a one-off accident. Thus, in order to appreciate this as a crisis, socially constructed knowledge is necessary. This knowledge is derived from our own normative framework, which guides our understanding of the world.

The policy stream

Further, Kingdon (1984) analyses how policy alternatives come into being. Generating alternatives and proposals in a certain policy community of decision-makers resembles a process of 'biological natural selection' (ibid., p. 116). As molecules float around in the so-called 'primeval soup' – to keep within the analogy – so ideas float around within these communities. He suggests that some ideas survive and prosper while others die, indicating that some are taken more seriously than others. If there is a feasible, available proposal which is taken seriously, then the problem will feature high on the agenda and may survive the politics stream.

Policy communities, in Kingdon's view, are composed of specialists in given policy areas. Some work in government positions, some in bureaucracy, some in think tanks, academia, etc. However, they are related mostly by their common interest in the policy area. Thus, they interact with one another often, and they know each other's ideas, proposals and research. According to Kingdon, this community 'hums along on its own' (ibid., p. 117) and merely reacts to events. Within this group, it appears that a wide range of ideas can be tested (p. 122). Policy entrepreneurs do not have to be within these communities, but certainly it can help to be there in order to make a significant impact.

What shapes people's thoughts within policy communities? Commonly held sets of beliefs and norms certainly seem to influence people's ideas and behaviours. Participants interact with each other and are socialised according to the prevailing norms within this reference group. Norms may even facilitate who participates in this group. Furthermore, norms do not just guide the behaviour of people in this policy community, but are also shaped by the discussions and the social interaction within this group. In short, the presence of social norms appears to influence the behaviour of people in these policy communities.

Moreover, Kingdon analyses the process of policy formation. In his view, it is a futile exercise to concentrate on the origins of ideas (ibid., p. 75). Ideas can come from anywhere, implying that tracing the origin leads into infinite regress. In addition, nobody really controls the information system and flow in a democratic society. No source monopolises the flow of information and ideas (ibid., p. 81). Thus, he suggests that this makes rational decision-making behaviour almost impossible. If decision-makers were to operate rationally, they would first define their goals and define the level of achievement necessary for goal satisfaction. Alternatives would be compared systematically, assessing costs and benefits, and the most cost-efficient alternative would be chosen. However, this is not the case due to the human inability to canvass and compare many alternatives simultaneously. Again, this makes the case for norms guiding human behaviour even stronger.

In order for ideas to survive the 'primeval soup', Kingdon (ibid., pp. 122–151) describes conditions that need to be fulfilled, i.e. (1) the technical feasibility (2) the value acceptability for the policy community, and (3) the anticipation of future constraints. Technical feasibility refers to its internal coherence of the proposal. However, only ideas that have been researched will be technically feasible, and often only acceptable ideas will be researched. Alternatives outside the mainstream will invariably become less technically feasible than mainstream alternatives due to a lack of investment. Thus, norms also influence technical feasibility. In addition, 'value acceptability' and 'norm compatibility' are very close concepts. Norms guide the preferences of specialists to decide on the policy alternatives. 'In some respects, the bulk of the specialists do eventually see the world in similar ways, and approve and disapprove of similar approaches to problems' (ibid., p. 133). In short, norms are vital for the policy stream too.

The politics stream

Finally, Kingdon (ibid., pp. 152–172) investigates how the politics stream works. The politics stream is composed of such things as public mood, pressure groups campaigns, election results, ideological distributions in the political institutions, and changes in the administration. Changes in the politics stream occur due to two different reasons: (1) a shift in the stream can occur due to shifts of important participants (administrations or legislators in Parliament); (2) changes can occur as a response to shifts in the political mood.

The political mood is a vital aspect in understanding the workings of the politics stream. Kingdon suggests that people in and around government sense a political mood (ibid., p. 146), which goes by different names, e.g. the national mood, the climate in the country, changes in public opinion, or broad social movements. Again, this actually underlines the importance of norms. As argued previously, indicators are important in measuring the extent of a problem. But the interpretation of indicators and the selection of questions asked depend invariably on pre-existing social norms. The same principle applies with political moods and public opinion, which are interpreted by the same decision-makers, guided by the aforementioned norms in their behaviour. These interpretations are then confirmed with opinion polls which act as a justification.

Political consensus, in this model, is built on persuasion (ibid., p. 167). In the politics stream a stronger emphasis is placed on bargaining than before. Coalitions are being built through the granting of concessions in return for support of a coalition. The proposals in the politics stream have already been discussed in the policy stream, and some people may have been convinced while others have not. So the remaining decision-makers that need to be convinced will need to be given something in return for their support. Actors pay a heavy price in the politics stream if they do not pay sufficient attention to coalition building (ibid., p. 160). The coalition building achieves a sort of bandwagon effect, where as some decision-makers join the coalition, more and more want to be on it.

Coupling streams, policy windows and supranational policy entrepreneurs

In the end, these three streams, i.e. problem, policy and politics, become coupled and form a policy window, providing an opportunity for advocates to push for their solutions. As Kingdon describes them, these policy entrepreneurs already have prepared solutions in hand for problems that still need to emerge. Thus, they need to wait in order to attach the former to the latter, necessitating a development in the politics stream (Kingdon, 1984, p. 165).

Streams become coupled as they come together at critical times. Once a problem is recognised, a solution is developed and available in the policy community, and then a change in the politics stream makes it the right time for overall policy change. This is the opening time for policy windows, which usually stay open only for a short period. The reasons for this shortness are due to four factors: (1) participants in the decision-making process may conclude that they have already addressed the issue, (2) nobody is willing to invest their resources, (3) there is no policy entrepreneur at this juncture to take advantage of the situation, and (4) the event which has led to the opening of the window passes without quick action.

According to Kingdon, these policy windows are vital for the adoption of any policy. The existence of policy windows mostly relies on the perceptions of participants (Kingdon, 1984, p. 171). Participants thus need to be convinced that there are open policy windows. If the participants themselves rely purely on their own perceptions to evaluate the openness of these windows, these perceptions may be shaped by norms again. Only if participants perceive them at the same time, will these windows become real for the participants. In brief, without the same shared norms these windows will not come into existence.

In Kingdon's view, political entrepreneurs are necessary for the coupling of streams. A political entrepreneur stands at the policy window in order to propose, lobby for, and sell a policy proposal. In Kingdon's definition (ibid., p. 181), political entrepreneurs need to possess resources which they are willing to invest, such as time, energy, reputation, money, and actively use these to promote a policy position in return for anticipated future gains. However, according to Kingdon, policy entrepreneurs do more than push, push, and push for their proposals. They also lie in wait for a window to open and therefore seize the right moment. With regards to the characteristics, the PE according to Kingdon has 'one of three sources: expertise, an ability to speak for others, or an authoritative decision-making position'. 'The person is known for his political connections or negotiating skills. ... Successful entrepreneurs are persistent' (Kingdon, 1984, p. 180).

Kingdon: from early constructivism to norms as analytical concepts

According to Alexander Wendt (1999), one can identify the defining characteristics of the constructivist approach as follows: first, that the structures of international life are primarily ideational and not exclusively material; and, second, that the contribution made by intersubjective shared meanings between purposive state actors decisively determines identities and interests in the international system. Wendt refers to this approach as 'structural idealism' (in opposition to existing structural realist theories such as those of Waltz). In a similar vein, Ruggie's (1998) classic description of constructivism notes 'that ideational factors have normative as well as instrumental dimensions'.

The argument in this chapter is that norms in effect guide the other three

(Kingdon) streams, i.e. the problem, policy and politics streams. They are guiding devices, as mentioned previously, for the recognition and appreciation of extraordinary crises and indicators, as well as for the search for policy alternatives, and the search for coalition partners. At the same time, norms do not determine precise outcomes. Actors still have a substantial degree of freedom within which to be guided by norms. In addition, as these norms do not just simply appear out of thin air, their social construction requires an agent – the SPE.

This relates very closely to Kingdon's original model, but, crucially, develops his thoughts on ideational factors affecting policy change further. In his book, Kingdon (1984) makes it also clear that agency is needed in the policy-making process and structural forces alone do not determine the policy outcomes. This is why he suggests the concept of the policy entrepreneur. Structural factors matter to Kingdon, particularly with regards to the section of indicators and crises, and cannot be entirely steered by the political entrepreneur. However, actors' interpretations of structural factors steers the process, not the factors by themselves. Clearly, this relates to Alexander Wendt's (1999) suggestion that agents and structures are mutually constitutive – one of the premises of International Relations constructivism.

Thus, clearly, Kingdon's model is closer to interpretive social science than to rational choice, despite attempts by Moravcsik and others to redefine supranational policy entrepreneurship. According to Kingdon, in practice, policy-makers do not have the time or the information to make 'rational decisions'. This does not mean they do not aim to do so, or may even think they do. However, ultimately, policy-makers are guided by ideational factors. As these factors are constructed and reconstructed over time, policy-makers are guided in their behaviour by social norms.

Norms are often defined as 'a standard of appropriate behaviour for actors with a given identity' (Finnemore and Sikkink, 1998, p. 891). One can distinguish between different types of norms. The most common distinction is between regulative norms, which order and constrain behaviour, and constitutive norms, which create actors, interests or action (Ruggie, 1998a). Actors 'are socialised to accept new norms, values and perceptions of interest' (Finnemore, 1996a, p. 5). It has been convincingly demonstrated how different types of actors, e.g. non-governmental organisations (NGOs), intergovernmental organisations (IGOs), and transnational advocacy networks, can contribute to major changes in norms and thus social actor behaviour (Finnemore, 1996a; Price, 1998; Keck and Sikkink, 1998).

According to Friedrich Kratochwil (1989, p. 6), norms influence choices through a reasoning process, implying a strong focus on the argumentative structure and the possible reasons for action. He assesses the impact of norms on decision-making, arguing that norms influence choices not by being causes for actions, but by providing reasons for actions. Consequently, he approaches the topic via an investigation of the reasoning process in which norms play a decisive role. His argument is developed through interpretation of the classical thinkers in international law (Grotius, Vattel, Pudendorf, Rousseau, Hume and Kant). Thus, norms shall be defined for the purpose of this book as follows: 'Norms are written and non-written rules which are reasons for action. They enable, restrain, or constitute different actions by providing a standard of appropriate behaviour for a particular reference group.'

But how do norms come about? Finnemore and Sikkink (1998) suggest a three-stage model of a norm 'life cycle'. According to this, the first stage involves 'norm emergence', the second stage involves 'norm acceptance', which she terms as 'norm cascade', and the third stage involves 'internalisation'. The second stage of the norm life cycle, according to Finnemore and Sikkink (ibid.), is characterised by a socialisation process – norm leaders are imitated by the followers. After a certain 'tipping point', more actors adopt the norm. In order to achieve this socialisation, praising as well as ridiculing those who deviate from the norm is involved. During the third stage – the internalisation – norms acquire a taken-for-granted status and are no longer an issue of public debate.

Payne (2001) explains how agents translate ideas into normative structures. Persuasion is considered the centrally important mechanism for constructing and reconstructing norms and hence social facts (ibid., p. 38). Persuasion is the process by which actions becomes structures, ideas become norms and the subjective becomes the intersubjective. He suggests that new ideas resonate because of some ideational affinity to other already accepted frameworks. This resonance is the work of political or norm entrepreneurs.

The mechanism of persuasion is an attempt to convince a critical mass of actors to embrace a norm by, what Finnemore and Sikkink (1998) term 'norm entrepreneurs'. These entrepreneurs have strong notions of appropriate behaviour, and are absolutely critical for success. Norms never enter a normative vacuum but instead access a highly contested space in which they need to compete with other norms. One condition for entrepreneurs at the international level is some kind of *organisational platform* from which to promote their norm. These can be specifically constructed for the aim, e.g. Greenpeace, or can be an established international organisation, e.g. the European Commission as an engine of European integration.

However, despite Finnemore and Sikkink's term 'norm entrepreneur', this chapter argues that the concept she refers to represents the activity of a (Supranational) policy entrepreneur in the norm stream. Political Entrepreneurial activities are not only related to the setting of the agenda, as discussed by Kingdon (1984), but they start already much earlier – in the construction and reconstruction of the reasons for action which constitute the norm environment for decision-makers. These norms then guide the other three streams, which means that they guide the recognition of crises and the appreciation of indicators, as well as the search for policy alternatives, and the search for coalition partners in the politics stream.

Supranational policy entrepreneurship: integrating norms into the three streams

This book suggests the following theoretical model of policy entrepreneurship. It takes the Kingdon (1984) framework as a fixed starting point; there are three streams, i.e. the problem, the policy and the politics streams, which operate simultaneously and in different ways. These streams operate exactly as conceptualised by Kingdon. However, in addition, a fourth stream guides (but does not determine) these streams – the norm stream. It is composed of existing norms within the reference group of decision-makers. These norms are generally stable and continuous. However (Supranational) Political Entrepreneurs can push for different reasons for actions in order to socially construct these reasons into the web of accepted norms. This then produces a change in the existing norm stream, which can then justify a different political course of action.

As suggested by Payne (2001), only reasons for actions which resonate with pre-existing norms can become norms themselves. These normative frames constrain actors as they provide limits to the establishment of new norms and also interpretation bands, which an SPE can use when they act as a *first mover*. However, once new norms are accepted, they guide the behaviour of policy-makers in any of the three following streams. They guide the interpretation of extraordinary crises and indicators in the problem stream, they limit the band of policy alternatives that are under close investigation, and they influence who can bargain with whom in the search for coalition partners in the politics stream. At the point where all streams are coupled, the SPE provides the impetus to push for detailed policy proposals which fit the other three streams. As soon as a policy window opens, the SPE gets an opportunity to succeed.

How can these norms be constructed and how can they be observed? Firstly, actors will provide reasons for action. There can be very differing reasons for action put forward by a certain number of actors. In the EU context this can be any one of the following: a Commission official, a member state Minister or head of state, an MEP, a judge of the European Court of Justice or of any of the constitutional courts of the member states, or indeed any actor involved in the policy process. The SPE in this regard will constantly push for his reason for action to become accepted as a norm. This is the first stage of norm creation in the norm life cycle as described by Finnemore and Sikkink (1998), and is followed by the norm socialisation stage. Once the reference group has accepted a particular norm, this does not in itself imply all actors will act upon it. It may still be in competition with other conflicting norms and deviation may still need to be eradicated by punishment. Finally, the norm becomes the dominant norm and is thus not challenged any more.

What is the content of the norms stream? Of course, this cannot and should not be pre-determined before any empirical investigation. Nonetheless, in the EU, as suggested before, on a very fundamental level, reasons for action range from the protection of national sovereignty (which is prevalent in the international system more broadly) to the pooling of national sovereignty at the supranational level. These reasons for action are clearly contested, yet over time with social acceptance by actors they will become less controversial, which signifies the gradual acceptance of a particular norm. In addition, these fundamental reasons for action are linked to other (second-order) reasons for action, and rarely are a goal by themselves. For instance, within the Single Market the pooling of national sovereignty is linked to liberal trade policies (though the EU services directive demonstrated the contested nature of some of these norms).

In order to operationalise norms and reasons for action, one needs to identify first the reasons for action put forward by the different actors. In the ongoing political debate, there comes a point where one can establish from the debate that certain reasons have been pushed for, but are still considered to be weaker arguments than the prevailing norm. Only at the point where decision-makers seem to accept a certain norm, can one speak of a valid norm. This acceptance should be prevalent in the statements that people make with regard to ongoing discussion. This needs to be cross-checked in interviews with decision-makers to follow through the whole process of the norm cycle.

What are the reasons for amending conceptualisations of supranational policy entrepreneurship? The answer is related back to the basic nature of the EU. At the political bargaining stage (within the politics stream), where decisions amongst different alternatives are taken, the EU is dominated by member states' preferences and interests within the Council of Ministers, especially regarding third-pillar decision-making in the AFSJ. While this would indicate the benefits of a liberal intergovernmental analysis for this policy area in principle, where European integration can best be explained as a series of rational choices made by national leaders and dominated by national interests (Moravcsik 1991, 1993, 1998, 1999a, b), and thus policy change is related to either (1) a change in interests within the member states, or (2) the result of a grand political bargain, this model only seems superficially convincing. EU institutions, in this conception, are merely there to bolster the credibility of interstate commitments (Moravcsik, 1998, p. 18) by ensuring that member states keep their promises and thus dare to agree to a mutually favourable solution without the fear of 'free-riders'.

However, where do member states' national interests and preferences originate from? Moravcsik (1998) assumes national interests to be exogenous from the EU process. The interests of the member states are stable before they come to the bargaining table. Yet, it does not seem reasonable to assert that preferences are exogenous. The EU has created a system whereby member states continuously interact at different levels. The claim that this could not alter preferences over time appears spurious. Even within the context of the international system with less social interaction amongst states, Katzenstein (1996) has convincingly demonstrated how norms and values shape national interests. Yet, if national interests and preferences are shaped by different norms and values, as argued in this chapter, this implies that a fourth stream – the norm stream – is underpinning the three other streams. Norms consequently influence the definition of political problems, the search for policy alternatives, and finally the national preferences in the politics stream where decisions are taken.

What are the ways in which the SPE can achieve policy change?

- *First-mover advantage.* It needs to be able to act promptly to construct issues and seize the right moment for political action in competition with other actors:
- *Persuasion strategy.* As suggested above, in order to achieve acceptance, other actors need to be convinced by the reasons for the action suggested. This requires the following:
    - *Legitimacy build-up.* Norms need to be anchored in existing norms, and changes to these need to be consistent in order to acquire legitimacy for the new norms.
    - *Expertise and information.* Only if the SPE has sufficient knowledge and is recognised as an expert, can it rely on actors to trust its authoritative judgement – information is crucial.
    - *Continued insistence.* New norms will encounter resistance at first, which means the SPE needs to insist significantly.
    - *Negotiation skills.* In order to persuade, the SPE needs to possess the social skills required to say the right things to the right people at the right time. A correct political assessment of the situation is crucial. This may also require some pressure at the right time.
    - *Alliances.* Once a problem is defined appropriately, and once other actors are somewhat persuaded, the negotiations in the political stream move towards bargaining efforts. In this process it is vital for the SPE to form initial alliance with powerful actors to create a bandwagon effect, whereby more actors will join the 'winning team'. Forming the right alliances at the right time will become crucial. This underlines the political skills needed for the SPE.

The next chapter will empirically analyse the institutional and normative changes in the Area of Freedom, Security and Justice (AFSJ) up to the Tampere Council Summit in 1999. In effect, this will be a reflection of the norm stream in the EU's AFSJ until the Amsterdam Treaty (1997) entered into force in 1999. As will be shown, the normative changes within this policy area enabled a political process towards supranational governance in the Area of Freedom, Security and Justice. SPEs in the AFSJ invariably build on this normative environment in order to facilitate policy change; thus a thorough understanding of it is indispensable in order to analyse the role of SPEs.

3

The historical genealogy of an Area of Freedom, Security and Justice

The Area of Freedom, Security and Justice (AFSJ) experienced significant growth in the late 1990s and the early part of the new millennium. This demonstrates an extraordinary dynamism as a special regime of European governance. According to Monar (1999a) this can be demonstrated empirically (1) in terms of its agenda and (2) in terms of its structure: the Council Secretariat, according to Monar's study, suggests that roughly 40 per cent of the meetings and the workload directly or indirectly relate to the AFSJ.

The AFSJ has been an anomaly as a policy-making area (see Joppke, 1998, 2001; Freeman, 1998; Guiraudon, 2000, 2001, 2003; Boswell, 2003a, b, 2008; Ellermann, 2008; Geddes, 2000, 2001; Stetter, 2000, 2007; Thielemann, 2001a, b, 2004, 2005, 2006; Thielemann and Dewan, 2006; Lavenex, 1998, 1999, 2001a, b, 2004, 2006; Occhipinti, 2003). The EU created the most complicated decision-making structures of all policy areas after the treaties of Amsterdam and Nice. There are a number of sophisticated and detailed analyses of asylum and migration in Western Europe and the EU (Huysmans, 2000, 2004; Bigo, 1996, 1998a, b, c, d, 2001a, 2002; Guild, 1999, 2002, 2003a, b, c, 2004, 2006; Guiraudon, 2000, 2003; Boswell, 2003b; Byrne et al., 2002; Cohen et al., 2001; Geddes, 2000; Guiraudon and Joppke, 2001; Stetter, 2000), yet they do not directly and systematically look at how the institutional arrangements in the AFSJ can be explained. Despite the significant growth that the area has seen recently, it is still comparatively under-researched.

The following chapter will analyse the institutional and normative changes in the social norms for decision-makers in the AFSJ up until the Tampere Council Summit in 1999, the first European Council to be entirely dedicated to the area. Firstly, an analysis of the legal norms in the policy area is used in order to demonstrate the changing nature of the 'constitutional' arrangements. Secondly, this chapter argues, that these legal and normative changes are indicative of a political process that could potentially lead to supranational governance in the AFSJ. This task has been conducted through a historical genealogy of the events and institutional changes. The aim of this chapter is to map the historical development of the political norms of decision-makers in order to understand the contextual environment in which the political entrepreneurs operate. Political agency in the AFSJ needs to build on this environment in order to facilitate policy change, thus a comprehension of the normative environment is indispensable in order to analyse agency.

How are norms operationalised? In order to identify norms, this chapter will examine the complementary, underlying normative questions around which the political 'grand debates' are structured. Methodologically, norm change has been examined through legal texts, policy documents, and elite interviews. A shift in the legal status of EU rules indicates a change in norms. Thus, a change in the legal status of those rules can be any one of the following: (1) the depth and the scope of the competences of the EU, (2) the legal instruments used, (3) the decision-making mechanisms, (4) the competences of the different institutions, and (5) the procedure on establishing those rules. The evolution of norms has been divided into four stages of development – the pre-1992 phase, the post-Maastricht phase up until 1997, the Amsterdam phase after 1997, and finally, the Tampere phase, starting with the Council Summit in 1999. When analysing these stages of development in the norms of decision-makers, the chapter will ask two important normative questions and examine the answers that the institutional structures give to both questions: (1) Should the EU be legislating in the AFSJ? (2) What are the main aims of EU legislation?

The argument of this chapter is that, despite clear normative developments up to Tampere in 1999, decision-makers remained attached to the norms of national sovereignty. The AFSJ became coupled to the Single Market in the 1980s and 1990s, and remained attached to the development of it until 1999. Later chapters will suggest more change in the policy-making area towards supranational governance, though incomplete, after 1999. In addition, this chapter will provide prima facia evidence to suggest that the EU institutions, in particular the European Commission, attempted to play the role of an SPE in the AFSJ since the beginning.

Stage 1: Justice and Home Affairs laboratories in the pre-1992 phase

In his widely cited and authoritative article 'The Dynamics of Justice and Home Affairs: Laboratories, Driving Factors and Costs' (Monar, 2001b), Monar claims that the rapid development of Justice and Home Affairs[1] into a major field of EU policy-making since the beginning of the 1990s can be explained by a combination of specific 'laboratories' and 'driving factors' which triggered development and expansion. This serves as an important reminder of how strongly decision-makers felt the social norms of national sovereignty, and how strongly it was protected against the background of developments in the economic integration in Europe.

Should the European Union be legislating in the areas of Area of Freedom, Security and Justice before Maastricht?

What are the implications for the norm structure that the institutional set-up of the 'laboratories' reflects? Firstly and unsurprisingly, it shows that from the beginning until before the end of the 1990s national sovereignty was treasured to a great extent. Internal security and the police were widely perceived to be vital and, indeed, core areas of the state. The same is true with regards to admitting foreigners on to the territory of the state – especially asylum and migration. Uncompromisingly so, the pooling of sovereignty in this vital area of the state was beyond inconceivable. This reluctance to pool sovereignty prevailed during times when first efforts to pool sovereignty in the area of the common market succeeded. It appears from this example that national sovereignty in internal security had to be protected and remained the core norm in the area. Examples of those laboratories are:

- *Interpol.* No sovereignty has been transferred to this international police institution. It may not even be described as intergovernmental in nature, as intergovernmental organisations are normally based on an international treaty or a convention according to international law. Interpol is not based on such a treaty, and entails no structure of national representation from the highest governmental levels, e.g. governmental Ministers, officials or ambassadors (Occhipinti, 2003, p. 29).
- *Council of Europe.* The continent's oldest political organisation, founded in 1949, is not an institution of the EU. It clearly displays most intergovernmental characteristics, which safeguard the norm of national sovereignty. With regard to JHA, a major part of the Council's activities have been dedicated to the fundamental establishment of a pan-European legal and judicial space, which coincides with the major aim of JHA policy since the coming into force of the Amsterdam Treaty (signed in 1997, in force since 1999).
- *The Trevi Framework* displayed most characteristics of safeguarding national sovereignty. The Rome European Council in 1975 created a body for co-operating and led to the creation of a multi-level intergovernmental forum under the umbrella of European Political Co-operation. But the EC institutions played a minor to no role at all in the group (Occhipinti, 2003). It represented the first attempt to deal with JHA matters in an EU-related format and dates back to the earlier Pompidou Group. The Pompidou Group was composed of Ministers and civil servants and largely concerned itself with studying drug education programmes and ways to collect data on drug trafficking and money laundering.
- *The Schengen Group* clearly safeguarded national sovereignty. It had its origins in the Saarbrücken Agreement of 13 July 1984, in which Chancellor Kohl and President Mitterrand agreed on the gradual abolition of controls at the Franco-German border (Geddes, 2000).

Shortly afterwards, the Benelux countries joined France and Germany on this initiative and the five countries signed the Schengen Agreement on 14 June 1985.

- *The Ad Hoc Group on Immigration* was set up in 1986 (ibid.) at the initiative of the British presidency, which wanted to foster co-operation on the compensatory measures necessary to achieve the Single Market. It was comprised of all of the twelve member states of the European Community at the time.

Monar (2001b) explains how the norm of national sovereignty had been weakened through a two-fold socialisation process. Firstly, a positive experience somewhat lessened the desire to safeguard national sovereignty, that is the experience of national Ministries of the Interior in being exposed to their European colleagues and hence the creation of a policy community where ideas can be exchanged. This change needs to be contrasted with the state of affairs of the rather inward-looking institutions before. It made the belief of co-operation in a field so close to the core of the nation-state a possibility. Secondly, a negative experience also added to the changes. Due to the larger membership and the purely intergovernmental basis of the proceedings in the various fora, even negotiations on more technical questions could take years. The negative experience can be seen as an impetus to move beyond these structures, but at the same time such a move would weaken the norm to protect the sovereignty of the nation-state in this area.

What are the main aims of this co-operation before Maastricht?

Before the Treaty of Maastricht (1992) the policy area was socially constructed as a spill-over from the Single Market programme. The normative construction was often referred to as 'the permanent security deficit' in the literature (Hebenton and Thomas, 1995; Mitsilegas et al., 2003; Occhipinti, 2003).

The first reason for action in the construction of the policy area relates to the famous 'four freedoms' introduced by the EEC Treaty of 1957 – the free movement of goods and of persons. The argument often suggested is that the full implementation of the freedoms required the dismantling of internal borders. The traditional approach of border controls was challenged by the Schengen process. France, Germany and the three Benelux countries signed the Schengen Agreement on 14 June 1985, and went ahead with the abolition of internal borders despite some resistance by other member states.

At this critical juncture the Commission proposed its famous 'White Paper' on the completion of the Internal Market (Mitsilegas et al., 2003, p. 28). Firstly, the document proposed the abolition of all internal border controls, which clearly would change the system of internal security. Secondly – rhetorically important – it also provided a political link between economic growth, border control abolition, and a whole range of compensatory measures. These included areas such as immigration, asylum, external border controls, and policies on visas, drugs and crime. While the Commission's proposals were embedded in an economic rationale of the completion of the Internal Market, it suggested a very wide range of common JHA measures. It is reasonable to assume that this may have been the first attempt by the Commission to change the norm environment for JHA issues.

Yet, none of the proposals made in 1985 were greeted with a great deal of success. In the European Community (EC) framework, the Commission's proposal relating to the abolition of border controls was met with strong opposition – in particular by the UK – which resulted in a rather vague reference to an 'aim of an area without internal frontiers' in the Article 8a Treaty establishing the European Communities (TEC) when the treaties were revised by the Single European Act (SEA) of 1986. The vagueness of the article represents possibly a failure for the Commission, but only at first sight.

The argument against the Commission proposals was always made on the grounds of preserving national sovereignty. As a result of the debate, neither the internal border controls were abolished, nor the JHA measures included in the treaty in 1986. But it went unquestioned that the abolition of internal borders would necessitate compensatory measures eventually. Indeed, this acceptance of the argument could be seen as a victory for the Commission. The implication is that once borders were abolished, JHA would become coupled to these changes. One must therefore logically deduce that norms changed. Despite the policy failure, the Commission managed to gain acceptance to politically link JHA to the Single Market. As the goals of the SEA regarding the free movement of goods, services and persons became a reality, the governments of the member states came to acknowledge the 'logical linkage between economic integration and co-operation and the maintenance of law and order' (Guyomarch, p. 137).

Stage 2: the Maastricht Treaty phase

The two Intergovernmental Conferences (IGCs), which prepared the Maastricht Treaty (on the economic and monetary union and the political union respectively), opened on 15 December 1990. The main objective was to deepen the internal market foreseen by the Single European Act and the establishment of the monetary union. In addition, it also established the area of Justice and Home Affairs institutionally for the first time as a policy-making area within the framework of the newly created EU.

At first sight, this appears ground-breaking with regards to the normative environment of decision-makers. However, the overarching normative question as to whether the EU should be legislating in Justice and Home Affairs matters was far from being settled conclusively. The following presents the arguments on which these suggestions are based.

Geddes (2000, p. 86) suggests that JHA co-operation was formalised but not supranationalised. To some, the Maastricht Treaty could be interpreted as a 'creeping supranationalisation' of JHA. Geddes rejects it on the grounds that it is founded on a teleological notion of inevitability of this fact. In his view, the agreements concluded reflect the desires of member states to free themselves from national judicial and political pressures. At the same time, the evidence produced can be interpreted to suggest that the Commission in particular had been arguing strongly for improved decision-making mechanisms due to the failure of the intergovernmental co-operation methods of the pre-Maastricht arrangements. This could be interpreted as early signs of entrepreneurial activities. Member states at the time, however, were not persuaded by the institutional arguments put forward by the Commission.

Geddes argues (ibid.) that the agreements made were the effects of the policy preferences of 'maximalist' and 'minimalist' member states arguing about the deepening of integration in the field. This can be corroborated by the fact that there were two different IGCs – one on economic and monetary union and one on political union – and four different institutional alternatives on the negotiating table, i.e. (1) maintenance of existing ad hoc arrangements, (2) a reference in the Treaty to co-operation without clear details, (3) more elaborate provision outlining areas of co-operation, and (4) full communitarisation. As member states were divided on the most fundamental questions as to whether the EU should have competence over these matters, the end result was a compromise.

Yet, what does this compromise reflect? The overarching normative question as to whether the EU should be legislating in Justice and Home Affairs matters had not been settled conclusively, as argued above, but rather incrementally advanced. The following presents the legal arguments on which to base these claims.

De Lobkowicz (2002) suggests that the twelve member states at the time could not agree on whether to transfer new competences to the EU. Therefore, they created a new legal concept, the so-called questions of 'common interest'. This does not represent what is commonly understood by a competence transfer to a supranational authority. In fact, it is only a catalogue of competences which are brought into a new institutional procedure, highly specific to those areas, and very different from supranational legislation. The competences only complement the other objectives of the EC. They are not objectives to be achieved by themselves, but only as a side effect of achieving the Community objectives.

Article K1 (3) of the Treaty of Maastricht specifies that the areas of common interest have an end goal in the implementation of the Union objectives, in particular the free movement of persons. It is hence a restricted approach, limited to the community objectives. The nine areas of common interests are: (1) asylum policy, (2) external border control, (3) immigration (entry, circulation, stay and fight against illegal immigration), (4) fight against drugs, (5) against international crime, (6) judicial co-operation in civil matters, (7) in criminal matters, (8) customs co-operation, and (9) police co-operation.

Effectively, these areas of common interest only bring existing forms of intergovernmental co-operation under the umbrella of the EU, with one main legislator, the Council of Ministers. It is important to be clear what this means in terms of the norms that decision-makers were following at the time. Justice and Home Affairs at the beginning of the 1990s was not an area that was marked by any significant evidence of a political will to transfer any competences upwards to the level of the EU. Indeed, in legal terms, there was a legal basis for co-operation within the umbrella of the EU, but the effect of this co-operation is not significantly different from co-operation outside the framework.

This condition can be further emphasised by a close look at the legal instruments available in the third pillar. These are not real EU legal instruments, but are far more like international law instruments. Within Community legislation, the Commission normally enjoys the monopoly of the right of legislative initiative, and the European Parliament now mostly enjoys the so-called co-decision power with the Council. Finally, the European Court of Justice has jurisdiction over all Community matters. Article 249 EC defines the legal instruments available within the Community framework. The EC institutions can adopt directives, which are binding for member states as to the results achieved, but the form and method are left to the member states. Secondly, regulations (directly binding) and decisions (binding for member states and individuals) can be used, as well as non-binding 'soft law'-like Conclusions, Recommendations and Resolutions (Shaw, 2000). In addition, EC Treaty articles have 'direct effect', meaning they form part of national law and can be pleaded in national courts directly or by individuals.

Within the area of JHA under the Maastricht Treaty, the legal instruments available underlined the fact that there was a basic disagreement as to whether the EU should legislate at all. For instance, Article K.3(2)(a) allowed the Council to adopt 'joint positions'. In addition, Article K.3(2)(b) allowed for 'joint actions' if EU objectives are better achieved together than on a individual national basis. This article implies that a justification on those grounds was needed for every proposal made, which is impossible to demonstrate conclusively either way. Article K.3(2)(c) referred to Conventions, which the Council could draw up and then recommend to the member states. However, the legal effect of all these instruments was rather cumbersome. Conventions were an established instrument in public international law, and measures were binding at the international level, but it was up to each country to determine the legal effect upon national law. While Community instruments are legally binding, these public international law instruments were not.

Again, this serves very well to underline the fact that the EU was not gaining legislative competence in JHA with the Treaty of Maastricht. The fact that the EU institutions were weak in the third pillar only follows as a logical consequence of the refusal to transfer legislative competence, and hence the refusal to pool national sovereignty in the area of JHA in the EU. To conclude, one faces the stark observation that legally the Maastricht Treaty did not mark a change in norms amongst decision-makers. National sovereignty remained intact; indeed most legal developments could have been achieved in theory before Maastricht just as well as after.

The most important victory for the Commission was the institutionalisation of what the aim of co-operation in JHA already signified, i.e. a flanking measure of the Single Market. This would make a roll-back of this aim very difficult for the future. This is precisely what the Commission had suggested back in 1985 in its famous White Paper.

Stage 3: the Amsterdam Treaty

Despite a commonly held assumption to the contrary, Geddes (2000, p. 110) demonstrates convincingly that the Treaty of Amsterdam did not supranationalise the policy-making area of JHA. However, it profoundly changed the objectives of the EU in JHA matters. As a consequence, it is worthwhile to examine the Treaty in greater detail. In addition, it also brought about a change of name – Justice and Home Affairs (JHA) became known as the Area of Freedom, Security and Justice (AFSJ).

What are the implications of the failure to supranationalise the area regarding the social norms of decision-makers? Firstly, national sovereignty remains the dominant norm. If decision-makers had wanted to pool national sovereignty at the EU level, the Treaty of Maastricht would have provided a possibility for this to happen. A so-called '*passerelle* clause' would have made it possible for the Council to unanimously decide to shift areas of common interest from the third pillar to the first pillar, the EC pillar, with the exception of criminal justice or police co-operation (De Lobkowicz, 2002, p. 96). Consequently, the non-use of the *passerelle* clause points to little normative change from Maastricht to Amsterdam.

Consequently, how can one establish the view of decision-makers regarding whether the EU should be legislating in the AFSJ? A range of views were reflected in the positions of the different member states during the negotiations of the Intergovernmental Conference (IGC) leading up to the treaty. A core of member states had expressed their support of a supranationalisation of immigration and asylum policy (Geddes, 2000). On the other side of the argument, the British Conservative government hung on to some minimalist positions instead, pointing to a spectrum of different positions of member states.

The IGC was launched at the Corfu European Council in December 1994, which established a reflection group chaired by the Spaniard Carlos Westendorp. The European Commission strongly criticised the then functioning of the decision-making procedures in the AFSJ in its May 1995 report (ibid., p. 119). It argued strongly for deeper European integration in the area – the full supranationalisation of AFSJ on the basis of democracy and efficiency. In particular, it suggested more effective legal instruments – the established EU legal instruments – combined with a strong role of the European Court of Justice (ECJ). This was also fully supported by the European Parliament (ibid., p. 120).

On the other side of the argument, the British Conservative position continued to block these EU competences, as outlined in its White Paper, *A Partnership among Nations*, in March 1996 (ibid., p. 116). The Danish and the Swedish governments supported the UK on the basis of national sovereignty concerns. Germany moved to oppose the supranationalisation of immigration policy towards the end of the negotiations. The Benelux countries, Austria, Italy, Portugal and Spain argued in favour of the supranationalisation of the policy area. Clearly, one can note that there was no normative consensus as to whether the EU should be legislating in this area. Consequently, the institutional architecture that was adopted would reflect this lack of consensus.

The most fundamental change of the Treaty of Amsterdam was the creation of an 'Area of Freedom, Justice and Security'. While the Treaty of Maastricht had only described common areas of interests, in which co-operation could happen in order to attain the Community objectives, the Treaty of Amsterdam made the concept of Freedom, Security and Justice an objective in itself. This implied legally that the EU would have to work to obtain these objectives. The legal basis of certain political actions could not be questioned any more on the grounds that it was not part and parcel of the 'flanking measures' of the Single Market. While the Treaty of Maastricht defined the general themes of co-operation in JHA, the Treaty of Amsterdam went beyond that. Consequently, it provided a first step to decouple the Single Market from the broader objectives in the AFSJ.

However, the legal mandate of the policy was much more restricted than its objective of an 'Area of Freedom, Security and Justice' would seem to suggest. With respect to asylum matters, Article 63 gave the EU competence to enact legislation on four specific issues: determining the member states responsible for considering asylum applications, as well as establishing minimum standards concerning the reception of refugees, the definition of 'refugee', and the procedures governing the asylum process. In addition, the article covered the establishment of minimum standards for giving temporary protection to displaced persons and persons who otherwise need international protection. The former concerned mass arrivals following a large conflict, such as the Kosovo conflict or the Bosnian War, while the latter was related to de facto refugees whose claim does not fulfil the criteria of the

Geneva Convention. It is also noteworthy that Article 63 emphasised the intention of the EU to respect all legal obligations under the Geneva Convention.

Concerning immigration matters, Article 63 stipulated the EU legal competence regarding measures on the:

- Conditions of entry into and residence in the EU.
- Conditions under which long-term visa and residence permits would be issued, including visas for family reunion.
- Conditions under which third-country nationals may reside in a member state other than that of their residence permit.
- Fight against illegal immigration and illegal residence.
- Expulsion of illegal immigrants.

De Lobkowicz (2002, p. 2127) confirms the view that the EU was given only a limited mandate. Article 63 EC required the Council to adopt within five years the variety of measures in the asylum field mentioned above, yet the majority of measures restricted the mandate to minimum standards of each measure (Peers, 2000). From the EU's point of view, it was a significantly restricted mandate, as it also implied that once the minimum standards were introduced no more action was needed. The same was true for legal and illegal immigration. Thus, De Lobkowicz argues that the Treaty of Amsterdam did not create a general legal competence for EU to create a common policy. Rather it created a work programme with specific tasks to fulfil. The Council had to complete the programme with EC-like instruments, but not real Community instruments.

The complexity of the newly created legislative procedure by the Treaty of Amsterdam only serves to conceal the fact that there were basic disagreements about the nature of the AFSJ. Should the EU be legislating in the area of JHA? The answer in the Treaty of Amsterdam was a 'maybe, maybe not'. Some policy matters were transferred to the first pillar while others were not.

Changes were also made to the legislative process, which came to be organised as follows (Kaunert, 2005, pp. 466–467; De Lobkowicz, 2002, p. 130; Peers, 2000, p. 40; Simpson, 1999, pp. 91-124):

- The Council acts unanimously in the consultation procedure with the European Parliament.
- The legal right of initiative lies with both the Commission and individual member states.
- From 1 May 2004, for the first pillar competences asylum and migration, the treaty establishes the sole right of legal initiative for the Commission.
- The Council could then also decide by unanimity to move towards co-decision with the European Parliament, and towards qualified majority voting as the decision-making mechanism in the Council.

- The European Court of Justice (ECJ), often the engine of integration, initially excluded in its jurisdiction from the area under the Treaty of Maastricht, gains more jurisdiction under Amsterdam, but remains strongly restricted.

However, as one significant drawback in the Treaty of Amsterdam, Article 69 includes three protocols attached to the treaty base (Simpson, 1999, p. 99). These exempt the UK and Ireland from all the provisions on asylum and migration (new Title IV), as well as Denmark from involvement in measures under the same title. All thee protocols are annexed to both the Treaty of Maastricht and Amsterdam, and have thus the legal force of the treaty itself. In essence, this is a trade-off from the negotiations between the integration-minded member states and the UK and Denmark (Ireland effectively bound to the UK position).

The UK demanded this exemption on the grounds of maintaining border controls with other member states, which practically obliged Ireland to follow suit in order to keep its Common Travel Area (CTA) with the UK (ibid., p. 100). Both member states are nonetheless permitted to opt into adopting and applying any measure proposed under the title as long as this decision is communicated to the Council Presidency three months after a proposal has been submitted. The Danish position is somewhat different. It requested the legal opt-out in response to concerns about a possible ratification failure for the Treaty of Amsterdam after the Treaty of Maastricht had been rejected in its first referendum. Consequently, the protocol exempts Denmark from all legal obligations from Title IV. However, this also means that, contrary to the UK and Ireland, Denmark did not receive an opt-in possibility. Thus, Denmark can only unilaterally implement legal decisions by doing this in the form of public international law.

In fact, the institutional arrangements of Amsterdam were even more complex than the ones in the Treaty of Maastricht. There is no generally accepted norm observable amongst decision-makers as to whether the EU should legislate or not. The arrangements represent an advance from the Maastricht Treaty where the answer to the aforementioned question was a clear 'no'. But the Amsterdam Treaty was by no means a 'yes' either. The institutional set-up of the third pillar, explained above, also underlines this argument. Even in this part of the Treaty, the answer to the normative question of EU competence was not a clear 'no' any more, yet it did not amount to a clear 'yes' either.

The incorporation of Schengen into the Treaty of Amsterdam

The scenario to integrate Schengen ('Schengen Acquis') into the EU only emerged at a very late stage during the negotiations for the Treaty of Amsterdam (Den Boer, 2001, p. 296), and was particularly pushed by the Dutch Minister of European Affairs, Michiel Patijn. The functional reason for the incorporation was the close relationship between the substance of the intergovernmental Schengen co-operation and the substance of the newly created AFSJ. However, the proposal was initially not received with much enthusiasm. Given this reluctance of some member states, in particular the UK and Ireland, the Dutch Presidency subsequently suggested a modest and global approach to integrate Schengen. The Treaty of Amsterdam would only stipulate the principle of incorporation and the application of the working method and procedures. The allocation of the Schengen texts would follow subsequently.

The legal mechanism of integrating the Schengen Acquis is a protocol (Simpson, 1999, pp. 106–107). The fifteen member states of the time would allow the thirteen Schengen states to establish closer co-operation amongst themselves within the institutional and legal framework of the EU, taking account of the respective opt-out and opt-in protocols of the UK, Ireland and Denmark. Article 2 of the protocol sets out the procedures to integrate the acquis into the treaty; essentially a work programme by the Council to identify the legal basis for each provision of the acquis, either pillar one or pillar three. Article 5 addresses the question of integrating the acquis under either of those pillars: 'the relevant provisions of the treaties shall apply'. The executive of the AFSJ hierarchy handled the incorporation process under two working groups (Den Boer, 2001, p. 298). The first 'Schengen I' group dealt with the incorporation of the acquis across the two pillars, and the possible opt-ins by the UK and Ireland. The second 'Schengen II' group examined the positions of Norway and Iceland as members of the Schengen Convention, but not of the EU. The work of both groups was finally completed under the German Presidency in the second half of 1999. With the integration of the Schengen Acquis into the treaties of the EU, it has become a legal obligation for all new member states of the different Enlargement waves of 2004 and 2007 (EU12) to fulfil. According to Geddes (2000, p. 125), the acquis comprises 172 documents covering all aspects of the 142 articles of the Schengen agreements.

The effect of the incorporation of the Schengen Acquis resulted in the fact that all decisions made by the secretive and largely opaque Schengen Executive Committee would become Community law with the entry into force of the Treaty of Amsterdam in 1999. Much of the Schengen decision had been taken outside the realm of democratic and judicial control (Den Boer, 2001, p. 300). The introduction of more solid and accountable responsibility within the supranational organisation EU with the judicial oversight of the ECJ was perceived to be preferable by policy-makers and academic scholars (Geddes, 2000, p. 126). The incorporation of Schengen also involved the merging of the Schengen institutions into those of the EU.

In conclusion, in the Treaty of Amsterdam, a number of incremental steps were taken towards supranationalisation. Yet it is difficult to overlook the fact that the question of EU competence was far from settled. If anything, it is was even more diverse after Amsterdam, in particular after the inclusion of the Schengen Acquis, which was split between the third and first pillars. The EU was given a broad objective in the AFSJ, but with a limited mandate in terms of competences and instruments.

Stage 4: the Council Summit in Tampere, 1999

The start of the Finnish Presidency on 1 July 1999 marks one of the most critical junctures in the history of the AFSJ. Norms of decision-makers changed significantly after Tampere, despite the fact that it is not a treaty building occasion. The conclusions of the Tampere Council (European Council, October 1999) are legally only 'soft law' (Shaw, 2000, p. 247), rules of conduct with practical effects. Yet, as decision-makers met to discuss the AFSJ for the first time in the EU's history at a summit entirely dedicated to the subject, important normative shifts occurred.

This section argues that the most important effect for the AFSJ has been the significant shift in norms for decision-makers at the Tampere Council Summit. At the Summit, decision-makers reconstructed the normative rationale as to why the EU should be involved in the AFSJ. As demonstrated in earlier sections, the AFSJ had been interpreted as a flanking measure for the Single Market. Despite the creation of an AFSJ, the Treaty of Amsterdam did not provide any new normative rationale independent of the former interpretation. The Tampere summit changed this normative rationale decisively. However, the summit did not change the legal competences of the EU, nor the decision mechanisms. Thus, the normative question as to whether the EU should be legislating still remained unanswered.

Several factors contributed to the heightened interest in the AFSJ around that time. Firstly, political events such as the disintegration of Yugoslavia and the ensuing refugee flows, as well as the Kosovo crisis, had propelled asylum and migration issues to the top of the political agenda in many European states. Secondly, the Amsterdam Treaty, as has just been explained, had increased the competences of the EU in this policy area and had established new policy objectives for the EU. Several member states considered that, in order to attain those, the EU needed to adopt a more precise work programme (including deadlines) to implement the treaty, in line with the system put in place for the development of the European Monetary Union (de Lobkowicz, 2002, p. 161; Occhipinti, 2003). The 1998 Cardiff European Council called for a plan outlining how best to implement the provisions of the Treaty establishing an AFSJ. The European Commission responded within a few months, delineating a precise agenda and proposing precise objectives.

The main outcomes of the Tampere summit were the so-called 'ten milestones' towards a union of 'freedom, security and justice'. In the conclusions of the summit, the milestones (European Council, October 1999) are preceded by ten introductory points, which explain the normative rationale for co-operation in the AFSJ. As pointed out in my previous analysis, this had been one of the main obstacles for progress before Tampere, i.e. the fact that the normative questions had not been decided. The first of the introductory points refers back to European integration as a process being based on human rights, democratic institutions and the rule of law, which are necessary for assuring peace and prosperity, and also for an enlarging Union. This elevates human rights as a basic objective of European integration, together with democratic institutions and the rule of law. The implication here is that the Union has to provide the remedies necessary to ensure the rule of law and democracy.

In addition, the rationale includes:

- Links to citizens outside the union due to Europe's humanitarian tradition.
- Commitments to international obligations such as the Geneva Refugee Convention.
- Freedom in a genuine area of justice, where criminals cannot hide behind differences in legal systems.
- The union as an actor on the international scene.

The following concrete objectives are new and thus redefine the AFSJ – a reconstruction from flanking measures to the single market to a free-standing area. However, the objectives go beyond the legal competences of the EU. In several cases, the objectives do not match the legal competences as provided by the treaties of Maastricht and Amsterdam. Thus, in a way, the Tampere Summit advances the normative question as to what the EU should aim for in its policy, but does not answer whether it should legislate per se. The absence of a precise legal basis for the following demands is a clear indication that the latter question still remains unanswered.

There are four milestones (ibid.) in Part A regarding a Common Asylum and Immigration Policy:

- Firstly, the goal of a 'partnership with countries of origin' is entirely new – not included in the Treaty of Amsterdam as an objective, nor given any specific competences. In fact, it neither follows logically nor legally that flanking measures for the single market would make this necessary. It follows, rather, from the humanitarian normative rationale of the Tampere conclusions.
- Secondly, the competence for a 'common European asylum' system is only partially covered by the Treaties. The legal competence only relates to minimum standards, but there is absolutely no legal basis for the long-term objective of a common asylum system with uniform status for those

that are granted asylum. This in effect means a different aim of the policy and does not necessarily follow from the Single Market argument, but rather from an argument about the AFSJ.

- Thirdly, the 'fair treatment of third country nationals', which includes the integration programmes for migrants, is not mandated with a clear legal competence either. Read in combination with the Tampere aims of a legal approximation on the conditions for admission and residence of third-country nationals, as well as the approximation of their status to EU citizens, it becomes clear that this does not follow logically from a normative rationale of flanking measures of the Single Market. Indeed, it rather follows the normative rationale of the Tampere conclusions.
- Fourthly, there is no clear legal basis for the objective of a 'management of migration' either. The demands are for close co-operation with countries of origins and transit, as well as for the combating of illegal trafficking. Border controls and illegal trafficking, for which there is a legal basis, are combined with migration flow issues, for which there is not. The latter also does not follow from arguments about flanking measures.

Part B (ibid.) calls for a genuine area of justice, in some way repeating the Treaty of Amsterdam. As above, a similar pattern of demands without legal competences emerges. These three milestones are particularly important:

- Better access to justice in Europe. In a pattern similar to the previous objectives, the legal basis for this objective is not clear.
- The principle of mutual recognition on judicial decision, which aims at preserving the different legal traditions within the EU. Again, this has not been mentioned in the treaties yet.
- Greater convergence in civil law.

Part C deals with the fight against crime, and also comprises three milestones. As above, a similar pattern of demands without legal competences emerges:

- The prevention of crime at the level of the Union becomes an objective. It has been partially recognised in the Treaties through criminal co-operation, but there is no clear legal basis for prevention.
- Stepping up co-operation against crime becomes an objective. Point 48 calls for common definitions, incriminations and sanctions. Yet, again, there is no legal competence for such measures.
- Special action against money laundering.

In addition to these three parts, Part D calls for stronger external action in the AFSJ: point 59 calls for all competences and instruments at the disposal of the EU to be used to build the AFSJ.

It has been demonstrated that there had been a significant shift in norms for decision-makers in the AFSJ at the Tampere Council Summit. From the conclusions, decision-makers reconstructed the normative rationale as to why the EU should be involved in the AFSJ. The AFSJ is no longer a flanking measure for the Single Market. The Treaty of Amsterdam did not provide this new normative rationale, but rather the Tampere Summit conclusions. Yet, the summit did not change the legal competences of the EU, nor the decision mechanisms. Consequently, the summit made demands, which have no legal basis in the existing treaties. Logically, the aim of the Tampere programme must then be to acquire such a legal basis.

What were the political dynamics at the Summit? Occhipinti (2003) explains that the origins of the idea to hold such a Summit dedicated entirely to the subject of AFSJ can be traced back to the Spanish government under Prime Minister Aznar. This then led to a commitment at the Vienna European Council 1998 to hold the Summit. The preparations were first made under the German Presidency and then under the Finnish Presidency in 1999.

Tampere coincided with the appointment of the new Commission in 1999, with its President Prodi and the new JHA commissioner Antonio Vitorino. For the first time there was a Commission Directorate entirely dedicated to the AFSJ, headed by Sir Adrian Fortescue as Director General. Commissioner Vitorino had been uniquely qualified to accelerate integration in AFSJ matters with his wealth of experience as a constitutional lawyer, as a parliamentary committee member in Portugal on European integration (1980–1984), and most significantly as the past chairman of the European Parliament's Committee on Civil Liberties and Internal Affairs (ibid., 2003, p. 81).

In the literature, the Commission is not widely attributed to have set the agenda very decisively in terms of themes of the summit – despite the positive changes mentioned above. Yet, it seems to have pushed important elements of its agenda into the Tampere conclusions. For instance, Occhipinti (ibid., p. 82) cites Prodi, who argued in a letter to the Finnish Prime Minister to not send out the impression of a Summit of repression, and, indeed, the conclusion reflected this humanitarian spirit. Furthermore, the Commission suggested the use of a 'scoreboard' system (interview CON 3, 2004) along the lines of a method used successfully for the internal market. This scoreboard could then be used as an instrument to exert pressure on areas of the AFSJ where progress was lagging behind, as suggested by Occhipinti (2003, p. 86). In the conclusions, the Council called upon the Commission to monitor a timetable of progress towards each of the goals and objectives in the Tampere conclusions.

During research interviews, an official from the Finnish delegation (interview PR12, 2004) present in Tampere suggested that, in particular, one Commission official responsible for asylum and migration matters had been particularly influential. He claimed that this Commission official had lobbied very hard and persistently for the inclusion of integration measures, and, in general, for a rather open and humanitarian wording of the conclusions with regards to asylum and migration. For this and other reasons to be discussed at a later point, the outcome of the Tampere summit and subsequent developments are suggestive of the Commission having acted in the role of a supranational policy entrepreneur. The next chapters will examine this in detail.

The Area of Freedom, Security and Justice until Tampere: towards supranational governance?

The aim of this chapter has been to provide a historical genealogy of the social norm environment of decision-makers in the AFSJ in the period until the Tampere Council Summit in 1999. This is particularly important in the light of a sharp increase of activity in this policy area within the framework of the EU. Most areas within the AFSJ are at the heart of the nation-state. Yet, how have norms developed until the Tampere Council Summit 1999, the point of departure for the research covered in the next chapters? In general, it has been demonstrated that norms until Tampere had evolved in two dimensions.

Firstly, one can note a development on the axis of whether the EU should be legislating at all in the AFSJ, where the normative debate had been structured between those wishing to preserve national sovereignty and those wishing to pool sovereignty at the EU level. Before the Treaty of Maastricht in 1992, national sovereignty was safeguarded very closely. Therefore, the first question would have been answered with a resounding 'No'. Internal security and the police were widely perceived to be vital and, indeed, core areas of the state. However, co-operation was perceived as increasingly more important as a counter-measure to the dismantling of internal borders at the heart of the Single Market.

The Treaty of Maastricht confirmed the preservation of national sovereignty and the purpose of co-operation as a flanking measure of the internal market. The Treaty of Amsterdam in 1997 created for the first time the grand objective of an AFSJ, but it did not supranationalise the policy area. The main normative change was a shift away from a full preservation of national sovereignty towards a partial pooling of national sovereignty with limited mandates and weak institutional instruments and structures. This indicates some normative movement, though limited in nature. Secondly, there was also some development on the axis of what the aims and the purpose of such legislation would be. Here, the evolution ranged from a flanking measure of the Single Market to a free-standing Area of Freedom, Justice and Security unrelated to the Single Market.

While this chapter has dealt with mainly structual developments amongst decision-makers, it is crucial to examine agency-oriented considerations of

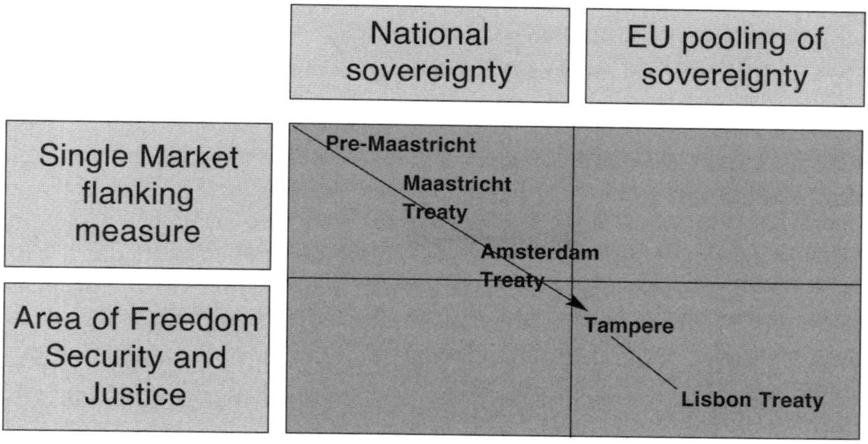

Figure 3.1 The norm matrix for the Area of Freedom, Security and Justice

policy entrepreneurship. Prima facia evidence suggests that the Commission, alongside other institutional actors such as the Presidency and the Council Secretariat, may have played a significant role in the area from its beginnings. While this was not the aim of this chapter, it has been raised as a possibility that merits closer attention throughout the next chapters.

The Commission had moved quickly with the famous White Paper on the Internal Market in 1985, where it argued strongly for the case of necessary flanking measures in the AFSJ due to the dismantling of internal borders. This functional logic became accepted even when it did not result in supranational competence for the EU. However, the increasing body of evidence described above suggests that the Commission has been pushing for its own policy solutions, which underlines the importance of this research.

Uçarer (2001a) also points to an increasing amount of evidence for an important role for the European Commission in the AFSJ. Her findings seem to suggest that the Commission had seen its involvement in the decision-making enhanced in the period until the Amsterdam Treaty in 1997. Her arguments relate to the fact that the institutional structure agreed in Maastricht made it awkward for the Commission to act efficiently in the third pillar of JHA. Thus, it put considerable constraints on its agency capacity and its ability to act as a 'competence-maximising' institution (ibid.). With Amsterdam, the Commission's institutional capacity increased quite markedly. Uçarer, in essence, argues that with this stronger constitutional and institutional basis, the Commission is 'no sidekick no more' (ibid., p. 1). The following chapters will establish whether and how this may hold for the role of EU institution in the process of creating an AFSJ more generally.

Note

1 JHA; with the Treaty of Amsterdam this area was renamed the AFSJ. Throughout this chapter JHA shall be used for before Amsterdam and AFSJ after.

Acknowledgement

Extracts from this chapter have been previously published in C. Kaunert, 'The Area of Freedom, Security and Justice: The Construction of a "European Public Order"', *European Security*, vol. 14, no. 4 (2005), pp. 459–483. Many thanks to Taylor & Francis for allowing its republication as part of this chapter.

4

EU counter-terrorism co-operation and the role of EU institutions

The European Union and the advent of international terrorism

Amongst scholars of EU counter-terrorism, there are diverging opinions as to which extent EU competences matter in the fight against the global terrorist threat (Reinares, 2000; Dubois, 2002; den Boer and Monar, 2002; Mitsilegas and Gilmore, 2007; Occhipinti, 2003; Deflem, 2006; Bures, 2006, 2008; Gregory, 2005; Zimmermann, 2006; Friedrichs, 2005; den Boer, Hillebrand and Nölke, 2008; Müller-Wille, 2008; Spence, 2006; Bossong, 2008; Kaunert, 2005, 2007, 2009). One the one hand, the EU is characterised as a 'paper tiger' (Bures, 2006, p. 57) and thus an ineffective counter-terrorism actor. On the other hand, scholars point out that the EU has taken great strides towards increasing integration and encouraging co-operation between member states since 9/11 (Zimmermann, 2006; Kaunert, 2007). Zimmermann (2006, p. 123) asserted that 'on 21 September 2001, the Union prioritised the fight against terrorism, and accelerated the development and implementation of measures deliberated on prior to the events of 9/11'. Yet, Zimmermann (2006, p. 126) makes an important caveat to all EU action in the field of counter-terrorism: '... the Union does not have a "normal" government at the supranational level with all the requisite powers, competences and, hence, capabilities of regular government; it is not a federal European state'. This means, a priori, one would not necessarily expect EU institutions to provide significant leadership in counter-terrorism.

EU counter-terrorism policy has also begun to receive significant scholarly attention recently (Spence, 2007). The *Journal of Common Market Studies* published a special issue on this topic in January 2008. The introductory article (Edwards and Meyer, 2008, p. 1) suggests that the entire 'governance of the European Union has been changed through its responses to international terrorism'. This is not a surprising claim when one considers that European security scholars frequently identify terrorism as one of the most salient security threats in the public perception across Europe. This leads Edwards and Meyer to present the surprising finding that 'the politics of counter-terrorism have contributed to the blurring of differences between the so-called three pillars established by the Maastricht Treaty' (ibid., p. 11).

However, counter-terrorism, while clearly one of the most crucial security policy fields within the EU, is also one of the most complicated areas in institutional terms. Counter-terrorism is, of course, a broad term which can encompass measures across all three pillars, from trade sanction of state sponsors of terrorism (in pillars 1 and 2), to the implementation of UN Security Council resolutions (pillar 2), to police and judicial co-operation (pillar 3). Therefore, it is important to keep in mind the cross-pillar character of the EU counter-terrorism policy when drawing conclusions on the role of EU institutions from the following analysis, as they can only be generalised to the pillar concerned. With this caveat, it must be underlined that the analysis of the EU counter-terrorism policy, precisely because of its institutional specificity, yields results of particular interest to those interested in EU policy-making more generally and in the AFSJ in particular.

Before analysing the role of EU institutions in counter-terrorism, it is necessary to clarify the understanding of terrorism underpinning the next two chapters. Whilst recognising that there is no globally agreed definition of terrorism (Wilkinson, 2006), this chapter will use the following working definition: 'the calculated use of violence or the threat of violence to inculcate fear, intended to coerce or intimidate governments or societies as to the pursuit of goals that are generally political, religious or ideological' (US Department of Defense, cited in Whittaker, 2003). This operational definition notwithstanding, it is recognised that an understanding of terrorism is an inherently political and calculated process (Hoffman, 2006). Depending on the side of the political argument, the term can acquire a different meaning. This can entail the negative connotation of 'terrorism' or the more positive uses as 'freedom fighters' (Arafat), 'urban guerrillas' (Brazilian revolutionary Carlos Marighela), and defence or revenge movements (Hoffman, 2006).

Forms of terrorism are often categorised according to the political motivations of the perpetrators (Whittaker, 2003; Wilkinson, 2006; Hoffman, 2006):

- *Ethno-nationalist groups.* These are secular terrorist groups aiming to achieve an ethno-nationalist ambition, such as the creation of a new state. Examples in this category are the group ETA in Spain, the IRA in Britain, or the PLO in Israel/Palestinian Occupied Territories.
- *Ideological groups.* These are secular terrorist groups motivated by different ideologies, such as Marxism, Maoism, Anarchism, etc. Examples of such groups are the former Red Brigades in Italy, the Red Army Fraction (RAF) or Baader-Meinhof Gang in Germany, the FARC in Colombia, or the Shining Path in Peru.
- *Religio-political groups*. These are non-secular, religiously motivated terrorist groups, such as Hamas with the objective of an Islamic Republic of Palestine, or Al Qaeda with the objective of a pan-Islamic Caliphate in the Middle East.
- *Single-issue groups.* These are secular terrorist groups with one particular

political objective (not covered above), such as the Animal Liberation Front (ALF). These groups have not yet caused any deaths, but only material damage.

With the terrorist attacks on the US (11 September 2001), Madrid (11 March 2004) and London (7 July 2005), as well as the failed attempts on 21 July 2005, Al Qaeda has increasingly emerged as the most dangerous terrorist organisation to EU member states. According to terrorism scholars (Hoffman, 2006; Wilkinson, 2006), Al Qaeda mainly aims to (1) establish the Shari'a religious law across Muslim lands in order to facilitate the arrival of the 'Messiah', (2) expel US and 'infidels' from Middle East and Muslim lands, (3) topple Muslim regimes that 'betray' true Islam, (4) ultimately establish a pan-Islamist 'Caliphate', reminiscent of the 'glorious days' of the Ottoman Empire, and (5) lead a Jihad ('holy war') against the US and its allies (the UK, Spain but increasingly also other European countries, such as Germany, France and Italy), and set up a 'World Islamic Front for Jihad'.

For EU member states, the danger that Al Qaeda represents mainly relates to its specific organisation and structure, which make European co-operation crucial in order to tackle it (Hoffman, 2006; Wilkinson, 2006). Its structure is that of a large transnational movement or network, rather than a traditional 'terrorist' organisation. This makes it more difficult to establish good intelligence in a mono-national setting. Al Qaeda's modus operandi requires a response based on strong transnational co-operation. Furthermore, Al Qaeda has a large presence in over sixty countries, making it the most widely dispersed terrorist movement in history. Whilst Osama Bin Laden and Ayman Zawahiri provide ideological and strategic leadership, assisted by a Shura (Council of Advisors), the networks of cells and affiliated organisations are responsible for their own operations. Thirdly, the political aims of Al Qaeda, which are absolutist in ideology, are generally perceived to be ultimately incorrigible (Hoffman, 2006). In contrast to this requirement of co-operation to effectively tackle the threat represented by Al Qaeda, the situation in the EU at the time of the terrorist attacks on 11 September 2001 was characterised by a general lack of co-operation in counter-terrorism.

One of the crucial elements of fighting transnational terrorism is extradition co-operation. Despite its importance, however, extradition between EU member states before the introduction of the European Arrest Warrant (EAW) was based on a set of different, inefficient conventions (Peers, 2001). All EU member states were bound by the 1957 Council of Europe European Convention on Extradition, seven were bound by a 1975 protocol to the convention, and eleven were bound by a 1978 protocol. In addition, all member states were bound by the 1977 Council of Europe European Convention on terrorism. The Schengen Implementing Convention of 1990 also contained provisions in this regard. In 1995 and 1996, EU member states agreed on two conventions, supplementing the aforementioned conventions with regard to extradition in cases where a fugitive consents to it. However, both of these were not ratified by all member states at the time of the European Commission's proposal on the EAW. This means that, at the time of the EAW proposal, EU member states were still relying on inefficient and ineffective international conventions in their extradition relationships. These, being constructed as international law, did not have a similar force in law as the EAW. This means, it is very clear how intergovernmental the area was designed at that point. It is difficult to find many other areas in which the institutional role of the Commission has been more restricted institutionally.

This chapter investigates the construction of an AFSJ in response to international terrorism, as outlined above. Since the terrorist attacks on 11 September 2001, the first and foremost security threat to enable the construction of the AFSJ is terrorism. Some authors have argued that it has become the 'greatest security threat of our times' (Hoffman, 2006; Wilkinson, 2006). This chapter will argue that EU institutions have capitalised on the presence of this 'security threat' in order to drive forward the process of European integration. The area of counter-terrorism can be described as the hardest case for the Commission, or any EU institution, to demonstrate its potential to act as a supranational policy entrepreneur. Nonetheless, it is precisely the area where the EU advanced most significantly after 9/11 with the agreement of the definition on terrorism and the European Arrest Warrant (EAW), as well as counter-terrorist financing, which will be analysed in more detail below. What has been the role of the European Commission, as well as the Council Secretariat, in establishing the EU as such a major actor in the field of counter-terrorism?

Policy entrepreneurship, policy advances and the role of EU institutions

The Tampere agenda

The Tampere European Council Summit of 1999 marks one of the most critical junctures in the history of the AFSJ. The origins of the idea to hold such a summit dedicated entirely to the subject of AFSJ can be traced back to the Spanish government under Prime Minister Aznar (Occhipinti, 2003). While the Commission is not widely credited to have set the political agenda, it appears to have pushed important elements of its agenda into the Tampere conclusions (Occhipinti, 2003, p. 82), such as the use of a 'scoreboard' system (interview CON 3, 2004) to monitor a timetable of progress towards each of the goals and objectives. This scoreboard was then used throughout the five-year programme as an instrument to exert pressure on member states if progress was lagging behind. However, the Commission also strategically used the openness of the Tampere conclusion on extradition matters in order to push for much more significant measures than member states initially asked for.

The adoption of the principle of mutual recognition of judiciary decisions is often seen as the major advance for European integration in criminal justice and counter-terrorism matters. Wagner (2003b) claims that this principle may play a role 'similar to the 1979 Cassis de Dijon judgement of the European Court of Justice ... which paved the way for the internal market'. In fact, according to Wagner (2003a) the Spanish government and the Commission both worked successfully on establishing this principle at the EU level, which had already been included in a series of Spanish bilateral treaties with Italy, France, the United Kingdom, and Belgium. This could be an indicator for Commission influence already at this early stage in the member state preference formation.

However, a closer look at the precise point regarding extradition in the Tampere Conclusions makes it clear how many options were still open on the road to the EAW:

> Point 35. With respect to criminal matters, the European Council urges Member States to speedily ratify the 1995 and 1996 EU Conventions on extradition. It considers that the formal extradition procedure should be abolished among the Member States as far as persons are concerned who are fleeing from justice after having been finally sentenced, and replaced by a simple transfer of such persons, in compliance with Article 6 TEU. Consideration should also be given to fast track extradition procedures, without prejudice to the principle of fair trial ... (European Council, October 1999, Tampere Conclusions)

This demonstrates the fact that the Commission's eventual EAW proposal went much further than the plans based on the 1999 conclusions of the Tampere European Council (Peers, 2001, p. 2; Wagner, 2003a, p. 706). Formal extradition was only planned to be abolished for convicted criminals, but not for crime suspects as covered by the EAW. The road from 'consideration of fast track extradition procedures' to the EAW is still very long. Research interviews (interviews PR1 to PR25) indicate that there were significant problems with the ideas in the EAW, such as the removal of the principle of double criminality and the effective removal of the political phase within the extradition procedure. For this and other reasons to be discussed below, the outcome of the Tampere summit and subsequent developments are suggestive of the Commission having acted in the role of a supranational policy entrepreneur.

11 September 2001

After the events of 11 September 2001 in the US, the EU adopted a framework to fight more effectively against terrorism. Immediately after the attacks on Washington and New York, the EU process went into action. The Justice and Home Affairs (JHA) Council met on 20 September 2001, agreeing on a package of measures in the fight against terrorism. These were endorsed by an extraordinary European Council meeting on the next day. In the extraordinary Council meeting on 21 September 2001, held a few days after the attacks in the US, the European Council launched an ambitious 'Action Plan to Combat Terrorism'. Its cornerstones were 'close co-operation between all the Member States of the EU' and the adoption of a 'co-ordinated and interdisciplinary approach embracing all Union's policies' (European Council, 2001). The European Council called for the use of all the tools at EU disposal, amongst which are legislative and operational, repressive and preventive, internal and external measures. This made the European collective response as comprehensive as possible and essentially multidimensional (Monar, 2007).

The conclusions from the special EU Council of Justice and Home Affairs Ministers on terrorism (Hayes, 2001) developed into a far-reaching action plan. The following legislative measures were proposed for the AFSJ:

- EU-wide definition of terrorism.
- European Arrest Warrant to replace extradition.
- Eurojust to become operational.
- EU mechanism for freezing assets of suspects.
- 1995 and 1996 EU Extradition Conventions to be ratified by member states.
- EU Mutual Legal Assistance (MLA) Convention, 2000, to be ratified by member states.
- Protocol extending obligations under 2000 MLA Convention to be ratified by member states.
- Immigration and asylum legislation to be examined with reference to the terrorist threat.
- Provisions of joint investigation teams in 2000 MLA Convention to come into force early.
- Mechanism for investigating attacks on computer systems and prosecuting computer crime.
- Ensure a balance between data protection and police efficiency with regard to the EC directive on data protection in the telecommunications sector.

Which measures in this list are significant? Firstly, the Framework Decision on Combating Terrorism is important. The European Commission presented a proposal to that effect to the aforementioned special meeting of EU Justice and Home Affairs Ministers in Brussels on countries in September 2001. It intended to put in place a definition of terrorism, alongside penalties and sanctions that come on extradition procedures and mechanisms for exchanging information. Effectively, this is the first time such a definition has been agreed to on a supranational level, especially in the light that a number of member states did not even have definitions of terrorism (Douglas-Scott, 2004).

The EU's Framework Decision on Combating Terrorism, agreed politically in December 2001, firstly defines what is meant by terrorist acts in three parts: (1) the context of an action, (2) the aim of the action, and (3) the specific acts being committed.

> They must be intentional acts ... which given their nature or context, may serve to damage a country or an international organisation. These acts must be committed with the aim of either seriously intimidating a population or unduly compelling a Government or international organisation to act or fail to act, or seriously destabilising or destroying the fundamental political, constitutional economic or social structures of a country or international organisation. (Bures, 2006, p. 68)

In addition, a list defines eight specific acts. The definition also covers behaviours which may contribute to terrorist acts in third countries.

The Framework Decision on Combating Terrorism thus ensures that terrorist offences are punished by heavier sentences than common criminal offences in all EU member states would have provided for. Furthermore, it approximates the level of sanctions between member states according to the principle that sentences have to be both proportional and dissuasive. Member states are legally responsible to act in cases of terrorist incidents that take place on their own territory or are committed against their own people. As pointed out by Dubois (2002, p. 326), this Framework Decision is also favourable for EU–US co-operation in the fight against terrorism as this offence is now recognised as a criminal offence on both sides of the Atlantic.

Yet, of the eleven measures above, six were proposed before 11 September and another four were already firmly on the EU's agenda. The 1995 and 1996 EU extradition conventions had not been ratified by member states at that point in time, thus making speedy ratification necessary. Of course, the EAW replaces those conventions and, in effect, makes them redundant. The rest of the measures were either operational (8, 9, 10, 11) or built on legal instruments of international law (5, 6, 7), which are neither very efficient nor under the supervision of the European Court of Justice. Consequently, in this chapter, mainly two significant measures will be analysed – the definition of terrorism and the European arrest warrant.

The European Arrest Warrant

This section will examine the importance of the EAW for European integration. The argument builds on two reasons: (1) The EAW is part of a traditional 'high politics' area very close to the heart of the nation-state, (2) the policy instrument itself is very far-reaching and restructures significantly the relations between the different EU member states in the area of extradition. Consequently, this important advance in European integration raises serious doubts about the interpretation that the pooling of national sovereignty is only possible in technocratic, uncontroversial policy areas of 'low politics'. European integration has reached the sphere of 'high politics'.

In the late 1960s, Stanley Hoffmann, a proponent of intergovernmentalism, advanced his famous distinction between 'high' and 'low' politics, which provides the basis for analysing the importance of the EAW for European integration: 'In areas of key importance to the national interest, nations prefer the certainty, or the self-controlled uncertainty, of national self-reliance, to the uncontrolled uncertainty of [integration] the untested blender' (Hoffmann, 1966, p. 882).

In his conception, European integration was possible in technocratic and uncontroversial policy areas. However, Hoffmann (1966) insisted that this approach could not work in areas of 'high politics', where the states would not give up national sovereignty under any circumstances. In his conception, 'high politics' refers to the politics of 'security'. Hoffmann's theoretical framework was inspired by scholars of the realist international relations tradition, thus explaining his strong insistence on 'security'. In his conceptualisation, the Hobbsian nation-state is clearly the main provider of security. Consequently, it is clear from this theoretical angle that intergovernmental scholars would not expect European integration to occur in 'security' areas.

However, this book argues that Hoffmann's theoretical expectations of European integration no longer sufficiently reflect the empirical record of the EU. While intergovernmentalists may have conceded that European integration is possible in areas where it is in member states' interest to co-operate, they would have argued that this could only occur in 'low politics' areas (ibid.), asserting the primacy of economic considerations, and assuming that national preferences in European policies are dictated by specific economic interests (Moravcsik, 1993, 1998).

However, European integration has reached the sphere's of 'high politics' as defined by Hoffmann (1966) by extending into extradition matters. Historically, the norm of national sovereignty meant that states did not share a common legal order and tended to perceive another state's legal order as 'alien'. Consequently, the decision whether to grant extradition to another state was traditionally an exclusive right of sovereign states (Wagner, 2003a). However, it is now the EU multi-level governance – the institutions and the member states – which is dealing with central defining elements of the Hobbsian state: the decision whether to grant extradition or not and thus by extension the provision of security against internal and external threats. Clearly, this demonstrates the importance of the European arrest warrant for European integration. European integration has reached the sphere of 'high politics'.

At the same time, related to the second part of the argument in this section, the European Arrest Warrant is also revolutionary per se, as it abolishes extradition amongst member states. This is in line with legal experts, such as Vogel, who have regarded the introduction of the principle of mutual recognition in the European Arrest Warrant to be a 'revolution in extradition law' (Vogel, 2001, p. 937). Of course, this does not preclude any such assessment for other instruments of the EU. Until the adoption of the

EAW, extradition between EU member states was based on several different intergovernmental measures based on international law (Peers, 2001), for instance the 1957 Council of Europe European Convention on Extradition, the 1975 and 1978 protocols to the convention, the 1977 Council of Europe European Convention on terrorism, the Schengen Implementing Convention of 1990, a convention in 1995 supplementing the aforementioned conventions, as well as a 1996 convention.

Unsurprisingly, all of these measures regarding extradition are based on sovereign nations agreeing to create international law between them to govern their relations with regards to extradition matters. The European arrest warrant is of a completely different kind. It does not create international law, but rather transnational or 'European' law (Wagner, 2003a). It replaces all of the aforementioned measures based on international law between the different member states with a legal instrument of the EU. In effect, this is a European extradition law.

The Commission's proposal went much further than the plans to simplify 'extradition law within the EU based on the 1999 conclusions of the Tampere European Council (Peers, 2001, p. 2; Wagner, 2003a, p. 706). Firstly, the EAW abolishes the term 'extradition' and replaces it with the term 'surrender' (Douglas-Scott, 2004). The national judicial authorities will be responsible for its enforcement, thus virtually excluding political decisions by excluding the national executives from the decision-making process. As mentioned above, this seems to suggest a change from international to transnational law (Wagner, 2003a, p. 707).

Secondly, the legal effect of this measure is subject to the jurisdiction of the European Court of Justice (Peers, 2001) if member states sign a declaration approving of this. This may be limited, but is an improvement to the previous legal position. The Commission chose to create the arrest warrant by means of a framework decision, one of the third-pillar instruments introduced by the Treaty of Amsterdam, which is binding on the member states as to the result to be achieved, leaving national authorities the choice of form and method of transposition (Peers, 2001; Wagner, 2003a).

Thirdly, the EAW abolishes the principle of double criminality for serious offences (Douglas-Scott, 2004). Thus, an arrest warrant may not be contested on the basis that it is for an activity not criminalised in the surrendering member states. In addition, the arrest warrant is applicable to all offences on a list, and not just terrorist offences. This applies to thirty-two different categories of crimes, thus, virtually all crimes apart from petty crimes. Examples of these categories of crime are: participation in a criminal organisation, terrorism, human trafficking, sexual exploitation of children and child pornography, and also corruption, fraud, money laundering, and counterfeiting money.

In conclusion, all these arguments corroborate the view that the EAW 'is a revolution in European extradition law' (Vogel, 2001) and that European

Integration has reached the sphere of 'high politics' – not expected or anticipated by scholars in the intergovernmental tradition of Hoffmann. All interviewees were in unanimous agreement about the significance and the importance of the EAW (interviews PR1 to PR24, NGO1 to NGO11, EP1 to EP5, COM 1 to COM 25, CON 1 to CON 9, IGO1 to IGO2).

Which way should the European Union go? The normative construction

Put simply, social and legal norms up until the Tampere Council Summit had evolved on two axes (Kaunert, 2005): (1) whether the EU should be legislating at all in the Area of Freedom, Security and Justice (AFSJ), where the normative debate had been structured between those wishing to preserve national sovereignty and those wishing to pool sovereignty at the EU level, and (2) what the aims and purposes of such a legislation are. This book suggests that regarding extradition matters, it is precisely this second dimension that was at the heart of the debate.

What happened in New York on 11 September 2001 had a significant impact on the norms of decision-makers in Europe. In simple terms, there were four general choices of direction available to the EU. The first option for EU member states may well have been to not join the 'war on terror' and continue to operate as before, adhering to the traditional principle of national sovereignty. This is represented by the first quadrant in the matrix. However, given the still positive state of transatlantic relations between Europe and America, this would have necessitated a clear rupture in relations. Hence, it was always unlikely to occur. The second option for EU member states would have been to build a counterweight against America's war and therefore not join in. Yet, in order to realise being a counterweight to the US, the EU would have had to integrate more politically. For the same reason as the first option, this was also unlikely to happen.

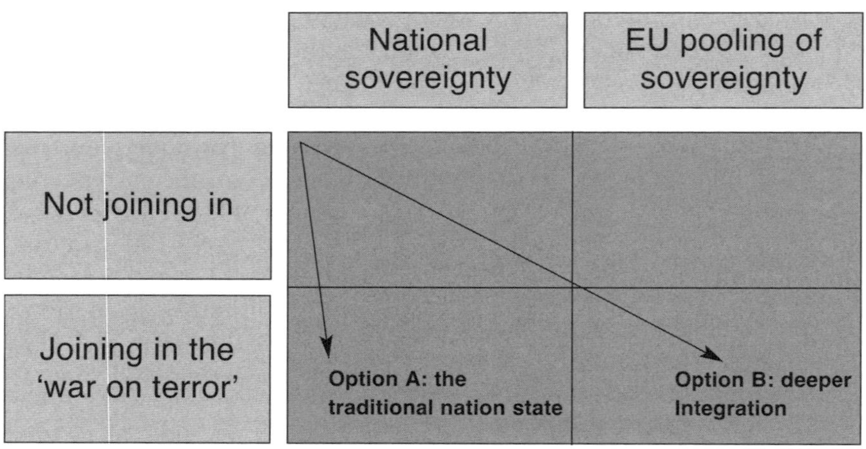

Figure 4.1 11 September 2001: the EU at a normative crossroads

This means that the norm to join the 'war on terror', which emerged after 11 September 2001, would make it difficult not to support the US. The only realistic options at this point in time were option A and option B. Option A represents what nation-states in Europe have traditionally practised for a very long time. This implies supporting the US while at the same time maintaining national sovereignty in the AFSJ. A good example here would be the provision of intelligence to the US government without any change of structures in intelligence relations. Option B represents the new option for European nation-states. It implies full support to the US and its 'war on terror' while restructuring the foundations of internal security relations in the EU. In essence, as argued in this book, the latter option was the one that was pursued by the European Commission and approved by the Council.

The European Union must join the 'war on terror'

The political norm that the international community needed to join the war against terrorism emerged with the attacks on the US on 11 September 2001. A close examination of the war discourse shows how the norm emerged, and ultimately made it difficult to do anything other than join it. This demonstrates the fact that, ultimately, the EU had to support the US – even if more in appearance than substance. In fact, the appearance of support would increase peer pressure for EU member states to adopt the EAW in the end.

The platform for the emerging norm to join the 'war on terrorism' was first established with Bush's 'act of war' speech (BBC News, 12 September 2001). In this, he declared: 'The deliberate and deadly attacks, which were carried out yesterday against our country, were more than acts of terror. They were acts of war.' ... 'This enemy attacked not just our people but all freedom-loving people everywhere in the world.' ... 'We will rally the world.' ... 'This will be a monumental struggle of good versus evil, but good will prevail.'

One should note the significant pressure for countries to adopt the norm to fight the 'war on terror'. Bush defined appropriate action in terms of fighting in the 'war against terrorism', and made an even stronger case by distinguishing between 'good and evil'. Later, Bush (BBC News, 12 September 2001) enforced this emerging norm by stating that 'you are either for us or against us'. Thus, the political pressure is such that the appropriate course of action became defined in its support of the US.

The rest of Europe rallied behind the US. For example, Germany's Chancellor Gerhard Schroeder called on European nations to band together within the framework of the EU to fight global terrorism (BBC News, 18 October 2001): 'Only if we put in place common policing and judicial resources can we ensure that there will be no hideouts for terrorists and other criminals in the European Union' ... 'We are ready to make Europe into an international player with global influence'. It was now quite clear that the EU would take part in the 'war on terror'. The question now was in which way the EU was going to take part.

The Commission, as a strategic first mover, constructs an EU version of the 'war on terror'

In speaking to the European Parliament, the commissioner responsible for the Area of Freedom, Security and Justice (formerly better known as Justice and Home Affairs), Antonio Vitorino, remarked (Norman, *FT*, 6 December 2001):

> Terrorist acts are committed by international groups with bases in several countries, exploiting loopholes in the law created by the geographical limits on investigators and often enjoying substantial financial and logistical resources. Terrorists take advantage of differences in legal treatment between States, in particular where the offence is not treated as such by national law, and that is where we have to begin.

Vitorino made the link that was established earlier very clear. In order to combat terrorism, these measures – the European Arrest Warrant – were vital (ibid.). Therefore, in Vitorino's view, anyone opposing these measures behaved out of line, inappropriately, and effectively supported terrorism indirectly by not closing the legal loopholes. The Commission moved extremely fast to make this link.

In the case of the European Arrest Warrant, the Commission followed this rhetoric up politically with a very timely proposal. This proposal for the policy had already been under preparation for about two years before it was launched. Vitorino initially intended to launch it under the Spanish Presidency in the first half of 2002 due to Spain's strong support of the issue in order to solve its own problems with the ETA terrorists. Yet, with the emerging norm of the 'war on terror', it became apparent that fast action was required. Ministers in the AFSJ would be under intense pressure to behave appropriately and settle their differences. Vitorino remarked: 'If we do not get agreement, and it should be a substantial agreement to cope with the global threat, it will be difficult to explain to the public why we failed' (Norman, *FT*, 6 December 2001).

Therefore, the Commission's strategy was for the arrest warrant to be presented as an anti-terrorist measure and to be amalgamated with other such measures, such as the Framework Decision on the Definition on Terrorism. During research interviews, this strategy could be triangulated from the information provided by the interviewees, as follows:

Firstly, officials in the Commission (COM 10, COM 14, COM 20, and COM 25) confirmed the political decision to bring the proposal of the EAW forward, as indicated above. Officials in the Directorate General JHA under Sir Adrian Fortescue had to work at full speed over the weekend before the proposal for it to be approved by the College of Commissioners on 19 September 2001 (Occhipinti, 2003, p. 149, also confirmed by interviews COM 10 and COM 25). The timing was crucial in order to construct the EU response to the 'war on terror'.

Secondly, the official who drafted the proposal (interview COM 20) confirmed the fact that there had been work on it for almost two years, which included bilateral meetings with the different member states, with national lawyers, academics and NGOs. Nonetheless, all these meetings made it very clear that the different national views were very, very far apart. These disagreements covered the most basic features of the EAW, including the maintenance of the principle of double criminality, the preservation of some political interference and even the choice of the legal instrument. All national representatives (interviews PR1 to PR24) had serious misgivings about the drafts of the EAW. This number is far larger than was commonly suggested by the reporting media, who mainly pointed at Italy. However, it seems clear that France, Ireland, the UK, Luxembourg, and even the Presidency at the time – Belgium – had severe political problems with significant parts of the draft. In the end, the Commission made the political decision to have a completely new extradition system and to convince member states through constructing the EAW into the 'war on terror'.

On 17 September 2001, the Commission drafted an internal strategy paper to amalgamate the EAW and the framework decision on a common definition of terrorism with several measures. This document, entitled 'Increasing the capacity of the EU to fight international terrorism' (Commission, 2001), was timed just ahead of the crucial extraordinary Justice and Home Affairs on 20 September as well as the European Council on 21 September. The document is highly indicative of the Commission's strategy at the time. It stated that the EAW and the framework decision on terrorism only addressed the internal dimension of the EU and were, thus, insufficient as a response to 9/11. Following the high-level political discourse of European leaders in the first days after the attacks, the EU needed to come up 'rapidly with a comprehensive and coherent response, internally and in co-operation with the US and other key partners, and moving beyond the narrow confines of a legal and political/security perspective' (ibid.). The Commission proposed that 'some areas' the 'EU [could] make a real contribution' and the US would welcome to deal with the Union as 'one interlocutor'. This argument could then be levelled against integration-sceptic member states (ibid.).

Thirdly, Commission officials accepted the fact that the speed of the negotiations was 'revolutionary' (interview COM 10 in particular, but also COM 20). This is perceived to have been in connection with the political mood of Ministers, who desperately wanted to demonstrate action (COM 10), and were persuaded by the Commission that the EAW had to be part of an anti-terrorist package. Subsequently, the Extraordinary (Emergency) European Council held in Brussels on 20–21 September set in motion a series of nine measures proposed by the Commission, of which the most notable items were the EAW and the definition of terrorism. This displayed the sense of action that national Ministers wanted. At the same time, it managed to blur the boundaries between the different contents – terrorism and crime more generally. The drafters of the EAW (interviews COM 20 and COM 12) accepted this fact. 'The European Arrest Warrant is not a specific instrument to fight terrorism, but to fight crime' (ibid.).

In conclusion, the norms changed demonstrably in the few weeks after 11 September 2001, and the Commission acted as an SPE in this process. It played the role of a strategic 'first mover' in order to shape the debate in a way that placed the EU at the centre of Europe's 'war on terror'. It also assessed very well politically how the norm environment would produce political pressure on member states to act. Consequently, the European Commission and its Commissioner Vitorino proposed action which clearly demonstrated its support for the US and its 'war on terror' (interviews COM 10, COM 25 and CON 7). Yet, it also constructed the EAW as an instrument to fight terrorism, thereby increasing political support for the project. From this evidence, it is clear that the Commission played the important role of a supranational policy entrepreneur at this stage.

The policy dimension of the European Arrest Warrant: the Commission as a supranational policy entrepreneur?

The European Arrest Warrant (EAW) was politically adopted by the Laeken Council Summit on 14–15 December 2001, with the formal legal adoption in June 2002 under the Spanish Presidency. The following section argues that the Commission managed to push through more advances than would have been theoretically expected by intergovernmentalist scholars, and thus it played the significant role of an effective SPE in the adoption of the EAW.

The negotiations start: alliance with the Presidency and the Council Secretariat first

The first post-9/11 opportunity for Justice and Home Affairs (JHA) Ministers to start negotiations on the ambitious anti-terrorist agenda in the Council was during its regularly scheduled session of 27–28 September 2001 in Brussels. It was of vital importance for the Commission to ensure the support of the six months rotating Presidency of the Council for the European arrest warrant until the summit would start.

In particular, there is one specific reason why the Commission needed to persuade the Belgian Presidency. Not only are Presidencies important in their gate-keeping and drafting roles, but the Belgians were known to be opposed to the European Arrest Warrant before it was proposed by the Commission. This is a fact that was not only confirmed by the Belgian delegation, but also reiterated by other national delegations (interviews PR1, PR3, PR5 and PR8), the Commission (interviews COM 10 and COM 20), and, in particular, staff of the Council Secretariat (interviews CON 3 and CON 7). According to the interviews (interviews COM 12 and CON 7), there was a long-running problem on extradition procedures between Belgium and Spain, where Belgium refused to surrender Basque terrorists to Spain due to the different interpretation of what constitutes 'terrorism', and whether they had in fact committed a crime under the Belgian law. The Belgian Justice Ministry was particularly opposed to the EAW (interview CON 7), and this fact was known to the European Commission before the negotiations. This was one of the reasons why the Commission initially wanted to propose the EAW under the Spanish Presidency six months later (interview COM 12). In these circumstances, it was a strategic gamble on the fact that it would manage to persuade Belgium in order to achieve greater EU integration in the area of criminal justice.

In the end, how did the Commission persuade Belgium? Firstly, it exploited a split between the Prime Minister, Guy Verhofstadt, and his own Justice Minister, Marc Verwilghen (interview CON 7). During the preparations of the Council agenda, the instructions of the Justice Ministry that were given to their staff were aimed to slow down progress in order to prevent the adoption of the EAW. In order to solve this potential problem, Vitorino personally intervened at the Prime Minister level (interview CON 7). In this struggle, the Prime Minister was convinced of the necessity to incorporate the EAW into the anti-terrorist agenda in order to advance to the EU's role in the 'war on terror'. It was only this direct intervention by the Belgian Prime Minister within his own national delegation that changed the negotiating stance of the Presidency.

As negotiations went on after the change in instructions the Belgians became co-operative towards the policy proposal (interview CON 9), and supported it due to the fact that they wanted to be perceived as driving the EU forward in the fight against terror. During the course of the negotiations, both the Belgian Presidency and the Council Secretariat greatly supported the Commission in its effort to persuade the other reluctant member states to adopt the European arrest warrant. Thus, the alliance with the Belgian Presidency and the Council Secretariat was highly significant. This was the essential first stepping stone to success for the Commission as a supranational policy entrepreneur.

This underlines the importance of the Commission's strategy of alliance with the Council Secretariat, which also held a very significant role in the third pillar. As argued in the theoretical chapter, an SPE needs significant allies in order to be able to push through its own proposals (Kingdon, 1984). While scholars traditionally have seen the role of the Council Secretariat to be to act as the Council's institutional memory (Christiansen and Vanhoonacker, 2006, p. 6), it has increasingly been argued to have become influential with the 'power of the pen' (Beach, 2004b), particularly in the area of security (Stetter, 2007). Therefore, it could be expected play a significant role. In this particular case, the Council Secretariat also had a direct influence on the Belgian Presidency.

Interviews (interviews CON 3 and CON 7) corroborated the input of the Council Secretariat officials who met the Belgian Presidency on the weekend after the attacks of 9/11 and thus allied themselves to the integration efforts of the European Commission. Key officials (ibid.) in the Council Secretariat negotiated up to the level of the Belgian Prime Minister Guy Verhofstadt. The Belgian Presidency, persuaded by the Commission, made clear that it was committed to rapid progress by significantly stepping up the rhythm and intensity of Council and working group meetings.

Furthermore, more evidence points to an entrepreneurial alliance of the Council Secretariat. A very high-ranking Council Secretariat official, Gilles de Kerchove, has been involved in the AFSJ since the late 1990s. His personal importance in EU counterterrorism policy has been corroborated throughout several interviews with the permanent representations of the member states in Brussels (interviews PR1–PR 25). In addition, in September 2007, de Kerchove has been appointed as the EU's counterterrorism co-ordinator. Due to his personal circumstances in which he had served as a Belgian Cabinet Minister in the past, this made a strong alliance between the Commission, the Council Secretariat and the Belgian Presidency much easier. In fact, the Council Secretariat proved to hold the 'power of the pen' (Beach, 2004b), as well as being capable to work in a strong alliance with the Commission and the Belgian Presidency.

Building broader support: coalition-building and negotiations in the Council

A statement made by David Blunkett, the British Home Secretary, makes the vital role of the Commission as an SPE very clear (BBC News, 20 September 2001): 'I'm hoping that the European Commission will be able to persuade those who are reluctant and fearful that there is nothing to fear from co-operation, there is everything to fear from allowing the terrorists to exploit our democracy.'

The Commission now bore the burden to make sure it would be adopted, which implied that it needed to persuade the big member states. Yet, even European Commission officials seemed to have been doubtful as to whether the difficulties in adopting their proposal could be overcome speedily enough. The late Director General of Justice and Home Affairs, Sir Adrian Fortescue, admitted, 'I am not confident that this proposal isn't going to run into considerable difficulties' (*European Voice*, 27 September 2001).

In addition, as part of the strategy to persuade the big member states, the Commission lobbied the US. The Director General of the Commission, Fortescue (*European Voice*, 27 Septyember 2001), had been part of an EU delegation meeting with Colin Powell, the US Secretary of State, in Washington the week after the events of 11 September. As a result of the terror attacks, Fortescue mentioned the fact that the EU and the US could be drawn together by co-operating. Furthermore, bilateral extradition arrangements between EU member states and the US could be replaced by an EU-wide system, thereby creating in the US the impression that it could demand support. Moreover, a letter (ibid.) was sent to Washington asking

President Bush how the EU could assist America.

Bush's reply in the form of a five-page letter angered several member states, but it gave the Commission another reason to press for the smooth adoption of its own proposals. Bush provided a long list of forty-seven demands covering judicial and diplomatic co-operation and other issues. In addition, the US would ask Europol to pass on to the US 'all information, including information about individuals, which it may have on terrorist cases and subsequently expand this co-operation to include criminal cases' (BBC News, 22 October 2001). Extradition processes from the EU to America should also be streamlined, the letter requested. However, this was not thoroughly considered at that time.

Most important, the letter asked the Union to ease extradition procedures internally. Again, welcome support for the Commission's cause. Leonello Gabrici, the Commission's Justice and Home Affairs spokesman, argued that 'the things that we are doing against terrorism ... will simplify life for the Europeans and make it easier for us to co-operate with the United States' (BBC News, 22 October 2001).

After the first discussion of the proposal at the extraordinary summit on 20–21 September 2001, a sizeable number of member states still reacted negatively to a blanket list of mutual recognition (interviews COM 12 and COM 20). At that point, the main debate evolved around the categories of crimes to be included in the warrant. The difficult political question was whether to establish a 'negative list' of offences to be exempt from the warrant, or to have a 'positive list' of crimes to be covered under the EAW. In its first draft, the Commission suggested the former (interview COM 12, and COM (2001) 521/522 final), as it was concerned that the latter would make surrender the exception, whereas extradition would stay as the rule.

By the time the Council met again in Ghent on 16 October 2001, the Commission supported by the Presidency had decided to change their strategy, and thus decided to abandon the 'negative list' in favour of a very long 'positive list' of crimes included in the EAW. According to Ludlow (2002, p. 109), this change of strategy occurred because they believed they could achieve more or less the same goal by compromising a little. Notwithstanding this change, discord continued over the different lists due to the lack of a common definition of some crimes, as well as the enduring insistence by some member states to maintain the principle of double criminality (Occhipinti, p. 162).

Yet, the Belgian presidency and the Commission managed to persuade thirteen out of fifteen member states to agree to a positive list of thirty-two categories of crimes included in the framework decision setting up the European arrest warrant (ibid.). As explained before, this means that the EAW would apply to almost all crimes other than petty crimes. The only countries still refusing to agree to the list were Ireland and Italy. Yet, Italy became the principal opponent of the persuasion efforts (Ludlow, p. 109).

While acknowledging the need to join the war on terrorism, the Berlusconi government insisted that instead of thirty-two categories of offences listed in the proposal, the EAW should only apply in six cases. Consequently, this created a situation whereby if Italy could be convinced, the EAW could be adopted.

Persuading Berlusconi and Italy: the final meeting at the Council Summit in Laeken, December 2001

The final part of the Commission strategy involved the aspects that Blunkett referred to earlier – persuading reluctant member states, especially Italy. This was achieved through a reinforcement of the norm to join the 'war on terrorism' and by putting considerable peer pressure on Italy from within the Council and the European Council (*Times*, 7 December 2001).

The next important negotiation opportunity was the Council session on 6–7 December 2001, with the aim of finalising the work before the Laeken summit of 14–15 December 2001. At that point, Ireland, which had been originally concerned about the proposal, dropped its objections and agreed to the warrant (Occhipinti, 2003, p. 170). This effectively left Italy as the only country still not agreeing. It still preferred a much shorter list of just six crimes, namely terrorism, child sexual exploitation, pornography, and trafficking in arms, drugs, and human beings. Berlusconi completely objected to the inclusion of fraud, money laundering and other crimes on the list of offences that would be subject to automatic extradition (Ludlow, 2002, p. 109).

The media linked these objections to the feud between Berlusconi, the Italian Prime Minister, and judges in Italy and Spain who were investigating his past business affairs. In fact, Berlusconi may well have feared being extradited himself one day for alleged tax-related financial wrongdoing. The Prime Minister remarked that 'there was a risk that judges in the country might abuse the law to oppress citizens' (Norman, *FT*, 6 December 2001). Of course, whatever the reasons behind Berlusconi's attempt to block the warrant, he underlined an important problem with the warrant. The automatic extradition for all crimes is not strictly relevant for fighting terrorism only. The statement made by Roberto Castelli, the Italian Justice Minister and member of the Northern League, is correct: 'I ask myself what sense there is in bracketing car theft with terrorism. What that would do is block everything without giving a proper response to the emergency of terrorism?' (Norman, *FT*, 6 December 2001)

However, the Commission and its allies amongst the member states, especially Belgium, were quick to apply peer pressure on Berlusconi. Commissioner Vitorino declared that 'we cannot be held hostage to Council unanimity' and indicated that the 'Council might try to proceed without Italy by using the option of enhanced co-operation to allow the fourteen member states to go ahead' (Occhipinti, 2003, p. 171). Marc Verwilghen – the Belgian

Justice Minister who initially opposed the EAW – warned Italy that the Laeken meeting on 14–15 December would be 'very difficult' for Silvio Berlusconi and that his behaviour was 'incomprehensible'. The German Interior Minister Otto Schily also complained that 'the Italian position is completely unacceptable' (ibid.).

But the Italian Prime Minister also came under intense pressure from the Italian media (Blitz, *FT*, 10 December 2001) in a public shaming process. Renato Ruggiero, Italy's Foreign Minister, played down the extent of Italy's problems in the EU in an interview with *Il Mattino* newspaper (ibid.): 'This is the first time that Italy has chosen to set itself apart and not participate in an agreed political and institutional development ... since the foundation of the European Community.' However, in a very outspoken front-page editorial in the Milan daily *Corriere della Sera*, Enzo Biagi accused his Prime Minister that he had the strong impression that when Berlusconi talked about defending the interests of Italy, he really meant defending his own interests (ibid.). Another leading columnist, Eugenio Scalfari, wrote on the front page of *La Repubblica* (ibid.): 'The damage is done, the international image of our government is already in ruins and the impact at home and abroad is devastating.'

In the end, the pressure applied on Berlusconi paid off, and Italy abandoned its opposition (*Irish Times*, 12 December 2001). Italy's official reversal of policy came during a visit to Rome on 11 December 2001 by Belgian Prime Minister Verhofstadt, the then leader of the Presidency. However, this section showed how the Commission and its ally – the Belgian Presidency – were able to organise pressure by hinting exclusion and by applying it in order to push for the Commission's proposal for the European Arrest Warrant. At the beginning, when Italy blocked the warrant, Berlusconi was shamed by the Commission, his fellow EU Prime Ministers, as well as the European media. The final outcome of the negotiations resembles the first proposal of the Commission in many major characteristics. This is the reason why the European Arrest Warrant provides an excellent example of the Commission as an effective SPE.

In conclusion, this section has demonstrated two points. Firstly, European integration is possible in areas of 'high politics', areas at the very heart of the nation-state. This finding would not have been predicted by intergovernmentalist scholars such as Hoffmann. The European Arrest Warrant provided an excellent case in point. Secondly, 'without the power of purse or sword' (Moravcsik, 1999a), the European Commission was able to significantly influence the decisions of the powerful member states. On the normative level, it managed to contribute significantly to a construction of the EAW into a European 'war on terror'. This significantly contributed to member states preference building, building up a momentum for intense peer pressure on reluctant member states. Equally, it managed to blur the boundaries between the 'war on terror' and the fight against crime in general, with the effect of creating a political momentum for the European Arrest Warrant. Despite the high speed of the negotiations, many defining features of its proposal remained in the final adopted version of the warrant, at least regarding the effect to be achieved. Consequently, it played the role of a supranational policy entrepreneur, as defined by Kingdon (1984) and further elaborated by Kaunert (2007), albeit in alliance with the Council Secretariat and the Belgian Presidency.

EU institutions in counter-terrorism

The purpose of this section is to evaluate to what extent the model of a supranational policy entrepreneur was indicative of the behaviour of the European institutions. The theoretical model suggested the following:

- *First-mover advantage.* It needs to be able to act promptly to construct issues and seize the right moment for political action in a competition with other actors.
- *Persuasion strategy.* As suggested above, in order to achieve acceptance, other actors need to be convinced by the reasons for the action suggested.
    - Legitimacy build-up. Norms need to be anchored in existing norms.
    - Expertise and information.
    - Continued insistence. New norms will encounter resistance at first, which means the SPE needs to insist significantly.
    - Negotiation skills.
- *Alliances.* Once a problem is defined appropriately, and once other actors are somewhat persuaded, the negotiations in the political stream move towards bargaining efforts. In this process it is vital for the SPE to form initial alliance with powerful actors to create a bandwagon effect, whereby more actors will join the 'winning team'. Forming the right alliances at the right time will become crucial. This underlines the political skills needed for the SPE.

A close examination of the summary of results substantiates the degree of success of the European institutions, in particular the Commission, in acting as a supranational policy entrepreneur. As explained above, the norms of decision-makers changed markedly with the start of the 'war on terror'. The events of 11 September 2001 were a normative defining point, and the role of the Commission was significant in constructing the EU into the 'war on terror'. Furthermore, the Commission influenced the political discussion in such a way that the European Arrest Warrant became connected to the European response against terrorism. Thus, the search for policy alternatives was very limited, especially given the time constraints at the time. It played the role of a 'strategic first mover' in order to shape the debate. As part of this

Table 4.1 European institutions as SPEs in EU counter-terrorism

Evidence for	
Long-term norm change	*Short-term policy advances*
Overall assessment	
Norms changed significantly after the Commission managed to construct the EU into the 'war on terror'	Significant policy advances: European Arrest Warrant
What changed?	
1 EU to legislate on counter-terrorism	EAW abolished extradition between EU member states
2 War on terror': the EU joined the 'war on terror', indeed it became a vital player	Jurisdiction of the European Court of Justice, and potential new legal precedents
3	Abolished the legal principle of double criminality
4	Cornerstone for the principle of mutual recognition
How did it change?	
1 First-mover advantage	Long consultation process and information build-up
2 Linking EU action with the 'war on terror'	Commission alliance with the Belgian Presidency and the Council Secretariat
3 Criminal justice measures included in anti-terrorist agenda to blur boundaries	Persuading big member states: bargaining and negotiation skills
4 Appealing to the US to put pressure on national governments	Isolating Italy, and rallying member states together to put pressure on it
5 Pushing at the right political moment	Compromised solutions are very creative and legally very sound
6 Negotiation skills	

strategy, it also appealed to the US in a letter, only to receive generous support to put pressure on EU member states to advance the EAW. However, the Commission achieved this only in an alliance with the Belgian Presidency and the Council Secretariat.

Successes in counter-terrorism financing

However, while the chapter predominantly focused on the Commissions successes in pillar three of counter-terrorism, it is important to note its successes also in pillar one. The Commission clearly also played the significant role of an SPE in the first-pillar area of implementing the FATF Special Recommendations, which represent international standards against the misuse of the global financial system by terrorist organisations. The FATF is an ad hoc intergovernmental body, which develops and promotes standards in the fight against money laundering and the financing of terrorism. It was created at the 1989 July Paris Summit meeting of the seven major industrialised nations (G-7), who were joined by the President of the European Commission (Fletcher et al., 2008). Its membership currently comprises thirty-two countries and territories and two regional organisations, including the fifteen 'old' member states of the EU and, interestingly, the European Commission. While it does not form part of any international organisation, it is organisationally attached to the OECD in Paris. Since the beginning of its activity in 1990, the FATF has drawn up forty Recommendations setting out the basic framework for international action against money laundering, whose implementation is monitored through a 'mutual evaluation process'. These recommendations were updated subsequently and in particular in October 2001, when the overall remit of the FATF was extended beyond money laundering in order to also include the fight against terrorist financing.

Following the US Congress's adoption of the 'International Money Laundering Abatement and Anti-terrorist Financing Act', which put increasing pressure on other governments to tighten their own legislation on money laundering and terrorist financing (Allen, 2003; Eling, 2006), the FATF on the extraordinary plenary session held in Washington in October 2001 adopted the so-called 'Eight Special Recommendations' on Terrorist Financing (FATF 2001). They established firm new international standards to detect, prevent and suppress the financing of terrorism and terrorist acts by denying terrorists and their supporters access to the international financial system, with specific regards to: (1) the ratification and implementation of UN instruments, (2) criminalising the financing of terrorism and money laundering, (3) freezing and confiscating terrorist assets, (4) reporting suspicious transactions related to terrorism, (5) international co-operation, (6) alternative remittance, (7) wire transfers, and (8) non-profit organisations.

Especially the Commission, more precisely DG Internal Market, utilised its expertise and competence from dealing with money laundering in order to initiate legislation related to terrorist financing. The Commission has the exclusive right to initiate proposals on terrorist financing with regards to first pillar provisions linked to financial crime. Consequently, it used this power and successfully persuaded the Council of Ministers and the European Parliament to approve its proposed laws. In addition, together with fifteen 'old' EU member states, it is also a member of the FATF itself. The Directorate General of the Commission DG Market leads the European delegation in these negotiations. It seeks to co-ordinate EU member states as much as possible negotiations start, despite their obvious jealousy to protect their national prerogatives.

Since the 2001 attacks, especially in the initial months of major political pressure for action, the Commission has been able to accelerate the adoption of some legislative measures with terrorist financing implications that were already under discussion before 9/11. It used the close link between money laundering and terrorist financing in order to push the European Parliament to agree on the text already approved by the Council. The success of this legislation has clear similarities with the Commission's policy entrepreneurship in the adoption of the European Arrest Warrant demonstrated earlier in this chapter. In the same way, the emerging international norm of joining in the 'war on terror' made it necessary to adopt the directive to counter-terrorist financing, even though it seemed implausible to adopt these instruments in the 'fight against money laundering' . In this way, the norm to participate in the war on terror (via EU mechanisms) was used strategically to convince the majority of member states of the political merits of the second anti-money laundering directive, and it allowed the Commission to use member states' peer pressure to convince the reluctant member states to participate. Thus, the Commission managed to play the role of an SPE and persuaded member states to promote European integration in counter-terrorist financing.

This process was pushed even more strongly when, in 2004, the Commission prepared a far-reaching Communication focused on the prevention of and the fight against terrorist financing through measures to improve the exchange of information, to strengthen transparency and enhance the traceability of financial transactions. Most of the elements included in the Communication were inserted also in the 2005 'third anti-money laundering directive' which repealed the previous two directives. The 'third directive' also made the title 'terrorist financing' more explicit, and, once again, reaffirmed the EU objective to comply with FATF standards. It clearly incorporated most of the latest version of the FATF Recommendations (as revised in 2003) into Community legislation.

In addition, it also integrated a number of associated measures aimed at implementing the FATF requirements: (1) Regulation (EC) No. 1889/2005 on the control of cash entering or leaving the Community (which implements SR IX on cash couriers), (2) Regulation (EC) No. 1781/2006 on information on the payer accompanying transfers of funds, and (3) Directive 2007/64/EC on payment services (PSD) in the internal market, which provides the legal foundation for the creation of an EU-wide single market for payments.

Finally, following the Council Decision 2000/642/JHA of 17 October 2000 concerning arrangements for co-operation between Financial Intelligence Units (FIUs) of the EU member states, the Commission launched the 'FIU.Net initiative', an EU-wide network of all national FIUs aimed at sharing information on terrorist funding in a secure environment and at supporting the co-operation between the various FIUs. In addition, the Commission set up a forum for discussion, the so-called 'EU FIUs Platform', aimed at enabling the EU FIUs to exchange views and experiences on technical issues. The FIU.Net project was co-financed by the Commission for a period of two years until the end of 2009. The Netherlands were the contracting party and co-financing was provided by Finland, Germany, Romania, the UK, France,

Greece and Italy (Council, 2009). The Board of Partners of the projects was formed by representatives of these eight member states. By May 2009, eighteen EU member states' FIUs had been connected to the FIU.Net and four were in the process of being connected. By August 2009, the CTC expected that twenty-two FIUs would be connected. In conclusion, the Commission managed to play a significant role in the area of transposing the FATF Special Recommendations at the EU level. It was evidently significant in designing and implementing the FATF recommendations and thus conformed to the model as a supranational policy entrepreneur.

Successes in the Area of Freedom, Security and Justice and the Lisbon Treaty
The European Commission (Commission, 2004, pp. 1–17) was very happy with all its achievements. European public opinion supported the development of European action in the field of AFSJ, the area was now firmly identified as one of the EU's priority policies, and the Commission argued that the EU reacted quickly and efficiently when the situation demanded it – after 11 September 2001 and 11 March 2004. However, the Commission constructed these successes together to the success of the Constitutional Treaty and, thus in parallel, to the Lisbon Treaty as its successor. By pointing out the institutional constraints, such as unanimity as a decision method in the Council, lack of co-decision with the European Parliament, and the Commission's sharing of the right of initiative with the member states; it queried the long-term viability of the area under the decision-making structure available.

On the basis of this communication, one can observe the relationship between the Tampere and the Hague programme's success and the Lisbon Treaty (LT). The former was vital for the Commission to demonstrate the usefulness of European co-operation in this field. If it could not demonstrate the Europe's use, it would have been impossible to argue for more legal competences in the LT. This is why the Commission underlined that the European public supported European action, while at the same time claiming that Europe acted when needed. In its political construction, terrorism became the main security threat. Therefore, this was the crucial moment when the Commission had to prove it could act quickly and efficiently. Only if Europe could act quickly and efficiently against this newly perceived common threat would it be relevant for both decision-makers and the general public. Yet, in the Commission's view, the institutional obstacles made it more difficult to achieve this progress. This is the link between the political success in the area of criminal justice, the AFSJ and the Lisbon Treaty.

Consequently, political success for the Commission depended quite clearly on the question of how the EU would act in the fight against terrorism, and whether it would become to be perceived as a serious actor in internal security matters. The defining moment of this action was 11 September 2001, the day New York and Washington were attacked by Al Quaida and Osama

Bin Laden. No matter how many successes were achieved in all the sub-areas of criminal justice, the crunch point was the action taken by the Commission after the attacks on the US. Therefore, one cannot overestimate the importance that the Commission had given to its proposals of the European Arrest Warrant and the definition on terrorism agreed in the months following September 2001.

Implementation, the German Constitutional Court, and the European Arrest Warrant

Despite the arguments above regarding the Commission as an SPE in an alliance with the Council Secretariat and the Belgian Presidency, it needs to be acknowledged that there are limitations to this argument. The Commission has acquired the capacity to act as an SPE as demonstrated by the case of the EAW. This implies a (potentially) significant role in the legislative process, even in institutionally difficult terrain such as the AFSJ. However, the thesis is limited to the legislative process. Institutionally, the Commission cannot take member states to the ECJ for failure to transpose the framework decision properly or on time as would be the case in infringement proceedings under the TEU. This makes its role somewhat unbalanced – stronger in the legislative process than in the implementation phase. Again, the EAW serves as a good case in point, as there were some important implementation problems after its adoption. Three member states experienced problems in the implementation of the EAW – Cyprus (7 November 2005), Poland (27 April 2005) and Germany (18 July 2005) – where it ended up in the respective national constitutional courts. Poland and Cyprus were consequently required to change their constitutions, while Germany had to adopt a new transposition law for the EAW which was adopted by the 'Grand Coalition' under Chancellor Angela Merkel in July 2006 (*Welt*, 8 July 2006). The interesting details of this case in Germany are discussed below.

The implementation problems of the EAW have been underlined by the court case before the German Constitutional Court (*Spiegel*, 14 March 2005). It evolved around Mamoun Darkazanli (No. 2 BvR 2236/04), who was viewed by terrorism investigators as a central figure in the Al Qaeda network. He was the first German arrested under the new provisions related to the European arrest warrant. Initially, Spain had issued an international arrest warrant for him in September 2003, but the German authorities refused to extradite him because the constitution bans the extradition of countries' own nationals. The Spanish judge, Baltazar Garzon, then issued a European arrest warrant due to the suspect's alleged support for Al Qaeda – despite the fact that supporting a foreign terrorist organisation was not yet considered a punishable offence in Germany at the time of the offence. In November 2004, a Hamburg court allowed the extradition based on the EU arrest warrant, which was blocked by the Constitutional Court following an appeal by the defence lawyers. It was argued that it is not possible for a German citizen to be extradited to another country for an act committed and considered lawful in Germany.

On 18 July 2005, the German Constitutional Court announced its verdict. 'German court rules EU arrest warrant invalid' (*FT*, 18 July 2005). According to the *Financial Times* (18 July 2005), the Federal Constitutional Court ordered the release of the suspect Mamoun Darkazanli. The BBC (18 July 2005) also seems to agree with this. 'Al Qaeda man wins German appeal' (ibid.). It is reported that the new European Arrest Warrant was invalid. Former German Justice Minister Zypries is cited to have said that the court ruling 'was a blow for the government in its efforts and fight against terrorism'. Earlier in the year, *Der Spiegel* (14 March 2005) cited her to have said that a negative decision would put 'Germany at the fringes of European integration'. This was because it was not possible for Germany to not adopt an instrument that was already adopted in the EU. This would put Germany in a direct collision course with the EU. What is more important, the EU or national law?

In theory, the German Constitutional Court had the option to declare the European arrest warrant invalid on the basis that extraditing German nationals to foreign powers is prohibited by the German Basic Law. Indeed, it could have cited Article 16 GG, which explicitly prevents extradition of German nationals. If it had declared the European Arrest Warrant framework decision invalid on the basis of this article, the European Arrest Warrant could not come into force in Germany. This would have indeed put Germany at odds with Europe, and could have had a 'domino effect' on constitutional courts across the EU, which might have referred to that decision. However, in the end, the verdict 2 BvR 2236/04 (BVG, 18 July 2005) strikes a different note.

On the basis of Article 16 GG, it declares that the German implementation law of the European arrest warrant is unconstitutional. At the same time, the majority view of the Supreme Court justices also declares that the European framework decision on the European arrest warrant is in fact constitutional, and thus it upholds the framework decision. The decision starts by stating that, in principle, a German national cannot be extradited to a foreign power. However, it acknowledges that this principle is not absolute. In the case of the EU, it is possible to extradite to foreign powers – and to international organisations, more generally – under the condition that citizens' rights that are protected by the German constitution are maintained.

The majority justices argue that the framework decision by the EU in fact upholds these protections. It is only the German implementation law that does not uphold them. Consequently, it declares the German implementation law null and void, with the consequence that the suspect must be released. At the same time, it leaves open the possibility for Germans to be extradited within the framework of the EU during the time that a new implementation law is adopted by the Bundestag, which takes these concerns into account. As cited above, this law was adopted in July 2006 (*Welt*, 8 July 2006). In essence, this means that the German Constitutional Court has upheld the European Arrest Warrant framework decision, but it also pointed to the implementation deficit in the EU's third pillar.

Acknowledgement

Extracts from this chapter have been previously published in C. Kaunert, '"Without the Power of Purse or Sword": The European Arrest Warrant and the Role of the Commission', *Journal of European Integration*, vol. 29, no. 4 (2007), pp. 387–404. Many thanks to Taylor & Francis for allowing republication as part of this chapter.

5

The external dimension of counter-terrorism co-operation

with Dr Sarah Leonard

The external dimension of EU counter-terrorism and international actorness

This chapter analyses the external dimension of EU counter-terrorism, a crucial aspect in the fight against international terrorism, which has been much and hotly debated (Reinares, 2000; Dubois, 2002; den Boer and Monar, 2002; Mitsilegas and Gilmore, 2007; Occhipinti, 2003; Deflem, 2006; Bures, 2006, 2008; Gregory, 2005; Zimmermann, 2006; Friedrichs, 2005; den Boer, Hillebrand and Nölke, 2008; Müller-Wille, 2008; Spence, 2006; Bossong, 2008; Kaunert, 2005, 2007, 2009). Following the 11 March 2004 attacks on Madrid, which killed almost 200 people, the EU stepped up its efforts against terrorism (Wilkinson, 2006, p. 172), with a particular emphasis on the international dimension. EU commitment in the field was subsequently reinforced by the shock of the terrorist attacks in Madrid. The 'solidarity' Declaration on Combating Terrorism of 29 March 2004, agreed upon by the European Heads of State and Government (European Council, 2004), strongly emphasised the need 'to reduce the access of terrorists to financial and other economic resources' and 'to address the factors contributing to the support for and recruitment into terrorism'. Accordingly, the European Council held in June 2004 included the combating of terrorist financing among the four priority areas of action. The subsequent revised Counter-terrorism Action Plan set out new proposals for tackling terrorist funding more effectively and called for the quick development of an EU ad hoc strategy (European Council, 2004a). The strategy on terrorist financing was swiftly drawn up by the Council on the basis of a proposal made jointly by the Council Secretariat and the Commission. It was adopted by the European Council in December 2004 (European Council, 2004b). The strategy provided a critical overview of the actions undertaken until then concerning the fight against terrorist financing. It also recommended a number of initiatives to be adopted to strengthen EU efforts. The EU underlined the importance of deepening the international consensus to combat terrorism, thereby reducing the access of terrorists to financial and other economic resources. The EU declaration on combating terrorism was later enshrined in the text of the Lisbon Treaty. The EU also made counter-terrorist clauses (CTC) an important element of the agreements concluded with third countries, which it described as 'a basis for political dialogue and a tool for EU external action' (Council, 2004, p. 7).

The external dimension of the EU counter-terrorism policy represents an important element in the possible construction of an Area of Freedom, Security and Justice, as making the EU secure depends at least to some extent on successful co-operation with countries outside the EU. This chapter examines different cases of this recent and comparatively less developed policy area. In his article 'The Absent Friend: EU Foreign Policy In Counter-terrorism', Keohane (2008) argues that, despite the international nature of the terrorist threat, foreign policy is surprisingly largely absent from the EU's counter-terrorism efforts. Keohane explains this absence by the leading role of Interior Ministers in the AFSJ, even in its external dimension. He also argues that the role played by the US and NATO in counter-terrorism has hindered the development of the external dimension of EU counter-terrorism.

In contrast to Keohane's argument, this chapter will show that the EU counter-terrorism policy has been characterised by an external dimension of growing importance. Recent EU Association and Co-operation Agreements with third countries include measures relating to the external dimension of the AFSJ, asking third countries to co-operate in the field of transnational threats such as terrorism and organised crime. Counter-terrorism has also been included in the European Neighbourhood Policy (ENP). However, as will be argued in this chapter, these counter-terrorism efforts lag significantly behind the most important counter-terrorism partnership that the EU has developed to date, i.e. EU–US co-operation. The chapter will also demonstrate that the EU institutions, in particular the Commission and the Council Secretariat, have played an active and significant role in these policy developments – the role of SPEs, albeit to different degrees across policy areas.

Legal basis and international actorness in the external dimension of counter-terrorism

It is important to analyse the external dimension of counter-terrorism in the wider framework of the creation of a European Foreign Policy. Indeed, the EU counter-terrorism efforts contribute to the establishment of the EU as an actor on the international stage, which, over time, may acquire the capability to conduct a *sui generis* foreign policy. Conventionally, with regard to the EU institutional structures, foreign policy is associated with the second pillar of the EU – the Common Foreign and Security Policy (CFSP). However, if one follows Hill's (2003) definition of foreign policy – 'the sum of all official external relations conducted by an independent actor (usually a state) in international relations' – it appears that there are some aspects of EU foreign policy that are conducted through either the first pillar (the European Community) or the third pillar (Justice and Home Affairs co-operation). Because of this institutional difference, they are often referred to as 'EU external relations', rather than 'EU foreign policy'. Nevertheless, this book takes a broad view of foreign policy as encompassing activities in the three pillars of the EU. As a result, an increase in the role of, for example, the European Commission in counter-terrorism external relations is interpreted as signalling an increase in the importance of the EU as an actor on the international stage.

Counter-terrorism, in turn, is a broad term which can encompass measures across all three pillars, from trade sanction of state sponsors of terrorism (in the first and second pillar) to the implementation of United Nations (UN) Security Council decisions (in the second pillar) to police and judicial co-operation (in the third pillar). Therefore, the debate on the external relations of EU counter-terrorism, despite (or perhaps precisely because of) its cross-pillar location, tells an important story about EU foreign policy more broadly. However, it is important to always bear in mind the EU pillar structure, as the conclusions of this analysis can only be generalised to foreign policy actions in the pillar concerned.

Therefore, can the EU act in counter-terrorism relations with external partners? The legal basis for external relations activities in Title IV TEC (first pillar) is mostly implicit in the EU's internal legal competences (Monar, 2004, p. 396). According to the EU treaties, first-pillar actions can be derived expressly through treaty articles, such as Article 133 TEC, which grants the EC the power to sign treaties concerning trade policy with third countries. However, according to European Court of Justice (ECJ) jurisprudence, legal competences can also be implicitly derived from the EU's internal competences – the 'doctrine of implied powers', which was derived from the AETR case (Eeckhout, 2004, p. 82).

Originally, the treaties of the EU did not contain many express provisions that would provide powers to the EU/EC to conclude international agreements with third countries. Only in 1970 did the Commission bring the AETR case to the European Court of Justice. This case was named after the European agreement concerning the work of crews of vehicles engaged in international road transport. The ECJ reasoned in two parts: (1) Article 281 EC provided the EC with a legal personality, enabling it in principle to act on the international stage, and (2) authority to conclude international agreements is not derived only from the express powers, but also from the measures of internal competences that would need to be exercised; after having exercised internal competences to agree on certain measures, the EC would have to have the capacity to defend those measures internationally, thereby enabling the EC to enter into international agreements.

The Lisbon Treaty foresees the abolition of the EU pillar structure. However, the pre-Lisbon legal framework for external relations activities in the third pillar remains more complex than that concerning the first pillar (Monar, 2004; Eeckhout, 2004; Stessens, 2008). The procedure used to conclude agreements on third-pillar matters with third countries is actually the procedure governing the signing of agreements with third countries in the second pillar of the EU. The legal competences of the EU for the conclusion of international agreements under the third pillar derive from Articles 24 and 38 EU. Article 38 EU stipulates that agreements listed in Article 24 EU, which is a second-pillar provision, can also cover matters in the third pillar (Fletcher et al., 2008, p. 153). This informs decision-making in the following way:

- If an agreement is deemed necessary, the Council may authorise the Presidency, assisted by the Commission, to open negotiations; agreements are concluded by the Council by way of Presidency recommendation.
- If an agreement for internal matter requires unanimity in the Council, the international agreement follows in parallel; if an internal matter requires qualified majority vote, the international agreement follows again.
- Agreements of this nature are binding on EU institutions, and on member states, unless they state in the Council that they have to comply with the requirements of their own constitutional procedure.

Although this provision outlines a clear procedure regarding the negotiation and the conclusion of agreements, it does not clarify on whose behalf these agreements are concluded. Yet, this issue is of utmost significance to the question of international actorness of the EU. As the EU does not have legal personality under the current treaties (i.e. until the entry into force of the Lisbon Treaty), does it mean that only the member states collectively, but not the EU itself, can conclude such agreements? Monar (2004, pp. 401–402) has criticised this idea on three grounds. First, the objectives outlined by Article 24 TEU are objectives that need to be attained by the EU, rather than a collection of member states. Second, decision-making authority rests with the Council of Ministers, an institution of the EU, rather than the member states as a group. Third, a change introduced by the Treaty of Nice, Article 24(2), provides for instances where a qualified majority voting shall be used in the Council for any measures implementing decisions adopted for purposes other than the approximation of the laws and regulations of the member states. Thus, it appears that this provision signals an implicit intention to provide the EU with an element of actorness in the third pillar at the international level.

Actors in the external dimension of counter-terrorism

Several actors across the three EU pillars are now dealing with terrorism in its internal and external dimensions. There are two Council working groups entirely devoted to the fight against terrorism: the third-pillar Terrorism Working Group (TWG), which is in charge of the internal aspects of counter-terrorism, and the second-pillar Working Party on Terrorism (External Aspects) (COTER), which is in charge of the external dimension of counter-terrorism (Council of the European Union, 2004). Furthermore, liaison officers have been designated in all the Permanent Representations of the EU member states in Brussels and meet in the 'Contact Group' to share information (Lugna, 2006, p. 108). In addition, a new ad hoc group, called the Situation Centre (SitCen) was established in 2005 in order to enable the security and intelligence services of the EU member states to co-operate. Based in the Council Secretariat, it co-ordinates national experts for intelligence assessment from the member states and assesses terrorist threats from outside the EU and, since 2005, from inside the EU's territory (Wilkinson, 2006, p. 175).

The negotiation and the conclusion of international agreements on third-pillar matters are decided by the Council (Stessens, 2008, pp. 344–345). Article 24 TEU states that the 'Council may authorise to open negotiations when it deems it expedient'. It normally decides by unanimity, except in a series of specific situations outlined by the Treaty of Nice. Firstly, the Council authorises the Presidency to open negotiations with a number of negotiation instructions, i.e. a mandate. The Presidency is assisted by the European Commission, and informally also by the Council Secretariat. The Presidency reports at regular intervals to the relevant Council working parties on the state of play of the negotiations. In the end, the Council agrees the text and adopts a decision authorising the signing of the agreement.

This chapter will focus on analysing the development of the external dimension of the EU counter-terrorism policy. It will be argued that the creation of internal competences made the EU an increasingly interesting partner in counter-terrorism for third countries. Amongst them, the US proved to be particularly keen to develop closer counter-terrorism co-operation with the EU after 9/11. In addition, the EU developed co-operation in counter-terrorism with its neighbours, as this issue was included in the agenda of the European Neighbourhood Policy (ENP).

This chapter will also examine the extent to which EU institutions have been significant in the development of the external dimension of counter-terrorism. It will show that the assistance provided by the Commission and the Secretariat to the Presidency during the negotiation of agreements allowed the European institutions to significantly influence the content of the negotiations, to link them to internal third-pillar policy in order to champion a 'European' solution in the negotiations with third countries, and to use these agreements to push forward the EU agenda on the internal dimension of counter-terrorism. Thus, it can be argued that the EU institutions have played the role of SPEs (in an alliance) in the external dimension of the EU counter-terrorism policy.

EU institutions in EU–US counter-terrorism relations

The purpose of this section is to examine the role of the EU institutions in counter-terrorism relations with the US. Many traditional terrorism scholars, such as Bruce Hoffman, have argued that the differences in terrorism perception have had negative implications on US–EU counter-terrorism relations. Yet, a survey conducted by the German Marshall Fund in 2004 seems to cast doubt on this analysis (Cameron, 2007). Both Europeans (71 per cent) and Americans (76 per cent) are found to share concerns about international terrorism, and thus have a similar perception of this threat. However, they differ markedly in their response to terrorism: Americans prefer a military response (54 per cent), whereas Europeans agree with this option only to a more limited extent (28 per cent). The conclusion that can be drawn from such a study is that EU–US co-operation on terrorism matters is not impossible, but, given these differences, is more likely to be achieved with regard to non-military measures.

The following section is divided into three parts. Firstly, EU–US counter-terrorism relations are examined in their contextual perspective, where the link between EU internal counter-terrorism and the precise foreign policy actions in EU–US counter-terrorism relations is also considered. Secondly, the main aspects of EU–US counter-terrorism co-operation are analysed in detail. Finally, the role played by the European institutions is scrutinised.

Contextualising EU–US counter-terrorism relations

It is a truism to say that the events of 11 September 2001 had a significant impact on foreign policy-makers in Europe and America (Cameron, 2007). For the first time since Pearl Harbor, Americans experienced a real sense of vulnerability. The terrorist attacks on the US homeland were seen by many analysts as a turning point in US history (Martin, 2006; Hoffman, 2006). In Europe, the terrorist attacks also had two main effects. Firstly, it became apparent that Islamist terrorism was a global problem and that fundamentalist terrorists could therefore strike in Europe as well.[1] Consequently, the EU had to act internally in order to create the competences necessary to protect Europe from this particular terrorist threat. Secondly, in foreign policy terms, this terrorist threat also had clear implications for Europe's relationship with the US, as it had to position itself towards the US response.

Indeed, Bush's 'act of war speech' (BBC News, 12 September 2001) and his depiction of Al Qaeda as threatening the very foundations of Western civilisation, led to the emergence of a political norm according, outlined in the previous chapter, to which the international community was expected to join the 'war on terror' (Kaunert, 2007). European states also felt this American political pressure and the EU rapidly found itself in a position where it had to show its support to the US in some shape or form. A reaction and an adaptation of the European and EU foreign policies were expected to demonstrate the European solidarity with the US.

Yet, as indicated above, there were clear philosophical differences between Europe and the US on how to deal with terrorism (Cameron, 2007, p. 131). In the US, the government's response to 9/11 was largely based on the concept of 'homeland security' (Cameron, 2007, p. 132). This led to a significant reorganisation in the counter-terrorism institutional structures. President Bush established a new Cabinet-level post for homeland security (Martin, 2006) and named Governor Ridge for this position. In October 2001, the US Patriot Act, intended to make the American 'homeland' safer, was also passed. This piece of legislation gave the US government significant new powers in dealing with terrorism, including the right to wire-tap, seize telephone and e-mail records, as well as medical, banking, educational and business files. 'We are at war and we have to do things differently' was the justification given by Attorney General John Ashcroft (Cameron, 2007).

In addition to such protective security measures, the US administration developed a range of responses against terrorism, including economic sanctions, international diplomacy efforts, and most notably the use of military force. The US launched a military campaign against the Taliban regime and the Al Qaeda network in Afghanistan in 2001 before invading Iraq in 2003. While the former was widely supported by the international community, the war on Iraq became a significant bone of contention between Europe and America. In contrast to the US administration – which hoped that the proof of US military success might deter groups and states from harbouring terrorists – European governments viewed the use of military force to tackle terrorism with far more scepticism.

Indeed, in Europe, responses to terrorism were primarily based on non-military means. While supporting the war in Afghanistan, many European governments opposed the war in Iraq. However, in non-military areas of counter-terrorism co-operation, in particular criminal justice, intelligence and police co-operation, Europe developed remarkably close relations with the US. In a similar fashion to the cases analysed in the previous chapter, the European Commission, in an alliance with the Council Secretariat, worked hard to push forward internal EU initiatives, which then supported the development of the co-operation with the US.

EU–US counter-terrorism and the role of EU institutions

The attacks of 9/11 have led to a significant increase in EU–US counter-terrorism co-operation. Two specific forms of structured dialogue have played an essential role in that respect: the Justice Dialogue and the Policy Dialogue on Borders and Transport Security (PDBTS) (Cameron, 2007). The former actually began in 1998, bringing together representatives of the US Department of Justice with EU colleagues from the DG Justice and Home Affairs. While it was initially established to ensure information flows to the US, it has increased in importance with the development of new EU competences in criminal judicial and police co-operation. Since 2002, this dialogue has also been held at ministerial level. The Justice Dialogue has been the central forum for negotiating the agreements on mutual legal assistance and extradition that will be examined below, as well as discussing the issue of liaison with Europol and Eurojust.

As the agenda of this dialogue became increasingly dominated by questions concerning US borders, it began to considerably overlap with other attempts to improve customs co-operation (ibid., p. 136). The US administration took several measures to increase the security of its borders, including the Container Security Initiative (CSI), the collection of Passenger Name Record (PNR) data and the use of biometric passports. By extending the American zone of security outward of its borders, the US homeland security policies had very significant implications for the EU and, as a result, provided strong incentives for reinforcing co-operation.

The present section focuses on four major aspects of EU–US counter-terrorism co-operation relating respectively to intelligence, police and law enforcement, the financing of terrorism, and justice.

Intelligence co-operation: the Passenger Name Record Agreement

In November 2001, the US Aviation and Transportation Security Act introduced the requirement that airline companies operating passenger flights to, from or through the US, provide US authorities with electronic access to PNR data, including passengers' names and addresses, bank numbers, credit card details, and information about meals ordered for the flights (de Hert and de Schutter, 2008). Such a requirement put EU-based airlines at risk of breaking the data protection legislation of their homeland. Consequently, the European Commission stepped in to open negotiations with the US to resolve the matter for all EU countries (Hailbronner et al., 2008, p. 189). Whilst US airlines were forced to rapidly comply with these new measures, the European Commission managed to negotiate with the US a delay for EU-based airlines, on the grounds that they were required to comply with the 1995 EU directive on the protection of personal data. The US Department of Homeland Security agreed to give the EU an extension until 5 March 2003 to comply with the new rules.

Therefore, while the PNR initiative clearly emanated from the US, the European Commission managed to construct a significant role for itself in the implementation of the PNR Agreement in Europe. In practice, it negotiated with US officials a series of requirements and adopted a decision on adequacy based on Article 25 of the EC directive on data protection (Commission Decision, 14 May 2004). This decision laid down a requirement for the US to ensure an adequate level of data protection for the data transferred from Europe. Following this, the Commission negotiated the Agreement on the transfer of data with the US government, assuming legal competence through the implicit legal power provided by community law regarding transport and data protection. The PNR Agreement was approved by the Council on 17 May 2004 and subsequently signed on 28 May 2004 in Washington.

However, the European Parliament, which had felt marginalised during the negotiations of the agreement, decided to start proceedings before the European Court of Justice (ECJ) to annul the agreement. Whilst it also objected to this agreement on the basis that the US authorities did not guarantee adequate levels of data protection, its complaint focused on the choice of legal basis, as it claimed that the agreement should not have been based on Article 95 TEU on approximation of laws. In May 2006, the ECJ did annul the agreement, but not on substantive grounds relating to issues of data protection. Instead, it ruled that the agreement was incorrectly based on EU transport policy (a first-pillar provision), as it mainly aimed to enhance security and to fight against terrorism. As a consequence, the concerned data transfers fell within the public security framework established by the public authorities (Guild and Brouwer, 2006, p. 3). Thus, despite achieving its aim of overturning the agreement, the European Parliament gained very little from the ruling. The ECJ did not address the issue of data protection guarantees by the US authorities. Moreover, one of the consequences of the judgement was that any new agreement had to be negotiated in the framework of the third pillar, in which the European Parliament is largely excluded from the decision-making process (de Hert and de Schutter, 2008, p. 328).

As a result of the ECJ judgement, what came to be known as the 'First PNR Agreement' had to be replaced. This Second PNR Agreement was to be based on third-pillar provisions, which meant that its negotiation had to be led by the Council Presidency with the assistance of the Commission (de Hert and de Schutter, 2008, p. 330). Given the tight deadline imposed by the ECJ to solve the legal problem, an Interim PNR Agreement was adopted in the meantime, which ensured similar levels of data protection as before. After several further negotiations, a final deal was reached by the end of June 2007, and approved by the Council of Ministers in July 2007. Under this Second PNR Agreement, the US government agreed to receive fewer fields of data: nineteen instead of thirty-four compared with the First PNR Agreement. In exchange, the Council agreed that American authorities would be able to share the data with an increased number of federal authorities and to store them for longer – fifteen years, instead of three and a half years (Occhipinti, 2008, p. 19).

Thus, despite a partial outmanoeuvring by the European Parliament, it can be argued that the European Commission, in alliance with the Council Secretariat, largely remained in control of the PNR negotiations, as 'the second Agreement ... is largely along the spirit and the lines of the original, Commission-negotiated EC–US Agreement' (Mitsilegas, 2009, p. 155). In fact, the Commission was even inspired to create EU legislation based on this experience of EU–US co-operation. In November 2007, as part of its new counter-terrorism initiatives, it suggested creating an EU PNR system, whereby PNR data concerning flights into and out of the EU would be collected and could be used in terrorist investigations (Occhipinti, 2008, p. 22). Furthermore, the Commission unveiled a package of proposals aiming to deal with terrorist threats, including a plan to implement a biometric system to monitor all entries into and exits from the Schengen zone by 2015.

Thus, the analysis of this policy area has demonstrated that, while the US may have initially irritated the European Commission by making demanding requests and approaching some EU member states on a bilateral basis, the US ultimately dealt with 'Europe' at the EU level and saw significant merit in dealing with the European Commission. In turn, such a position made the US a welcome partner for the European Commission. As a consequence, the Commission pushed very hard to ensure the conclusion of EU–US agreements and also used US pressure to advance European integration on these policy issues.

Police and law enforcement co-operation

EU–US co-operation in police and law enforcement has mainly developed through agreements between the US and the European Police Office (Europol). Before analysing how the co-operation between Europol and the US has developed, it is necessary to briefly explain the functions of Europol and the legal framework that allows this organisation to co-operate with third states.

Europol is a European Law Enforcement Organisation that aims to support co-operation amongst EU member states with regard to terrorism, drug trafficking and other serious forms of international organised crime. It was set up on the basis of an international Convention that came into effect in 1999. Europol has legal personality and can therefore enter into binding agreements under international law. A significant proportion of Europol staff comprises Europol liaison officers, which represent the national law enforcement agencies from all EU member states. The main control mechanism for Europol is its Management Board, which brings together high level representatives of the member states from the Ministries of Interior or Justice, and from operational law enforcement organisations. While the Council of Ministers is responsible for the main control of Europol, the Management Board has some important functions such as approving Europol's work programme. With regard to Europol's external relations, it can identify priorities for the negotiation of agreements with third states and bodies.

According to Article 42 of the Europol Convention, Europol can establish relations with third states and bodies. While the Management Board establishes rules for contacts with EU-related bodies, it is the Council that is responsible for establishing the rules on co-operation with non-EU related bodies and third states (Heimans, 2008, p. 374). Consequently, in 1998, the Council adopted three regulations concerning, respectively, the receipt of information by Europol from third parties, the governance of Europol's external relations with third states, and the transmission of personal data by Europol to third states and non-EU related bodies. When it comes to the signing of agreements with third states, the procedure starts with a unanimous decision of the Council on the list of states with which an agreement should be negotiated. The agreement is then negotiated by the Europol Director, who can only sign the agreement once it has been authorised by the Council (Heimans, 2008, p. 374).

Having established these legal foundations, which enable and at the same time constrain Europol's actions, it is now possible to examine the development of police co-operation between the EU and the US in the wake of 9/11. As early as 20 September 2001, the JHA Council, which was eager to demonstrate the EU's solidarity with the US, invited the Director of Europol to establish informal co-operation with the US – pending the conclusion of a formal agreement – and 'to finalise the formal agreement with the US as quickly as possible so that the Council may authorise its conclusion at its meeting on 16 November 2001' (Council of the European Union, 2001). The Council also indicated that the agreement was to provide, inter alia, for the exchange of liaison officers between Europol and US agencies concerned with policing. Moreover, the Council invited the Director of Europol to open negotiations with the US on an agreement covering the transmission of personal data.

The first of the two agreements was indeed promptly adopted on 6 December 2001. It mainly focuses on the exchange of strategic and technical information concerning 'serious forms of international crime', which include 'crimes committed or likely to be committed in the course of terrorist activities against life, limb, personal freedom or property' (Article 3). The agreement provides for the identification of points of contact, information exchange, mutual consultation, exchange of expertise, as well as the exchange of liaison officers.

The second agreement between Europol and the US, called the 'Supplemental Agreement on the exchange of personal data and related information', took longer to negotiate. This was mainly due to the differences in the approach to personal data issues between Europe and the US. As explained by Rees (2006, p. 92), in Europe, a significant amount of legislation on data protection has been adopted, as states have tended to hold rather large amounts of information on their citizens. In contrast, in the US, the approach towards data protection has been more ad hoc and relaxed, as relatively few data on citizens are held by the authorities. Despite this complex situation, the agreement was eventually signed on 20 December 2002 (Mitsilegas, 2003, p. 319).

Although it was criticised by civil liberties campaigners, this Europol–US agreement actually contains a significant number of data protection safeguards that had not previously been conceded by US authorities, including the important principle of 'purpose limitation', according to which information obtained for a specific purpose can only be used for that purpose. In addition, Article 7 stipulates that all federal authorities which receive information are bound by this principle and only those US agencies that agree to it can be provided with information under the terms of the agreement. This Europol–US agreement was the first international agreement in which US authorities agreed to apply such specific data protection provisions.

This analysis has demonstrated that EU–US co-operation on police and law enforcement to combat terrorism has considerably developed in the aftermath of 9/11. What is also distinctive about this area, in comparison with other dimensions of the EU–US counter-terrorism co-operation, is the lack of direct involvement of the European Commission in the policy developments. However, this does not mean that the Commission had no influence on this area at all, as it was still able to influence negotiations indirectly through the setting of the larger agenda in EU–US counter-terrorism relations. In contrast, Europol was able to exercise influence on the development of the EU–US co-operation more directly. The legal rules governing Europol's activities give it a certain degree of independence from normal EU institutional structures. It can even be argued that, to a limited extent, Europol was able to act as an SPE in an alliance with the Council Presidency and the Council Secretariat. Yet, in the end, no agreement can be signed by the Director of Europol without at least three Management Board and Council decisions. This means that, in order to act as an SPE, it is necessary for Europol to forge an alliance with the Presidency of the Council and the Council Secretariat.

Co-operation on combating the financing of terrorism

Since 9/11, targeting the financing of terrorism has become an increasingly important dimension of the fight against terrorism. On 28 September 2001, the UN Security Council adopted Resolution 1373, which requires all states to take several measures to combat the financing of terrorism, including the prevention and the suppression of the financing of terrorist acts, the criminalisation of the financing of terrorism and the freezing of the funds of individuals and entities involved in terrorist activities. In October 2001, the US Congress adopted the 'International Money Laundering Abatement and Anti-terrorist Financing Act' and put increasing pressure on other governments to tighten their own legislation on money laundering and terrorist financing.

In addition, in October 2001, the Financial Action Task Force (FATF) held an extraordinary plenary session in Washington to adopt eight Special Recommendations on Terrorist Financing, which established international standards with regards to: (1) the ratification and implementation of UN instruments, (2) criminalising the financing of terrorism and money laundering, (3) freezing and confiscating terrorist assets, (4) reporting suspicious transactions related to terrorism, (5) international co-operation, (6) alternative remittance, (7) wire transfers, and (8) non-profit organisations.[2]

As shown by Eling (2007, p. 105), the EU rapidly decided to tackle this issue of terrorist financing very seriously, which was positively seen by the US authorities. EU–US co-operation on the financing of terrorism has significantly grown. EU experts have been invited to participate in US terrorist financing assessment missions and to send trainers to support the delivery of US training programmes for financial regulators (Council of the European Union, 2006b, 2007b). The EU and the US have also held a series of joint workshops on financial sanctions to combat terrorism (Council of the European Union, 2006b, 2007b). In April 2007, the EU and the US also adopted a joint Public Outreach Paper, which aims to outline an efficient, fair and clear procedure for targeted sanctions to combat terrorist financing. These examples demonstrate that the EU and the US have developed close relations in the fight against the financing of terrorism.

Judicial co-operation

In addition to the policy areas already examined, the events of 9/11 have also led to an increase in EU–US co-operation in justice matters. As early as 20 September 2001, 'in a spirit of great transatlantic solidarity following the tragic events of 11 September 2001' (Stessens, 2008, p. 342), the JHA Council 'agreed on the principle of proposing to the US that an agreement be negotiated between the EU and the US, on the basis of Article 38 of the TEU, in the field of penal co-operation on terrorism' (Council of the European Union, 2001). Following a positive response from the US, negotiations led by the Presidency of the Council – assisted by the Commission and the Council Secretariat – started and led to the signing of the Extradition Agreement and the Mutual Legal Assistance Agreement in June 2003 (Stessens, 2008). These were the first agreements between the EU and a third country concerning criminal justice co-operation. Nevertheless, the negotiation of these agreements proved to be challenging at times, as there are some significant philosophical differences between Europe and America on judicial and extradition matters. In particular, Europeans tend to be very critical of the existence and execution of the death penalty in several US states, whereas Americans tend to perceive European penal codes as unjustifiably lenient, especially concerning sentencing in relation to murder (Rees, 2006, p. 86).

In terms of content, the EU–US Extradition Agreement aims to facilitate the extradition of persons having committed any offence punishable by deprivation of liberty of one year or more (Mitsilegas, 2003, p. 526). As far as the Mutual Legal Assistance Agreement is concerned, it foresees co-operation between the EU and the US on a wide range of issues including evidence-sharing for criminal investigations and prosecutions, the streamlining of extradition arrangements, the establishment of central points of contact between judicial authorities, and the sharing of sensitive data (Rees, 2006, p. 89). The adoption of both agreements was controversial (Gregory, 2005, p. 116), because their negotiation was conducted in secret and their text remained confidential for a long time, making parliamentary scrutiny very difficult (Mitsilegas, 2003, p. 525). In addition, concerns relating to human rights and data protection were also raised, notably by the European Parliament's Committee on Citizens' Freedoms and Rights, Justice and Home Affairs, in its report adopted in May 2003. It is important to note that, at the time of writing, both agreements have yet to enter into force (Stessens, 2008, p. 349).

In addition, an agreement between Eurojust and the US was signed in November 2006. Eurojust is an EU body whose main task is 'to enhance the efficiency of the national investigating and prosecuting authorities, when dealing with serious cross-border crime' (Helmberg, 2007: 246). The Council decision setting up Eurojust authorises it to negotiate co-operation agreements with third states, which require the approval of the Council before their final adoption (Council of the European Union, 2002). The main aim of the agreement between Eurojust and the US is to improve co-operation between the competent authorities to facilitate the co-ordination of investigations and prosecutions involving the US and one or more member state. Amongst the different measures foreseen by the agreement, one can note the following: the secondment of a Liaison Prosecutor from the US to Eurojust, the appointment of at least one contact point to Eurojust within the office of the competent authority in the US, and the exchange of information in compliance with the existing data protection rules.

Thus, the EU has also developed the judicial dimension of its co-operation with the US, in particular through the adoption of three important agreements. With respect to them, the Council has evidently played a major role, as it is required to authorise their conclusion. Yet, this does not mean that the Commission had no influence on this area at all, as it was still able to influence negotiations indirectly through the setting of the larger agenda in EU–US counter-terrorism relations. However, it is also important to note that Eurojust has been given some autonomy by the decision that established it. As a result, it is able to exercise a certain degree of autonomy when negotiating co-operation agreements, which emphasises the important role that EU bodies and institutions can play in the development of the EU counter-terrorism external relations. Thus, Eurojust was very influential on the development of the EU–US co-operation. The legal rules governing Eurojust activities give it a certain degree of independence from normal EU institutional structures, similar to Europol. Consequently, it can be argued that, to a limited extent, Europol was able to act as an SPE in an alliance with the Council Presidency and the Council Secretariat.

How important were the European institutions in the development of EU–US counter-terrorism co-operation?

The EU required a clear strategy and leadership after the terrorist attacks of 11 September 2001. As explained in the previous chapter, the European Commission and the US co-operated very closely. This continuous co-operation was consistently supported by the Council Secretariat, or as demonstrated above also, by EU bodies such as Europol and Eurojust.

On the one hand, one needs to acknowledge a certain rivalry for competences between these institutions at the EU level. For instance, the Commission had been cautious about the idea of a special representative for terrorism outside the Commission framework (Spence, 2007, p. 18). When the former Dutch deputy Interior Minister, Gijs de Vries,[3] was appointed as counter-terrorism co-ordinator within the Council in order to drive forward the EU action plan on terrorism, the Commission was rather lukewarm (interviews COM 25, 12, CON 6). It feared that the Council Secretariat would propose structures that increased its own powers over the Commission (ibid.).

However, despite these misgivings, the Commission and the Council Secretariat both support stronger powers and competences for the EU on counter-terrorism, internally and externally (interviews COM 5, 7, 9, 12, 25; CON 1–9). Officials in both institutions are clearly aware that a close alliance on matters of counter-terrorism is vital. The Commission depends on the Council Presidency, which in turn depends on the Council Secretariat. While the Presidency rotates every six months, staff in the Commission and the Secretariat remain largely constant. Consequently, the need to work closely together is perceived by many officials (interviews COM 5, 7, 9, 12, 25; CON 1–9). In other words, there are structural conditions favourable to the development of an alliance between both EU bodies.

The EU Commission also responded very quickly to the attacks of September 11 with legislative proposals, as analysed in the previous chapter. An exceptional EU JHA Council Ministers met on 21 September 2001 and developed a far-reaching action plan. In this document measures in five areas were proposed: (1) police and judicial co-operation enhancement, (2) the development of international legal instruments, (3) putting an end to the funding of terrorism, (4) strengthening air security, and (5) co-ordinating the EU's global action (Council of the European Union, 2001). Especially the latter point points clearly to the intent to construct an international role for the EU. Dubois (2002, p. 324) thus asserts that 'the events of 11 September have indirectly allowed the EU to become a consistent actor in the fight against terrorism'.

The first attempt to link the construction of internal EU counter-terrorism competences to the construction of an international role for the EU occurred shortly after 9/11 when the Director General of the Commission, Sir Adrian Fortescue (*European Voice*, 27 September 2001), attended a meeting with Colin Powell, the US Secretary of State, on 21 September, as analysed in the previous chapter. In a personal interview, the late Sir Adrian confirmed that the Commission's strategy to work closely with the US also partly aimed to enhance internal competences for the EU in the field of counter-terrorism.

However, the European Commission had to use a 'carrot and stick' approach in its relations with the US. Thomas Ridge, the former US Homeland Security Secretary, stated in his farewell speech that his greatest regret was not to have worked more closely with the EU from the start (Lebl, 2006, p. 125). Initially, US officials were rather cautious to engage with the EU institutions in order not to damage their bilateral relationships with EU member states. They also worried that dealing with the EU would be less efficient, or even counterproductive compared to working with national and local officials. This is where the Commission used the 'stick' approach, in particular regarding the container security agreements. In 2002, the US negotiated bilateral agreements with several member states on container security, culminating in the decision to admit Belgium, France, Germany and the Netherlands to the US Container Security Initiative by June 2002, and the UK, Italy, Spain and Sweden by January 2003 (Faull and Soreca, 2008, p. 409). Holding the view that this would infringe EC exclusive legislative competence, the European Commission began legal infringement proceedings against these member states before the ECJ. Threatened with this stick, the US and the EU expanded their own 1997 co-operation agreement to include transport security, and in particular elements of the US Container Security Initiative. Consequently, the Commission withdrew its legal infringement procedures, having amply made its point. The Commission was ready to help the US in order to increase its legal competences in the AFSJ, for as long as the US respected the role and competences of the EU (Lebl, 2006) – which the US did after this episode.

The Commission also invited the US to provide information as to how the EU could help and support its counterterrorism efforts after 9/11 – the 'carrot' approach. President George Bush listed forty-seven demands in a letter to the EU, covering judicial and diplomatic co-operation, data protection, the proliferation of biological weapons and other issues, and hence strengthening co-operation with the EU in fighting terrorism. It also mentioned that extradition processes from the EU to America should be streamlined, in addition to asking the EU to facilitate extradition procedures internally. The fact that the EU agreed on EU-wide extradition policy from December 2001 onwards, with the EAW analysed previously, enabled the EU to start negotiations on extradition with the US. Without the EAW, the political consensus to conclude an international extradition agreement between the EU and the US would not have existed. For the EU, this would have meant that it might have become sidelined in future counter-terrorism agreements.

In conclusion, this section has demonstrated the fact that the EU has made significant progress in counter-terrorism in order to show its support for the US. This was a necessary first step in order to facilitate counter-terrorism relations. There were advantages stemming from this co-operation for both sides, with the EU being recognised as an important international actor in counter-terrorism by the only remaining world superpower. Yet, it also demonstrated the importance and political significance of three actors. Firstly, the US put significant pressure on the EU to strengthen co-operation. In the war on terror it was a case of 'for us or against us'. The EU chose to support the US as much as possible, without offering military means. However, the EU bodies and institutions have had a significant impact on the ways in which the EU has provided its support, including Europol and Eurojust. Significantly, for the European Commission in particular, support for the US became equated with advancing European integration. This included internal action, as well as EU external action on counter-terrorism with the US. The larger global agenda of the 'war on terror' was seized as a promising opportunity to advance European integration in the counter-terrorism field.

Counter-terrorism in the European Neighbourhood Policy

This section will examine how the EU has also developed counter-terrorism co-operation with neighbouring states through the framework of the European Neighbourhood Policy (ENP) and the role that EU institutions have played in the development of this policy. The ENP was launched by a Communication of the European Commission entitled 'Wider Europe – Neighbourhood: A New Framework for relations with our Eastern and Southern Neighbours' in 2003. This document argued that, as it was about to enlarge to ten new member states, '[the] EU should aim to develop a zone of prosperity and a friendly neighbourhood – a "ring of friends" – with whom the EU enjoys close, peaceful and co-operative relations' (European Commission, 2003c, p. 4). It argued further that '[in] return for concrete progress demonstrating shared values and effective implementation of political, economic, and institutional reforms, all the neighbouring countries should be offered the prospect of a stake in the EU's internal market' (European Commission, 2003c, p. 10). Thus, in practice, the ENP has aimed to offer these 'friends' a 'privileged relationship' involving deeper co-operation on a wide range of policy issues, but falling short of offering them full membership of the EU.

Since then, the ENP has become one of the most important foreign policy instruments of the EU and the main policy framework for its relations with several states. Those can be organised into two categories: the eastern ENP countries (Ukraine, Belarus, Moldova, Georgia, Armenia and Azerbaijan) and the southern Mediterranean (Med) ENP countries (Morocco, Algeria, Tunisia, Libya, Egypt, Jordan, Lebanon, Syria, Israel, and the Palestinian Authority). This chapter will focus on the importance and the modalities of counter-terrorism co-operation in the relations between the EU and the Med ENP countries. There are several reasons for focusing on this group of countries. First of all, strengthening political dialogue and co-operation on combating terrorism is a priority that has been identified for the relations between the EU and all the Med ENP countries. In contrast, counter-terrorism has not been identified as a priority for action in the case of several eastern ENP states (Balfour and Missiroli, 2007, p. 36). Moreover, several scholars have argued that, in contrast with the emphasis of the EU's official discourse on political and economic reforms, the EU policies towards its Mediterranean neighbours are actually mainly concerned with tackling security issues such as terrorism (Dannreuther, 2006; Bosse, 2007; Joffé, 2008; Wolff, 2009).

This section will start by examining the broader context in which the ENP and its counter-terrorism dimension have developed. Then, it will consider the institutional aspects of the ENP, before analysing the development of counter-terrorism co-operation between the EU and its Med ENP partners.

The European Neighbourhood Policy and counter-terrorism in context

Before examining the development of the ENP towards the EU's southern neighbours and the importance of counter-terrorism in these relations, it is important to consider the broader context in which these policy developments have taken place. Indeed, the ENP builds upon pre-existing co-operation between the EU and its southern neighbours. The first attempt to develop such co-operation was the launch of the Euro-Arab Dialogue in December 1973. This initiative aimed to provide a forum for dialogue and co-operation between the EC and the League of Arab Nations. However, it proved to be largely unsuccessful because of international tensions relating to the Arab–Israeli conflict and the Gulf War (Youngs, 2006, p. 19).

A significant attempt was subsequently made to relaunch co-operation between the EU and its southern neighbours at the Barcelona Conference. In November 1995, the Barcelona Declaration was adopted at this Euro-Mediterranean Conference and established the Euro-Mediterranean Partnership (EMP) or 'Barcelona Process'.[4] The EMP aims to enhance co-operation between the EU and southern Mediterranean countries with regard to three key areas: political and security issues, economic and financial issues, and social, cultural and human issues. Migration was added as a fourth key area for co-operation in 2005 (see Euro-Mediterranean Partnership, 2007). The issue of terrorism was explicitly mentioned in the Barcelona Declaration, alongside many other policy issues. The signatories announced their intention to 'strengthen their co-operation in preventing and combating terrorism, in particular by ratifying and applying the international instruments they have signed'.

With regard to its implementation, the Barcelona Process involves multilateral and bilateral actions. The multilateral dimension of the EMP comprises regular Euro-Mediterranean conferences, which bring together the Ministers of Foreign Affairs of all the countries concerned to monitor the application of the Barcelona Declaration and to define actions for its implementation. These meetings are complemented by ad hoc meetings of Ministers, senior officials and experts in charge of the various sectoral policies. Over the years, terrorism has increasingly moved towards the top of the agenda of the Euro-Mediterranean conferences. This has been particularly highlighted by the adoption of a Euro-Mediterranean Code of Conduct on Countering Terrorism at the 2005 Barcelona Summit (Euro-Mediterranean Partnership, 2005).

The other important aspect of the implementation of the Euro-Mediterranean Partnership has been the conclusion of bilateral Association Agreements between the EU and its Mediterranean partners. Based on Article 310 TEC, these Association Agreements have replaced the Co-operation Agreements previously adopted. They have been negotiated by the European Commission with the partner countries on an individual basis, following the Council's authorisation to open negotiations.

At the time of writing, Euro-Med Association Agreements are in force between the EU and the following countries: Tunisia, Israel, Morocco, Jordan, Egypt, Algeria, as well as the Palestinian Authority on an interim basis. These agreements cover a wide range of policy areas, such as trade, agriculture, environment, energy, customs, etc. Most Association Agreements that have been signed to date do not explicitly mention the issue of terrorism. However, they all contain a clause relating to the establishment of a regular political dialogue between the two parties aiming to enhance the stability, security and prosperity of the Mediterranean region. Evidently, terrorism could be one of the issues included in this political dialogue. Only two Association Agreements, which are also amongst the most recent ones, contain specific provisions relating to terrorism. Article 59 of the EU–Egypt Association Agreement, which entered into force in 2004, foresees counter-terrorism co-operation between the two parties, particularly with regard to 'exchange of information on means and methods used to counter terrorism; exchange of experiences in respect of terrorism prevention; joint research and studies in the area of terrorism prevention'. Article 90 of the EU–Algeria Association Agreement, which entered into force in 2005, also concerns the fight against terrorism. However, it foresees different co-operation measures, such as the implementation of terrorism-related UN Security Council resolutions, the exchange of information on terrorist groups and their support networks, and the sharing of experience in combating terrorism.

Thus, the analysis of the development of the EMP has shown that terrorism has become an increasingly important issue in the Euro-Mediterranean relations over the last few years. However, Joffé's claim (2008, p. 147) that 'co-operation to achieve economic and political development between South Mediterranean states has been effectively replaced by co-operation to combat a shared threat: transnational terrorism' appears to be exaggerated. It is true that terrorism has grown in importance in the Euro-Mediterranean political statements. However, in practice, counter-terrorism co-operation between the EU and its southern Mediterranean partners has remained very limited. Actually, this is not a problem specific to this policy area, as the EMP in general has been harshly criticised for its effectiveness (Pardo and Zemer, 2005; Del Sarto and Schumacher, 2005). In that respect, the ENP, which was launched in 2003, was also an attempt – largely developed by the European Commission – to address the shortcomings of the EMP with respect to its southern neighbours.

With regard to the relationship between the two policy initiatives, the EU has presented the ENP as complementing the multilateral framework of the Barcelona Process and building on its bilateral dimension. Indeed, the existing Euro-Med Association Agreements provide the legal basis for the development of the ENP towards southern Mediterranean states, including counter-terrorism actions. This means that the ENP can only be 'activated' towards countries which have concluded an Association Agreement with the EU, setting aside Libya and Syria at the moment, although they are officially recognised as participants in the ENP. In addition, the ENP is seen as allowing for more differentiation amongst southern Mediterranean states, as some are able to progress towards closer ties with the EU without the constraints of a multilateral framework (Balfour, 2007, p. 16).

Institutional aspects of the European Neighbourhood Policy

The key instruments in the ENP are the Action Plans that are developed in partnership with each of the countries concerned. These plans are not treaties that are binding under international law (Emerson et al., 2006, p. 4). They are jointly agreed policy documents that identify priorities for actions to be achieved within three to five years (Balfour, 2007, p. 16; Emerson et al., 2006, p. 4). The European Commission plays a prominent role in the development of these Action Plans. First of all, it is responsible for preparing individual 'Country Reports'. Each of these reports aims to analyse various factors (political situation, economic and social situation, institutional and sectoral aspects) in order to assess how the EU can further develop its relations with the country concerned. The Commission published seven Country Reports in May 2004 (Moldova, Ukraine, Israel, Jordan, Morocco, the Palestinian Authority and Tunisia), before releasing a further five in March 2005 (Egypt, Lebanon, Georgia, Azerbaijan, and Armenia).

The Council has a responsibility to consider these Country Reports. If it decides to proceed to the next stage of relations, the Commission prepares a draft ENP Action Plan for each country, with the input from its delegations abroad and the member states (Balfour, 2007, p. 16). Based on the principle of 'joint ownership' (see European Commission, 2006c, p. 3), these Action Plans are negotiated with each neighbouring country under the leadership of the Commission. According to Johansson-Nogués (2007, p. 33), the fact that the European Commission leads the consultations with the ENP partners on Action Plans that concern policy matters across the three EU pillars has already 'unnerve[d] the Council'. Once the text of the ENP Action Plan has been agreed with the ENP partner, it has to receive the approval of the Council in order to be considered for final adoption in the respective EU-partner Association Council. In another example of the close relationship between the EMP and the Barcelona Process, Association Councils are also tasked with the promotion and the monitoring of the implementation of the Action Plans (Johansson-Nogués, 2007, p. 33). These matters are reported upon in both joint assessments and unilateral EU reports, called 'regular country reports'. A first report is to be published two years after the start of the Action Plan, followed by a second report in the following year (Kelley, 2006: 33).

Counter-terrorism in the European Neighbourhood Policy

All the Med ENP Action Plans contain measures aiming to develop counter-terrorism co-operation between the EU and its neighbours. This section analyses the four main areas of counter-terrorism co-operation covered by the Action Plans: political dialogue and co-operation, co-operation on combating terrorism financing, police and law enforcement co-operation, and judicial co-operation.

Political dialogue and co-operation

A large number of measures on counter-terrorism contained in the Med ENP Action Plans concern political dialogue and co-operation. Each Action Plan analysed contains the general aim of strengthening co-operation between the EU and its neighbour in the fight against terrorism. The importance of '[ensuring] respect for human rights in the fight against terrorism' is also mentioned in all the Plans, although this measure is expressed in different terms in the Action Plan for Israel – namely 'exchange views on the dilemmas and concerns of democracies in their fight against terrorism while ensuring the safeguarding of human rights in that pursuit, and protecting the rights of those targeted and affected by acts of terror'. In line with the EU's traditional support for multilateralism (Eling, 2007), all the Med Action Plans contain measures aiming to reinforce the role of the UN in combating terrorism, including, in some Plans, more specific actions, such as the full implementation of the UN Security Resolutions (Action Plans for Morocco and Tunisia) and the enhancement of efforts to reach an agreement on a Comprehensive

UN Convention on Combating Terrorism (Action Plans for Egypt and Lebanon). Most Plans also contain measures calling for the exchange of views on the methods to counter-terrorism (Action Plans for Morocco, Tunisia, Israel, Egypt and Lebanon), whilst some of them also contain measures on co-operation with regard to terrorism prevention (Action Plans for Israel, Egypt and Lebanon).

Thus, it clearly appears that the European Commission, whilst developing the Action Plans with the countries concerned, has set an ambitious agenda for the development of counter-terrorism co-operation, which covers a wide range of issues for political dialogue. However, one can also question the vagueness of some of these objectives, such as 'ensuring respect of human rights in the fight against terrorism'. The plans do not contain any indication of how this is to be achieved in practice, which raises important questions about the likelihood of major changes in this area in the countries concerned.

Co-operation on combating the financing of terrorism

Another policy area in which the EU has aimed to develop co-operation with its Med ENP partners is the fight against the financing of terrorism. All the Action Plans for the Med ENP partners contain measures relating to this area. Some of them are included in the section on 'justice and home affairs actions', whereas others are mentioned as part of the 'political dialogue and co-operation'. The relatively large number of actions pertaining to this policy area indicates that it has been identified as one of the most important aspects of the EU's counter-terrorism co-operation with the Med ENP countries.

There are arguably two main reasons for which the fight against the financing of terrorism has been emphasised in the ENP framework. Firstly, the fighting of terrorism financing has been internationally recognised as an important component of combating terrorism. As explained earlier, international standards have been established, with which all states have been expected to comply, including the EU's Med ENP partners. It is not surprising that the EU would strongly push for the implementation of these global standards, as it has traditionally been a strong champion of multilateralism and international norms and, in particular, has 'sought to be an exemplary "implementer" for the prescriptions issued by the Security Council after 9/11' (Eling, 2007, p. 119). Secondly, specific characteristics of the economic and banking systems of these countries – in particular, the important role played by Islamic charities and the *hawala* networks[5] (Gardner, 2007, p. 342; de Moraes Ruehsen, 2007, p. 165; Gunning, 2008) – have made their problems of money laundering and terrorism financing particularly acute and the compliance with international standards defined in this area all the more challenging. From the EU's point of view, this situation has reinforced the importance of developing co-operation on these matters with the Med ENP countries.

Before examining the measures aiming to combat terrorism financing in the Med ENP Action Plans, it is necessary to briefly recall the respective roles of the main international organisations involved in this policy area. First of all, the UN Security Council has adopted Resolutions 1267 and 1373. The former was adopted in 1999 and established sanctions against the Taliban regime in Afghanistan for its support of Osama bin Laden and Al-Qaeda, whereas the latter has a far broader scope (Thony and Png, 2007, p. 154). It requires states to take concerted actions to prevent support to terrorist organisations, including financial support. It imposes the criminalisation of terrorism financing, as well as the freezing without delay of all assets of terrorists and terrorist organisation. Thus, it does not target any specific individuals or organisations, but all forms of terrorism. As a result of the adoption of these standards and sometimes under considerable external pressure, Mediterranean and Middle Eastern states have adopted or amended their national legislation on money-laundering and the financing of terrorism. However, Western officials have often criticised these reforms for their shortcomings (de Moraes Ruehsen, 2007), in particular their over-reliance on anti-money-laundering measures which are not sufficient to efficiently combat terrorism funding (United Nations Security Council, 2004).

The other major international player in the field of terrorism financing is the FATF. It is an intergovernmental body, which develops and promotes standards in the fight against money laundering and the financing of terrorism. Its membership currently comprises thirty-two countries and territories and two regional organisations, including the fifteen 'old' member states of the EU and, interestingly, the European Commission. In addition to its forty Recommendations concerning the fight against money-laundering, FATF has adopted nine Special Recommendations (SRs) on Terrorist Financing, which have become internationally accepted best practice. The implementation of the FATF standards is monitored through a 'mutual evaluation process', which has revealed considerable deficiencies in the only two Med ENP countries that have already undergone it (Morocco and Tunisia) (Middle East and North Africa Financial Action Task Force, 2007a, b).[6]

In line with the importance of these new standards on the financing of terrorism and the significant problems of compliance that have affected several Middle Eastern and Mediterranean states, the financing of terrorism – alongside money laundering – has been identified as a policy issue in all ENP Action Plans, apart from that for the Palestinian Authority. Moreover, all the ENP Action Plans, apart from that for Tunisia (and evidently that for the Palestinian Authority), contain measures which make explicit references to the FATF standards.

In practice, several Action Plans contain measures involving changes to national legislation on the financing of terrorism. For example, Lebanon is asked to implement the counter-terrorism related UN Resolutions and Conventions. The Action Plan for Tunisia calls for the implementation of the legislation on money laundering and the financing of terrorism, whereas

Morocco is asked to 'continue the development of an effective legal framework in the field of money laundering and the financing of terrorism in accordance with FATF recommendations' – an implicit recognition that it lags behind other countries in the region when it comes to fighting the financing of terrorism.[7]

In addition, some Action Plans contain measures regarding information exchange and co-operation with the EU on combating the financing of terrorism. The Action Plans for Jordan, Egypt, Lebanon, and Morocco foresee the exchange of information on 'European legislation and international instruments (FATF recommendations)' and the legislation of the ENP partner on money laundering and the financing of terrorism. Those for Israel, Jordan and Lebanon call for the development of co-operation to strengthen the fight against the financing of terrorism 'in line with standards laid down in the FATF recommendations on terrorism financing'.[8] Furthermore, the Action Plan for Israel is unique in containing a provision calling for the 'mutual exchange of information and practices on supervision and monitoring methods regarding money laundering and the financing of terrorism'.

Thus, the issue of terrorism financing has received a lot of attention in the ENP Action Plans. The high number of measures relating to this policy issue indicates that it has been identified, notably by the European Commission, as an important area of counter-terrorism co-operation between the EU and the Med ENP countries. Nevertheless, it is also true that the level of co-operation envisaged with the Med ENP countries is lower than that between the EU and the US. Several measures contained in the Med ENP Action Plans are also rather vague – with the possible exception of the Action Plan for Israel – as they do not indicate the precise actions involved to achieve them. This can be explained by the fact that these states are not as advanced in the development of their policies against terrorism financing, which means that there is less scope for co-operation on specific aspects of the fight against the financing of terrorism. Nevertheless, despite the current modest level of co-operation, it is interesting to note the growing role that the European Commission has managed to construct for itself in this policy area by including the issue of terrorism financing in the negotiations with the Med ENP countries.

Police and law enforcement co-operation

Another dimension of counter-terrorism co-operation included in the ENP Action Plans concerns police and law enforcement. Several Action Plans, i.e. those concerning Israel, Jordan, Egypt and Lebanon, contain a broad measure that calls for the development of co-operation between law enforcement agencies to combat terrorism. Two Action Plans go further than this general declaration of intent to develop co-operation. First of all, the Action Plan concerning Morocco contains a more specific measure calling for the adoption of an agreement with Europol, the European Police Office, including 'action on combating terrorism'. Furthermore, the Action Plan for

Israel states the common goal of the parties to enhance co-operation between the relevant services of the EU and Israel 'including specialised bodies at European level' – a phrasing that can be interpreted as referring notably to Europol.

Indeed, Europol is the likely body through which co-operation between the EU and the Med ENP countries would be channelled. In practice, co-operation between Europol and a third country can only start after an agreement has been signed between both parties concerned, because an agreement is essential for the secondment of liaison officers of Europol to third states and vice versa (Article 3 of the Council Act of 3 November 1998 laying down rules governing Europol's external relations with third states and non-EU-related bodies). The procedure for the adoption of agreements foresees that the Council unanimously determines the third states with which agreements are to be negotiated by the Director of Europol. In recent years, Europol has concluded two different types of agreements with third countries: operational agreements – which authorise the exchange of personal data – and strategic agreements – which do not include the exchange of personal data. The latter can only be signed with countries whose data protection standards are satisfactory.

To date, Europol has not signed any agreement with Med ENP countries yet. However, as has just been explained, the adoption of an agreement is envisaged with Morocco and Israel. In the case of the former, this is actually no new development, as the Director of Europol has had a negotiation mandate for a co-operation agreement with Morocco since March 2000 (Council of the European Union, 2000). The negotiations are still ongoing at the time of writing. With regards to Israel, the Council authorised the Director of Europol to negotiate an operational agreement with this country in February 2005. Following this decision, Europol has been assessing Israel's data protection legislation, whilst Israel has received funding for a €1 million twinning project entitled Strengthening Data Protection in Israel (Austrian Ministry of Justice and Interior, 2007).

Apart from the cases of Morocco and Israel, it is likely that, in practice, police and law enforcement co-operation with the Med ENP countries will remain rather limited in the near future. The main reason is that 'Europol and [its] Management Board have expressed the views that, from a law enforcement point of view, there is far more interest to have operational agreements rather than strategic agreements. The general rule should therefore be the negotiation of operational agreements (subject to the existence of an appropriate data protection framework)' (Europol, 2006, p. 5). However, apart from Israel, no Med ENP country could be viewed as having an 'appropriate data protection framework', i.e. a framework that would comply with the regulatory framework governing the exchange of information between Europol and its partners. This does not make them attractive partners for Europol as it could only sign a strategic agreement with them.

However, it is interesting to note that the existence of appropriate data rules is only required for the exchange (or sharing) of information. It does not apply to the receipt of information by Europol. As a result, a co-operation agreement is not essential for Europol to receive information from third partners. The only obligations of Europol in such a case is '[to check] the completeness and the correctness of the data supplied by third partners and to pay specific attention not to accept information which was obviously obtained in violation of human rights' (Europol, 2006, p. 6). Thus, if these conditions were fulfilled, the Med ENP countries could transmit information to Europol if they so wished, which could be a first step towards the establishment of mutual co-operation at a later stage.

Thus, it is fair to say that the current level of police and law enforcement protection in counter-terrorism between the EU and the Med ENP countries is still rather low at this stage. Nevertheless, the inclusion of measures relating to this policy area in the Med ENP Action Plans indicates that it is an area in which the EU is keen to develop co-operation in the future. What is also remarkable is that these Action Plans have been elaborated under the leadership of the European Commission whilst it is actually a policy area in which the Commission has traditionally not had a strong position. By placing police and law enforcement on the ENP agenda, the Commission has increased its status in this specific policy area and has, more generally, reinforced its role in the external relations of both the second and the third pillars.

Judicial co-operation

Judicial co-operation is another aspect of counter-terrorism co-operation covered by the ENP. Given the absence of judicial co-operation between the EU and Mediterranean and Middle Eastern countries traditionally, it is remarkable that some of the ENP Action Plans, i.e. those for Israel, Jordan, Lebanon and Egypt, indicate that such co-operation in the field of counter-terrorism should be developed. However, it is true that, at the same time, this is a rather vague objective, as the ENP Action Plans do not contain any more precise details on how such co-operation would be implemented in practice.

Nevertheless, one can argue that such judicial co-operation in counter-terrorism would be likely to develop through Eurojust, given its growing role in criminal justice co-operation in the EU. Eurojust is an EU body that was established in 2002 to improve the co-ordination of investigations and prosecutions of serious cross-border and organised crime between competent authorities in the EU member states. It has a potential role to play in the development of judicial co-operation in the area of counter-terrorism with ENP countries as it is allowed to co-operate with the authorities competent for investigations and prosecutions in third states. According to Article 27 of the Council Decision setting up Eurojust, it may sign co-operation agreements with third countries, as well as 'exchange any information which is necessary for the performance of its tasks' with the authorities competent for investigations and prosecutions in third states. Normally, Eurojust would first sign a co-operation agreement with a third country before exchanging information with its competent authorities. However, the Decision that set up Eurojust authorises it to co-operate with third countries even if an agreement has not been signed 'to resolve urgent matters', with the exclusion of personal data. Nevertheless, 'by way of exception and with the sole aim of taking urgent measures to counter imminent serious danger threatening a person or public security', Eurojust is authorised to carry out an exchange of personal data even if it has not signed a co-operation agreement with the competent authorities of the third state (Article 27).

To date, Eurojust has not signed an agreement with any of the Med ENP countries. In addition, as in the area of police and law enforcement, the underdevelopment of data protection rules in these countries represents a significant obstacle to the development of judicial co-operation, although the existence of an emergency or of serious and imminent threats can justify exceptional measures. In practice, it is mainly with Israel that judicial co-operation has developed so far, with the appointment of a contact point for Eurojust in Israel. Nevertheless, like in the other areas of counter-terrorism co-operation, the mere fact that judicial co-operation has made its way into some of the ENP Action Plans is already a remarkable development, given the lack of such co-operation to date.

EU institutional entrepreneurship in the external dimension of counter-terrorism

In conclusion, it is clear that the EU has significantly expanded its co-operation with third states in the field of counter-terrorism since 9/11. It is also evident that co-operation with the US has developed far more significantly than co-operation with the Med ENP countries. Nevertheless, the mere fact that co-operation on terrorism is now firmly on the ENP agenda, even if it has not yielded many results to date, is remarkable. Although one may criticise the counter-terrorism measures contained in the ENP Action Plans for their vagueness, they are considerably more precise than what was ever agreed by the EU and its southern neighbours in the past. In addition, the inclusion of counter-terrorism issues in the ENP has reinforced the role of the EU in the global efforts against terrorism, which has increased its status of attractive partner for the US.

Having established the success of the EU in developing co-operation in counter-terrorism with third states, it is important to examine the role played by the European institutions toward this achievement in the light of the model of SPE. A close examination of the summary of results substantiates the degree of success of the European institutions in acting as an alliance of SPEs. The strategy of the EU institutions, in particular the Commission and the Council Secretariat, was again to use a 'first mover' advantage in order to construct for themselves a 'foot in the door' of the external dimension, and to push for a 'European approach', facilitated by the anchoring of EU policy in the prevailing 'war on terror' discourse, analysed in the previous chapter. First of all, the Commission managed to set the agenda in defining the problems in the problem stream, along the model suggested by Kingdon (1984, p. 90). In this particular case, similarly to the preceding chapter, the

Table 5.1 European institutions as SPEs in the external dimension of counter-terrorism relations

Evidence for	
Long-term norm change	*Short-term policy advances*
Overall assessment	
Norms changed significantly after the Commission managed to construct the EU into the 'war on terror'	Significant policy advances:
What changed?	
1 EU–US transatlantic counter-terrorism co-operation building on previous bilateral relations	Europol–US agreement
2 Counter-terrorism becomes more important in the ENP	EU–US mutual legal assistance agreement
3 EU's promotion of multilateralism and global norms	Eurojust–US agreement
4	EU–US extradition agreement
5	EU–US PNR agreement
6	Countering the financing of terrorism through EU–US co-operation and the ENP
How did it change?	
1 First-mover advantage	Networks of EU experts: Commission, Council, national Ministries, Europol, Eurojust
2 Linking EU action with the 'war on terror'	Commission alliance with Presidency and Council Secretariat; help from Europol and Eurojust
3 Preventing the US to use bilateral channels (container security)	Persuading big member states: bargaining and negotiation skills
4 Appealing to the US to put pressure on national governments	Proposed solutions for a compromise are very creative and legally sound
5 Pushing for policies at the right political moment	
6 Negotiation skills	
7 Strong legitimacy of the proposed solutions drawing upon global norms	

Commission managed to rapidly construct a 'European dimension' to what was previously perceived as a national problem. Subsequently, over the years, the Commission and the Council Secretariat continued to push for an increase in the role of the EU in the global fight against terrorism, sometimes with the help of other actors, such as Europol.

As a striking example, both the Council Secretariat and the Commission have agreed on terrorist financing as an inherently cross-pillar issue due to its link to money laundering, as well as foreign policy. They both recognised that the adoption of a really comprehensive approach was unquestionably the best way to address the problem as well as to increase their own influence. The Council Secretariat, in a paper submitted to COREPER on 8 March 2004, points out that 'the fight against terrorism is a cross-pillar activity engaging many EU actors and instrument'. It also highlights the manifold problems of co-ordination encountered so far which have challenged the EU capacity to respond coherently and effectively to international requirements. On 25 March 2004, the new Office of the EU Counter-terrorism Co-ordinator (CTC) was created with the aim to improve co-ordination in EU counter-terrorism policy. This office is based in the Council Secretariat under the leadership of the High Representative for Foreign and Security Policy, Javier Solana . The EU CTC was tasked together with the Commission to ensure the follow up of the strategy on terrorist financing on a cross-pillar basis, and was also required to report on a six monthly basis to the Council. The most recent version of this strategy (European Council, 2008) stated that most of the actions mentioned in the 2004 strategy have been carried out and that co-ordination has considerably improved. This is a clear sign that the two institutions are continuously working better with one another.

In the specific case of the ENP, the Commission was very active in shaping an ambitious and cross-pillar agenda for future co-operation with the Med ENP countries, drawing upon the 'knowledge capital' that it acquired whilst managing the enlargement process (Balfour, 2007, p. 16). In addition, the Commission has made frequent references to international law instruments, such as UN Security Council resolutions and conventions, or recommendations and global standards from other institutions such as the FATF. By using those as reference points for the standards to achieve with the Med ENP countries, the EU has increased the legitimacy of its actions, which appear to pursue universal standards rather than working towards European interests only (Balfour, 2007, p. 18).

Another important factor to bear in mind is that solutions to policy problems are shaped in the same policy communities of EU counter-terrorism experts, ranging from the civil servants in the Commission, the Council Secretariat, to Europol and national JHA Ministries. Commonly held sets of beliefs and norms influence people's ideas and behaviours. Participants interact with each other and are socialised according to the prevailing norms within this group. In the end, the necessary political consensus is built on persuasion (Kingdon, 1984, p. 167) in the politics stream, with a stronger emphasis on bargaining. The coalition building achieves a sort of bandwagon effect: the more decision-makers join the coalition and the more attractive it becomes to other policy-makers. It is precisely this effect that can be noted in the construction of the external dimension of counter-terrorism. Experts from the Commission facilitated the development of a 'transatlantic counter-terrorism agenda' in the external dimension of counter-terrorism, aided by experts in the Council Secretariat, Europol and Eurojust. With regard to the Med ENP countries, the Commission has developed a rather ambitious agenda for developing counter-terrorism co-operation in partnership with the countries concerned. This important role has reinforced the status of the EU as an important international actor in counter-terrorism, making it more attractive as a co-operation partner to countries such as the US. It has also enabled the European Commission to be politically stronger to push for a European counter-terrorism agenda, in both is internal and external dimensions.

Notes

1 In general, Al Qaeda aims for co-ordinated attacks with massive casualties (Hoffman, 2006). It has between 5,000 and 12,000 members in at least twenty-four groups (James and Brenda Lutz, 2004, p. 82). These groups are scattered all over the world, and this number relates only to the recognised groups.

2 A ninth Special Recommendation was adopted in October 2004, concerning cash couriers.

3 His successor is now Gilles de Kerchove, a formidable civil servant from within the Council Secretariat and a clear driving force for European integration. (Interviews CON1–CON9.)

4 The Barcelona Conference brought together the Foreign Affairs Ministers of the then fifteen EU member states and the following twelve Mediterranean non-member countries: Algeria, Cyprus, Egypt, Israel, Jordan, Lebanon, Malta, Morocco, the Palestinian Authority, Syria, Tunisia and Turkey. Mauritania, the League of Arab States and the Arab Maghreb Union (AMU) were also invited. Since then, Cyprus and Malta have become members of the EU, whilst Turkey has been officially recognised as a candidate for EU membership. In addition, Libya was granted observer status in the EMP in 1999.

5 It has been alleged that donations to Islamic charities, which are often made in cash and with little regulation, may have been used to finance terrorism. As far as the hawala networks are concerned, they are informal value transfer systems operating outside the formal banking system. It has also been suspected that they may have been used by terrorist organisations.

6 As the membership of FATF is largely Westerncentric, its actions are complemented by those of the so-called 'FATF-style regional bodies' (FSRBs) which organise the mutual evaluation process at the regional level. All the Med ENP partners, apart from the Palestinian Authority – which has the status of observer – and Libya, are members of the FSRB covering the Middle East and North Africa, i.e. MENAFATF (the Middle East and North Africa Action Task Force).

7 At the time of the mutual evaluation process Morocco was found to be 'non-

compliant' with five SRs, 'largely compliant' with one SR and 'partially compliant' with three SRs. In contrast, Tunisia has received a better assessment, as it was found to be 'compliant' with two SRs, 'largely compliant' with three SRs, 'partially compliant' with one SR and 'non-compliant' with three SRs.

8 The Action Plan for Egypt contains a similar provision, although there is no mention of the FATF recommendations.

6

The Common European Asylum System and border management: EU policy entrepreneurship?

This chapter investigates the potential second step in the construction of an Area of Freedom, Security and Justice. The first major security threat has been terrorism as analysed in the two preceding chapters. However, more quietly, asylum and migration has also become to be seen as a significant security threat which has supposedly influenced the first phase of the Common European Asylum System (Huysmans, 2000, 2004; Bigo, 1996, 1998a, b, c, d, 2001a, 2002; Guild, 1999, 2002, 2003a, b, c, 2004, 2006; Guiraudon, 2000, 2003). Policy developments after 9/11 have prompted a series of scholars (Faist, 2004; Karyotis, 2003; Huysmans, 2000; Ceyhan and Tsoukala, 2002; Kostakopolou, 2000) to argue that migration have been constructed as a security threat in Europe. These scholars often drawn upon the Copenhagen School's securitisation theory and argue that migration issues have been securitised in the EU. Levy (2005, p. 35) comments that 'the trend towards liberalisation seemed to be stopped dead in its tracks by the events of 9/11', whereas Boswell (2008) remarks that while EU migration policies were not securitised since 9/11, this does not hold for asylum policies.

However, this fear should be counter-intuitive. Especially the European Commission is well known for its legalistic approach to policy problems, always following the letter of the law, in fact the Commission is often derided for being technocratic. It seems thus counter-intuitive that the Commission would 'securitise' the EU Asylum Policy. According to the Copenhagen School, who argue that an issue is transformed into a security issue (i.e. securitised) after a securitising actor presents it as an existential threat and this 'securitising move' is accepted by the audience, this would mean that EU institutions, such as the Commission, deliberately construct refugees as a security threat in order to be able to use 'emergency measures' (Buzan, 1991; Buzan et al., 1998; Waever, 1993, 1995). Buzan, Wæver and de Wilde (1998, p. 25) note that 'the existential threat has to be argued and just gain enough resonance for a platform to be made from which it is possible to legitimise emergency measures or other steps that would not have been possible ...' (ibid.). This means that the same EU institutions that want to give the impression of following the letter of the law want to construct a situation in which the letter of the law can be disregarded ('emergency measures'). The way in which the EU institutions would aim to achieve this would be through a discursive construction of threats, thereby lifting the issues 'outside the normal realms of politics' (Buzan, 1991; Buzan et al., 1998; Waever, 1993, 1995). On the face of it, this seems plausible for right-wing politicians at the national level, but rather unlikely for EU bureaucrats, who loathe nothing more than the 'political limelight'.

Moreover, this goes against several academic arguments that were often made about asylum co-operation in Europe. Amongst academic scholars in the field of immigration and asylum, the argument has been advanced that EU governments decided to 'venue shop'; they decided to circumvent domestic pressures and obstacles, and therefore 'escaped' to legislate at the EU level where they were protected from these issues (Joppke, 1998, 2001; Freeman, 1998; Guiraudon, 2000, 2001, 2003; Boswell, 2003a, b, 2008; Ellermann, 2008; Geddes, 2000, 2001; Stetter, 2000, 2007; Thielemann, 2001a, b, 2004, 2005, 2006; Thielemann and Dewan, 2006; Lavenex, 1998, 1999, 2001a, b, 2004, 2006; Occhipinti, 2003). EU member states, in this argument, have decided to enhance their co-operation in the field of asylum and migration (ibid.) in a process driven by national bureaucracies. These state-centred accounts (esp. Joppke, 1998; Freeman, 1998) stress the resilience of nation-states, their ability to control 'unwanted immigration' and the use of the EU by its member states as a device for attaining immigration and asylum (see Thielemann, 2001a, b) policy objectives that are unlikely to be achieved at the domestic level alone. If indeed, national policy-makers are perfectly able to circumvent national pressures in order to restrict immigration and asylum at the EU level, why should they then 'securitise' the issues in order to achieve what they are already achieving? Why should national policy-makers go to a forum where technocracy is valued in order to securitise, which would be far easier in a national context? What are the constraints to securitise at the EU level, notably the Commission and its strong links to non-governmental organisation?

This chapter will make two significant points. Firstly, the Common European Asylum System (CEAS), other than in its intrinsic value, is a very significant case for demonstrating that even with the 'war on terror' on the political agenda (see also Lodge, 2004, 2007), the asylum policy in its first phase remained within the constraints of the Geneva Convention, and actually strengthened it. The balance between security and liberty, as a result, did not go as far towards security as some scholars may have feared, despite the importance of warning against such a possibility. Secondly, the role of the EU institutions in EU asylum and migration has been significantly underestimated. Contrary to expectations, EU institutions, and especially the European Commission, played the significant role of a supranational policy entrepreneur in this policy area. However, the strategy of the Commission in

EU asylum policy was significantly different from its counter-terrorism strategy. While the Commission actively constructed terrorism politically as a 'European threat' rather than providing space for national threat constructions, it never attempted to construct asylum as a threat. Thus, its policy strategy was more difficult to achieve than in counter-terrorism. This is due to the fact that 'security threats' create a sense of urgency in the political system. At the same time, the Commission contributed to the construction of a 'European approach' on asylum matters.

Historical background to the Common European Asylum System

From the European Community to the European Union: borders, Schengen and visa policy

When it was established by the Treaty of Rome in 1958, the European Community (EC) did not receive any formal competence on asylum matters. Though the preamble of the treaty stated that its signatories were 'determined to lay the foundations of an ever closer union among the peoples of Europe', the EC started as an essentially economic enterprise, the main purpose of which was to set up a common market. At the time, asylum matters seemed to fall beyond the scope of this project and the EC was thus not granted any competence in this area. This was also in line with the attitude of most, if not all, governments that considered asylum a matter of national sovereignty. Therefore, the EC institutions did not play any noticeable role in the field of asylum for almost three decades, with some minor exceptions.

The main political impetus in the 1980s for asylum co-operation derives from the so-called 'Schengen zone', which originated in the Saarbrücken Agreement of 13 July 1984, in which Chancellor Kohl and President Mitterrand agreed on the gradual abolition of controls at the Franco-German borders. Shortly afterwards, the Benelux countries joined France and Germany on this initiative and the five countries signed the Schengen Agreement on 14 June 1985. Five years of negotiations were then necessary to adopt the Convention applying the Schengen Agreement on the Gradual Abolition of Checks at the Common Borders. This document, drafted mostly by representatives of the national Interior Ministries, widely focused on compensatory measures necessary to safeguard internal security after the lifting of checks at the internal borders. 128 articles of the 142 article Convention were dedicated to those compensatory measures (Berthelet, 2003, p. 220). Thus, the Schengen Convention comprised a substantial number of provisions relating to the entry, movement and expulsion of non-EC citizens, notably asylum seekers. Firstly, the Schengen Convention contained several measures aiming at strengthening the controls at the external borders. They notably included using mobile units to patrol the borders between crossing points, increasing co-operation to make checks and surveillance more effective, exchanging relevant information, and establishing liaison officers (Title II, Chapter 2).

Secondly, Title II, Chapter 7 of the Convention laid down provisions concerning the responsibility for processing applications for asylum. The members of the Schengen group decided that only one state should be responsible for examining an asylum claim, namely the state 'which had played the main role in authorising entry either by issuing a visa, or having issued the visa of longest duration, or by not requiring any visa'. In the case of illegal entry, 'the first border reached would determine which state was responsible'. The main purpose of those rules was to curb the growing phenomenon of 'asylum shopping', i.e. multiple applications for asylum in several states simultaneously or successively. It is noteworthy that, regarding the procedures for the handling of applications, the members of the Schengen Group did not develop any common approach. They decided that each state would process asylum claims in accordance with its national law (Article 32).

While the Schengen Convention was initially outside the framework of the EU, it became of vital importance with the Treaty of Amsterdam 1997, when it was integrated into the framework of the EU. Despite the fact that EU institutions had not been very influential in its conceptions until then, the Tampere programme, which started with the entry into force of the Treaty of Amsterdam in 1999, created significant new opportunities for EU-level actors, such as the European Commission. Yet, in addition to these Europe-wide intergovernmental conventions, the EU asylum policy is even more fundamentally embedded in international regimes, as analysed below.

The Geneva Convention and international regimes

The Common European Asylum System is embedded in a long-standing international regime of refugee protection (Loescher, 1989, 1992, 1993, 1995, 2004; Marrus, 1985, 1988; Noll, 2000; Peers, 2002, 2004, 2006; Peers and Rogers, 2006), which aims to keep the balance between security and liberty firmly towards liberty and the rights of victims of persecution. The international regime was established on 14 December 1949, when a resolution of the UN General Assembly created the office of the United Nations High Commissioner for Refugees (UNHCR). The first instrument was created in 1951, when the Geneva Convention relating to the Status of Refugees was adopted for Western Europe. Ever since, it has been the cornerstone of contemporary international refugee law, only supplemented by the 1967 New York Protocol, which extended the Geneva provisions to the rest of the world.

Signatories to the convention, which include all EU member states, are required (according to Article 1A (1) of the Geneva Convention) to offer refuge to a person who:

- has a well-founded fear of being persecuted

    - for reasons of race, religion, nationality, membership of a particular social group or political opinion,
- is outside the country of his nationality and is
    - unable or (due to such fear) is unwilling to avail himself of the protection of that country
- or who, not having a nationality, and being outside the country of his former habitual residence, is unable or unwilling to return to it due to such fear.

Despite being the cornerstone of international refugee protection, not all member states interpret and apply the Geneva Convention in the same way. According to one NGO (interview NGO 8), 'some EU states' interpretation of the law has no basis in the wording of the 1951 Geneva Convention, is not in the spirit of that convention and is in contradiction to UN High Commissioner for Refugees' official advice'. Differing definitions of 'refugee' create different levels of protection and an uneven sharing of the responsibility. Most member states have a range of statuses to confer on refugees, with varying socio-economic and judicial rights. They differ sharply on whether to award refugee status (which confers full legal protection and access to social security and the labour market) in cases of persecution by non-state agents, such as warlords, paramilitary groups or mafia organisations. This gap in interpretation provides clear opportunities for a progressive EU asylum policy.

Yet, more recent 'asylum crises' led some member states to perceive the Geneva Convention on refugees to be out of date. In a past UK election campaign, the then opposition leader Michael Howard (BBC, 22 April 2005) called for the UK's withdrawal from the Geneva Convention on numerous occasions. This only reflected statements by David Blunkett, then Home Secretary, in 2003 (BBC, 5 February 2003). Consequently, it is reasonable to suspect some EU governments – especially the UK – to think that the EU framework provides an opportunity to create measures that replace, amend or supplement the Geneva Convention. Chapter 7 will, in fact, demonstrate evidence to make this more plausible, most notably the UK attempt to establish external 'refugee camps' outside the EU. Prima facia evidence would therefore suggest that the EU, through its member states, could conceivably be attempting to reduce the rights of refugees as demanded by the Geneva Convention.

The Common European Asylum System

The Tampere Presidency conclusions of October 1999 identified a number of policy aims. Paragraph 14 of the conclusions emphasises:

> This system should include, in the short term, a clear and workable determination of the State responsible for the examination of an asylum application,

> common standards for a fair and efficient asylum procedure, common minimum conditions of reception of asylum seekers, and the approximation of rules on the recognition and content of the refugee status. It should also be complemented with measures on subsidiary forms of protection offering an appropriate status to any person in need of such protection. ... In the longer term, Community rules should lead to a common asylum procedure and a uniform status for those who are granted asylum valid throughout the Union.

What are the advances of the first phase of the EU asylum policy during Tampere? This section will analyse the legal advances of the first phase of the Common European Asylum System (CEAS) in more detail below. However, let's first underline the importance of the CEAS. According to Hailbronner (2004), the CEAS is important, even in the short term. The prospect of a CEAS has already produced harmonising effects in national legislations. With agreed common minimum standards, this will prevent a 'race to the bottom' between national legislators. They are not competing with each other anymore for more restrictiveness, and thus do not need to lower their standards below their neighbours in order to reduce the numbers.

Moreover, Ackers (2005, p. 33) makes a strong case for the importance of the CEAS in the longer term. The adoption of the four directives is of historical importance for the EU as it opens up the road to a new period in decision-making on the CEAS. The area becomes communitarised, which signifies transfer of national sovereignty to the EU level. Consequently, asylum policy is now in the EU order – very different from international law (Shaw, 2000). Therefore, the Geneva Convention is now cemented in EU law, and the legal value is much stronger than it was before the Tampere programme. This is due to the distinction between international law and EU law – and the principle of national sovereignty compared to an EU pooling of sovereignty (Kaczorowska, 2003; Shaw, 2000).

Thus, the legal doctrines of the direct effect of EU law and its supremacy will apply to the area for the first time. This creates enforceable legal obligations not only in vertical relations between public authority and individuals, but also in horizontal relations between individuals inter se (Weiler, 1991, 1999). Community principles with direct effect can be invoked before domestic courts, which must provide adequate legal remedies. This is crucial, as it alters the public international law assumption that legal obligations are addressed to states only, and thus do not create direct effects for nationals of that state. This has changed with the CEAS. These laws are now directly enforceable in domestic courts with little discretion. Individual asylum seekers can take states and individuals to the domestic courts. Thus, in addition to the EU supremacy of law, this provides a certain force to asylum rights which was previously missing under international law.

One example is the frequent discussion on whether the UK may leave the Geneva Convention. In the 2005 UK election campaign, the opposition leader, Michael Howard (BBC, 22 April 2005), called for the UK's withdrawal from the Geneva Convention on numerous occasions. This only reflected statements by David Blunkett, then Home Secretary, in 2003 (BBC, 5 February 2003). While withdrawal from the Geneva Convention would be possible under international law prior to the CEAS, it is not possible any more under the current rules. As the UK opted into all of the EU asylum rules, these are now fully binding and enforceable in UK courts. This hypothetical scenario makes it much clearer how the legal value of the Geneva Convention refugee protection has increased with the CEAS.

Moreover, the communitarisation of asylum matters also implies that decision-making procedures have now changed. Future legislation in the area will include the co-decision procedure between the Council and the European Parliament, which was previously only consulted on the matter. In the Council, the voting procedure is now qualified majority voting (Peers, 8 November 2004). This then removes any blocking possibilities by any of the twenty-seven member states. Therefore, on the institutional level, the CEAS represents a clear step forward and represents the hope that, with more and more involvement of other 'refugee-friendly' EU institutions, such as the European Parliament, the future of the CEAS is progressive.

However, as the analysis below will demonstrate, the current legislation already provides of a certain degree of progressive elements. The emphasis in the analysis below is only on the adopted legislative instruments – the four directives. The directives discussed below are: (1) the temporary protection directive', (2) the 'reception conditions directive' (3) the 'asylum qualification directive', and (4) the 'asylum procedures directive'.

The 'temporary protection directive'

The temporary protection directive (Council Directive, 20 July 2001, 2001/55/EC) was the first legal instrument in asylum law since Tampere. Its content was influenced by the experience of the reception of displaced persons from Yugoslavia in the 1990s (Hailbronner, 2004, p. 68). Thus it is intended as an effective instrument of temporary protection in the context of mass refugee movements for people not falling under the remit of the Geneva Convention.

How does it work? The Commission first proposes the existence of a situation of mass influx, which is then adopted by the Council by qualified majority and which is binding on all member states. However, the number of persons to be admitted is not specified as mandatory. The time limit of the duration of this scheme is one year with the extension possibilities of six months or one year by the Council. Member states admit according to the information provided by them on their reception capacity.

There are a number of rights given to persons in need of protection through this scheme, which are: residence rights, employment rights, and family reunification rights. In addition, all admitted persons are not prejudiced in their rights to apply for refugee status under the Geneva Convention.

In this regard, their status determination can be delayed for the period of their temporary protection (Peers, 2002, p. 89).

In essence, this directive has been criticised for window-dressing by Guild (2004, p. 211). She criticises the very fact that this directive represents an alternative for protection under the Geneva Convention. Either a person is a refugee, in which case they would need the protection of the Geneva Convention, or the person is not. In the former case, she demonstrates very succinctly that the person would receive higher benefits under the Geneva Convention than under this temporary protection directive. This echoes Peers (2002, pp. 89–90), who also warns of the danger of this instrument replacing the refugee rights under the Geneva Convention.

Guild's argument has one important drawback. Firstly, as suggested by Hailbronner, temporary protection is a complementary right which does not prejudice an application for refugee status, as the person can still apply for it after two years (Hailbronner, 2004). As it is a complementary right, the person receiving this protection would probably not fall under the Geneva Convention as a refugee – a case which Guild does not consider. In conclusion, the temporary protection directive is a clear advance for people in need of protection compared to the situation prior to the legislation. It is the first legislation of the EU in the area (Monar, 2002). Nonetheless, it is only a stepping stone towards EU legislation in substantive areas of asylum policy.

The 'reception conditions directive'

The reception conditions directive (Council Directive, 27 January 2003, 2003/9/EC) of 27 January 2003 lays down minimum standards for the reception of asylum seekers across member states. Monar (2004, p. 118) describes this directive as an important new legal element of the common asylum system. It is the first element of three closely linked legislative initiatives: the asylum qualification directive, the reception conditions directive, and the asylum procedures directive.

Hailbronner (2004: 78) explains the reasons why the reception conditions directive is such an important one. Firstly, the substantial differences in reception conditions in the various EU member states can be a factor for migratory movement of refugees within the EU. Logically, based on the Dublin convention and now the Dublin regulation, asylum seekers can only apply for asylum once in the EU, and thus the conditions in which they are being received matter significantly in their choice. In 2001, the Commission initiated this legislation, which was subsequently passed by the Council in January 2003. It defines certain key terms of the Geneva Convention, such as applicants for asylum, family members, unaccompanied minors, reception conditions, and detention.

The directive only applies to applicants for asylum, which has been criticised (Guild, 2004, p. 213), especially as it does not apply to the temporary protection directive. The question of which basic rights and benefits asylum seekers deserve should be based on their needs rather than on the grounds on which the claims are based, according to this argument. This is a valid argument, but as the competent authorities in member states always have to presume an application for asylum, this should address the issue.

The directive generally accords freedom of movement to asylum seekers within the territory of the host state or within an area assigned to them by that state. This addresses more restrictive regulations of some EU member states (Hailbronner, 2004, p. 79). Detention will only be allowed in order to check the identity of the applicant for asylum. Refugee organisations have rightly criticised the practice of restricting the freedom of movement as being contrary to human rights provisions. Yet, as Hailbronner (2004, p. 80) demonstrates, some member states' practices (for instance, Germany) tended to be even more restrictive.

Member states must guarantee several reception conditions:

- Material reception conditions, such as accommodation, food and clothing.
- Family unity.
- Medical and psychological care.
- Access to the education system for minor children and language courses.
- Lodgings in a house, accommodation centre or hotel.
- In all cases, applicants must have the possibility of communicating with legal advisers, NGOs and the UNHCR.
- Access to employment.

The most heavily disputed provision concerns the access to employment – criticised for the delay in access to it (Guild, 2004). At the same time, member states have been generally reluctant to grant access to the labour market in the field of migration. In this directive, they are at least obliged to open access to the labour market and vocational training to applicants for asylum twewlve months after they have lodged their application. Thus, despite the criticisms related to its complicated procedure (Guild, 2004, p. 215), and the UNHCR argument that a six-month delay would have been preferable, it is already significant that throughout twenty-seven EU member states this was possible at all. In addition, as with all reception conditions, member states will be free to apply more favourable conditions of reception.

In conclusion, this directive rectified one particular problem within the member states – the wide variance of reception conditions. It is clear from the evidence presented that this is an advance in those conditions across the EU-27. For most member states, they will need to be higher than before the directive. Equally, there is no obligation to lower any favourable conditions. Consequently, the directive is beneficial for the EU.

The 'asylum qualification directive'

The asylum qualification directive (Council Directive, 29 April 2004, 2004/83/EC) addresses three important elements of asylum: (1) the recognition of refugees, (2) the content of refugee status, and (3) the approximation of rules. In addition, the directive highlights the grounds for qualification for subsidiary protection.

In order to make the distinction between subsidiary protection and refugee status clear, the directive provides definitions of both concepts. A refugee is defined exactly as in Article 1A of the Geneva Convention. On the other hand, a person eligible for subsidiary protection is a:

> third country national or a stateless person who does not qualify as a refugee but in respect of whom substantial grounds have been shown for believing that the person concerned, if returned to his or her country of origin, or in the case of a stateless person, to his or her country of former habitual residence, would face a real risk of suffering serious harm.

As Hailbronner (2004: 58) suggests, both protection as a refugee within the terms of the Geneva Convention, and subsidiary protection – for those who fall outside the convention – are included in this legislation.

The directive addresses many of the issues in substantive asylum law which have had forced divergences in national practices before, and it increases protection. Firstly, the established grounds for persecution are the same as in the Geneva Convention, thereby solidifying the group of people qualifying for refugee status. In addition to the generally accepted forms of persecution, the directive sets out three principles, which have not been applied by member states prior to it (Hailbronner, 2004, p. 60). For the first time, 'persecution can stem from non-state actors' where the state is unable or unwilling to provide protection. Given the increase in people fleeing on such grounds, this is a significant widening of the concept. Secondly, the directive also includes child specific and gender specific forms of persecution, not in existence prior to the legislation (Monar, 2005, p. 132). Finally, persecution may take place even though all persons in a particular country face generalised oppression. In essence, the effect of all these legal changes means that the directive goes beyond existing refugee rights enshrined in the Geneva Convention.

Balzacq and Carrera (2005, pp. 48–49), however, are concerned why refugees and persons under subsidiary protection are not treated equally. They demonstrate that some rights accorded to persons granted subsidiary protection are below the rights of refugee protection. Consequently, they wonder whether this is a 'double standard consistent with the general philosophy of equality of treatment for people in need of and who qualify for international protection'. Yet, persons who are granted subsidiary protection do not qualify for international protection under the Geneva Convention (Hailbronner, 2004, p. 62). The provisions in this directive represent the first concrete European initiative to protect those who fall outside the refugee definition.

In an ideal world, one could conceive of rewriting the Geneva Convention to broaden the concept of asylum. However, this has not happened to date, and the alternative to this directive is only the member states' discretion as to how much they want to help. Under this directive, there is no discretion anymore, and subsidiary protection rights are codified. Consequently, this is a substantial success in expanding rights for people in need of protection.

The 'Asylum Procedures Directive'

On 9 November 2004, the Council agreed politically on the directive on minimum standards for procedures – the Asylum Procedures Directive (Balzacq and Carrera, 2005, p. 50). The Commission had first presented its proposal for the directive in September 2000, and submitted an amended version by June 2002. After intense negotiations, a 'general approach' was agreed in April 2004, and politically confirmed in November 2004. The directive had not formally been adopted by the end of 2004 due to the lack of agreement on a list of 'safe country of origin'. Yet, on 1 December 2005 it was finally formally adopted, leaving the list to the side.

The harmonisation of asylum procedures is of vital importance for a common asylum system together with the reception conditions directive. Firstly, it contributes to the prevention of secondary movements of asylum seekers. Secondly, it is vital for the asylum seekers themselves as they are no longer able to freely choose their country of application under the Dublin Regulation. As they cannot chose their country anymore, it is vital to harmonise procedures in order maintain fairness towards people in need of protection. Thirdly, this legislation will enable follow-up legislations in the area in the longer term (Hailbronner, 2004, p. 70).

Monar (2005, p. 133) describes how both the Treaty of Amsterdam and the Tampere programme demanded the adoption of policy instruments within the transitional period of five years ending on 30 April 2004. This put considerable pressure on the Council for the adoption of the directives in time, which was managed in a meeting on 29–30 April. The Asylum Procedures Directive defines minimum standards for procedures, which include:

- Access to the asylum process.
- The right to interview.
- Access to interpretation and legal assistance.
- Detention circumstances.
- The appeal procedure.
- In addition, it defines controversial concepts, such as:
- 'First country of asylum': this allows applications to be rejected where

applicants have been recognised as refugees in another country with sufficient protection in that country.
- 'Safe country of origin': this allows considering a group of applications of nationals of one country to be unfounded, thereby entering into an accelerated procedure. The failure to agree on a specific list of countries in this category has delayed its formal adoption.
- 'Safe third country': this allows the transfer of responsibility for the processing of an asylum application to countries of transit to the EU.

This directive has been more severely criticised by NGOs (ECRE et al., 2004) and academics than the other three directives. The main arguments relate to a supposed incompatibility with international obligations (ECRE et al., 2004, p. 51). Costello (2005) criticises the three controversial concepts: (1) first country of asylum (2) safe country of origin, and (3) safe third country. In her view, these provisions threaten to undermine many of the other laudable features during the Tampere process, in particular the Asylum Qualification Directive (ibid., p. 36). According to Costello, these three provisions will undermine access to and the integrity of asylum procedures in the EU.

Doede Ackers (2005), negotiating the Asylum Procedures Directive on behalf of the Commission, disagrees. He explains the rationale for adopting it and the different stages in the negotiations. Firstly, Ackers (2005, p. 32) disputes that the politically agreed general approach breaches international human rights obligations. It is argued that for each of the safe third country provisions, certain safeguards should be laid down to ensure that if member states properly implement these rules, no breaches of international law occur.

Secondly, as it stands the approach adds value to the soft-law standards already agreed, including the procedures according to the UNHCR Handbook (Ackers, 2005). On the question of appeals procedures, the general approach even introduces the obligation to ensure an effective remedy before a court or tribunal, which goes beyond the standards in the Handbook. It is vital to note at this point that the Handbook is only soft-law in international law, and thus left to the individual interpretation of domestic courts, which can vary significantly across the EU.

Finally, Ackers (2005) argues that several member states will have to raise their standards to comply with the provisions in the general approach. Thus, a framework which requires higher standards than the previous practice of member states can hardly be described as a breach of international law – certainly not of customary international law. Fullerton (2005) fully agrees with this view. In her article, she analyses the asylum situation in Spain and Portugal. Although the Iberian Peninsula is closer to regions of conflict and migratory routes than most EU states, the numbers of asylum seekers registered in Spain and Portugal are far lower than in other member states of comparable size and economic development (Fullerton, 2005, p. 659). While multiple factors deter refugees from seeking asylum in Spain and Portugal, their inadmissibility procedures are the most important. Both states employ an inadmissibility procedure which results in the rejection of a substantial majority of applicants for asylum prior to any hearing on the merits.

The Asylum Procedures Directive limits the grounds for rejecting a claim as inadmissible, whereas the Spanish and Portuguese procedures dismiss asylum applications on far broader grounds. Consequently, they will contravene the Procedures Directive. As a consequence, an asylum procedures directive that increases the number of asylum seekers who will be able to apply for refugee status in a number of member states – such as Spain and Portugal – is a clear legal advance for refugee rights.

In conclusion, this section has demonstrated that the CEAS has brought very clear legal advances in terms of refugee protection. The CEAS has produced harmonising effects in national legislations, and, with agreed common minimum standards, it is likely that this will prevent a 'race to the bottom' between national legislators. Moreover, the CEAS is also of importance for the EU as it opens up the road to the communitarisation of asylum policy, which signifies transfer of national sovereignty to the EU level. Thus, the legal doctrines of the direct effect of EU law and its supremacy will apply to the area for the first time. Therefore, individual asylum seekers can take states and individuals to the domestic courts. In the next section, it will be argued that the European Commission played an important role in the legal advance.

The European Commission: a supranational policy entrepreneur in the Common European Asylum System?

This section will assess the extent to which the European Commission, in both its normative and policy dimension, has been able to play the role of an SPE with regard to the CEAS.

Asylum policy is a very difficult field with complex decision-making rules (Noll, 2000), as outlined above. Article 63 TEC sets out a framework agenda for the transitional period of five years; it requires the Council to adopt a variety of measures within five years. However, it is striking that the majority of measures contain the mandate of minimum standards. Article 63 TEC asks the Council to adopt the following four measures 'within a period of five years after the entry into force of the Treaty of Amsterdam':

1. criteria and mechanisms for determining which Member State is responsible for considering an application for asylum submitted by a national of a third country in one of the Member States;
2. minimum standards on the reception of asylum seekers in Member States;
3. minimum standards with respect to the qualification of nationals of third countries as refugees;

4. minimum standards on procedures in Member States for granting or withdrawing refugee status;

However, according to article 67 TEC, 'during a transitional period of five years following the entry into force of the Treaty of Amsterdam, the Council shall act unanimously on a proposal from the Commission or on the initiative of a member state and after consulting the European Parliament.' It is only after this period of five years that the Commission gains its usual sole right of initiative. While this article is often seen as a 'break' on the Commission in order to curb its legislative powers, in practice, as the subsequent section shows, this has not had this effect necessarily. In fact, it encouraged the Commission to have the most competitive proposals, which in the area of the CEAS meant that no member state actually thought it was able to present better proposals than the Commission (interviews PR 1–26).

The legal instruments available to the EU pre-Tampere used to be very weak with little legal effect – mainly conventions, which had to be ratified by each member state individually. These were replaced with new instruments (directives) in 1999. Nonetheless, during the Tampere programme from 1999 to 2004, the decision-making procedure was based on the so-called 'consultation procedure'. This meant that the European Parliament only had to be consulted, but was left with no decision-making power. The sole legal decision-maker was the Council of Ministers, which had to vote by unanimity. Very clearly, this meant that every proposal by the Commission has to be negotiated upon, and often this involved significant changes (Batjes, 2006; Lambert, 2004), which could appear to limit the argument that the Commission would play a significant role in the CEAS.

Yet, the next section argues that despite this institutionally weak(er) position by the Commission, compared to the first pillar, it managed to significantly influence the policy shape of the CEAS. Institutionally, it possesses the key role as political 'monitor' and legal 'enforcer' of the law in the asylum area. The Commission has the legal power to investigate claims that member states are failing in their EC law obligations and to bring them before the European Court of Justice (ECJ) for such alleged failures. While this formal instrument also remained largely untouched, the Commission nevertheless managed to shape the policy direction through a series of soft law measures over a prolonged period and through consensus-building by developing and funding pro-migrant organisations.

The Commission as a strategic first mover

The Commission's strategy was twofold: firstly, 'a persuasion strategy' as a 'first mover' in order to get the foot in the door. It socially constructed the functional link between a 'moving policy train' – the single market – and EU action in asylum matters. It pushed for this starting in the 1970s, throughout the late 80s and early 90s. It published communications that became the reference points for later legislation in the CEAS. Secondly, the Commission also constructed EU asylum action into the international prevailing norms on refugee protection – the Geneva Convention – which gave it more legitimacy as an actor. Norms only develop gradually, and therefore the Commission would have to act pragmatically in the meantime. The following section will demonstrate both of these aspects.

The first serious attempt to shape the EU asylum agenda was the Commission's famous 'White Paper' (COM (84) 310 final) on the completion of the Internal Market in 1984 (Mitsilegas et al., 2003, p. 28; Mitsilegas, 2009; Geddes, 2000, p. 70). It is significant for this research as it represents the origins of the Commission's attempts to gain competences for the EU in asylum policy. The document proposed the abolition of all internal border controls, but also provided a link between the former and economic growth, as well as a whole range of compensatory measures – such as immigration, asylum, external border controls, and policies on visas and drugs, and crime. Yet, none of the asylum proposals made succeeded due to the gradual nature in which norms often develop (Geddes, 2000, p. 71, 2001, p. 24). Yet, member states accepted the link between the internal market and the EU asylum policy – and in time the success of the single market would drag along the EU asylum policy – as long as the European Commission kept pushing.

In 1991, the Commission took the next steps in its persuasion strategy – constructing the link to both the single market and international refugee norms. The communication (Commission, 1991, SEC(91) 1857 final) acknowledged the fact that the political and social importance of the right of asylum had increased in Western Europe. It was claimed that, as a consequence, individual states were less able to deal with the problem caused by the increased influx of asylum seekers. However, the Commission insisted that humanitarian standards would need to be maintained, and took the 1951 Geneva Convention as a starting point. The communication also underlined the humanitarian objectives of the Convention.

The following common actions were envisaged in the short term in order to cope with the increase in asylum seekers (ibid.):

- speeding up administrative and judicial decision procedures
- harmonisation of the conditions under which people can be turned down at the external borders
- effective return policy of the rejected asylum applicants
- exchange information procedure

The following actions were envisaged with regards to the harmonisation of asylum law in the internal market (ibid.):

- harmonising the national criteria and practices regarding the determination of refugee status

- harmonising the rules with regards to the stay of 'de facto' refugees (those who do not qualify for Convention refugee status)
- harmonisation of the reception conditions for asylum seekers

These suggestions are already exceptionally close to the objectives of the Tampere programme of 1999. The communication in 1991 even includes its outcomes in 2004 – the directives on asylum qualification, asylum procedures and reception conditions. The suggestions by the Commission had no clear legal basis in the Treaty of Maastricht in 1992 and certainly not before Maastricht in 1991, and were extremely ambitious. While not being pursued in policy terms, they clearly did affect the norm environment of decision-makers. The issues never slipped off the agenda from the day of this communication – which the Commission ensured with future communications.

The communication in 1994 (COM (94) 23 final) represented another important step in the persuasion strategy. With a view to stimulate discussion and debate, it followed on from the earlier document of 1991 (also referred to in COM (94) 23 final, pp. 23–27). It built on the suggestions made in 1991. The communication called for the following measures:

- Harmonised application of the definition of a refugee in accordance with article 1 a of the Geneva Convention.
- The development of minimum standards for fair and efficient asylum procedures.
- The elaboration of a convention on manifestly unfounded asylum applications.
- The harmonisation of policies concerning those who can be admitted as refugees, but may be in need of help.
- A measure harmonising schemes of temporary protection.
- A European fund for refugees.

These measures all represent the basic foundation of what became the Tampere programme in 1999, and, finally, the outcomes of it in 2004 – the directives on temporary protection, asylum qualification, asylum procedures, and reception conditions, and even other adopted instruments, such as the European Fund for Refugees. Indeed, all of the aforementioned communications display the determination of the Commission to drive forward the process of EU integration in EU asylum matters. Yet, an efficient EU asylum policy would only be possible with a major treaty change (Gradin, 1999). Therefore, it was implicit in the strategy of the Commission that it could compromise as long as the goal of full communitarisation was reached.

Connecting the asylum policy with international human rights norms in the face of the 'war on terror'

In the previous section, it was demonstrated how the European Commission managed to connect the EU asylum policy to the single market. Acceptance of this fact led to increasing dynamics in the area. Yet, it was equally important for the Commission to link asylum policy to the Geneva Convention. This was particularly important after 11th September 2001 – the terrorist attacks on New York and Washington. The following section will demonstrate the strategy used in this endeavour – divided into two parts: (1) the anchoring of EU asylum policy before Tampere 1999 by relying on civil society and NGOs, and (2) the continued insistence on international human rights standards after 11 September 2001, despite shifts in rhetoric to accommodate the 'war on terror'. This is in contrast to the area of criminal justice, where the 'war on terror' was pushed strongly as a reason for action (Kaunert, 2007).

Firstly, when the Commission started to construct a role for the EU into national asylum policy, it had decided to link it to both the single market – to push the project – and the internationally prevailing refugee protection norms – to gain legitimacy. The latter is particularly important as the Commission has been frequently attacked for not being democratic since the 1990s. The essence of its legitimacy problem is that the 'unelected' Commission is widely perceived as detached from the concerns of EU citizens. Thus, its own legitimacy needed to be increased through the legitimacy of other actors in the field – the UNHCR, NGOs, and the European Parliament. The literature has established that the Commission often aims to use NGOs to improve its own legitimacy (Greenwood, 2003). Both Hix (1999) and Geddes (2000) have pointed out their importance for the Commission, particularly in the areas of asylum and migration.

Yet, European integration always remains the most important objective above all for the Commission. Geddes (2000, p. 134) suggests the success of this strategy. While NGOs criticise current EU policy, the answer to the problem tends to be more, not less, 'Europe'. This was confirmed throughout interviews (interviews NGO 1 to NGO 11). There was widespread support for a communitarisation of asylum matters in particular. As described by Geddes, the mood of NGOs was one of frustration because of the lack of what they perceived to be progress in the asylum policy. At the same time, they did not attribute the blame on the European Commission, which was perceived as an ally. The blame was usually attributed to the Council of Ministers and member states.

Some NGOs were under no illusion of their own ability to influence the Commission, asserting that they were mostly utilised by the Commission when it was useful to do so (interview NGO 2) – to gain information and legitimacy. Despite this realisation, they represented an important ally for the Commission, being useful on two fronts (Geddes, 2000, p. 136): (1) they push for asylum solutions based on the Geneva Convention, and (2) they implicitly support European integration by operating at the EU level, thus making the political issues de facto 'problems of Europe'.

It is important to note at this point that the Commission partially created this useful ally (Geddes, 2000, p. 143). A significant number of NGOs (interviews NGO 1 to NGO 11) indicated that the Commission was actively involved in the creation of their EU structures or their organisation in general, and continues to finance the majority of them. These findings also confirm Geddes' suggestion of some 'top-down' influence of the Commission on pro-migrant groups (Geddes, 2000, p. 143).

Secondly, the anchoring of the EU asylum policy within the international prevailing refugee rights norms became vital after 11 September 2001. At this point, norms could have easily shifted towards a securitisation of asylum – the construction of asylum as a security threat. Yet, from the documentary and interview evidence presented below, it is clear that the Commission took the political decision at that time to not link the asylum issue to the 'war on terror' (interviews COM 10 and COM 16).

Van Selm (2003, p. 143) describes it as remarkable that the Commission's proposal for a Framework Decision on combating terrorism made no mention of refugees, asylum, or the exclusion of any person seeking refugee status. In her view, this was particularly remarkable as the Geneva Convention did provide grounds for exclusion from refugee status for terrorists. Yet, the Commission decided not to link the issues of asylum and terrorism.

Nonetheless, in agreement with the NGOs' (interviews NGO 1 to NGO 11) views, the war on terror did influence the policy area (Boswell, 2008). The conclusion of the 20 September 2001 meeting reflected mainly judicial and criminal co-operation, but also asylum matters (Van Selm, 2003, p. 145). The conclusions, amongst others, invited the Commission to examine the relationship between safeguarding internal security and complying with international protection obligations and instruments. This is of particular importance. It appears as an attempt by member states to put internal security above international protection norms, and thus effectively to securitise asylum.

Yet, in the end the Commission managed to keep the policy anchored within international norms, and thereby prevented a shift into security (COM (2001) 743 final). Consequently, in the working document entitled 'the relationship between safeguarding internal security and complying with international protection obligations', the Commission did not advocate any change in international refugee protection, and bases the Geneva Convention at the heart of any response. This was written in response to the Council conclusion mentioned above.

There are two main premises of the Commission working document: (1) bona fide refugees and asylum seekers should not become victims of the recent events, and (2) no avenues should exist for the supporting of terrorist acts. The document made it clear that a scrupulous application of the exceptions to refugee protection available under the current laws is the appropriate response. It was therefore an outright rejection of placing security in contradiction to existing refugee protection instruments. This was confirmed in an interview with the author of this document (interview COM 16). Moreover, while the Commission acknowledged that terrorists might use asylum channels, it considered this as not likely, as other channels would be more discreet and more suitable for criminal practices.

It was suggested for the member states to use existing legal instruments (COM (2001) 743 final) – based on the Geneva Convention – such as:

- Article 1(f), the exclusion clause, should be used within the asylum procedure in order to avoid refoulement.
- If sufficient grounds are known for exclusion, an accelerated procedure should start

There were suggestions for the following policy alterations (ibid.):

- The creation of EU-level guidelines on the use of exclusion clauses.
- The proposal on minimum standards for asylum procedures should include provisions for the cancellation of status on the grounds of information coming to light after processing of claims

In essence, this document followed up on the somewhat harsher language of 20 September 2001 conclusions of the European Council. Yet, contrary to the initial demand which seemed to indicate an attempt to present asylum as a security threat in the war on terror, the working document did not deviate from accepted international norms. In fact, it demonstrated the legal value of the Geneva Convention, and thereby strengthened it. It resisted the temptation to move an issue into the security area when it was perceived as a human rights issue. In fact, the Commission rescued this political perception by trying to reconcile the demands for greater security with the international refugee protection norms.

It would have been difficult for the Commission to do otherwise, as it had consistently anchored the EU asylum policy in international refugee norms. Consequently, it could have been perceived as inconsistent and thus less credible. It would have lost legitimacy in the eyes of the NGOs, who have been supporting the Commission in its efforts to create an EU asylum policy. Any deviation from this established position would have damaged the Commission politically. Yet, the demands by member states seemed to go into that direction – attempting to place security above refugee protection. In the end, the Commission managed to please both by presenting harsher rhetoric using the language of security, while maintaining the Geneva Convention as the bedrock of the EU asylum policy.

Communitarising the EU Asylum Policy as the main strategic goal

Previously, it was demonstrated that norms up until Tampere had evolved in two dimensions. Firstly, on the axis of whether the EU should be legislating at all in the AFSJ, where the normative debate had been structured between those wishing to preserve national sovereignty and those wishing to pool sovereignty at the EU level. Secondly, on the axis of what the aims and the purpose of such legislation would be. For the area of asylum policy, it is precisely this second dimension that was at the heart of the change during the Tampere programme.

Sandra Lavenex (2001a, b, p. 852) describes how a normative paradox exists among two dimensions: the tension between state sovereignty and supranational governance, as mentioned above, and the tension between internal security and human rights institutionalised in refugee rights. Emek Uçarer (2001b) echoes the normative description by Lavenex and analyses how the global refugee protection regime was characterised by two principles, i.e. humanitarianism and state sovereignty. Indeed, these two axes provide a lucid analytical point of reference for the development of norms in the area.

Figure 6.1 maps the development of norms in the area of asylum during the Tampere programme, summarising the main developments of the two previous sections. Initially, EU co-operation on asylum before the Tampere programme had been mainly in quadrant II of the matrix. It was characterised by an anchoring in the internationally prevailing norm on national sovereignty and the refugee protection norm – the Geneva Convention. At this point, there were three different possibilities for norms to develop if there was any change at all.

Firstly, the policy could develop from Q0 to Q3. This change would imply that national sovereignty would remain the bedrock of asylum polices in Europe, and thus there would be no movement on the axis of whether the EU

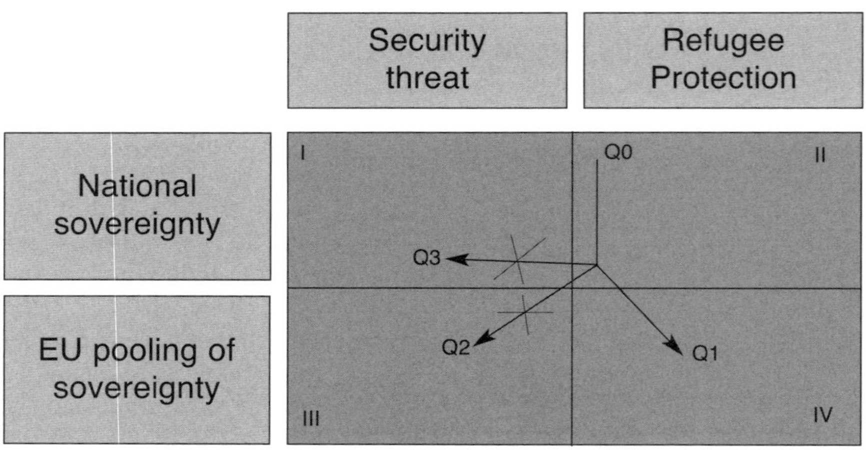

Figure 6.1 **Mapping developments in EU asylum policy**

should be legislating in the area of asylum. In fact, this would imply that no EU legislation would be possible, or indeed the legislation efforts would be meaningless.

The second alternative would have been a development from Q0 to Q2. This change would imply that a supranational policy entrepreneur had managed to persuade the European member states to pool national sovereignty in the area. However, the implications of 11 September 2001 would have been used politically in such a way as to construct asylum as a security threat in order to achieve this goal. In some sense, this was the most likely scenario, as it is similar to the area of counter-terrorism.

Nonetheless, it is the third alternative that the Commission managed to achieve, which involved movement from Q0 to Q1. This implies that the Commission managed to persuade member states of the pooling of national sovereignty at the EU level. At the same time, this pooling is firmly anchored in international refugee protection norms – especially the Geneva Convention. The Commission played the role of a strategic first mover in order to shape the debate in a way that placed the EU at the centre of the policy. In the area of asylum, these norms developed incrementally. The norm of national sovereignty still remained very sticky and difficult to change.

In fact, this has changed by the end of the Tampere programme, and the EU asylum policy has been established. It was a significant success and the main goal of the Commission – the full communitarisation – has been achieved. Nonetheless, contrary to expectations, this has not been achieved by going from Q0 to Q2, but rather to Q1. The Commission never attempted to construct an EU asylum policy based on the perception that it was a security threat. Even after 11 September 2001, it pushed for the fulfilment of international obligations under the Geneva Convention.

Evaluating the policy dimension of the European Asylum Policy: the Commission as an supranational policy entrepreneur?

In this section, it will be argued that the Commission managed to push through more advances than expected. It will deal with all four directives, but not with each individually as it is impossible to analyse all possible details due to space restrictions. Consequently, this section is not structured chronologically, but according to the themes raised by the research. This represents empirically the problem, the policy and the politics stream in the model presented in Chapter One. In the interviews, one official described the Commission's strategy during the negotiation process as 'listen, learn and defend' (interview COM 7). Other interviews confirmed this (interviews COM 2, COM 10, COM 16, COM 20 and COM 23). The following section will refer to all four directives without necessarily giving each an equally detailed analysis of the negotiations – but it will include them in the broader themes that are raised.

The 'listen' phase

The listening phase is the start of the legislative process within the institution of the European Commission. In this regard, it is vital to underline the point of departure of the negotiations in asylum policy. Ackers (2005, p. 2) describes how the national systems significantly differ from one another. The administrative framework for decisions on asylum applications has been developing purely within a national domestic context in all member states. Asylum procedures are embedded in general administrative law, national administrative traditions and specific constitutional arrangements. A view across member states, for instance, France, the UK or Germany, clearly demonstrates very different administrative traditions. Therefore, Ackers (ibid.) argues that such procedural law is very difficult to harmonise. This view was unanimously shared across member states throughout the interviews (interviews PR 1 to PR 24). At the level of practitioners, it was always clear how difficult these negotiations were going to be.

Consequently, it is all the more important to provide excellent legislative proposals. Throughout the interviews, all member states acknowledged the fact that the Commission's proposals were significantly superior to anything they could have proposed themselves. In fact, this was so clear that no attempt was ever made, despite the fact that it would have been possible (interviews PR 1 to PR 24). This is also quite different from other policy areas, where member states do make proposals. The asylum area was perceived to be better led by the European Commission (ibid.). Informally, member states agreed to not even attempt to make a proposal, as this would have distracted discussion time from the better proposals made by the Commission (interviews PR 1, PR 3, PR 4, PR 8, PR 10, PR 11, PR 12 and PR 13).

All of the original proposals were based upon consultations with member states, the European Parliament, and useful allies, such as the UNHCR, following the initial working document by the Commission in March 1999 (Ackers, 2005, p. 3). All of these actors were invited to bring forward their views, resulting in member states submitting written comments, the European Parliament adopting a resolution, and the UNHCR expressing its point of view. The Commission services then analysed and compared the positions expressed, and made a comparison between member states' practices. Ackers (ibid.) describes this process in detail for the asylum procedures directive. Nonetheless, the interviews also demonstrated this process for the other directives (interviews COM 1 to COM 25). However, what seemed to be a simple consultation, also resulted in an initial alliance building, the reasoning for which has its roots in the Commission's legitimacy problem explained above.

Firstly, the Commission managed to use the European Parliament (EP) as an ally. This opportunity resulted from the relative neglect of the Parliament as an actor by the member states in the Council. As member states had to approve legislation in the Council of Ministers unanimously, they would regularly agree politically before the Parliament's opinion was received (interviews PR 1 to PR 14). The only way the Parliament could be effective was through the Commission, as the decision-making procedure for the area was consultation with the Council. Once political agreement in the Council was reached, member states were generally unwilling to change their positions due to the implications of further negotiations (ibid.).

This opened an opportunity for the Commission to take account of the views of the EP, and amend the proposal in the light of this. Consequently, the Commission had an ally that would support its position when needed (interviews PR 1 to PR 24), and that could 'shame' member states for their too restrictive behaviour. It also lent legitimacy to the Commission. At the same time, when the EP was not needed, the Commission could always rely on some very restrictive member states in order to make the point why certain positions could not be reflected in its proposal. Overall, the European Parliament was satisfied with the work of the Commission (interviews EP 1 to EP 2), resulting in good inter-institutional relations and respect.

Secondly, a similar logic also applies to using the UNHCR as an ally. As the institutionalised representative of the norm of international refugee protection, the UNHCR would be present throughout the negotiations to give legitimacy to the EU asylum policy (EAP). In fact, unusual for non-EU actors, it would even sit at the negotiation table at times, represented by the High Commissioner Lubbers, a former Dutch Prime Minister (Ackers, 2005, pp. 24–25). In this way, the UNHCR put pressure on the Council by bringing up issues concerning international refugee protection, such as their aide-mémoire on the directive on asylum procedures (ibid.). It is clear that it was vital for the Commission to maintain a strong alliance with the UNHCR throughout the negotiations.

As described above, the UNHCR gave legitimacy to the Commission, which also supported international refugee protection norms. The former confirmed during the interviews (interview IGO 1) its close working relationship with the latter. The UNHCR perceived relations to be excellent, and only had praise for the Commission and Vitorino. It confirmed the Commission's reputation as excellent negotiators, whereas the blame for restrictive measures was put only on member states. It also praised the European Parliament's role, while it acknowledged the lack of direct influence. Overall, this alliance worked as a second shaming instrument for the Commission along the lines of the scoreboard that was explained before. Whenever member states would become too restrictive, the Commission could count on the 'shaming efforts' of the EP and the UNHCR.

However, despite this initial alliance building, only one directive had been agreed by July 2001, the start of the Belgian Presidency – the temporary protection directive. The pace of negotiations was very slow and no member state wanted any change at all in national practices (Ackers, p. 7). In fact, this is the point where the recollection of interviewees diverges somewhat. One

Commission official claimed that there had been the opening of a policy window just before September 2001 (interview COM 2), which closed again after the terrorist attacks. However, this is not the generally accepted view by member states (interviews PR 1 to PR 14), who think there was never any window there in the first place. The evidence seems to agree with the latter, as only one instrument had been agreed at the time. In the end, it is agreed throughout the interviews that 11 September did alter the policy environment towards more security concerns (interviews PR 1 to PR 14). As explained above, the Commission managed to steer normative views in this process towards international refugee protection norms, in alliance with the UNHCR and the EP.

According to Ackers (2005, p. 6), at the time of the Belgian Presidency in July 2001, the wishes of member states were contradictory to one another, resulting in the Commission having to reconcile the draft. At that point, the Council did not continue the examination of individual provisions of proposals, but focused on the underlying themes in the directives – for instance, at the JHA Council of Ministers session of 27 September 2001. Commissioner Vitorino defended the political ideas behind some of the choices in the original proposal.

The 'learn' phase

In this phase, the Commission had to learn to deal with domestic political problems, often anti-asylum populism, and needed to convert them into 'European' solutions. Negotiations would get stuck frequently due to national domestic problems, and member states wanted to give very little. Without the Commission at the centre – aiming to bring back deviating member states towards the Tampere programme – aimless piecemeal legislation could have been the result of the negotiations. Yet, the Commission remained successful in its attempts.

In January 2002, the Commission acquired a useful ally in the incoming Spanish Presidency (Ludlow, 2002b). Significantly, the Spanish Presidency strongly prioritised the AFSJ as a whole (ibid., pp. 7–8). Given the Spanish interest in prioritising the 'war against terrorism', it came as a surprise when the government signalled that asylum and migration would be on top of the Council agenda for the Seville Summit on 21 and 22 June 2002. Ludlow describes a good working alliance between the Spanish Presidency and the European Commission in arguing for a balanced and nuanced approach.

Before the Seville Council Summit, the Commission was determined from the outset that the single most important priority in the whole process was to adopt what was already going through the EU legislative machinery – the three remaining directives on asylum reception conditions, asylum qualification, and asylum procedures (Ludlow, 2002b, p. 19). This was particularly emphasised by Commissioner Vitorino, whose 'magnificent mastery of technical issues and his marvellous political nose' were also praised in an interview with Ludlow (ibid.). At this stage, the reception conditions directive was given priority for adoption over the two other directives and was finally adopted in January 2003 under the Greek Presidency.

In the end, the Commission strategy of focusing on the main message managed to set a political impulse for the negotiations to follow. Indeed, it even achieved deadlines for the adoption of the directives, which often works as a pressure device for member states (Ludlow, 2002b, pp. 88–89). The Tampere conclusions remain the basic point of reference for every aspect of the AFSJ, and thus asylum policy. Paragraphs 28 and 29 of the conclusions make specific reference to the Geneva Convention. This is a particular victory for the Commission, having argued for this all along and despite the ongoing 'war on terror'. In addition, the Council conclusions followed the Commission's priority for legislative Acts entirely. A demand for new legislation would have effectively put up serious hurdles for the three outstanding asylum directives.

According to Ackers (2005, p. 13), the Greek Presidency took up the negotiations on the proposals by way of priority when they started in January 2003. The Greek Presidency made the strategic choice for a new focus on the first part of the asylum procedures directive, with the remainder left to the Italian Presidency in the second half of 2003. As a result, negotiations moved more smoothly. However, the Italian Presidency was universally condemned as catastrophic by all member states (interviews PR 1 to PR 24) except Italy. Negotiations were chaotic, with no clear priorities. For the asylum procedures directive, the discussions predominantly evolved around the safe country of origin principle, as well as accelerated procedures (Ackers, 2005, p. 180). Despite their best efforts, problems proved insurmountable at the Council of Ministers session of 27 November 2003, and were thus passed on to the Irish Presidency at the start of January 2004.

The 'defend' phase

On 29 April 2004, the EU Interior Ministers managed to forge a deal on the asylum qualification directive and a political agreement on the asylum procedure directive. In fact, this was only two days before 1 May 2004, the deadline set by the Amsterdam Treaty, and the day of EU Enlargement. Thus, the pressure of enlargement seems to have had an accelerating effect. After the temporary protection directive of 2001 and the reception directive in January 2003, this resulted in the conclusion of the first phase of the EU asylum legislation (interviews COM 7, COM 10 and COM 16).

In the end, the Irish Presidency from January 2004 also contributed to the conclusion of the negotiations, as it was universally (interviews PR 1 to PR 24) recognised as an efficient, unpretentious and result-oriented presidency. It did not get politically too involved, but rather tried to be an efficient broker. Yet, the Irish used the deadline of 1 May 2004 as a great tool to put pressure on member states to agree, as they perceived it politically embarrassing to go beyond the deadline. It was thus a second shaming device, working similarly to the Commission's scoreboard, which had continuously applied pressure throughout the negotiations (interview COM 24).

In the end, the efficiency of the Irish Presidency paired with the negotiation skills of the Commission managed to achieve agreement (interviews PR 1 to PR 24). For the Commission, it was vital to compromise as well as defend their red lines. At this point, it was more important to defend their position in order to secure an EU policy on asylum matters (interview COM 7). In the end, it was very successful in defending these red lines, with the occasional intervention by the UNHCR.

The Irish Presidency soon realised the fact that in order to be efficient and achieve agreement, it had to resort to unconventional measures (interview PR 6). It considered the normal legislative machinery as far too cumbersome. Ackers (2005, p. 25) argues that experts on the technical levels seem to have an insufficient mandate to broker compromises. Thus, the Irish decided to take the talks forward on the basis of a combination of informal consultations, regular discussions and orientation debates in the Council of Ministers. Indeed, success would never have been achieved under normal procedures (interview PR 6). This meant that meetings could be called quickly, without the normal agendas, rules and room bookings procedures. The Irish aimed to have a general approach on the directives at the 30 March 2004 Council, and failing this, again at the 29–30 April 2004 Council of Ministers. Indeed, the latter session proved decisive, with a general exhaustion of all member states (interview PR 6).

At this point, the UNHCR also put pressure on member states (Ackers, 2005, p. 29). It had brought forward a paper in which it outlined their outstanding key issues of concern, in particular the danger of indirect refoulement through the directives. In the light of the concerns of the UNHCR, shared by the Commission and one anonymous member state (probably Sweden), there were drafting sessions which resulted in considerable improvement of the text above the level of international law (ibid., p. 30). In addition, formulations appeasing both Germany and the UK could also be found. Sweden then lifted their reservation about the compatibility of the legislation with international law.

Consequently, the Irish Minister was able to conclude in the afternoon of 29 April 2004 that the Council had reached a general approach on the asylum procedures directive – political agreement with formal adoption pending. Equally, the asylum qualification directive had been agreed. The reason for the time gap between the political agreement and the formal adoption of the asylum procedures directive was the fact that the Council wanted to agree on a list of 'safe third countries' as well – before the formal adoption. However, no agreement could be reached. Thus, the Council established the list of 'safe third countries' later with a changed institutional mechanism by qualified majority vote on a proposal from the Commission, after consultation with the

European Parliament and after the formal adoption of the asylum procedures directive. The procedures directive was then formally adopted without discussion on 1 December 2005.

In conclusion, it has become clear that the Commission played a crucial role in the negotiations. In the listening phase, it consulted widely amongst member states, and established initial alliances with the European Parliament and the UNHCR, as well as inheriting the support of NGOs through its activities in the 1990s. In this process, it was crucial to not push too much too fast, but rather to consolidate and keep a steady course. Nonetheless, under and with the help of the Spanish Presidency, the Commission managed to get negotiations back on track, which had been very slow previously. The Irish Presidency was essential as an efficient, effective and unconventional administrator of the negotiations. Yet, the Commission managed to mediate between member states and achieved a significant political success with the adoption of the four asylum directives. It was an incremental success, but an important one nonetheless.

EU institutions in the Common European Asylum System

The purpose of this section is to evaluate to what extent the European institutions, in particular the European Commission, have played the role of a supranational policy entrepreneur (Table 6.1).

A close examination of the summary of results substantiates the degree of success of the European Commission acting as a supranational policy entrepreneur in the area of EU asylum policy. Nonetheless, there were two differences compared to the area of counter-terrorism. Firstly, the success of the four asylum directives was a long and tedious process. It took almost five years to achieve the four directives, whereas the European arrest warrant took less than one year of negotiations and two years of preparation. This appears to suggest the fact that it is easier to achieve progress in the area of security than in granting refugee rights.

Secondly, however, it was far less clear whether the Commission would push for the rights of refugees with the emerging narrative of a 'war on terror'. The easy political solution would have been to link asylum to security and terrorism. This made perfect sense when the European arrest warrant was pushed and linked to terrorism. However, while it may have worked well, it was not what the Commission decided to do in the area of asylum. Even under difficult circumstances it pushed to include refugee rights under the Geneva Convention, and opposed the perception of asylum seekers as a security threat. In the end, this strategy paid political dividends. In fact, all four asylum directives actually increased the legal value of the Geneva Convention.

In addition, there are several implications of these findings. Firstly, the

Table 6.1 The Commission as an SPE in EU asylum policy

	Evidence for	
	Long-term norm change	*Short-term policy advances*
	Overall assessment	
	Norms changed significantly. The Commission successfully constructed the EU into refugee protection. This resulted in a normative shift towards the pooling of national sovereignty in the area	Significant policy advances: four asylum directives, i.e. the temporary protection, the asylum qualification, the reception conditions and the asylum procedures directives
	What changed?	
1	EU to legislate on asylum policy	Temporary protection is entirely new instrument
2	Value added from the EU pooling of sovereignty	Standards for reception conditions higher
3	'Protection of international refugee norms'	New concept of subsidiary protection
4	EU laws are linked to international refugee law, strengthening the force of international law	Harmonised definition of refugee concept
5		Persecution can stem from non-state actors – first-time recognition of this empirical fact
6		Effective communitarisation of EU asylum policy
	How did it change?	
1	First-mover advantage	Long consultation process and information build-up
2	Linking EU action with the 'single market' as well as international refugee protection	Close alliances with UNHCR and EP
3	Persuasion strategy, incremental and pragmatic	Strategically persuading member states first: impulses through Spanish Presidency and wrap up by Irish Presidency
4	Anchoring in existing international norms to gain legitimacy	Persuading and accommodating big member states with domestic problems, e.g. Germany: bargaining and negotiation skills
5	Alliances with NGOs, UNHCR and EP	Strategy: listen, learn, defend
6	Continued insistence on human rights	Compromise solutions are very creative and legally sound
7	Negotiation skills	

institution of asylum has developed very significantly in the EU measured by its standing amongst professionals in the field (interviews PR 1 to PR 24). It is clear that they consider this to be the area where European action is now the most accepted course of action. It is no surprise that this perception was then reflected in the negotiations of the Constitutional Treaty and subsequently in the Lisbon Treaty, which will be analysed in detail in Chapter 8. The Commission is unanimously perceived to become even stronger in the area over the coming years (interviews PR 1 to PR 24).

Moreover, these developments were reflected in the Hague programme from 2005 until 2009 (Peers, 5 November 2004). The decision was taken to communitarise the area after the first-phase instruments of the Tampere programme. The Hague programme contained the political commitment to do so. For any future European asylum policy, the decision-making procedures have changed. The Commission is the only actor left for making legislative proposals, and thus will be further strengthened. All member states unanimously predicted that the Commission would become even stronger in the area after its communitarisation with the Hague programme (interviews PR 1 to PR 24). The general feeling was that the Commission deserved it on the basis of its excellent work during the Tampere programme. The Council of Ministers is co-legislator with the European Parliament, and decides by qualified majority voting rather than unanimity. This will make future blocking of the area by one national veto impossible.

However, despite the fact that the Commission acted as an SPE in the asylum area, it is clear from this chapter that asylum policy is a highly complex area, with a multitude of actors: member states in the Council of Ministers, the European Parliament, the UNHCR and the NGOs, in addition to the Commission. These all form a part of the decision-making in a direct or indirect way.

7

The external dimension of EU asylum policy and border management

with Dr Sarah Leonard

This chapter will analyse the external dimension of asylum and migration. The external dimension of asylum and migration represents an increasingly important element of EU policy activity, and is clearly embedded in one of the most interesting and important policy areas, which a large number of scholars have been debating (Joppke, 1998, 2001; Freeman, 1998; Guiraudon, 2000, 2001, 2003; Boswell, 2003a, b, 2008; Ellermann, 2008; Geddes, 2000, 2001; Stetter, 2000, 2007; Thielemann, 2001a, b, 2004, 2005, 2006; Thielemann and Dewan, 2006; Lavenex, 1998, 1999, 2001a, b, 2004, 2006; Occhipinti, 2003). With the establishment of internal competences in the area of asylum policy, it represents the acceptance of third countries of EU actorness in the Area of Freedom, Security and Justice (AFSJ). However, as is argued in this chapter, contrary to the security threat of terrorism, the AFSJ is not constructed against refugees as a security threat; in fact, it is even resisted by the European institutions, notably by the European Commission.

As suggested in this book, it is the response to a 'security threat' that enables political actors to construct an 'Area of Freedom, Security and Justice'. Asylum and migration have indeed come to be seen as security threats (Huysmans, 2000, 2004; Bigo, 1996, 1998a, b, 8c, d, 2001a, 2002; Guild, 1999, 2002, 2003a, b, c, 2004, 2006; Guiraudon, 2000, 2003). However, as suggested in this chapter, this responsibility does not rest with the EU institutions, and is actively resisted by the European Commission. Especially the European Commission played the significant role of a supranational policy entrepreneur in the policy area; yet, it changed its strategy significantly from its role in counter-terrorism. It never attempted to construct refugees as a threat, and even actively resisted this.

The so-called 'external dimension' or 'internationalisation' of the EU immigration and asylum policy has become increasingly important in recent years from both policy and scholarly points of view (van Selm, 2002; Boswell, 2003a; Lavenex, 2006). There is no precise definition of this concept, which broadly refers to external relations in the area of border, asylum and migration. As migration issues, by definition, concern the crossing of borders and involve different states, the definition of the 'external dimension' of the EU asylum and migration policy could cover a very large number of issues, if not the policy as a whole. This would decrease its usefulness as a concept. In this chapter, therefore, it is decided to adopt the following narrower definition: 'co-operation with third countries (countries of origin and transit) in the field of asylum and migration', as it seems to be the understanding of 'external dimension' that underpins the EU policy on asylum and migration (European Council, December 2004).

Whatever the precise definition of the external dimension of the EU asylum and migration policy, it is often considered that it has two main components (see notably Boswell, 2003a; Lavenex, 2006):

- *A 'control' approach*, which aims to co-operate with third states to insert them in the defensive system that the EU has gradually established against 'unwanted migration', notably through the conclusion of readmission agreements.[1]
- *A 'root causes' approach*, which aims to co-operate with third countries to tackle the root causes of migration (poverty, war, violence, unemployment, etc.) in third countries in order to decrease the incentive to migrate for the local population.

This chapter argues that mainly the European Commission played the role of a supranational policy entrepreneur in the external dimension of asylum policy. As demonstrated in the previous chapter, the Commission aims to keep the EU asylum policy anchored in the prevailing international norms, such as the Geneva Convention. Consequently, the Commission's role is often more associated with the 'root causes' approach in the external dimension of asylum. In this area, the Commission achieved two main successes: (1) it pushed for, and succeeded partially, with its 'root causes' approach, while at the same time (2) managing to divert the attention from the extra-territorial control approach advocated particularly by the UK. It is important to note that the role of an SPE in this particular case involves the shaping of the agenda through the pushing of its policies, as well as through the diversion of the actions of rival policy entrepreneurs, such as the UK government.

EU institutions in the external dimension of the asylum policy: a place for the Commission as a supranational policy entrepreneur?

As explained in the previous chapter, the European Commission played an active role in shaping the development of the EU policy on asylum, migration and borders from its origins by issuing a series of Communications.[2] In these documents, it consistently emphasised the idea that this policy should have an external dimension, which should itself be based on a 'comprehensive approach' to migration. This section outlines the development of the external dimension of the EU policy on asylum, migration and borders through an analysis of both its normative and policy dimensions, as well as the role of EU institutions, in particular the European Commission, in the policy-making process.

The European Commission as a strategic first mover

The Commission's strategy was again to use its 'first mover' advantage in order to construct for itself a 'foot in the door' of the external dimension, and to push for a 'root causes' approach, facilitated by the anchoring of EU asylum policy in prevailing international norms. Firstly, the Commission managed to set the agenda in defining the problems in the problem stream, along the model suggested by Kingdon (1984, p. 90). How do problems capture the attention of decision-makers? In this particular case, similarly to the preceding chapter, the Commission managed to construct a 'European dimension' to what was previously perceived to be a national problem by way of producing a multitude of communications and suggestions that clearly laid out the problem. Subsequently, over the years, the Commission continued to push for the same solutions following the same policy direction – towards greater European competences.

This is particularly important due to the fact that solutions to policy problems are shaped in the same policy communities. What shapes people's thoughts within these policy communities? Commonly held sets of beliefs and norms certainly seem to influence people's ideas and behaviours. Participants interact with each other and are socialised according to the prevailing norms within this reference group. Furthermore, norms do not just guide the behaviour of people in this policy community, but are also shaped by the discussions and the social interaction within this group.

In the end, the necessary political consensus is built on persuasion (Kingdon, 1984, p. 167) in the politics stream, with a stronger emphasis on bargaining. The coalition building achieves a sort of bandwagon effect, where as some decision-makers join the coalition, more and more want to be on it. It is precisely this effect that can be noted in the construction of the external dimension of asylum and migration. Through the constant pushing for a certain asylum policy agenda, i.e. the anchoring of the asylum policy in prevailing international norms, the Commission facilitated the development of a 'root causes' approach in the external dimension of asylum and migration. This enabled it to build a winning coalition with the support of other actors, the UNHCR and the European Parliament, but also a significant number of member states, through an increase in legitimacy. Thus, the success in anchoring the four asylum directives of the preceding chapter in the Geneva Convention also enabled the Commission to be politically flexible enough to push a limited element of the 'control agenda', notably the negotiation of readmission agreements to reduce irregular migration, in order to construct a role for the EU. Essentially, a role for the EU, over time, would imply the role of the EU institutions, especially the Commission, the Parliament, and the European Court of Justice, to strengthen, and would lead to a furtherance of the process of European integration.

The 1991 Communication of the European Commission on Immigration

The first significant attempt to develop the external dimension of the EU asylum and migration agenda was the Commission's first Communication on Immigration (1991), released in the run-up to the Maastricht Treaty.[3] In this document, the European Commission called for 'making migration an integral element of the Community external policy' in order to act on 'migration pressures' (European Commission, 1991, p. 2). More precisely, it suggested using development actions, such as projects targeting poor regions identified as important migration sources, in order to '[counter] migration pressure' (European Commission, 1991, p. 20), as well as including migration issues in future co-operation agreements. The Commission also proposed to conclude readmission agreements with third countries in order to facilitate the repatriation of immigrants in an irregular situation (European Commission, 1991, p. 22).

This Communication of the European Commission was discussed by the EU member states at the Edinburgh European Council in December 1992. After debating what they called the issue of 'migration pressures', they adopted a 'Declaration on Principles Governing External Aspects of Migration Policy', which was annexed to the Conclusions of the Presidency (European Council, 1992). It is particularly interesting to note that the Declaration emphasised the commitment of member states to honour their full obligations under international human rights and refugee law (European Council, 1992, p. 46), as well as combat racism and xenophobia. This was a particular victory for the Commission, which had itself emphasised the importance of 'improving control over immigration, without in any way prejudicing the right of asylum' in its 1991 Communication (European Commission, 1991, p. 19).

The main thrust of the Declaration was to delineate a broad approach to tackle migration pressures, going beyond an exclusive focus on the control of migration channels. It notably identified eight principles aiming to guide the development of the Community's external relations. Whilst some of them related to the control of migration flows, including the conclusion of readmission agreements with third countries, others aimed to tackle the 'causes of migratory movements' (European Council, 1992, p. 47) – what has been identified in the literature as the 'root causes' approach to migration control (see for example Spencer, 1996; Lindstrom, 2003). In that respect, member states notably agreed that they should give an appropriate amount of development aid in order to promote sustainable social and economic development. However, the Declaration did not set any specific objectives or deadlines for the implementation of this 'root causes' policy. This arguably contributed to the slow progress recorded in this area in the following years (Boswell, 2003a, p. 626), as will be shown later in this chapter.

In contrast, the 'control' approach received more immediate attention in practice. The first Council of Justice and Home Affairs adopted a set of principles for possible readmission agreements with third countries in order to combat illegal immigration. It also adopted several conclusions on the desirability of linking Community external agreements with third countries to readmission agreements (European Commission, 1994, p. 5/Annex II). Nevertheless, this initial relative lack of enthusiasm of the member states to implement the 'root causes' approach to migration did not discourage the Commission. As indicated by Kingdon (1984), one of the defining characteristics of political entrepreneurs is persistence. The Commission certainly displayed this quality as it drafted and tabled another major Communication on asylum and migration matters.

The 1994 Communication of the European Commission on Immigration and Asylum Policies

In its 1994 Communication on Immigration and Asylum Policies, the Commission called again for the development of a comprehensive approach to migration issues. In addition to outlining several measures on controlling migration in the short term, it underlined the need to co-ordinate 'traditional areas of activity, such as social policy, aspects of common foreign and security policy and trade, co-operation and development instruments as well as migration and migration management policies' (European Commission, 1994, p. 5). The Commission explained that 'the basic philosophy of this approach is that short-term control measures, including admission measures need to be matched by long term co-operation with countries and regions of origin ...' (European Commission, 1994, p. 11) with regard to the demographic, economic, environmental, political and human rights causes of migration (European Commission, 1994, pp. 13–19).

Despite these detailed proposals from the Commission and a certain level of interest in them in the Council, the 'root causes' approach was not implemented in practice at the time. This was mainly due to the institutional context, which was not favourable to the development of a broad approach to migration. Firstly, the European Commission, which was the champion of the 'root causes' approach, was in a relatively weak institutional position as it did not have the monopoly on the right of initiative in this policy area yet (see also the previous chapter). Secondly, according to Boswell (2003a, p. 626), development and external relations officials in the Commission were reluctant to integrate migration issues into the EU external relations policy because they were afraid that development goals might be 'subverted' through the use of development instruments to prevent migration flows. Consequently, the 'root causes' approach' largely remained at the level of rhetoric in the early 1990s.

However, at the same time, the Commission managed to anchor the development of the external aspects of the Community asylum and migration policy in the prevailing international refugee norms, including the Geneva Convention. The Commission's emphasis on international norms is an important similarity in its strategies towards the development of the internal aspects of the EU asylum policy and the external dimension of asylum and migration respectively. Nonetheless, the Commission also developed the 'control' aspect of the external dimension of the asylum and migration policy. It called for the conclusion of readmission agreements with third countries in order to ensure that illegal migrants and the asylum seekers whose claim had been rejected could be returned to their country of origin. Following the signing of the first multilateral readmission agreement between the Schengen states and Poland in 1991, similar agreements were signed with other Central and Eastern European candidate countries in the 1990s.

First steps towards the consolidation of the external dimension of the EU Asylum and Migration Policy

The external dimension of the EU asylum and migration policy received a new impetus following the signing of the Treaty of Amsterdam in 1997. Actually, this Treaty did not explicitly mention the issue of co-operation with third countries on asylum and migration. Nevertheless, the subsequent Council and Commission's Action Plan for implementing the Treaty, which was adopted at the Vienna European Council in December 1998, included several measures in this area such as the 'assessment of countries of origin in order to formulate a country specific integrated approach' and 'information campaigns in transit countries and in the countries of origin' in order to discourage illegal immigration (Council of the European Union and European Commission, 1998).

The adoption of this Action Plan had been preceded by months of intense debates on the controversial 'Strategy Paper on Migration and Asylum Policy' tabled by the Austrian Presidency (Council of the European Union, 1998a). This paper emphasised the importance of 'curbing illegal migration and combating facilitator networks' (Council of the European Union, 1998a, p. 20), notably through the conclusion of readmission agreements. It brought both approaches together in its model of 'concentric circles of migration policy':

> the Schengen States currently lay down the most intensive control measures. Their neighbours (essentially the associated States and perhaps also the Mediterranean area) should gradually be linked into a similar system which should be brought increasingly into line with the first circle's standards, particularly with regard to visa, border control and readmission policies. A third circle

> of States (CIS area, Turkey and North Africa) will then concentrate primarily on transit checks and combating facilitator networks, and a fourth circle (Middle East, China, black Africa) on eliminating push factors. (Council of the European Union, 1998a, p. 19)

Thus, according to this model, the 'root causes' approach was to be applied exclusively to countries of origin such as the Middle East and sub-Saharan Africa, whereas the control approach would be applied to neighbouring countries, including in North Africa. Drawing on some of these ideas, the Dutch government proposed to create a working group on the external relations of the EU asylum and migration policy.

On 7 December 1998, the Council of the EU decided to set up a task force on asylum and migration in order to tackle what it described as the 'problem of mass influxes of asylum-seekers and illegal immigrants' (Bulletin EU 12–1998, Justice and home affairs co-operation 5/18). This 'High Level Working Group on Asylum and Migration' (HLWG), comprising high-level officials of each member state and of the Commission, aimed to 'establish a common, integrated, cross-pillar approach targeted at the situation in the most important countries of origin of asylum-seekers and migrants'. Its mandate covered both the 'control' approach and the 'root causes' approach.

The first countries to be selected for the elaboration of Action Plans were Afghanistan/Pakistan, Albania and the neighbouring region, Morocco, Somalia and Sri Lanka. The HLWG also decided to update the Action Plan on Iraq that had been previously drawn up. The first Action Plans on these countries were submitted on schedule to the Tampere European Council in 1999. Again, the idea of securing readmission agreements with third states received a lot of attention in the work of the HLWG (Boswell, 2003a, p. 630). This development was certainly linked to the composition of the group, which mainly comprised JHA officials.

Moreover, the composition of the HLWG had an impact on budgetary issues and this also significantly influenced the course of its work. Originally, the HLWG did not possess its own budget to implement its proposals tackling the root causes of migration. Therefore, it depended on co-operating with those working on external relations or development for funding its actions (van Selm, 2002). However, these other groups were reticent to co-operate with the HLWG for various reasons. First of all, officials from the Commission DGs for external relations and development considered that they had not been sufficiently involved in the drawing up of the plans. External relations staff in the Commission also criticised the fact that the HLWG proposed to use financial programmes dedicated to development in order to implement the Group's own proposals in the field of asylum and migration (Boswell, 2003a).

In sum, the establishment of the HLWG was a significant initiative as an attempt to institutionalise the external dimension of the EU asylum and migration policy in order to overcome the fragmentation of previous initiatives. However, it lacked both a broad support base and the financial resources necessary to implement effectively a comprehensive approach to migration. Nevertheless, its misfortunes did not prevent the external dimension of the EU asylum and migration policy from continuing to grow in importance. This was notably the result of its prominent place in the Conclusions of the Tampere European Council in October 1999. On this occasion, EU member states emphasised the importance of both the 'control' and 'root causes' approaches'. Indeed, in addition to highlighting the new powers of the Community with regards to the conclusion of readmission agreements, the Conclusions emphasised the idea of 'partnership with countries of origin' through the development of 'a comprehensive approach to migration addressing political, human rights and development issues in countries and regions of origin and transit' (European Council, October 1999). Thus, it is remarkable to observe the very significant impact that the European Commission's ideas on a 'comprehensive approach to migration' had on the Tampere Conclusions, which constituted themselves the political basis of the EU's work programme on asylum and migration for the following five years.

The Tampere programme, 1999–2004

In practice, however, the first years of the Tampere programme were still characterised by an emphasis on the 'control' approach on the EU member states' part. In 2000, the Council approved mandates for the Commission to negotiate readmission agreements with Russia, Pakistan, Sri Lanka, and Morocco. This was later followed by the adoption of negotiation mandates for readmission agreements with Hong Kong and Macao in 2001 and five more countries in 2002 (Ukraine, Algeria, Albania, China, and Turkey). However, negotiations proved far more difficult with those third states than they had previously been with candidate countries to the EU. Out of eleven mandates, only three readmission treaties had been agreed by May 2003 (with Hong Kong, Sri Lanka, and Macao). Of the other eight states, four of them had not even agreed to begin negotiations by October 2002 (Peers, 2004, p. 196). This was not surprising as it is well known that such agreements are of virtually no interest to the third countries concerned (Trauner and Kruse, 2008, p. 11). Without any strong incentive or counterpart such as the prospect of EU membership or substantial visa facilities, third countries remained reluctant partners in these negotiations on readmission.

This emphasis on the 'control' approach in the development of the external dimension of the EU asylum and migration policy was also evident in the run-up to the Seville European Council of June 2002. This summit was characterised by controversial debates on an initiative of the Spanish Presidency of the Council – with the support of the British government – aiming to significantly reshape the external dimension of the EU asylum and migration policy (Peers, 2004, p. 209). Whilst reaffirming the importance of the 'root causes' approach', the Spanish Presidency proposed to add a 'complementary' dimension to the policy in order to ensure the co-operation of third states with the EU. It suggested establishing a list of conditions relating to migration control that third states should fulfil, notably with the EU's financial support; otherwise, the Council would take specific foreign policy measures towards the states concerned and would invite the Commission to decrease its aid to these countries. The Spanish Presidency suggested that such a clause on migration management should be included in all future co-operation and association agreements.

After heated debates, the member states finally reached a compromise at the end of the European Council. The Council Conclusions started by recalling the importance of 'an integrated, comprehensive and balanced approach to tackle the root causes of illegal migration' as the EU's 'constant long-term objective'. Nevertheless, they also referred to the control dimension of the policy as they emphasised the need to include a clause on joint management of migration flows and compulsory readmission in the event of illegal immigration in all future agreements of the EU. They also indicated that the EU would provide the necessary technical and financial assistance to third states for this purpose (European Council, 2002, p. 11).

In December 2002, in response to the Seville European Council's conclusions, the Commission adopted the Communication 'Integrating migration issues in the European Union's relations with third countries' (COM 2002 (703)). This Communication contained two main parts. Whilst the first one provided a thorough analysis of the migration–development nexus, including important issues for the countries of origin such as migrant remittances and brain circulation, the second part focused on assessing the effectiveness of the financial resources available to manage migration in a rather control-oriented approach. The importance of the section on the migration–development nexus demonstrates how the Commission has continued to consistently emphasise the 'root causes' approach in order to make it a very significant component of the EU policy on asylum, migration and borders. In line with this analysis, the Communication concludes that co-operation with third countries should take three main forms:

- A balanced overall approach that addresses the root causes of migratory movements.
- A partnership on migration stemming from a definition of common interests with the countries concerned.
- Specific and concrete initiatives to help these countries to increase their capacity in the area of migration management.

Following a survey of the financial resources available for this policy area, the Commission also announced in its Communication that it would propose a multi-annual co-operation programme with third countries to finance targeted operations, in order to complement other operations on migration that were funded by other co-operation and development instruments.[4] This programme was to replace budget line B7-667, which had been created in 2001 to finance preparatory actions concerning asylum and migration in association with third countries and regions for which the Council had agreed Action Plans on migration (prepared by the HLWG). It concerned three priority areas: (1) the management of migratory flows, (2) voluntary return and the efficient fulfilment of obligations arising from readmission, and (3) the fight against illegal immigration.

The successor to budget line B7-667, the so-called 'AENEAS programme', was established in March 2004, following the adoption by the Council of Regulation EC 491/2004. Its overall indicative budget of €250 million for the period 2004–2008 represented a substantial increase compared to the previous B7-667 budget line of the years 2001–2003 (€10 million in 2001, €12.5 million in 2002, and €20 million in 2003). It also had a bigger remit than its predecessor, as it was established with the five following aims:

- The development of the legislation of third countries in the field of legal immigration, including admission rules, integration and non-discrimination measures, as well as the fight against racism and xenophobia.
- The development of legal migration, notably the raising of public awareness of the advantages of legal migration and the consequences of illegal migration.
- The development of the legislation and practices of third states regarding international protection, as well as the building of reception capacities for asylum seekers and refugees.
- The development of an effective policy against illegal immigration in the third countries, including the fight against the smuggling and trafficking of human beings.
- The readmission into the third countries concerned of 'persons who have illegally entered or remained on the territory of member states or of persons who have unsuccessfully applied for asylum in the EU or benefited from international protection there'.

In conclusion, the Commission's strategy to use a 'first mover' advantage in order to construct a role for itself and the EU in the external dimension of asylum and migration succeeded partially at the end of the Tampere programme. Most important, it managed to set the agenda in defining the problems by constructing a 'European dimension' to a 'national' problem through a multitude of communications and suggestions. Through the constant and consistent pushing for a certain asylum policy agenda, i.e. the anchoring of the asylum policy in prevailing international norms, the Commission facilitated the development of a 'root causes' approach in the external dimension of asylum and migration. Due to this, the Commission was also able to push the negotiation of readmission agreements to reduce irregular migration in order to construct a role for the EU. Yet, this enabled it to build a winning coalition for its 'root causes' agenda through increased legitimacy and bargaining with member states, which will be demonstrated below.

The Hague programme

On 4 November 2004, the Council adopted the Hague programme, which established the objectives to be implemented in the whole AFSJ, including the asylum and migration policy, in the period 2005–2010. In May 2005, the Commission presented a list of detailed measures and a schedule for the implementation of the Hague programme. This Action Plan was approved by the Council in June 2005 and became the reference point for the development of the external dimension of the EU asylum and migration policy in subsequent years.

The Action Plan implementing the Hague programme identified three main components of the external dimension of the EU asylum and migration policy:

- Co-operation with third countries in managing migration and asylum, including the external relations and development dimensions.
- Development of EU Regional Protection Programmes.
- Intensified co-operation with countries of transit to enable these countries to better manage migration and to provide adequate protection for refugees (in particular the actions taken in the context of the European Neighbourhood Policy).

The objective of signing Community readmission agreements was also included in the Action Plan, but under the heading of 'fight against illegal immigration' rather than that of 'external dimension of asylum and migration'. Interestingly, the Action Plan did not include any precise target date for the conclusion of the agreements, but only indicated that it should be 'timely'. This was an implicit recognition by the EU member states of the difficulties encountered by the European Commission in the negotiations of readmission agreements with third countries.

In practice, since the adoption of the Hague programme, the EU has continued to combine both measures on migration control and measures aiming to tackle the root causes of migration in the external dimension of the EU asylum and migration policy. Nevertheless, although both aspects are present in the external dimension, it appears that the concrete implementation of the 'control' approach' has continued to prove very challenging for the EU, the 'root causes' approach has grown in importance and in precision over the years.

As far as the 'control' approach is concerned – which is often referred to as the 'effective management of migration flows' in EU documents – one of its main aspects is the conclusion of readmission agreements with third countries. As previously mentioned, the European Commission has found it very difficult to lead successful negotiations on readmission agreements, because of the lack of incentives for third states to sign up to such agreements that are not to their advantage. As indicated earlier, during the Tampere programme, only three agreements were signed, which, in addition, concerned countries of limited importance in terms of flows of illegal migrants (Hong Kong, Macao and Sri Lanka). Further to these three treaties, two more readmission agreements were signed, respectively with Albania (2005) and Russia (2006). The latter case is important, as the conclusion of this readmission agreement was considerably facilitated by its linkage to the negotiations on an agreement on visa facilitation from July 2004 onwards. Drawing upon this experience with the Russian Federation, the EU offered this incentive of the visa facilitation to Ukraine in 2005 and also decided to start parallel negotiations on both the readmission agreement and the visa facilitation with Bosnia, Macedonia, Moldova, Montenegro, and Serbia in 2006 (Trauner and Kruse, 2008, pp. 10–11). This strategy proved successful with these countries, which all agreed to the readmission agreement.

However, as far as other countries are concerned, namely Algeria, China, Morocco, Pakistan and Turkey, the EU has not linked the negotiation of the readmission agreement to that of the visa facilitation. As a result, negotiations with these countries – some of which are important countries of origin and/or transit for many migrants to the EU – are still ongoing after a considerable time (e.g. seven years in the cases of Pakistan and Morocco at the time of writing). Thus, overall, although the EU has managed to conclude further readmission agreements in recent years, it still has not managed to do so with several countries that are crucial, from the EU's perspective, to control migration flows. This aptly illustrates the limitations of the 'control' approach in the external dimension of the EU asylum and migration policy, as some third states are reluctant to co-operate with the EU for its implementation.

As a consequence, it has become all the more necessary for the EU to approach migration from a perspective other than that of control. Therefore, it is perhaps not so surprising that recent years have seen a growing emphasis being placed on the 'root causes' approach to migration in the EU. In September 2005, the European Commission (2005c) issued a Communication on 'Migration and Development: Some Concrete Orientations' – a title that reflected the Commission's willingness to give a strong impulse to the concrete implementation of the migration–development agenda. Focusing on North–South migration, it proposed to take actions in the following areas: remittances, the role of diasporas in the development of their home countries, 'circular migration' and 'brain circulation', as well as measures for mitigating the effects of 'brain drain' in developing countries. Thus, in general, these measures aimed to increase the flexibility of migration policy in order to allow people to circulate more easily between developing countries and the EU, although some have criticised their relatively narrow scope.

In November 2005, the Council encouraged the Commission to 'give concrete expression to the orientations contained in its Communication, in particular with regards to migrant remittances, diaspora and "brain drain" issues'. It also invited the Commission to develop further its ideas on temporary and circular migration, as well as return migration (Council of the European Union, 2005: 5–6). Following this request, the Commission presented a Communication 'On circular migration and mobility partnerships between the European Union and third countries' in May 2007, which aims to facilitate and encourage circular and temporary migration between the EU and third countries.

In parallel with all this work on the migration–development nexus and tackling the root causes of migration, there have been a lot of debates in the EU on the so-called 'global approach to migration'. As the name suggests, the 'global approach' aims to formulate a comprehensive migration policy that addresses the broad range of issues relating to migration in different fields, including development, social affairs and employment, external relations, justice and home affairs, etc., from both short-term and long-term perspectives. To be precise, it does not only refer to the external dimension of the EU policy on asylum, migration and borders, as it also concerns the co-operation and solidarity that member states are expected to develop amongst themselves. Nevertheless, the 'global approach has a strong theme of working in partnership with countries of origin and transit' based on 'partnership, solidarity and shared responsibility' (European Commission, 2007a, p. 1).

The origins of the current debates in the 'global approach' are to be found in the British Presidency of the EU in the second half of 2005. At the Hampton Court European Council in October 2005, the EU Heads of State or Government asked the European Commission to issue a paper on migration which would identify priority actions for improving global migration, with a specific focus on Africa. The European Commission responded to this request in November 2005, when it issued a Communication on 'Priority Actions for responding to the Challenges of Migration: First Follow-up to Hampton Court'. In an implicit acknowledgement that the EU policy on asylum and migration comprises two main strands, 'root causes' and 'control', the Commission indicated that its Communication addressed 'both the security and development aspects of migration' in an attempt to take a 'balanced and comprehensive approach' (European Commission, 2005b, p. 2). It called for increased co-operation on migration issues amongst member states, but also with neighbouring countries and countries of origin in Africa.

At the Brussels European Council in December 2005, member states discussed the Communication of the Commission and decided to endorse a series of priority actions focusing on Africa and the Mediterranean, in line with the Commission's proposals. Details on the priority actions that the member states intended to take in the field of asylum and migration were included in a document bearing the title 'Global Approach to Migration', which was annexed to the Presidency Conclusions. Since then, the 'global approach to migration' has become a concept widely used in EU policy documents, including those issued by the European Commission. In particular, in November 2006, the Commission (2006a) issued a Communication on 'The Global Approach to Migration one Year on: Towards a Comprehensive European Migration Policy', in which it assessed the progress that had been accomplished towards the implementation of the global approach in Africa and the Mediterranean region. It concluded that significant progress had already been made to develop concrete co-operation on migration issues, but that actions needed to be enhanced in order to meet all the challenges associated with migration flows.

This Communication was complemented by another Communication issued in May 2007, on 'Applying the Global Approach to Migration to the Eastern and South Eastern Regions neighbouring the European Union'. It responded to the request of the European Council to extend the global approach beyond its initial scope, which had been limited to Africa and the Mediterranean region. In December 2007, the Commission (2007b) also published a new 'Interim Progress Report on the Global Approach to Migration', which surveyed the progress accomplished in 2007 with regard to both the migration–development agenda and the control of migration, in particular the fight against illegal migration, in the two main geographical areas covered by the global approach (Africa and the Mediterranean region, and the eastern and south-eastern regions neighbouring the EU).

It is interesting to note that the European Commission has also adopted the slogan of the 'global approach to migration', but has tended to juxtapose it with its traditional idea of a '*comprehensive* approach to migration'. In terms of content, both approaches are remarkably similar. Many of the actions currently developed under the umbrella of the 'global approach', and perhaps even more important the very idea underpinning the global approach, i.e. linking all the various policy fields upon which migration touches for the EU policy to be effective, had consistently been put forward by the European Commission since 1991.

The development of this comprehensive approach towards migration, including a growing emphasis on development issues, has been reflected in changes in financial instruments. A new programme entitled 'Thematic Co-operation Programme with Third Countries in the Development Aspects of Migration and Asylum' has been established to replace the AENEAS programme, as part of broader changes by the Commission aiming to simplify its external co-operation programmes from 2007 onwards (European Commission, 2006b). Its objective is to assist third countries – with the exception of countries with an EU membership perspective – in the areas of asylum and migration 'through an integrated, coherent and balanced approach' (p. 3). The programme has five main objectives: to foster the links between migration and development, to promote well managed labour migration, to fight illegal immigration and facilitate the readmission of illegal migrants, to protect migrants against exploitation and exclusion, and to promote asylum and international protection. The all-encompassing character of this financial programme testifies to the impact that 'global approach' thinking has had on the development of the external dimension of the EU asylum and migration policy.

In conclusion, the Commission has managed to set the agenda on the development of the external dimension of the EU policy on asylum, migration and borders. It has consistently called for the strengthening of the 'root causes' approach to migration and for its inclusion in a comprehensive approach to migration, which would link together the various policy issues which have an impact on migration. In that respect, the Commission has certainly displayed one of the major qualities of political entrepreneurs according to Kingdon (1984), namely persistence.

Nevertheless, this has been a slow and incremental process and, at the time of writing, a lot still remains to be done for the 'global approach' to be implemented effectively in all its aspects. This has been mainly due to the difficulties inherent to the co-ordination of all the different institutions and actors involved in this approach which crosses various fields (development, external relations, social and economic affairs, trade, justice and home affairs). Furthermore, some of these actors, in particular in the development community, were initially reluctant to become involved in migration matters and took some time to embrace the comprehensive (or 'global') approach to migration (Boswell, 2003a, 2008).[5] Nevertheless, with the strengthening of its position in this policy area, the Commission has been able to strengthen the 'root causes' approach to migration and to make the Council endorse the comprehensive approach to migration that it had been calling for since 1991, albeit under the slightly different label of 'global approach' to migration.

Consequently, this section confirms that the Commission has been able to act as an SPE, in a similar fashion to the role that it has played in the making of the EU asylum policy. Moreover, the next section will demonstrate that the Commission, in addition to being able to set policy agendas to a considerable extent thanks to its consistency and persistence, is also able to divert the attention of EU policy-makers away from proposals of rival policy entrepreneurs, such as the British government. In other words, not only is the Commission able to establish detailed agendas for policy areas that are new for the EU – as it did for the external dimension of the EU asylum and migration policy, even before the EU received formal competences on asylum and migration, it is also able to push for its policy agenda even with the presence of rival political entrepreneurs.

The extraterritorial processing of asylum claims: Commission entrepreneurship in different ways

According to the SPE model, a political entrepreneur stands at the policy window in order to propose, lobby for, and sell a policy proposal. In Kingdon's definition (1984, p. 181), political entrepreneurs (PE) need to possess resources which they are willing to invest, such as time, energy, reputation, money, and actively use them to promote a policy position in return for anticipated future gains. However, according to Kingdon, PEs also lie in wait for a window to open and therefore seize the right moment.

This section will illustrate Kingdon's idea that political entrepreneurs, whether supranational or national, are often in competition against one another. As suggested, they also need to wait for the right moment. More precisely, the section below will demonstrate how the European Commission skilfully exploited the problems encountered by a radical British proposal on asylum and migration to push for some of the ideas that it had previously developed. It will show how the British government failed to wait for the right moment and did not manage to convince enough of its fellow governments to support its proposal. In doing so, it opened the policy window for the Commission. This managed to successfully divert the attention away from the British proposal towards its own proposal, which itself drew upon previous work. While the aim of the Commission in this case was not to push through a particular proposal, but rather to stop the British proposal, it also fits in with the Commission's general approach to the area of EU asylum discussed in the preceding and the present chapter, i.e. anchoring this policy in international refugee norms and pushing for a 'root cause' approach. In contrast, the British proposal aimed to push the EU in the opposite direction and ultimately failed. This case can also be seen as a form of policy entrepreneurship of the Commission aiming to protect its other achievements in the field of asylum. The British proposal, if successful, would have had the capacity to considerably undo these achievements.

The EU debates on the British proposal on the extraterritorial processing of asylum claims

As the EU was about to enter the final year of the 'Tampere programme' and member states were engaged in the long and complicated negotiations of several directives in the area of asylum as seen in the previous chapter, the British government made a proposal on asylum that dominated the EU debates in this policy area for a few months in 2003. It suggested processing the claims of asylum seekers having reached the EU – or on their way to the EU – *outside* the territory of its member states, a policy known as the 'extraterritorial processing of asylum claims'.

This idea proved to be highly contentious (interviews NGO 1 to 10, IGO 1, COM 2, COM 7, COM 12, and COM 16) and gave rise to intense debates amongst the member states of the EU, the European Commission, the UNHCR, and the NGOs active in the field of asylum and migration. The proposal, described by some as aiming to 'radically change European Union asylum policy' (BBC News, 19 June 2003), was harshly criticised on legal, moral, economic, and practical grounds (interviews NGO 1–10). Amnesty International (2003) branded it 'unlawful' and 'unworkable', whilst a document jointly signed by several NGOs claimed that it 'sen[t] a dangerous signal about the UK's commitment to human rights' (British Refugee Council, 2003).

This section opens with a chronological presentation of the debates in the EU on the British proposal in 2003. It outlines the evolution of the EU debates on the British proposal with regards to the extraterritorial processing of asylum claims. It also presents in detail the British proposal, as well as the two other proposals on the same topic that were considered at the same time, which had been tabled by the UNHCR and the Commission respectively. In effect, there was a competition between these three proposals as to which one would shape the future development of the external dimension of the EU asylum policy.

The British proposal 'New International Approaches to Asylum Processing and Protection', March 2003

On 10 March 2003, Tony Blair sent a letter to Greek Prime Minister Costas Simitis – the then President of the Council of the EU – asking for a discussion at the upcoming Brussels European Council on an idea developed 'to help deal with the problems of refuges and migration'. Attached to the letter was a six-page document bearing the title 'New International Approaches to Asylum Processing and Protection' (UK Government, 2003).

This document started by highlighting the premise underpinning the British proposal, namely that the 'current global [asylum] system [was] failing' for various reasons (UK Government, 2003, p. 1). Firstly, financial support for refugees was inequitably distributed, as Western states devoted a lot of money to processing asylum applications, whereas little money was spent in the regions of origin of the refugees. Secondly, the current system required asylum seekers to enter the West illegally, often with the help of criminal organisations. Thirdly, between half and three-quarters of those claiming asylum in Europe did not meet the criteria of 'full refugees', whereas 12 million 'genuine refugees' remained in their region of origin to find protection. Finally, there were high costs and difficulties involved in returning the asylum seekers whose application had been rejected, which, in turn, undermined the confidence of the public in the asylum system.

Based on this assessment, the British proposal aimed to develop a 'better management of the asylum process globally' (UK Government, 2003, p. 1), through a reduction in the number of unfounded applications and the improvement of the protection granted to genuine refugees. For this purpose, it proposed the establishment of a new asylum system, whereby asylum seekers would no longer arrive illegally in Europe in order to claim asylum, but would rather arrive through legal channels, including refugee resettlement.

In what can be interpreted as an attempt to increase the legitimacy of its proposal, the British government claimed that it drew on the 'Convention Plus' initiative of the UNHCR (UK Government, 2003, p. 2). The 'Convention Plus' is an initiative that was launched by the UNHCR in 2002. It aimed to build on the Geneva Convention, by creating special agreements on the secondary movements of asylum seekers (i.e. movements of asylum seekers from a first country of refuge to another country) and ensuring lasting solutions for refugees in regions of origin.

The British proposal had two complementary components, namely (1) the adoption of measures to improve the regional management of migration flows, including the establishment of 'protected areas' for asylum processing, and (2) the establishment of processing centres on transit routes to Europe. The British government emphasised in the document that its ultimate objective was 'to deal more successfully with illegal migrants within their region of origin' through the adoption of four types of measures (UK Government, 2003, p. 2). Those respectively aimed to tackle the root causes of migration, improve the protection capacities in the source regions, establish better managed resettlement routes to Europe on a quota basis, and raise the awareness and acceptance of the states of origin of their 'responsibility to accept returns' (UK Government, 2003, p. 4), possibly through the conclusion of new readmission agreements.

However, the British government was aware that its proposal could only be implemented in the long term. It rested on the idea that countries of origin would have protection standards high enough to convince European domestic courts of the lawfulness of the transfer of asylum seekers over there. Given the currently low protection standards of many of these countries, this could only be considered a remote perspective. Therefore, the proposal of the British government also suggested medium-term action in order 'to deter those who enter the EU illegally and make unfounded claims' (UK Government, 2003, p. 4), whilst preserving the right to protection for those who are genuinely entitled to it.

More precisely, the suggestion put forward was the creation of so-called 'Transit Processing Centres' (TPCs) for asylum seekers. Such centres would be established outside the EU, for example on migration transit routes to the EU. They could be managed by the International Organisation for Migration (IOM) and financed by the participating states, with perhaps – at least, this is what the British government seemed to hope – some financial support from the EC budget. Asylum seekers arriving in the UK (or in another EU participating state) would be transferred to those TPCs, where their application for asylum would be processed, 'with a screening system approved by the

UNHCR' (UK Government, 2003, p. 5). Those persons granted refugee status would be resettled in the EU on a quota basis. The asylum seekers whose application had been rejected would normally be returned to their country of origin. Only in the case where they could not be returned safely to their country of origin might asylum seekers be given temporary refuge in the EU, until the situation in their country of origin improved. The British proposal also mentioned the idea of sending to the TPCs 'illegal migrants intercepted en route to the EU before they had lodged an asylum claim' (UK Government, 2003, p. 5), if they appeared to have a clear intention to do so.

This proposal had been developed over the previous months by a joint Cabinet Office/Home Office Committee. It had already been presented to Ruud Lubbers (interview IGO 1), the UN High Commissioner for Refugees, at a meeting in London on 10 February 2003, as the British government hoped to get the UNHCR's endorsement and its agreement to participate in the implementation of the proposal.

At the Brussels European Council on 20–21 March 2003, there was only a brief and preliminary discussion of the British proposal. The Heads of State and Government decided to invite the European Commission to 'explore these ideas further, in particular with UNHCR' (Council of the EU, 2003a, p. 30) and to report to the next European Council in June 2003.

The Veria Council: debates on the British proposal and the UNHCR's 'three-pronged' proposal

At the informal meeting of the EU Justice and Home Affairs Council in Veria on 28 March 2003, it appeared that EU member states were divided on the British proposal (*Financial Times*, 28 March 2003; *Independent*, 29 March 2003). Some member states indicated their support for the proposal, in particular Italy, Denmark and the Netherlands, and also, although to a lesser extent, Finland, Spain, Ireland, Austria and Belgium.[6] Some of them made their approval conditional upon the approval of the plan by the UNHCR (*Financial Times*, 28 March 2003). In contrast, German Interior Minister Otto Schily expressed his scepticism towards the plan and received the support of other member states, notably Sweden and Portugal. European Commission officials also had reservations about the British proposal, which, in their view, was not fully thought through and raised numerous legal and budgetary questions (*Financial Times*, 28 March 2003).

The media reported that Ruud Lubbers, the UN High Commissioner for Refugees, took part in the Veria meeting (*Financial Times*, 28 March 2003). What the media did not explain at the time was that, at the Veria Council, Lubbers did not merely comment on the British proposal. He also tabled a rather comprehensive counter-proposal, the so-called 'three-pronged' proposal, the content of which suggested that the UNHCR largely shared the British government's appraisal of the state of the global asylum system. The documents in which it was exposed in detail were not made public by the

UNHCR and only became accessible after they were leaked to Statewatch. The 'three-pronged proposal' was named after its three prongs or main dimensions: (1) improving the national asylum systems of the destination states (2) improving access to solutions in the regions of origin, and (3) processing the 'manifestly unfounded' cases in EU-operated closed reception centres within EU borders.

The first prong, the 'regional prong', aimed to improve access to protection and solutions in the regions of origin of refugees 'while addressing certain asylum dilemmas confronting host States' (UNHCR, 2003a, p. 1). The purpose of the second prong, called the 'domestic prong', was to improve the national asylum systems of the destination states. The UNHCR argued that, after the wide array of asylum reforms adopted by many states, the time had come 'to refocus efforts to establish clearer and simpler procedures, which concentrate on well resourced, and faster yet quality initial decision making with appropriate safeguards' (UNHCR, 2003a, p. 11). The third prong, called the 'EU prong', proved to be the most controversial. Its aim was to encourage EU member states to address the issue of 'mixed movements', i.e. migratory flows of both asylum seekers and economic migrants, by processing jointly presumed 'manifestly unfounded asylum claims' from selected non-refugee-producing countries of origin. In other words, persons originating from designated countries of origin would be considered as economic migrants resorting to the asylum channel. Upon arrival anywhere in the EU, they would be immediately transferred to a joint EU centre for the processing of their claim, with the exceptions of persons medically unfit to travel or stay in a closed centre.

Such a centre would be a closed reception and EU-funded centre, where interpretation services and legal counselling would be available for asylum seekers. The processing of applications would be conducted in accordance with 'commonly agreed procedures respecting international standards' (UNHCR, 2003a, p. 7). First instance decisions would be taken promptly and appeals could be limited to a simplified review. The UNHCR would monitor the determination process and could also be part of the review process. In contrast to the British proposal, which foresaw centres located outside the EU, the UNHCR proposed to create centres 'initially in one or two EU Member States' (UNHCR, 2003a, p. 7). Those found in need of protection would be distributed within the EU in accordance with pre-agreed criteria, as there would be expanded resettlements quotas in the EU. The asylum seekers whose claim was rejected would be returned through operations jointly organised by the EU member states, in co-operation with the IOM.

Thus, in addition to the British proposal, there was now a second proposal on the negotiation table, that of the UNHCR. In some respects, it was in broad agreement with that of the British government, notably with regard to the current problems of the global asylum system, the importance of strengthening protection in the regions of origin and the need to implement reforms. The UNHCR's proposal also contained the idea of establishing processing centres, as had been suggested by the British government.

By the end of the Veria Council, member states had not been able to reach a common position on these proposals for the extraterritorial processing of asylum claims. They decided that these matters should be discussed again at the Thessaloniki Council in June. It was expected that, by that time, the European Commission would have published a new Communication exploring these ideas further, as requested by the European Council in March.

The role of the EU institutions and the UNHCR

As explained earlier, the British proposal was received with interest by some EU governments, although some of them insisted on its endorsement by the UNHCR. The European Commission stated that the proposal gave rise to several legal and practical issues. This opinion may have been shared by several governments, but only two made their opposition to the British proposal publicly known, namely Germany and Sweden (*Financial Times*, 16 June 2003; *Independent*, 19 June 2003; *Guardian*, 20 June 2003a). Consequently, it was the Commission that played a key role in the evolution of the discussions by tabling a proposal that would divert the attention away from the British proposal, thereby reducing its chances of success. In so doing, the Commission would manage to protect its own achievements in the asylum field, which have been analysed before.

The European Commission's counter-proposal

In the following weeks, as the Thessaloniki Council drew closer, the idea of the extraterritorial processing of asylum claims dominated the European asylum and migration debates. The media regularly reported on this topic, notably the *Observer* (15 June 2003), which claimed that the British proposal was already being implemented as a '[s]ecret Balkan camp [was being] built to hold UK asylum seekers' in Croatia. This turned out to be wrong, but other media outlets had already reproduced the story (BBC News, 15 June 2003; *EUobserver*, 16 June 2003).

According to several media reports, the British government continued to champion the idea of creating 'zones of protection' for asylum seekers near conflict areas, an idea which, it claimed, had the support of the UNHCR, the European Commission and 'a number of [Britain's] EU partners' (*Guardian*, 16 June 2003a; see also *EUobserver*, 17 June 2003; *Financial Times*, 16 June 2003; *Guardian*, 18 June 2003). As a first step in that direction, it hoped to gain EU political support and funding for pilot projects, the first of which was expected to be carried out in the Horn of Africa (*Financial Times*, 16 June 2003; *Guardian*, 20 June 2003a).

However, at the Thessaloniki Council on 19–20 June 2003, the idea of 'zones of protection' 'did not ... make it past the first working session of the three-day summit' (BBC News, 19 June 2003; *Guardian*, 20 June 2003). After hearing the objections of the European Commission and several other EU member states, notably Sweden and Germany, at the pre-Summit dinner, the British government decided to withdraw its proposal (BBC News, 19 June 2003; *Guardian*, 20 June 2003a). Nevertheless, it announced its intention to form a 'coalition of the willing' with other like-minded member states, such as Denmark, Austria, the Netherlands, and Ireland, in order to pilot some trial schemes of regional protection zones (BBC News, 19 June 2003; *Financial Times*, 16 June 2003; *Guardian*, 20 June 2003a).

As the British proposal was being withdrawn from EU debates the Commission capitalised on the policy dynamics of the time to push the policy in a different direction (interview COM 16). At the Thessaloniki Council, member states began to discuss a Communication on asylum that the European Commission had published on 3 June 2003 under the title 'Towards more accessible, equitable, and managed Asylum Systems' (European Commission, 2003) (interviews PR 1, 4–8, 15). Although this document started by analysing the British proposal, as well as UNHCR's contribution to the debates, it would be misleading to interpret it as a purely ad hoc reaction to these developments. It actually built on a series of Communications on asylum that the Commission had been releasing since 2000. Before examining this 2003 Communication in greater detail, it is necessary to present briefly the Communications that preceded it in order to understand its foundations.

In 2000, the Commission tabled a Communication entitled 'Towards a Common Asylum Procedure and a Uniform Status, valid throughout the Union, for Persons granted Asylum' (COM (2000) 755). It notably argued that processing asylum claims in the region of origin of refugees and facilitating their arrival into the EU through the establishment of a resettlement scheme would allow them to access protection rapidly, without having to migrate illegally or use the services of criminal gangs. The Commission underlined that this option could only be complementary to the treatment of spontaneous applications for asylum on the territory of the EU member states. Subsequently, it commissioned two feasibility studies on the processing of asylum claims outside the EU and on an EU-wide resettlement scheme respectively.

In 2001, the Commission published another Communication on asylum, bearing the title 'On the Common Asylum Policy, introducing an open Co-ordination Method' (COM (2001) 710). Again, it mentioned the idea of 'evaluating the merits of resettlement programmes [and] the possibility of processing asylum applications outside the Member States (. . .)'. In the same year, the Commission also published a Communication 'on a common policy on illegal immigration', in which it suggested that

> Member States should . . . explore possibilities of offering rapid access to protection so that refugees do not need to resort to illegal immigration or people smugglers. This could include greater use of Member States' discretion in

> allowing more asylum applications to be made from abroad or the processing of a request for protection in the region of origin and facilitating the arrival of refugees on the territory of the Member States by resettlement scheme. Such approaches could ensure sufficient refugee protection within and compatible with a system of efficient countermeasures against illegal migratory flows. (European Commission, 2001b, p. 8)

In its Communication of June 2003, the Commission drew on the results of the two feasibility studies commissioned earlier to develop these ideas further (European Commission/Danish Centre for Human Rights, 2003). It mentioned that it agreed with the assessment of the British government that asylum procedures were being abused in Europe and that 'new avenues' ought to be explored. However, it differed from the British proposal by emphasising again the 'need to fully respect international legal obligations of Member States' (European Commission, 2003, p. 11) – a concern ignored in the British proposal. The Commission also emphasised that 'managed entry' proposals should be complementary to the traditional territorial processing of asylum claims. It criticised the British idea to replace, rather then complement, the existing asylum system by a 'new approach to the international protection regime'. More important, it radically dissociated itself from the British government's idea of 'Transit Processing Centres' by not considering this policy alternative at all.

The two main proposals that the European Commission put forward in this Communication were the introduction of Protected Entry Procedures (PEPs) and the creation of an EU-wide resettlement scheme. PEPs would allow a non-national to approach a potential host state outside its territory with a claim for asylum (or other form of international protection) and to be granted an entry permit in case of a positive response to that claim, be it preliminary or final. In a refugee resettlement scheme, refugees would be transferred from a first host country to a second country where they would enjoy guarantees of protection, including residence, and prospects for integration and autonomy.

At the Thessaloniki Council, member states asked the Commission to 'explore all parameters in order to ensure more orderly and managed entry in the EU of persons in need of international protection, and to examine ways and means to enhance the protection capacity of regions of origin' with a view to present a report to the Council before June 2004 'suggesting measures to be taken, including legal implications' (Council of the European Union, 2003b, p. 8). A draft text of the Presidency Conclusions read differently as it called on the European Commission to 'examine ways and means to enhance the protection capacity of regions of origin and first countries of asylum, in particular on the basis of experience gained by pilot projects to be conducted in full partnership with countries concerned and in close co-operation with UNHCR' (*Financial Times*, 16 June 2003). However, several member states rejected the mention of the pilot projects, which explains why only the broader and less committal reference to the 'protection capacity of regions of origin' remained in the final text (*Guardian*, 20 June 2003). In sum, the Thessaloniki Council brought an end to the discussions of the British government's ideas of 'transit processing centres' and 'regional protection areas (or zones)', as the European Commission and several other EU member states expressed their scepticism or, in some cases, strong opposition. Instead, it was the Commission's proposal, which notably suggested strengthening the protection capacity of regions of origin, which took centre stage in the development of the external dimension of the EU asylum policy.

The Commission: Supranational Policy Enterpreneur in a different policy direction?

On 1 October 2004, the European Commission announced at the informal JHA Council that it had decided to fund the €1 million UNHCR project 'Towards a Protection Space in North Africa' in conjunction with the Netherlands (*Bulletin Quotidien Europe*, 2 October 2004). This project concerned Morocco, Libya, Tunisia, Mauritania, and Algeria. Its objectives were to enhance knowledge of transit migration, to develop basic protection mechanisms in North Africa, to examine media and public attitudes, to support NGOs, and to prepare a multilateral approach to protection on the high seas.

In September 2005, the European Commission announced that it was to develop 'Regional Protection Programmes' (RPPs) in close co-operation with the UNHCR and the third countries involved (European Commission, 2005a). RPPs would aim to deliver direct benefits to refugees and to contribute to improving the protection and human rights situation in third countries hosting large populations of refugees. Each RPP would focus on five or six actions, including the delivery of practical benefits such as training, infrastructure building, the provision of equipment, etc. The Commission announced that the first pilot RPP would be implemented in the Western Newly Independent States (WNIS) (Ukraine, Moldova, and Belarus), as this region emerged as a clear priority in the discussions between the Commission and the member states. This RPP would focus on strengthening already existing protection capacity, notably by giving practical support to the examination of asylum applications, the reinforcement of subsidiary protection, integration and registration. The identification of a second pilot RPP was also discussed in the Commission's Communication. It mainly discussed the suitability of the Great Lakes region, in particular Tanzania, for this purpose, but also mentioned other possibilities such as North Africa, the Afghanistan region and the Horn of Africa. In practice, at the time of writing, RPPs have been implemented in the three WNIS and in Tanzania on the basis of the AENEAS programme (European Commission, 2007b)

Therefore, the development of the Commission's idea of RPP and its subsequent implementation demonstrate that, with regards to this crucial stage in the development of the external dimension of the EU asylum and border management policy, the Commission was able to push its own proposals forward to a considerable extent. Moreover, what is remarkable is that these proposals were significantly different from those made by the British government, which was the main rival of the Commission for agenda-setting in this policy area at the time. Thus, this section demonstrated how the European Commission skilfully exploited the problems encountered by the British proposal on asylum and migration to push through its own ideas. This underlines the need to wait for the right moment, which the British government had failed to do, and to convince enough of its fellow governments to support its proposal. Consequently, this case is a form of policy entrepreneurship of the Commission aiming to protect its other achievements in the field of asylum, while pushing further its own agenda.

EU institutions in the external dimension of asylum and border management

This section aims to evaluate the extent to which the European institutions, in particular the European Commission, have played the role of a supranational policy entrepreneur. The theoretical model suggested the following:

- First-mover advantage.
- Persuasion strategy: (1) legitimacy build-up, (2) expertise and information, (3) continued insistence, (4) negotiation skills.
- Alliances.

As explained above, the Commission skilfully fulfilled the first condition, as it acted as a first mover and managed to construct a role for the EU in the external dimension of asylum and migration. It also pushed successfully for the 'root causes' approach, as well as a limited control approach by way of promoting readmission agreements. In this endeavour, the Commission followed a similar strategy as in the preceding chapter on internal EU asylum policy. However, being an SPE in this area was an even greater challenge given the existence of powerful rivals for the definition of the policy agenda. In this area, the Commission had to prove even more – that it could succeed as an SPE even with powerful rivals for the policy agenda. The Commission successfully raised to the challenge proved this very skilfully when it effectively stopped the British proposal for extraterritorial processing of asylum claims with the help of some allies – even under conditions where the UNHCR was favourably inclined towards it. This proved to be the ultimate success for the Commission.

Table 7.1 The Commission as an SPE in the external dimension of EU asylum policy

Evidence for	
Long-term norm change	*Short-term policy advances*
Overall assessment	
Norms changed significantly. The Commission succeeded in constructing the EU into the external dimension of asylum	Significant policy advances: emerging root cause approach, development–migration nexus on the policy agenda, readmission agreements
What changed?	
1 Emerging development–migration nexus	Co-operation with third countries in managing migration and asylum, including the development and external relations dimensions (what could be called the 'root causes' approach)
2 'Protection of international refugee norms'	Development of EU Regional Protection Programmes
3	Intensified co-operation with countries of transit to enable those countries to manage migration better and to provide adequate protection for refugees (in particular the actions taken in the context of the European Neighbourhood Policy)
How did it change?	
1 First-mover advantage	Long consultation process and the production of many communications
2 Linking EU action with the 'root causes' approach as well as international refugee protection	Close alliances with UNHCR and NGOs
3 Persuasion strategy, incremental and pragmatic	Strategically persuading member states first, in particular Germany and Sweden
4 Anchoring in existing international norms to gain legitimacy	Compromise solutions are very creative and legally sound
5 Alliances with NGOs, UNHCR and EP	
6 Continued insistence on human rights	
7 Negotiation skills	

Notes

1 According to the Glossary of the International Organisation for Migration (IOM), a readmission agreement is an agreement that addresses procedures for one State to return aliens in an irregular situation to their home State or a State through which they passed en route to the State that seeks to return them.

2 In this chapter, the concepts of European Community (EC) and the European Union (EU) are used interchangeably, as it is the EC that signs readmission agreements.

3 To be precise, a Resolution of the European Parliament on the right of asylum had already highlighted the need for economic and political co-operation with countries of origin in order to stabilise their economies and to guarantee the protection of human rights in 1987 (European Parliament, 1987, paras B–E) (Lavenex, 2006, p. 233).

4 Indeed, external relations assistance programmes such as TACIS (Eastern Europe), CARDS (Western Balkans) and MEDA (Mediterranean countries) have also financed action in the field of asylum and migration. These cannot be considered in this chapter for lack of space.

5 As Boswell (2008) has argued, there have been divisions within the Commission itself, amongst various Directorates-General (DGs). However, this is beyond the scope of this book.

6 Interviews (PR 3, 7, 8, 9, 12, and 16) confirmed the fact that certain member states were in favour of the proposal, at least in principle. However, individually this was not confirmed by their Permanent Representation.

8

The Lisbon Treaty and the institutionalisation of the Area of Freedom, Security and Justice

The Lisbon Treaty and the constitutionalisation of the European Union

When final result showed 67.1 per cent of Irish voters in favour of the Lisbon Treaty, with 32.9 per cent voting against, Irish political elites were visibly relieved. Irish Taoiseach Brian Cowen celebrated that 'today we have done the right thing for our own future and the future of our children' (Euractiv, 3 October 2009). Irish Foreign Minister Michael Martin concurred: 'I am delighted for the country.' Thus, fortunes reversed by a massive 20 per cent swing towards the 'yes' campaign compared to the first Lisbon referendum in June 2008. Voter turnout was up by 6 per cent to reach 58 per cent. European Commission President José Manuel Barroso celebrated that the support for the treaty 'shows the value of European solidarity and I am really glad with the result we are receiving from Ireland … it shows the very positive response that Europe is bringing to the economic and financial crisis.' In agreement, Guy Verhofstadt, leader of the Liberal ALDE group in the European Parliament and former Belgian Prime Minister expressed his joy:

> Today is a beautiful day for Europe. Today is the first day of a new future for Europe, united, democratic, effective and strong. With this new Treaty the European Union will be able to tackle important problems such as the financial and economic crisis in a more European, coherent and effective way. We will be able to speak with one voice in the world and to provide the answers our citizens need. (*Ibid.*)

Jerzy Buzek, President of the European Parliament, even suggested that 'Europe is back on track' (*Euractiv*, 3 October 2009).

However, the road to the entry into force of the Lisbon Treaty has been very long and hard. The aim of this section is to establish the larger context in which the Lisbon Treaty has been negotiated, before analysing its precise details related to the AFSJ. The Lisbon Treaty has evolved out of the rejected 'Treaty establishing a Constitution for Europe' and is part of what is commonly referred to as the process of treaty reform. This includes all EU treaties from the Treaty of Rome (1957) to the Single European Act (1986), the Maastricht Treaty (1992), the Amsterdam Treaty (1997), and the Nice

Treaty (2001). However, very soon after the Nice Treaty was signed, the so-called 'post-Nice process' was launched to start a significant debate about the future of Europe (Christiansen and Reh, 2009). Christiansen (2008) suggests that this debate about a 'European Constitution' was deeply embedded in an active process of politicisation by EU elites, in particular the inclusion of language, symbols and other trappings of statehood in that particular treaty. The outcome of this debate was first included in the Convention on the Future of Europe, which provided the blueprint for the Constitutional Treaty (CT). However, when the treaty was rejected in two separate referenda in France and the Netherlands in 2005, a 'period of reflection', followed by another Intergovernmental Conference (IGC), led to the Lisbon Treaty, signed on 13 December 2007.

Christiansen and Reh analyse the process of treaty reform as a process of 'constitutionalisation' (Christiansen and Reh, 2009, p. 4) on the basis of three major premises: (1) constitutionalisation is a continuous process whereby Europe's normative basis is being transformed driven by formal and informal, explicit and implicit mechanisms, with each reform being connected to the previous one, (2) treaty reform is an important mechanism behind constitutionalisation, amongst others, and (3) constitutionalisation is a struggle between various actors over institutional choices overlapping with EU policy-making. Further, they distinguish between three different key mechanisms in this process: (1) formal and explicit constitutionalisation, which is the process most closely modelled on the domestic constitution-founding experience, leading to a 'European *finalité*' (the Constitutional Treaty falling into this category), (2) formal and implicit constitutionalisation, which is the process which generates an 'EU constitutional order' through international treaties whereby the legal order increasingly moves away from traditional international law (successive EU treaties from Rome, to Maastricht, Amsterdam, Nice and Lisbon), and (3) informal and incremental constitutionalisation, which de facto move the EU's legal order towards a constitutional order without relying on EU treaty reform (such as European Court of Justice verdicts).

Christiansen and Reh (2009) conclude that the process of formal and explicit 'constitutionalisation' failed. This links to the argument advanced by Christiansen (2008) that the experiment of 'politicisation' of treaty reform was unsuccessful. The constitutional debate had been a radical departure from the previous practice of avoiding politicisation at all costs. Yet, the success of the Lisbon Treaty indirectly confirms also the failure of the Constitutional Treaty. Reforming the treaties of the EU is possible only under conditions of low politicisation, despite the lessons of Nice which had seemed to indicate that a greater involvement of the European public would be beneficial for the European integration project (Christiansen, 2008).

How did the EU reach this point at which Lisbon, the failure of the formal and explicit constitutionalisation, would be seen as a success in Brussels? At the very minimum it is still a formal and implicit step towards greater European integration via treaty reform. Initially, the outcomes of Nice were perceived as questionable, in both content and process in which they had been negotiated. The actual experience of the final summit was damaging, when negotiators bargained for three entire days (and nights) over the final issues, and were perceived to be more concerned with individual member state interests than 'European' interests as a whole. Consequently, the Nice summit ended in Declaration 23, intended to launch a wider debate about the 'Future of Europe' (Christiansen, 2008, p. 40). Belgium, the EU Council Presidency in the second half of 2001, ensured a 'maximalist' interpretation of the post-Nice process. The decision to entrust the preparation of an Intergovernmental Conference (IGC) to a Convention was taken in Laeken (Norman, 2003, p. 24). This Convention started in February 2002 and produced the first incomplete draft of the Constitutional Treaty (CT) on the 13 June 2003 in time for the Thessaloniki Council a week later. Subsequently, the Convention gained two more sessions to finish by 10 July 2003 for some 'purely technical' (ibid., p. 301) work. Under the Irish Presidency, the IGC finally approved the CT on the 18 June 2004.

The participants of the Constitutional Convention were of considerable significance. Valery Giscard d'Estaing, a former French President, was nominated as the chairman of the Convention, with Jean-Luc Dehaene and Guiliano Amato, former Prime Ministers of Belgium and Italy respectively, as vice-chairs. Sir John Kerr, a former UK Permanent Representative with excellent connections to the British establishment, was appointed as Secretary General. Thus, the Convention had considerable and clear political and administrative leadership (Christiansen, 2008, p. 40). The Convention was composed of national governments, members of the European Commission, and members of national parliaments and the European Parliament. While members of the Convention organised themselves in different sectoral working groups, the Convention can be seen as a top-down affair with the 'Presidium', bringing together the twelve key members of the Convention, steering the drafting of the treaty (ibid., p. 40).

In the end, the Convention managed to set the agenda decisively for the Constitutional IGC. The IGC had the formal powers to decide on treaty reform, and followed the Convention in most respects. The Italian Presidency during the IGC in the second half of 2003 followed more or less a strategy of avoiding reopening individual articles. While it practically failed in December 2003, it handed over the same strategy to the Irish Presidency, which succeeded in June 2004. However, as Christiansen suggests (2008, p. 41), given the constitutional aspirations of the CT, the Convention created significant public interest in a large number of member states, which subsequently made referenda a much-used method of ratification. Spain, France, the Netherlands, Britain, Ireland, Luxemburg, Portugal, Sweden, Denmark, and Poland all agreed to hold referenda in order to ratify the CT. However, during their respective referenda, on 29 May 2005 France voted 'No' with 55 per cent, on 1 June 2005 the Netherlands voted 'No' with 62 per cent, and, subsequently, Britain froze ratification of the Treaty on 6 June 2005. Subsequently, the feeling across member states became clear that France and the Netherlands were so central to the European integration project that the treaty would have to be renegotiated, deemed necessary and possible (ibid., p. 42). The Commission identified a gap in the communication between the EU and its citizens, which was aimed to be filled through a programme of dialogue between citizens and elites, the so-called 'Plan D'.

The European Council summit of 17 and 18 June 2005 decided that a 'reflection period' lasting until 2007 was necessary, which would enable a renegotiation of the Treaty before the June 2009 European Parliamentary election. As a result of this reflection, the Lisbon Treaty was signed by the Heads of State or Government in December 2007. While the precise AFSJ content of the signed Lisbon Treaty will be discussed in the next section, it is notable that the vast majority of provisions of the CT were also included in the Lisbon Treaty (LT). This is especially remarkable for the AFSJ (Donnelly, 2008).

However, how important are supranational actors in EU Treaty reform? Christiansen (2002) challenges aspects of Moravcsik's theory of liberal intergovernmentalism (1998) in this context. He explains the limits of 'intergovernmental bargaining', as the process of treaty reform includes a wider process of issue-framing, agenda-setting, decision-making, as well as implementation and legitimation. This implies that the whole policy process prior to the Intergovernmental Conference can be seen as part and parcel of the bargaining itself. Indeed, taking this point seriously, this book examines the role of European institutions is in both arenas: (1) the policy-making in the AFSJ as outlined in the previous chapters, and (2) treaty reform and the AFSJ in this chapter. Yet, 'can faceless bureaucrats, unelected and without power of purse or sword really influence the decisions of powerful nation-states? Are we seeing the emergence of a "new statecraft" grounded in international networks managed by supranational political entrepreneurs?' (Moravcsik, 1999a).

Moravcsik (1999a) certainly questions whether unelected bureaucrats without financial and legal enforcement powers would actually be able to influence political decisions made by national governments. Yet, this debate has produced different outcomes (Haas, 1958, 1964, 1967; Lindberg, 1963; Lindberg and Scheingold, 1970, 1971; Puchala, 1971, 1984; Moravcsik, 1999a; Hix, 1994, 1998; Pollack, 1997a, b, 2003; Tallberg, 2002, 2003, 2006, 2008; Beach, 2004b, 2005a; Stone Sweet and Sandholtz, 1997, 1998; Stone Sweet et al., 2001; Kaunert, 2005, 2007, 2009). When examining the role of European institutions in detail, notably through the prism of Supranational Political Entrepreneurship (SPE), this book builds on the conceptual framework put forward by John Kingdon (1984).

This chapter investigates the role of EU institutional actors at the treaty level in the process of constructing an 'AFSJ'. What is the role of the European institutions, in particular the Commission, in this treaty-building process? This chapter argues that the Commission in particular (through alliances with other institutional actors during the Convention phase) managed to incrementally contribute to a shift in norms. This shift derived from the policy-making level from 1999 onwards. It manifested itself specifically during the negotiations of the Constitutional Treaty and the subsequent renegotiation of the Lisbon Treaty. Here, the Commission acted with the support and the use of other supranational actors during the Convention, without which this result would have been difficult, if not impossible, to obtain. Thus, the role of EU institutional actors is significant for as long as they act in unison. Firstly, the chapter will deal with the main advances of the Constitutional Treaty which resulted in the Lisbon Treaty. Subsequently, the role of the Commission and other EU institutional actors will be examined. Finally, this will lead to an overall evaluation.

The Lisbon Treaty, the Constitutional Treaty and the AFSJ

Monar (2005) claims that future historians are likely to regard the EU's creation of the AFSJ as one of the most significant developments in the European integration process. He bases these claims on three considerations. Firstly, the creation of the AFSJ touches upon essential functions and prerogatives of the modern nation-state. Secondly, the area touches upon a number of very sensitive political issues. And thirdly, the area is now one of significant growth and development of EU action.

But what precisely are the advances with regards to the Lisbon Treaty (LT)? Whatever the achievements of the treaty in other areas, the main focus of this section is on the relevant part of the AFSJ institutional architecture in the LT. The following section will analyse the finally agreed text of both the Constitutional Treaty and it will substantiate the argument that the Lisbon Treaty remained substantially the same 'beast' as the Constitutional Treaty (CT), at least regarding the AFSJ, though it even went beyond its advances.

The final draft of the CT relied very significantly on the report produced by the Working Group X of the Convention (CONV 426/02), which provided the rationale for the draft treaty section. The final outcome (Conference, CIG 87/04, 2004) in this section was not significantly different from the draft. An analysis of the final report of the working group (CONV 426/02) confirms that the normative question of whether the EU should be legislating is now settled for decision-makers. The introduction starts by referring to the normative rationale of the Tampere conclusions:

> If the European Union is to win the maximum support of its citizens, it must show that it can deliver concrete results on issues that really matter. The

> Convention will be deemed to be a success if it is seen to have put in place means to ensure that freedom can be enjoyed in conditions of security and justice is accessible to all. (CONV 426/02, 2002, p. 1)

Again, this emphasises the main objectives put forward by Tampere. Yet, it even goes one step further when proclaiming a 'proper sense of European Public Order' (ibid., p. 2).

General provisions

The Lisbon Treaty amends two separate bodies of treaties: (1) the Treaty on European Union (TEU), and (2) the Treaty on the Functioning of the Union (TFEU). The latter, replacing the current Treaty establishing the European Community (TEC), contains the title 'AFSJ'. It includes five chapters and brings together the currently dispersed AFSJ policies (Carrera and Geyer, 2008).

Article 3(2) TEU (formerly Article I-3 CT; Conference, CIG 87/04, 2004, p. 15) elevates the 'AFSJ' to become an objective with the same status as the Internal Market (Article 3 (3) TEU).

> The Union shall offer its citizens an area of freedom, security and justice without internal frontiers, in which the free movement of persons is ensured in conjunction with appropriate measures with respect to external border controls, asylum, immigration, and the prevention and combating of crime.

The very first time in the history of the EU, the AFSJ has been legally attributed the same status as the single market.

EU legal competences in the AFSJ are now clarified. Article 4(2j) TFEU (formerly Article I-13 CT; under B. Specific amendments, pp. 46–47) puts the area as one of shared competences. Article 2(2) TFEU (formerly Article I-11(2) CT; under B. Specific amendments, p. 45) stipulates:

> When the Treaties confers on the Union a competence shared with the Member States in a specific area, the Union and the Member States may legislate and adopt legally binding acts in that area. The Member States shall exercise their competence to the extent that the Union has not exercised its competence. The Member States shall again exercise their competence to the extent that the Union has decided to cease exercising its competence.

The article thus states that once the Union has legislated in the area, member states are bound to that legislation, which creates a pre-emptive legal effect. Thus, member states can no longer exercise full legal sovereignty in the area from that point onwards.

Furthermore, the Lisbon Treaty creates a simplified decision-making procedure (Carrera and Geyer, 2008). Firstly, the pillar structure will be formally abolished, which results in the communitarisation of the areas of criminal justice, policing and terrorism. Secondly, the standard decision-making procedure in the AFSJ will be co-decision according to article 294 TFEU (present Article 251 TEC) and qualified majority voting (QMV) in the

Council. This gives the European Parliament joint decision-making power. Thus, an important number of measures concerning issues like border controls, immigration and asylum, will be taken by qualified majority vote in the Council. The Commission will be given the exclusive power to propose legislation. In criminal justice and policing legislation, the latter power is shared with a quarter of the member states. This is in line with the stipulations in the CT (Article III-396). In addition, national parliaments will be more involved in the EU's AFSJ policies. The Lisbon Treaty goes beyond the Constitutional Treaty in relation to national parliaments' role in scrutinising the principles of subsidiarity and proportionality.

Thirdly, the disappearance of the pillar structure leads to a commonality of legal instruments between titles that were formerly pillar one and pillar three. In the LT, this is achieved under the name 'ordinary legislative procedure'. It is important to note that for the first time the Union can use the 'ordinary legislative procedure' in principle for the whole area. But rather than a case-by-case approach, as agreed in the Amsterdam Treaty, this is the first time that it is recognised as a principle. Nonetheless, instead of using the new terms of the CT, i.e. European laws, European framework laws, European regulations, the LT will retain the traditional community instruments, i.e. regulations, directives, decisions, etc. The Amsterdam instruments, i.e. framework decisions, common positions, conventions, etc., will disappear. Judicial control will be expanded by applying the normal court rules on the European Court of Justice's jurisdiction to all AFSJ matters in all member states (including the possibility for all national courts or tribunals to send questions to the ECJ).

Finally, the legal status of the Charter of Fundamental Rights of the Union will be clearer for the majority of member states. The new Article 6 TEU will provide a cross-reference to the Charter on Fundamental Rights which renders the Charter directly legally binding for the European institutions, Union bodies, offices and agencies as well as member states when they implement Union law (except those that have exceptions to various degrees, such as Britain, Ireland and Poland). This will put EU actors and member states under a clear legal obligation to ensure that fundamental rights are respected and will thus strengthen the freedom dimension of the AFSJ.

Asylum, migration, and civil law

In the areas of asylum, migration and external border controls (art. 77–80TFEU), significant new competences are transferred to the EU level (Carrera and Geyer, 2008). Legally, according to the Amsterdam and Nice Treaties, it is only possible to legislate on minimum standards for asylum measures. Given that the Tampere conclusion demanded a much broader objective, this requires a legal change of the treaties to make it possible. Thus, this involves a further transfer of competences to the EU level. The Lisbon Treaty (as well as the Constitutional Treaty) provides the competence to adopt, acting in accordance with the ordinary legislative procedure, laws for a uniform status of asylum valid throughout the Union, a uniform status of subsidiary protection, a common system of temporary protection, common procedures for the subsidiary protection, standards for reception conditions (formerly only minimum standards), and partnership and co-operation with third countries for the purpose of managing inflows of people. These are identical to the new objectives of the Tampere, and are now enshrined in the Lisbon Treaty.

The areas of migration and illegal migration bring similar new competences for the EU, in particular the combating of trafficking in persons, which did not even feature in the Convention draft. In addition, according to the LT (and previously the CT), incentives for integration measures for third-country nationals can now be legislated by the EU. Both treaties also provide for a burden-sharing mechanism within the EU member states.

Similarly, the competences of the Union in civil law matters have increased. Firstly, the Lisbon Treaty and the Constitutional Treaty provide the EU with competences over cross-border civil matters based on the principle of mutual recognition. The list of objectives has been clearly expanded. However, despite the general simplification of decision-making procedures, family law remains outside this communitarised framework, and maintains the old unanimity rule in the Council and the Parliament consultation procedure. In fact, it is one of the last remaining intergovernmental areas of the AFSJ. This relates to the fact that the concept of family still remains very differently understood in the different member states – notably with regard to same-sex marriage. Going beyond the intergovernmental character in the Constitutional Treaty, the Lisbon Treaty makes this provision even slightly more intergovernmental by including a provision requiring the Commission to notify national parliaments regarding proposals in this area. This provision also provides national parliaments with an effective veto right by making their opposition known within six months.

Criminal justice, policing and counter-terrorism

The Lisbon Treaty (as well as previously the Constitutional Treaty) constitutes a big leap forward towards the full communitarisation, i.e. the full transfer of the competences to the Union level, for the area of criminal justice, policing and counter-terrorism (Articles 82–89 TFEU). The provision regarding procedural criminal law, which is often mentioned as one of the cornerstones in developing mutual trust among member states, stipulate the following:

- Article 82(1a, b, c) TFEU opens up the legal possibility to establish rules and procedures to ensure the recognition of all forms of judgements and judicial decisions throughout the union, to prevent and settle conflicts of jurisdiction, and to support the training of the judiciary.

- Article 82(2a, b, c, d) TFEU provides the competences to establish minimum rules in criminal matters with a cross-border dimension. This concerns the admissibility of evidence, the rights of individuals in criminal procedure, the rights of victims of crimes, and any other aspect of criminal procedure for which the Council has adopted a unanimous European decision in advance.
- Hence, this includes potentially every aspect of criminal procedure, as long as the Council identifies a cross-border dimension. This catch-all paragraph gives the legal possibility to extend Union competences in the field of procedural criminal law quite far.

Article 83 TFEU opens up the legal possibility for the union to establish minimum rules concerning the definition of criminal offences and sanctions. It then lists the areas where these definitions would fall into: terrorism, trafficking in human beings and sexual exploitation of women and children, illicit drug trafficking, arms trafficking, money laundering, corruption, counterfeiting of means of payments, computer crime and organised crime. This list is significantly more inclusive than the Amsterdam Treaty. In addition, the Council can adopt a unanimous European decision to include more crimes to this list. This is again the same catch-all clause as in procedural criminal law, which can push EU competences quite far.

Consequently, the area of criminal justice has been effectively communitarised, and the EU has acquired legal competence over a whole set of new areas. These are legally extendable without a change in the LT, but by unanimous Council decision. Therefore, the normative +question has been conclusively answered for this aspect of the AFSJ; indeed, for EU and national decision-makers, the EU should be legislating in the area.

However, there is a drawback to this in the area due to the so-called 'emergency brake' and 'accelerator' procedures – two of the compromises of the Constitutional Treaty IGC, which have been slightly modified for the Lisbon Treaty ('less brake and more accelerator').

- Paragraph 3 of Article 82 and 83 TFEU provides the 'emergency brake' in both the aforementioned articles. A member of the Council can refer the framework law to the European Council – which decides by unanimity and thus keeps some form of veto – but only if an aspect of that law affects a fundamental aspect of its criminal justice system. The framework law then remains suspended for four months. Yet, this provision is restrictive, and the European Court of Justice (ECJ) could potentially establish case law regarding the definition of what constitutes a fundamental aspect of a national system. In the CT, the European Council could decide to terminate the suspension and continue the negotiations, or demand a new draft. However, in the LT, the European Council 'shall, within four months of the suspension (after discussion and in case of consensus), refer the draft back to the Council, which shall terminate the suspension of the ordinary legislative procedure'.

- Paragraph 4 provides for the so-called 'accelerator'. If after the four months no decision can be made by unanimity (CT and LT), or after twelve months no new framework has been adopted (not in the LT anymore), then an accelerated form of enhanced co-operation can start. This means that nine member states (LT; one-third of the member states in the CT) could go ahead and adopt the legislation for themselves. Authorisation would be automatically granted through the fulfilment of this paragraph. De facto, this means that the national veto will no longer exist in the area of criminal justice. Yet, instead of a veto, this area creates a de facto 'opt-out' possibility for every member state – with restrictions possibly established by a future ECJ decision.

According to Article 87 TFEU, the EU shall establish police co-operation involving all the member state's competent authorities, including police, customs, and law enforcement. According to the ordinary legislative procedure, the EU may establish measures concerning the collection, storage, processing, analysis, and exchange of relevant information, as well as support for the training of staff and staff exchange, and common investigative techniques in the detection of serious forms of crime. According to the special legislative procedure (i.e. unanimity in the Council), the EU may also establish operational co-operation between the above authorities. In the original CT, this was a strict unanimity provision, which meant this operational co-operation had not been communitarised. However, the Lisbon Treaty goes a step further than the Constitutional Treaty, and introduces an element of the accelerator analysed for the area of criminal justice. In the absence of unanimity in the Council, nine member states may send this measure to the European Council, which needs to send it back to the Council after four months. In case of continuing disagreement, nine member states may then proceed on the basis of enhanced co-operation, and the authorisation for enhanced co-operation is deemed to apply automatically. This means, in the area of operational police co-operation, these are the first attempts at communitarisation, though through the mechanism of enhanced co-operation. Thus, the Lisbon Treaty is a significant advance to the Constitutional Treaty in the area of operational police co-operation, which was already an advance to the Amsterdam and Nice Treaties in the area of data exchange.

In addition, the status of Europol has been strengthened in both the LT and the CT – though much more cautiously – as Europol no longer just facilitates co-operation. Its future mission indicates that it will support and strengthen action by member state police authorities. This implies a wider mandate than before. The precise extent of this mandate will be determined by the ordinary legislative procedure (LT). Again, this implies the EU should legislate in the area; not to replace national police, but to complement it. In addition, Europol will become fully accountable to the European Parliament together with national parliaments. However, any operational activity must be in agreement with national police authorities, and coercive measures are excluded from their list of responsibilities.

Furthermore, the Lisbon Treaty (as well as the CT) creates the legal possibility of establishing a European Public Prosecutor out of Eurojust under Article 86 TFEU. Initially, the competences of such a prosecutor would be related to crimes affecting the financial interests of the Union. However, paragraph 4 provides the legal possibility to amend the competences by a unanimous European decision to include serious crimes with a cross-border dimension. This paragraph was added in the CT Intergovernmental Conference and did not feature in the original Convention draft. The function of such an office would include the investigation, prosecution and bringing to justice the perpetrators and accomplices of serious crimes. It would exercise the functions of a prosecutor in a national court. This would be decided unanimously by the Council with the consent of the European Parliament. However, the Lisbon Treaty goes even beyond the Constitutional Treaty. In paragraph 1 (Article 86 TFEU), two new paragraphs have been added to circumvent the unanimity requirement through the 'accelerator procedure' in order to establish this European Public Prosecutor. Again, as the case above, in the absence of unanimity in the Council, nine member states may send this measure to the European Council, which needs to send it back to the Council after four months. In case of continuing disagreement, nine member states may then proceed on the basis of enhanced co-operation, and the authorisation for enhanced co-operation is deemed to apply automatically. This means the likelihood of establishing a European Public Prosecutor is much increased in the Lisbon Treaty compared to the Constitutional Treaty. Thus, the Lisbon Treaty is a significant advance in this area.

Indeed, were such an institution created at any point in time – for which there is now a legal competence of the Union – this would be the most radical step towards a 'European Public Order'. The Charter of Fundamental Rights is now also included in the LT and can be considered an integral part of the new legal framework. By fully incorporating the Charter, the treaty clearly creates a better basis for the comprehensive protection of fundamental rights at the EU level. Despite the insistence by the British government to make it 'toothless', most Commission lawyers interpret it as very powerful. In fact, they are expecting important future judgements by the European Court of Justice (interview COM 10). All advances taken together, define important elements of a foundation stone of an emerging European Public Order.

Finally, the introduction of an explicit principle of solidarity into the context of AFSJ legislation is one of the most significant innovations of the Lisbon Treaty. The creation of a solidarity clause can have important implications on the AFSJ. The clause stipulates that in the case of a terrorist attack or a natural or man-made disaster the Union shall act jointly to mobilise all instruments at their disposal. It clarifies how this procedure would occur in practice. Firstly, it would require a European decision by the Council on a proposal from the Commission and the High Representative for Foreign Affairs for cases with military implications. In addition, the European Council is now legally required to regularly assess the threats facing the Union in order to take effective action. One could imagine scenarios where a 'man-made disaster' could mobilise either the police or the judiciary within the EU. Clear avenues have opened so that this legal competence could be used not only for catastrophes, but also for terrorist attacks and, thus, present emerging opportunities for a European Public Order to resemble more closely to a European Homeland Security.

In conclusion, the normative question has now been conclusively answered as a political consensus of decision-makers; the EU should be legislating in the AFSJ. Why? The political aims are clear and enshrined in the Lisbon Treaty. The substantial legal advances underline the fact that, for decision-makers, the EU should legislate in the AFSJ. The area is one of shared competences between the EU and the member states – which effectively transfer highly significant competences to the EU level. This occurred throughout all substantial parts of the area: asylum, migration, civil and criminal law, and even to some extent police co-operation. Indeed, the AFSJ has experienced its biggest advances in historical terms. The AFSJ is the 'big winner' of the Lisbon Treaty.

The role of the EU institutions

This section will analyse the role of the European Commission, acting to initiate and push for a process of normative change among EU decision-makers, as well as concrete institutional change, which is both part of its role as a supranational policy entrepreneur.

Prior to the Convention: Commission entrepreneurship by officials?

According to Sir Adrian Fortescue (1995), then the Director of the General Secretariat of the Commission and later the first head of the JHA Directorate of the Commission, in the early days the Commission had been under close scrutiny by the European Parliament and by the Council of Ministers, but for opposing reasons. On the one hand, member states tended to see the Commission as a competence-maximising institution that, in their view, lacked credible expertise in the area. On the other hand, the European Parliament tended to see the Commission's ambitions as too modest, and suspected it of pleasing member states too much.

Consequently, Fortescue (1995) argues that it needed to square the circle, not to be torn between these different expectations in the process of establishing its credibility. This was initially done through communication papers rather than legislative proposals in order to open the public debate on some subjects and in order to work against the prevailing image of working behind closed doors. In the abstract, this can be seen as attempts to change underlying norms rather than jumping into the bargaining directly.

At the beginning of co-operation in the 1980s, the European Commission had to force its way into the area and had to push strongly for any role at all. The key moment in the evolution of the EU's role in the area of Justice and Home Affairs, according to Fortescue (interview COM 25), was, when in 1985, instead of just talking about the internal market as a place in which goods and services circulated, the Commission was the first to start putting forward the phrase 'Europe without frontiers'. This can be demonstrated by examining Lord Cockfield's famous 1985 White Paper on completing the internal market (Commission (85) 210 final).

The Commission started to focus institutionally on 'Europe without borders' in 1989 when it appointed Fortescue (interview COM 25) and one other person to begin thinking through the consequences of getting rid of frontier controls. Fortescue's initial small team of people was transformed into what came to be known as the Justice and Home Affairs Task Force, but it was still located in the Secretariat General. Initially, the Commission had to bring in national experts from the member states. This created a network of great advantage for the Commission in its strategy. This link between the national and supranational was vital in order to establish trust and legitimacy vis-à-vis member states.

However, in the early days, the Commission had limits imposed upon what it could do legally; in particular, its usual right of initiative had to be shared with the member states, thus not being able to guarantee that its proposals rather than the ones suggested by member states received attention. The Commission was consequently forced to always table a better and more competitive proposal than any member state would and could. The interviews with permanent representations of twenty-four member states confirmed the fact that the Commission was able to do this during the Tampere programme (interviews PR 1 to PR 24). Indeed, each member state confirmed that the proposals of the Commission, in general, were of much higher quality than any other state's proposal. This implies that there was a clear and widespread acknowledgement of the expertise that the Commission had acquired over the years.

This was particularly attributed to Commissioner Vitorino (1999–2004 Commission), but it was largely confirmed by member states representatives in to be present throughout the Commission services. All permanent representations (interviews PR 1 to PR 24) unanimously confirmed that it did not matter that the Commission had to share their right of initiative because it would almost always table the proposal of the highest quality anyway. In addition, the Commission scored very highly regarding its negotiations skills throughout the Tampere process (interviews PR 1 to PR 24 and NGO 1 to NGO 11). This is particularly true for the Commissioner Vitorino, who was unanimously applauded for his efforts by everyone – all member states and all NGOs. Thus, there is a unanimous acceptance of the central role of the Commission in the future direction of the AFSJ (interviews PR 1 to PR 24).

Yet, the Commission's position also depends on its legitimacy towards civil society, and on the input it receives from civil society. Indeed, it worked very hard over the years to build up good relations with the plethora of non-governmental organisations (NGOs) in the field of AFSJ (interviews NGO 1 to NGO 11). There are instances where important actors of NGOs had even become important members of the services in the Commission (interview COM 16). Consequently, this led to a widespread support for a communitarisation of AFSJ matters by NGOs (interviews NGO 1 to NGO 11). In addition, NGOs provided it with invaluable supplementary input of information through informal information channels and job changes. Consequently, they represented an important ally for the Commission, and were thus invited to participate in the Future of Europe debate for civil society in parallel with the Convention that drew up the first draft of the Constitutional Treaty. This gave increased weight to the Commission's position in the Convention and perceived legitimacy.

The European Commission had another strong natural ally throughout the years in its efforts to supranationalise the AFSJ with the European Parliament (interviews EP 1 to EP 5) and the Committee on Citizens' Freedoms and Rights, Justice and Home Affairs (Commission des libertés et des droits des citoyens, de la justice et des affaires intérieures, LIBE). The alliance with the European Parliament is of particular importance regarding the LT, as a significant number of MEPs were also in the Convention that drafted the CT. The EP, as the only directly elected institution of the EU, was best placed to support changes to the treaties on the grounds of efficiency, accountability and democracy, and support the Commission in its efforts. From the interviews (EP 1 to EP 5, COM 1 to COM 25, PR 1 to PR 24), it is important to note that the relations between the Parliament and the Commission are perceived to be very good by both sides, contrary to the relations between the Parliament and the Council. It also helped that the Commissioner Vitorino (1999–2004) had previously been the chairman of the LIBE Committee in the European Parliament (1994–1999). His knowledge, skills and political credit with the EP have been vital elements of the Commission's success.

In conclusion, the normative advancements of the AFSJ can be directly related to the strategy employed by the Commission throughout the 1990s, but in particular its constructive role during the Tampere programme. It adopted a strategy of pragmatism and trust-building and was very successful with it. It is evident from the interviews that the Commission has managed to manoeuvre itself into the centre of the area and managed to create and maintain trust from all sides. It has managed to establish trust with the twenty-seven member states, as well as maintain the trust it had been endowed with by civil society represented by the plethora of NGOs in Brussels. Moreover, it had its natural ally – the European Parliament – by its side in this battle.

The run-up to the Convention, 2002–2003

Why was the IGC prepared by a Convention for the first time in the history of the EU? According to Christiansen (2002), this is important in order to appreciate the role that the Commission played in the process of treaty-building. Derek Beach (2005a), in his comparative study across five different EU treaties, suggests the fact that the 'convention method' was used before a subsequent IGC was already quite a revolutionary procedural change (ibid., p. 178). According to Beach (ibid.), this method had been pushed by the Commission, the European Parliament, and federalist-oriented governments. The work of the Convention was divided into three phases: (1) listening from the start in early 2002 until the summer of the same year, (2) studying working groups' discussions until autumn 2002, and (3) the final or deliberation phase until June 2003.

But what was the chain of events that led to this establishment? In 2001, the words 'convention' and 'constitution' were becoming buzzwords amongst decision-makers and were gradually gaining acceptance. The decisive move towards the Convention occurred during the second half of 2001 under the Belgian Presidency. Building on the rhetorical legacy of the aforementioned speeches, Belgian Prime Minister Verhofstadt managed to establish agreement on a Convention with the Laeken Council declaration of 15 December 2001 (ibid.).

Peter Ludlow (2002) demonstrates how two Commission documents were closely knit with the eventual Council declaration for the establishment of the European Convention. While the Laeken declaration appeared to condemn the EU for its problems, as a consequence the mandate for reform became rather wide. It portrayed Europe as being at a crossroads, claiming that the unification of Europe was near. A number of challenges were drawn out; in particular, how to bring EU citizens closer to the EU, how to better divide and define the competences of the EU, how to simplify the legal instruments, how to increase democracy, transparency and efficiency, and how to reorganise the treaties of the EU into one single constitution. It also set out the working mechanism of the Convention.

The most important Commission document mentioned in the Laeken declaration is the 'White Paper on Governance' (2001). A close examination of it reveals that it prepared some ground for the debate. It suggested better involvement of and more openness to citizens by the EU institutions, better policies, global governance, and refocused institutions. A large part of the document was on the Commission itself and how it can improve without any treaty change. Nonetheless, it asserted that the Commission alone cannot improve European governance (Commission, 2001, p. 9). Change required concerted action by all the European institutions, all its member states and civil society at large. And it defined five principles of good governance: openness, participation, accountability, effectiveness, coherence. In essence, this was an anticipation of the Laeken declaration.

Let us also recall the context of the Laeken declaration. It was only a number of months after the attacks of 11 September 2001. In speaking to the European Parliament, the commissioner responsible for Justice and Home Affairs and the Commission representative in the Convention, Antonio Vitorino, remarked soon afterwards:

> Terrorist acts are committed by international groups with bases in several countries, exploiting loopholes in the law created by the geographical limits on investigators and are often enjoying substantial financial and logistical resources. Terrorists take advantage of differences in legal treatment between States, in particular when the offence is not treated as such by national law and that is where we have to begin. (Norman, 2001)

In the aftermath of the terrorist attacks, the European Commission managed to construct European integration as a necessary policy tool to fight terrorism, as demonstrated in Chapter 4. Therefore, one must deduce that the European Commission was far from unimportant in framing the issues that went on to dominate the Convention. It constructed itself into the centre of the fight against terrorism on the one hand, and the fight for democracy and transparency on the other.

During the Convention, 2002–2003

But what was the role of the European Commission during this Convention? The notion of the Commission playing an important role in the Convention has been popularly caricatured by journalists who tend to cite the supposedly failed 'Penelope' feasibility study led by Commission President Romano Prodi (BBC, 5 December 2002). It is perceived as an attempt that antagonised member states rather than convinced them. Peter Norman (2003, p. 162) seems to echo those concerns. He describes how the Commission was internally divided over which drafts to push – its first contribution or Penelope.

Norman argues that the Commission's first document for the Convention (COM (2002) 247 final) was far from comprehensive. Yet, a close reading of both of the aforementioned documents with a focus on the AFSJ reveals another highly significant fact which raises doubts over the common interpretation of these by journalists. In fact, the documents could be described as focused and prioritising – with fewer but more important objectives. The main focus of the first document was the AFSJ. At the beginning, it argued that Europe had achieved a lot, in particular enlargement and the introduction of the euro. Then it prioritised the AFSJ as well as the Charter of

Fundamental Rights. It also asserted that integration in the AFSJ was strongly desired by public opinion. Consequently, the document spelled out a clear policy goal – the full communitarisation of the area.

Similarly, the 'Penelope' feasibility study of December 2002 can also be seen in this light, if one reads the parts on the AFSJ. Other than creating a supposed federalist vision of the EU, the study prioritised the AFSJ yet again. The aims and objectives were very much in line with the conclusions of the working group in the Convention. In fact, the draft articles in the document were not significantly different from the Convention draft. In some parts, the document even fell below the Convention draft in its ambitions. Needless to say, it did not contain some of the major compromises of the IGC of early 2004. Nonetheless, it was a highly significant paper for the AFSJ, which makes it difficult to sustain the argument that both the May and December studies of 2002 did not somewhat influence to debate in the Convention – at least for the AFSJ. The important question is – to what extent?

Derek Beach (2005a) examined the role of the different EU institutions during the Convention and the following IGC. His analysis provided a mixed picture of the Commission's leadership during the Convention. On the one hand, he suggests that the Penelope study 'alienated even its allies' (ibid., p. 199). On the other hand, he asserts that the Commission was able to influence better when playing a low-profile and realistic role. He suggests its successes included the Charter of Fundamental Rights.

Besides all the available policy documents, there is further significant evidence of the Commission's importance during the Convention:

Firstly, the choice of which commissioner would represent the institution in the Convention was not accidental, but rather led by a clear choice of priorities. Antonio Vitorino was chosen due to his prior involvement in the Convention which led to the Charter of Fundamental Rights, but also due to his legal expertise, and his responsibility and long-standing expertise in the AFSJ (interview COM 10). Overall, this was a reflection of the priorities of the Commission for the Constitution which was demonstrably reflected in their earlier documents. And it certainly did no harm that he was very well respected amongst member states (interviews PR 1 to PR 24), as demonstrated above.

Secondly, the commissioner's attendance record was impeccable and unsurpassed, thus providing ample opportunity to push the Commission's viewpoint. The Working Group X on the AFSJ met nine times from September to December 2002 (CONV 256/02). The Convention Secretariat provides the minutes of the meetings and the participants who attended. Examining all these documents, one may notice two people who attended every meeting. One was the chairman of the Working Group X, John Bruton, who had to attend every meeting in his chairing capacity. The second was the commissioner responsible for the AFSJ, Antonio Vitorino, who also attended every meeting. From this one can deduce that at the very least he acquired the best grasp of the ongoing negotiations. But more likely, this provided significant opportunities to push the Commission's arguments, both during the official debate and more informally with the individual working group members. It is not a huge surprise if constant attendance finally pays off in terms of substantive policy gains.

Thirdly, the selection of experts was favourably inclined towards the Commission's arguments. Amongst others, these included Mr de Brouwer, who was responsible for asylum and migration in the Commission, and Mr de Kerchove from the Council Secretariat, responsible for criminal justice and well known amongst decision-makers for his positive views towards further integration (interviews PR 1 to PR 24), now the EU's counter-terrorism co-ordinator. In addition, experts included EU representatives from Eurojust. Moreover, federalist-inclined academic scholars were also invited, such as Professor Henri Labayle, who has previously made forceful legal arguments for full communitarisation of the area. This certainly underlined the arguments already presented by the European Commission. In essence, the sum of all these people represented a policy community which was closely knit and favourably inclined towards further communitarisation of the AFSJ. Hence, as suggested by Kingdon (1984), in the problem stream where problems are defined, one can empirically encounter a close-knit policy community in which a supranational policy entrepreneur can shape the way problems are defined.

The intervention by Antonio Vitorino during the deliberation and his recommendations (Convention, 2002, WGX-WD14) were in line with previous documents and the advice given by his civil servants. The interventions advocated a full communitarisation of the AFSJ, including a common policy on asylum, a European immigration policy, a genuine area of justice both in civil and criminal law matters, enhanced police and judicial co-operation and full judicial oversight by the European Court of Justice. The Commission also submitted a document (Convention, 2002, WGX-WD27) on the European public prosecutor. In his changes to the final working group report draft (Convention, 2002, WGX-WD30), Antonio Vitorino reiterated some of the Commission priorities, including the EU Public Prosecutor and the policy objectives of the AFSJ. The Franco-German intervention (Convention, 2002, WGX-WD32) by Foreign Ministers Joseph Fischer and Dominique de Villepin resembled the prior contribution by the Commission.

But where in the debate do the final working group report and the final draft of the AFSJ article stand? Overall, the Commission had a significant impact first on the debate, then on the working group report, and finally on the final draft. The final outcome (Conference, 2004) for the AFSJ was not significantly different from the Convention draft. The final Convention draft relied significantly on the report produced by the Working Group X of the Convention (Convention, 2002, CONV 426/02), which provided the rationale for the draft treaty section. In turn, the working group report resembled the interventions of the European Commission. Thus, one can clearly trace the impact of the interventions made by the Commission.

Overall, Working Group X on the AFSJ proposed sweeping changes. It reinforced the drive for simplification of the treaties by proposing a common legal framework bringing all treaty provisions under a single title. It pushed for simplification of decision-making mechanisms, which meant a qualified majority vote in the Council in co-decision with the European Parliament. All major parts of the AFSJ were significantly strengthened. Mutual recognition of judicial decisions was eventually enshrined in the treaty, as advocated by the Commission. In order to make this possible, some legal harmonisation was included with regards to criminal and civil judicial co-operation – again in line with the Commission proposals.

In addition, there was consensus that unanimity voting in the Council could not be sustained after enlargement. To the annoyance of Commissioner Vitorino, the Commission now has to share its right of initiative with a quarter of the member states in parts of the former third-pillar areas. However, this is a small price to pay given that all interviewees suggest that the sharing of the right of initiative did not influence the Commission in a negative way (interviews PR 1 to PR 24). Even the Commission agreed with this assessment internally (COM 10). The working group report was divided over whether to create a European Public Prosecutor, but the final draft included the possibility of establishing one and hence fulfilled one of the most crucial aims of the Commission in the area (interview COM 10).

In conclusion, in the light of the evidence presented, one must deduce that the Commission with its representative, Antonio Vitorino, played a highly significant role during the Convention. It provided significant input papers before the Convention and shaped the discussion, despite some misunderstandings caused by Penelope. Indeed, the AFSJ had been a top priority from the beginning, which lasted until the end. Vitorino demonstrated a great amount of determination, full participation and a constant engagement in the debate. The Convention draft can certainly be seen as a victory for the Commission. Did member states change that during the course of the IGC?

During the CT Intergovernmental Conference, 2003–2004

The Intergovernmental Conference is the most difficult part to analyse for any researcher of the EU due to the lack of open source documents. In essence, this project had to rely on comparing the version of the draft before the IGC to the final version of the Constitutional Treaty. This was triangulated with some interviews (in particular COM 10), and some of the media coverage – which did not focus much on the details of the AFSJ.

IGCs are based upon Article 48 of the TEU (Beach, 2005a, p. 8). Governments of any member states may propose to the Council to amend existing treaties. They are convened either by agreement in the Council under

Article 48 TEU, or by a binding legal commitment included in the treaty. In the case of the CT, it was convened due to both the Laeken declaration and the commitment in the Nice Treaty. There are no formal provisions for how the agenda for an IGC should be prepared; here the agenda was already set by the Convention draft. Nonetheless, IGCs are formally outside of the institutional framework of the EU, thus effectively being an international/intergovernmental negotiation. While there are EU norms governing IGCs, all internal documents are under diplomatic secrecy.

How did the media report on the negotiations for the EU constitution with regards to the AFSJ? When the IGC started in September 2003, convention member expressed the hope the conference would only rubber-stamp the conventional draft. Nonetheless, media commentators suggested 'the constitution was in tatters' when the first summit in December 2003 under the Italian presidency failed due to the lack of compromise on voting weights (*Economist*, 16 December 2003). *The Economist* commented that after eighteen months of hard work by 105 delegates from twenty-five countries in the Convention, member-state negotiations collapsed by lunchtime on Saturday 13 December. The main disagreements had been between France and Germany on one side and Spain and Poland on the other over voting arrangements. At that point in time, this suggested the British had kept their so-called red lines. The Italian presidency accepted Tony Blair's insistence that member state countries keep their vetoes, amongst others, in judicial co-operation. This would suggest that the British had succeeded in redrafting parts of the articles on the AFSJ. A week prior to the summit, *The Economist* (11 December 2003) also suggested that Britain had strong reservations about the Charter of Fundamental Rights, and that the UK, Ireland, Sweden and Denmark also opposed the European Public Prosecutor and further criminal law harmonisation. Apparently, these issues did not end the negotiations.

An interview with a senior Commission official present at the negotiations in the Convention and during the IGC (COM 10) confirms that the British delegation had been the biggest obstacle in finding a solution for the outstanding issues in the AFSJ. According to him, they were supporting the Convention proposals during the Convention, which included a general move towards qualified majority voting throughout the area coupled with co-decision with the European Parliament. They also supported the jurisdiction of the European Court of Justice. During the Italian presidency in late 2003, the British delegation rediscovered their dislike of some of the advances in the area. In particular, this included the European Public Prosecutor (to which they had acquiesced previously), the move to qualified majority voting in the Council in the area of criminal justice, and the legal inclusion of the Charter of Fundamental Rights. Indeed, they had succeeded in redrafting some of the aforementioned articles, though not as fundamentally as the newspapers would suggest.

In February 2004, the European constitution was 'back from the dead'

(*Economist*, 5 February 2004). During the Irish Presidency, the negotiations had been quietly resurrected with a low-profile strategy by claiming that they were not able to do it until a year later. This is in contrast to the high-profile strategy by the Italians, absolutely wanting a deal under their Presidency. *The Economist* suggests that the parties who blocked a deal in December 2003 were then ready to talk again. By March 2004, all twenty-five member states had committed themselves to agreeing on a final text for the Constitution by their next summit on 17 and 18 June 2004 (*Economist*, 26 March 2004). Now with the Spanish and Polish delegation looking more likely to compromise on voting, the British red lines could become more difficult to maintain.

In the interview, the senior Commission official (COM 10) argues that the British delegation had again become the biggest obstacle just before the summit. Despite the fact that the media at the time claimed the UK was opposed to the European Public Prosecutor, the official asserted that the British had already accepted its inclusion just before the summit. Similarly, a solution for the legal inclusion of the Charter of Fundamental Rights had already been found as well – and the British agreed to the compromise. The remaining sticking point was therefore the move to qualified majority voting in the area of criminal justice. The British insisted on their principled opposition to it, while the Commission insisted that unanimity would be unacceptable. A large number of member states agreed with the Commission's arguments.

A compromise solution was found in the form of a so-called 'emergency brake'. The British wanted the latter to work in a way that would have meant that any member state could have blocked QMV by shifting the decision upwards to the European Council and its unanimity rule – on the legal grounds of a fundamental of national law being under threat. This would have effectively meant a continuation of unanimity in a different way. The Commission was fiercely opposed to that solution and the official predicted that the final solution would be different. He predicted – prior to the summit – that the eventual solution would also include an accelerator procedure. This would mean a member state could initially block QMV in the area of criminal justice. Yet, at the European Council, the decision would have to be sent back to the Council of Ministers within a tight deadline. The Commission was particularly insistent on this deadline. After that point, the accelerator would kick in – and the formerly blocking member state would be effectively excluded from the legislative procedure. Therefore, the fact that the prediction by the Commission official became a reality in June 2004 – only a month after the interview took place – is a highly significant piece of evidence. It clearly points to how closely involved Commissioner Vitorino was in the solution finding at the IGC, and how influential he was in pushing through his solutions. The remainder of the AFSJ institutional architecture did not change significantly compared to the Convention draft.

'Finally, a Constitution – Now the hard part' (*Economist*, 22 June 2004);

'A difficult birth' (*Economist*, 24 June 2004). Those headlines express the feelings of commentators after the agreement on the treaty. While the EU summit in Brussels did not nominate a Commission President on 18 June 2004, nonetheless it agreed on the Constitutional Treaty. The articles on the AFSJ remained significantly intact compared to the conventional draft, in particular due to the negotiation skills of Commissioner Vitorino and his staff. It has become apparent how much the Commission acted as an SPE throughout the whole constitutional process.

During the reflection period, 2005–2007

During their respective referenda, on 29 May 2005 France voted 'No' with 55 per cent, on 1 June 2005 the Netherlands voted 'No' with 62 per cent, and, subsequently, Britain froze ratification of the Treaty on 6 June 2005. The immediate reflex of the EU institutions was to persist with the ratification process, including Luxemburg with a 'yes' vote. However, as mentioned before, France and the Netherlands were so central to the EU that the treaty had to be renegotiated.

While the Commission developed the so-called 'Plan D' to improve communication between the EU and its citizens, the European Council Summit of 17 and 18 June 2005 decided that a 'reflection period' lasting until 2007 was necessary. This could then enable a renegotiation of the Treaty before the June 2009 European Parliamentary election. The Council conclusions (Luxembourg Presidency, 18 June 2005) asserted that the ratification would continue after a reflection period of one year. The conclusions alluded to the fact that ten member states by then had already successfully concluded ratification procedures. The Council, however, did not call into question the attachment of EU citizens to the construction of Europe. It was agreed that those member states wishing to continue ratification during this reflection period were free to do so, while other member states might respond differently. The Council decided to respond to all developments and make an overall assessment of the national debates on how to proceed by June 2006.

Despite this official reflection amongst member states in the hope of better domestic conditions for renegotiation and ratification, a possible renegotiation of the Constitutional Treaty was very much helped along by EU-level factors. These pre-empted the CT to some extent, and therefore made it easier to portray the Lisbon Treaty as less radical, especially in the AFSJ. Thus, in fact, it was possible to portray it as only a 'mini-treaty' in Sarkozy's words, or as it was called until the signing, a 'reform treaty'. This argument relies on two developments in 2005. Firstly, the so-called 'Hague programme' pre-empted the ratification of the CT to a large extent. Secondly, landmark decisions of the European Court of Justice on 16 June and 13 September 2005 created case law that solidified the advances made in the area of criminal justice. This legal precedent made ratification of the CT less necessary in order to achieve a similar institutional architecture.

Consequently, the treaty could be portrayed as less significant, and thereby ratifiable through parliament.

The Hague Programme

One of the key outputs of the Dutch Presidency of the EU in the second half of 2004 was the adoption of a new multi-annual programme, referred to as 'the Hague programme' on the AFSJ. It provided a new agenda for building on the recent policy and legislative achievements of the Tampere programme (1999–2004).

The programme abolished the requirement of unanimous voting in the Council on all EU immigration and asylum law, except illegal immigration. This also meant co-decision powers for the European Parliament. The exception was family law, which would still remain under unanimity. In fact, the programme itself did not abolish the voting requirements, as it is not legally binding and only a political commitment to act. The actual change in the decision-making rules was made by a Council decision, as it was urged by 'the Hague programme'. The Hague Programme pre-empted some of the innovations of the CT as it was based on the its compromises. The legal advances followed the relevant provisions of the Amsterdam Treaty and the Nice Treaty (Peers, 5 November 2004), which provided a so-called *passerelle* clause. As these legal changes brought about by 'the Hague programme' pre-empted the ratification of the CT, the need to ratify the same treaty to change the decision-making in the area of asylum and migration was much reduced.

European Court of Justice decisions

Furthermore, on 16 June and on the 13 September 2005, the European Court of Justice (ECJ, 16 June 2005) issued two groundbreaking judgments, which changed the legal instruments available in the area of criminal justice significantly. The so-called 'Pupino case' before the ECJ (ECJ, 16 June 2005) concerned an Italian nursery school teacher accused of maltreating a five-year-old child.

The judgement stated that a Council framework decision concerning police and judicial co-operation in criminal matters must be respected in a national criminal court case. Commission spokesman Martin Selmayr suggested consequently that this was a historic decision which would considerably strengthen the legal instruments available in the field of police and judicial co-operation in criminal matters (*Euractive*, 18 June 2005). Under the EU treaties as per Amsterdam and Nice, framework decisions adopted under the third pillar have no such direct effect – they cannot normally be directly invoked by individuals in national courts. However, the European Court of Justice (ECJ) pointed out that framework decisions are binding on member states in that they have a bearing on the interpretation of national law. Mueller (16 June 2005) explains how this fundamentally altered the legal instruments available for the EU in the area of criminal and judicial co-operation, one of the biggest advances of the CT (de facto de-pillarisation). This judgement significantly altered the legal instrument that were available under the previous treaties and changed them into instruments that are very close to what is available under the CT. This means, effectively, that the ECJ introduced elements of a de facto de-pillarisation.

The ECJ (ECJ, 16 June 05) noted in its verdict that the framework decision was adopted on the basis of the EU Treaty provisions regarding police and judicial co-operation in criminal matters, which means its jurisdiction to give a preliminary ruling, was subject to a declaration by a member state to accept that jurisdiction – which Italy made. The ECJ decided that the formulation of what is meant by a framework decision is sufficiently close to that of a 'Community directive' in the first pillar – despite its acknowledgement of the intergovernmental nature of the third-pillar instruments. It further stated that the second and third paragraphs of Article 1 of the Treaty on the European Union marked a new stage in a process of creating an ever closer union among the peoples of Europe. As it would be difficult for the Union to carry out its task effectively if the principle of loyal co-operation did not require third-pillar instruments to be binding (as directives are), they therefore would have to become binding. Thus, the court deduced that national law had to be interpreted as far as possible in the light of the wording of framework decisions. This effectively turned framework decisions into directives, which pre-empted the ratification of the CT to some extent.

Furthermore, the second landmark decision by the European Court of Justice (ECJ, 13 September 2005) also changed the nature of the legal instruments and decision-making procedures in criminal justice along the lines suggested by the CT (Castillo Garcia, 2005). In 2002, the Commission had tabled a proposal to step up environmental protection through the application of criminal sanctions in case of severe pollution after the oil tanker *Prestige* sank off the Galician coast of Spain. Brussels asked for environmental offences to be incorporated into the EC Treaty as part of its exclusive powers ('first pillar'). But member states in the EU Council of Ministers later amended the proposal and decided that environmental crime should instead be treated by EU member state governments on an ad hoc basis ('third pillar'). The landmark judgement by the European Court of Justice granted the Commission the power to require criminal sanctions for environmental offences. By finding that the adoption of criminal penalties in areas of Community policies was a matter for Community law – and not for intergovernmental co-operation – the judgement conferred on the European Parliament a decisive role in the adoption of such measures, whenever they are made in a field governed by co-decision. One of the major institutional consequences of this judgment was that the co-decision procedure would apply in areas which were previously subject to a procedure of unanimous voting in the Council and EP consent. This is a significant step forward towards the communitarisation of the area of criminal justice.

Both judgements put together meant that third-pillar legal instruments had become like first-pillar instruments, and confirms the idea of a de facto de-pillarisation. This made it much easier for member states to argue that, while the 'reform treaty' was important for EU decision-making, in fact, the changes were only minor. While the changes in the AFSJ dimension had been very significant indeed, the policy entrepreneurship by the European Court of Justice, acting on a request by the Commission, made it easier to present abolition of the pillar structure as a modest endeavour. Thus, this increased the likelihood of the renegotiation of the treaty to succeed at the end of the reflection period.

Renegotiation, the Second IGC, 2007, and ratification of the Lisbon Treaty, 2009

As a result of the reflection period, the Lisbon Treaty was signed by the Heads of State or Government in December 2007. A number of domestic factors made this signing more likely. Firstly, France elected Nicolas Sarkozy as President, who argued successfully for a smaller 'reform treaty' in the French presidential (May 2007) and parliamentary elections (June 2007). He suggested that he would choose to ratify this 'mini-treaty' by parliament. Given that France presented the most significant stumbling block to ratification of the CT, this became a formidable chance for the EU to maintain the momentum for treaty reform. EU political elites still regarded treaty reform as necessary, but following Sarkozy, they argued that the new treaty should not be presented as a constitutional project, but rather a 'mini-treaty'. Ratification of an 'ordinary' treaty was perceived to be more easily achievable. This resulted in a strategy of active depoliticisation of negotiations towards a 'reform treaty' (Christiansen, 2008, p. 42).

Due to this official strategy to depoliticise the new 'reform treaty', efforts made by the Finish Presidency with the support of the European Commission in 2006 to introduce some of the communitarising provisions of the CT did not receive a majority of member states in its support (Donnelly, 2008). This attempt aimed to bring in QMV in the Council and co-decision with the Parliament through the back-door route of the passarelle clause in the Amsterdam and Nice Treaties. Yet, these suggestions were resoundingly denied out of fear that it might have made it less likely to renegotiate a 'reform treaty'. It would have also meant that the increase in EU AFSJ competences would have been lost, as well as the ECJ jurisdiction.

Under the German Presidency of 2007, rapid progress was made to renegotiate what was eventually to become the Lisbon Treaty, which included all major AFSJ provision from the CT, and even went further, as explained in the second section of this chapter (including even the Prüm Convention acquis). In addition to positive domestic conditions with the fresh election of French President Sarkozy, a number of other coincidental factors also helped. Firstly, it is often easier to agree on a raft of measures in a treaty, where different interests of member states are balanced against each other, than to agree on specific AFSJ provision (as attempted during the Finish Presidency). In addition, UK Prime Minister Tony Blair had announced his forthcoming resignation from government, which may have provided him with more room for manoeuvre to take political decisions that his successor would have to implement (Donnelly, 2008, p. 21). Finally, German Chancellor Angela Merkel proved to be an expert and very skilled negotiator, especially to overcome Polish obstructions against the new voting procedure. The fact that the German 'Grand Coalition' proved much more stable than expected added a sense of leadership from Germany.

However, despite some Polish obstructions by President Kaczynski, it was in fact (again) the British delegation that had again become the biggest obstacle just before the IGC summit. Within the British domestic political debate, the extension of the Community method to the AFSJ was widely under attack for infringing British national sovereignty, despite the safeguards that were already in the CT (Donnelly, 2008, p. 22). While the Lisbon Treaty communitarises the AFSJ for most member states, the British government insisted a generalised opt-in/opt-out from all newly communitarised parts of the AFSJ. At the back of this concession to Britain, Ireland also received the same protocol due to its 'common law' position (or the possibility of an Irish referendum, in other words). This significant new opt-in/opt-out mechanism, even in areas that Britain and Ireland had not previously received such a mechanism,[1] meant that the Lisbon Treaty was a 'different beast' to the Constitutional Treaty, at least in the British and Irish version. In the British context, this was a vital concession to make the domestic argument against holding a referendum as a method for ratification, subsequently often used by PM Gordon Brown to ensure British ratification. Given the British historical record of opting into almost all measures outside the Schengen framework, it is doubtful whether this will make a concrete difference for Britain, but it might provide its government with a stronger hand in any future AFSJ negotiations.

Reacting to the first Irish referendum: persuading Ireland to vote again

Unfortunately, again, referenda appeared as crucial obstacles in the way of ratifying the Lisbon Treaty. This treaty can enter into force only after it has been ratified by all of the twenty-seven EU member states. The first Irish 'no' vote (53 per cent) in a referendum on the Lisbon Treaty on 12 June 2008 made ratification of the treaty uncertain. Subsequently, Eurosceptic commentators (again) called for abandonment of the treaty, as indicated by the main headline in *The Economist* (20 June 2008): 'Just bury it.' However, in sharp contrast to the aftermath of the 'no' votes in France and the Netherlands, no member state stalled ratification. To reinforce this point, the European Council encouraged all member states to continue ratifying the Lisbon Treaty (*Die Presse*, 10 September 2008).

This meant that Ireland (similarly to the situation after the first Nice referendum) became the most significant and obvious obstacle to ratification. Fifty-three per cent of voters rejected the Lisbon Treaty either because of a tangible lack of knowledge about the treaty or because they felt they had not been properly informed. Consequently, this became one of the most important issues for the Irish government to tackle. Several other reasons for the 'no' vote included widespread fears about the alleged 'militarisation of Europe' and its impact on Irish neutrality, as well as ethical issues pushed by ultra-Catholic pressure groups, such as alleged threats to the restrictive Irish abortion laws and laws outlawing euthanasia. One of the main cited reasons for voting 'no', however, was the envisaged reduction in the size of the European Commission.

Subsequently, this presented the EU (*Die Presse*, 10 September 2008; *EUobserver*, 31 July, 4, 18 September 2008) with only one realistic option of persuading Ireland to vote again, along the lines of the Nice Treaty, which also had to be voted on twice. For such an event, options of how the Irish electorate might be persuaded to ratify (*Die Presse*, 10 September 2008) were the following:

- The European Council could decide to revert back to the principle of 'One country – one commissioner', if the Treaty of Lisbon was approved, contrary to the provisions of the Nice Treaty (which obliges the number of commissioners to be reduced).
- The Irish could receive special protocol assurances of their neutrality, their tax sovereignty and their abortion regulatory sovereignty (though unaffected by the Lisbon Treaty).
- The Irish could receive an all-encompassing opt-out from all defence co-operation to assure it of its neutrality (to counter the scare strategy of the 'no' side to depict a 'militarisation of Europe')

Given the fact that there was absolutely no appetite for renegotiating the Lisbon Treaty (again) amongst other EU governments, the Irish government decided to enter into non-treaty negotiations, in which it secured a series of legal guarantees. At the EU summit on 18–19 June 2009, the Taoiseach, Brian Cowen, received a declaration designed to reassure the Irish principal reservations derived from the first referendum (Hierlemann, 2009). The European Council clarified that Ireland's abortion laws remained intact and would not be affected by the Lisbon Treaty. Furthermore, Ireland would keep its right of tax sovereignty and its traditional policy of military neutrality. Furthermore, the European Council confirmed that every member state would continue to be able to nominate its own commissioner if and when the Lisbon Treaty would come into force. In addition, it adopted a 'Solemn Declaration on Workers' Rights, Social Policy and other Issues'. These decisions are legally binding coming into effect the day of the entry into force of the Lisbon Treaty. To ensure full treaty status for these guarantees, they will be attached as a protocol to the Lisbon Treaty after the ratification of the next accession treaty (Hierlemann, 2009).

This resulted in an overwhelming success for the 'yes' campaign, as indicated at the beginning of this chapter. 'The Irish people have spoken with a clear and resounding voice.' Taoiseach Brian Cowen called the Irish vote a 'declaration of intent to remain at the heart of Europe'; 67.1 per cent of the Irish electorate voted in favour of the Lisbon Treaty, while 32.9 per cent voted against. This represents a 20 per cent swing to the 'yes' side, when compared to Ireland's rejection of the Lisbon treaty in June 2008 (*EUobserver*, 3 October 2009). As a result, Jerzy Buzek, President of the European Parliament, even suggested that 'Europe is back on track' (*Euractiv*, 3 October 2009). Nonetheless, there were other hurdles to overcome still.

Further obstacles: from Karlsruhe to Warsaw and Prague

Prior to the Irish referendum, the German Constitutional Court had to decide whether the Lisbon Treaty could be seen as compatible with the German 'Basic Law', i.e. the German Constitution. The Second Senate of the Federal Constitutional Court decided on 30 June 2009 that the Act Approving the Lisbon Treaty (*Zustimmungsgesetz zum Vertrag von Lissabon*) was compatible with the Basic Law (BVG, 30 June 2009). In contrast, the Court ruled the 'Act Extending and Strengthening the Rights of the Bundestag and the Bundesrat in European Union Matters' (*Gesetz über die Ausweitung und Stärkung der Rechte des Bundestages und des Bundesrates in Angelegenheiten der Europäischen Union*) unconstitutional; it ruled that it infringed the German Basic Law (*Grundgesetz*, GG). The reasoning provided in its ruling has been mainly the alleged facts that Bundestag and Bundesrat would not have been accorded 'sufficient rights of participation in European lawmaking procedures and treaty amendment procedures'. As a consequence, although it was proclaimed that 'Das Grundgesetz sagt "Ja" zum Vertrag von Lissabon,' the German Constitutional Court ruled that that the accompanying laws passed by the Bundestag to incorporate the Lisbon Treaty needed to be revised before German ratification could be completed (BVG, 30 June 2009). Hoffmann (2009) argues that the seventy-two pages of 'small print' by the judges turned the 'Ja zu Lissabon' effectively into a 'Ja, aber ...'.

The ruling led to strong differences of opinions in Germany. The former Foreign Minister Joschka Fischer criticised the verdict strongly; 'Karlsruhe simply does not like the EU's progress towards deeper integration' (*Die Zeit*, 9 July 2009). The Second Senate of the Constitutional Court 'had attacked the phantasmagoric vision of a European "federal state"' merely in order to lend legitimacy to its view that in future European integration policy would not be formulated in Berlin by democratically legitimated bodies, that is, the German government, the German Parliament and the Federal Council, but by the court in Karlsruhe (*Die Zeit*, 9 July 2009). European Commission President Barroso also expressed concern at the judgement by Germany's constitutional court on the Lisbon Treaty, fearing it could undermine the 'European project'. President Barroso elaborated that the judgement raised 'very important and sensitive issues in terms of the competence of the EU and other competences, namely on the understanding of the principle of subsidiarity' (*EUobserver*, 15 July 2009). He continued to state that the judgement was 'extremely important' for the way member states 'understand respect for Community law'.

Hoffmann (2009) suggests that the Court used its Lisbon verdict to expand on its 1992 Maastricht decision, in which the Maastricht Treaty was declared compatible with the *Grundgesetz*, yet the Constitutional Court claimed a legal supervisory role over potential infringements by the EU into areas of German national competences. Yet, this verdict aims to contain European integration in a 'list of areas that have always been deemed especially sensitive for the ability of a constitutional state to democratically shape itself' (Hoffmann, 2009): (1) criminal law, (2) the use of force (police and military), (3) fiscal policy, (4) the social state, and (5) cultural policies including education, family and religious law and laws regulating religion. While the list seems arbitrary, the verdict makes no attempt to provide reasons behind this selection.

Since the verdict, the German Bundestag reconvened for a special session before the elections in September 2009 in order to amend the accompanying laws as demanded by the Lisbon verdict. In September 2009, just before the Irish referendum on 2 October 2009, the Bundestag and Bundesrat passed three new laws in relation to the co-operation between the government and the Parliament, as well as three new laws in relation to the co-operation between Bundestag and Bundesrat on EU matters. The laws, in line with the Court verdict, require explicit instruction by the legislature for the government to act in areas of the *passerelle* and flexibility clauses. As a consequence of these new laws, German President Horst Köhler signed the Lisbon Treaty at the end of September 2009, and the German ratification documents were deposited in time before the Irish referendum. However, the new rules of the game as stipulated by Karlsruhe will have clear consequences for future German EU policy: (1) the German government will find European policy (more) complicated, and (2) debates in the Bundestag and the Bundesrat will become more strongly focused on EU matters. Every German Chancellor will have to bear in mind the Eurosceptic consequences of this Karlsruhe ruling.

However, the last remaining obstacles to the ratification of the Lisbon Treaty were to be found in Warsaw and Prague, where Presidents Kaczynski and Klaus had refused to sign the Lisbon Treaty prior to the Irish referendum on the basis that 'the Treaty was dead'. Nonetheless, on the 10 October 2009, the Polish President Lech Kaczynski signed the Ratification Act of the Lisbon Treaty, which concluded a long and painful ratification process in Poland (Zwolski, 2009). While the President had waited for the result of the second Irish referendum, despite the fact that the Polish parliament ratified the

Treaty already in April 2008, ultimately he did not give the impression that he would block the ratification process in Poland. In a 'pro-European ceremony', with the Commission President Barroso and the European Parliament President Buzek present, he finally ratified the Lisbon Treaty.

This left the Czech Republic as the last country not to ratify the treaty under the strongly Eurosceptic President Klaus. Kratochvil and Braun (2009) suggest that the resistance to ratifying the Lisbon Treaty cannot be explained due to a particularly Eurosceptic public opinion; Eurobarometer polls indicated that the Czech population belongs to the EU mainstream. They suggest that the political elites in the Czech Republic are rather specific. The Civic Democratic Party (ODS), on the right, is commonly described as being Eurosceptic. However, President Klaus has become one of the 'heroes' of pan-European Euroscepticism.

The Lisbon Treaty was ratified in both chambers of the Czech parliament during spring 2009. Yet, in this ratification process, the Treaty was brought to the Czech Constitutional Court three times, each time with a clear verdict in favour of the treaty. During the first challenge by Klaus-loyal senators to the Constitutional Court, the senators posed six specific objections to the Treaty (Kratochvil and Braun, 2009): (1) the division of competences, (2) the flexibility clause, (3) the *passerelle* clause (which also caused problems in Germany), (4) EU legal personality for international agreements, (5) the increased competences of the EU in the former third pillar, and (6) the status of the Charter of Fundamental Rights. President Klaus put the argument forward to the Czech Constitutional Court that the Treaty would give the EU a competence – competence through the flexibility clause and the so-called *passerelle*, which enables smaller revisions of the treaty without the normal process of treaty ratification. The general argument put forward by President Klaus and his loyal supporters is based on the assumption that the Lisbon Treaty moves the EU one step further towards becoming a state.

However, finally, as the Lisbon Treaty was approved by both chambers of the Czech parliament, only two actors remained: the Czech Constitutional Court and President Klaus. In the end, the Czech Constitutional Court found three times in favour of the Lisbon Treaty. In its first verdict, the outcome was decided by a seven-to-zero decision in favour of the Lisbon Treaty. The Czech Constitutional Court clearly did not follow the German Constitutional Court in its Euroscepticism. The court examined whether the treaty was compatible with the Czech constitution for a final time at a hearing on 27 October 2009, two days before a crucial EU summit in Brussels. As with the other challenges in the past, the Czech Constitutional Court gave its positive verdict shortly after this hearing. Yet, once the Constitutional Court decided in favour of the Lisbon Treaty, the political pressure became substantial on President Klaus; some parts of the Czech political elite even advocated his removal from office in case he did not want to sign the treaty.

Although the Czech parliament ratified the treaty in May 2009, President

Klaus initially refused to sign the Lisbon Treaty until after the second Irish referendum in October 2009. Subsequently, he refused to sign suggesting his hands were tied until the final verdict of the Czech Constitutional Court. However, in addition to this, Klaus created another unexpected obstacle for ratification by demanding that the Czech Republic needed an opt-out from Lisbon Treaty's charter of fundamental rights due to fears of property claims by expelled former refugees from the Sudetenland. Klaus suggested that he wanted to ensure that, by ratifying the Lisbon Treaty, the Czech Republic would not open the door to a mass of claims on Czech property from ethnic Germans expelled from the former Czechoslovakia after 1945, or from their descendants. In order to de-escalate this stand-off between Klaus and the rest of the EU, the Czech Prime Minister Fischer agreed that his government was willing to discuss a possible solution to this situation with its European partners during the EU summit at the end of October 2009. In return, Klaus agreed to sign the Lisbon Treaty quickly after the Czech Constitutional Court approved the treaty: 'The Lisbon Treaty cannot be stopped any more ... the process is already too far advanced to be stopped ... I will not wait for a potential new British government to call for a referendum ... They should have done something about this earlier' (*Tagesschau*, 17 October 2009). Thus, the Czech government agreed to draft a declaration that would satisfy objections raised by the Czech President Klaus.

Intense political pressure, from EU partners and the Czech political elites ensured that he would keep his promise. After intense consultations between the Czech government and its European partners, and strong criticism of Klaus, this pressure paid off. Former President Havel, for instance, criticised him very strongly for his role in obstructing the ratification process. He suggested his successor Klaus was damaging the country's name in Europe by refusing to sign the Lisbon Treaty. He stated that Klaus's attitude 'was dangerous' (BBC, 15 October 2009). French President Sarkozy also criticised the Klaus' refusal to sign the Lisbon Treaty and warned him of the repercussions. 'Decision time is coming for him and it will not be without consequence ... and whatever happens, this issue will be resolved by the end of the year' (BBC, 15 October 2009).

Thus, shortly after the Czech Constitutional Court´s positive ruling, Klaus finally completed the ratification process for the Lisbon Treaty in the Czech Republic. Having received legal assurances in the form of a declaration at the EU Council Summit at the end of October 2009, Klaus finally decided to sign and fulfil his legal obligation according to the Czech Constitution. While he was certainly not in a hurry with his signature, all the conditions that he defined as necessary for his signature (the Irish yes, the Court´s approval, and the EU Council declaration) were in place. As a consequence, Klaus signed the treaty, which was subsequently ratified by the Czech Republic as the last member state to ratify. The Lisbon Treaty entered into force on the 1 December 2009.

Evaluating the role of EU institutions as supranational policy entrepreneurs

The purpose of this section is to evaluate to what extent the European institutions have played the role of a supranational policy entrepreneur. A close examination of the summary of results substantiates the degree of success of the European institutions, in particular the Commission, as a supranational policy entrepreneur in the AFSJ dimension of the Lisbon Treaty. Antonio Vitorino in particular – the commissioner responsible for the AFSJ from 1999–2004 – and his organisation qualify for this category. The Commission achieved significant policy advances in the institutional architecture of the area. This was often due to the valuable negotiation skills of Commissioner Vitorino and his staff. However, especially during the reflection period in the run-up of the Lisbon Treaty, the European Court of Justice also displayed clear signs of policy entrepreneurship, prompted by the action of the Commission. It is clear that an alliance of European institution is often necessary to advance European integration.

Note

1 The original opt-in/opt-out mechanism was initially only linked to areas that were brought into the EU from the Schengen framework, which Britain and Ireland had opposed in the negotiations on the Amsterdam Treaty.

Table 8.1 The Commission as an ideal SPE in the AFSJ on the constitutional level

	Evidence for	
	Long-term norm change	*Short-term policy advances*
	Overall assessment	
	Norms changed significantly during the Tampere programme culminating in the Constitutional Convention and the CT and LT IGC	Significant policy architecture advances
	What changed?	
1	EU to legislate in the AFSJ. Norm of national sovereignty reconstructed	AFSJ same status as the single market
2	Purpose of EU legislation. From flanking measure of single market to an AFSJ and 'European public order'	Significant increases in legal competences (asylum, migration, criminal justice, police)
3		EU decision-making procedure applicable throughout the AFSJ; ECJ oversight
4		European Public Prosecutor
5		Solidarity clause
6		Charter of Fundamental Rights
	How did it change?	
1	Change in strategy: gradualist, pragmatic	Commission communications and papers in the run-up of the Convention
2	Expertise and knowledge build-up: central role through highest quality of proposals	During Convention: • High-quality contributions • Commissioner Vitorino as a representative • Full attendance, hardworking, good negotiations
3	Legitimacy build-up: NGOs, civil society, European Parliament	During IGC: • Strong pushing for Commission viewpoint • Bargaining and negotiation skills of Vitorino • Compromise solutions very creative and legally very sound
4	Vitorino negotiation skills	During reflection: • Insistence on LT • Further development of CT into LT • ECJ as SPE in addition to Commission
5	Scoreboard: naming and shaming	

9

Conclusion: Towards supranational governance in the Area of Freedom, Security and Justice?

Supranational policy entrepreneurship and the Area of Freedom, Security and Justice

This book has analysed the role of strategic EU institutional actors, in particular the European Commission, in the process of constructing an 'Area of Freedom, Security and Justice'. The book has argued that the EU policies on counter-terrorism, asylum and border management, as well as the institutional arrangements in these areas, are the expression of a political process attempting to construct such an 'area' for different political communities by ensuring their security from external security threats. This threat perception has arguably influenced the negotiations of the Lisbon Treaty, which contains a solidarity clause.

This book has further argued that EU institutional actors, especially the European Commission, have played a crucial role in shaping the development of the AFSJ in particular ways. Member states have often been pushing towards dealing with these new items on the political agenda as security threats, which have traditionally called for national solutions. The European institutions, in particular the European Commission, have managed to channel this process towards developing a 'European' – rather than a 'national' – solution. Thus, the aim of this book was to analyse the political role of the EU institutions in the AFSJ. The overarching question in the analysis of this process of constructing an AFSJ was: do European institutions have an emerging capacity to act as supranational policy entrepreneurs?

The answers provided in this book are affirmative, and thus suggestive of increased supranational governance in the AFSJ. The transition to supranational governance has been reached in two ways. Firstly, cross-border security issues pushed towards greater demand for EU legislation. Supranational organisations, like the European Commission, had considerable influence on the supply of this legislation; their acknowledgement is therefore clearly very important (Stone Sweet, Sandholtz and Fligstein, 2001). Institutional change has been facilitated by the (1) exogenous shocks like 11 September, and the terrorist attacks on Madrid and London, and (2) policy entrepreneurship. 'Policy entrepreneurs generate and attempt to propagate ideas that will define problems and solutions in ways that other actors find convincing and useful' (ibid.). This book has demonstrated how the concept of political entrepreneurship has been increasingly reinterpreted by scholars such as Moravcsik in order to dismiss the notion of the EU institutions' capacity to act as supranational policy entrepreneurs. Furthermore, the book has brought the concept back into the policy-making model where it originated from (Kingdon, 1984). The first chapter established the fact that the significance of European institutions, in particular the Commission, in the EU's policy process was well documented and widely recognised, despite some caveats. However, the picture differed regarding the process of treaty reform. Some scholars argued for the importance of the Commission (Beach, 2005a, Stone Sweet and Sandholtz, 1997, 1998; Stone Sweet et al., 2001), whereas others dismissed it (Moravcsik, 1999a; Pollack, 2003).

Functions and delegated powers to the EU institutions, have been the subject of fierce academic debate since the beginning of European integration (Haas, 1958, 1964, 1967; Lindberg, 1963; Lindberg and Scheingold, 1970, 1971; Hoffman, 1966, 1982; Moravcsik, 1993; Stone Sweet and Sandholtz, 1997, 1998; Stone Sweet et al., 2001; Pollack, 1997a, b, 2003; Hix, 1994, 1998; Tallberg, 2002, 2003, 2006, 2008; Beach, 2004b, 2005a; Kaunert, 2005, 2007, 2009). Three main points had emerged from the literature on European integration: (1) EU institutions, in particular the Commission, play a significant role on the policy level in areas of low politics (e.g. the single market); (2) EU institutions are less likely to play the same role on the treaty level; and (3) they are least likely to play that role in areas of high politics (security), either on the policy level or on the treaty level. As a result, it has been widely assumed that the role of the EU institutions, including the European Commission, in treaty-making and in security policies is minor, which had resulted in a lack of research on this topic.

Consequently, the book has made an original and much needed contribution to the literature. It has analysed cases that have received little academic attention – the AFSJ and the political role of European institutions, in particular the Commission and the Council Secretariat, and has generated original insights based on a wide range of interviews with policy-makers in Brussels. In addition, this book suggested a model built on John Kingdon (1984), but one that, crucially, develops his thoughts on ideational factors affecting policy change further. Agency factors are equally important in the policy-making process; structural forces alone do not determine the policy outcomes. Political entrepreneurial activities are not only related to the setting of the agenda, as discussed by Kingdon (1984), but they start already much earlier – in the construction and reconstruction of the reasons for action which constitute the norm environment for decision-makers. This model is useful for analysing how the role of a political entrepreneur is vital in the construction and reconstruction of norms alongside the pushing for specific policies. Consequently, this book has made an original contribution to the literature on European integration (Haas, 1958, 1964, 1967; Lindberg, 1963; Lindberg and Scheingold, 1970, 1971; Hoffman, 1966, 1982; Moravcsik, 1993; Stone Sweet and Sandholtz, 1997, 1998; Stone Sweet et al., 2001; Pollack, 1997a, b, 2003; Hix, 1994, 1998; Tallberg, 2002, 2003, 2006, 2008; Beach, 2004b, 2005a; Kaunert, 2005, 2007, 2009).

Finally, this book has made a strong empirical contribution by analysing the role of the European Commission, the Council Secretariat, and partially the European Court of Justice in the AFSJ. This clearly indicates the empirical significance of both – the European institutions and the AFSJ for the EU of the early twenty-first century. In particular, the change in the institutional architecture of the AFSJ in the Lisbon Treaty (LT) is very significant, as argued in Chapter 8. The legal changes introduced by this Treaty provide for a full pooling of sovereignty at the EU level regarding the AFSJ – termed a 'European Public Order' in the Convention for the Constitutional Treaty.

Two analytical levels have been used to determine the EU institutions' influence on policy – the level of social norms of decision-makers in the norm stream, and the level of policy outcomes. The use of a case study approach has facilitated the analysis of these two analytical levels, which were used consistently across the three case studies: (1) EU counter-terrorism and criminal justice, (2) EU asylum and border policy, and (3) the institutional architecture of the AFSJ in the LT.

The analysis of these cases has demonstrated that the political activities of a European institution are more likely to be successful if it uses:

- *A first-mover advantage.* The EU institution comes forward quickly and with persistence and draws upon its first-mover advantage.
- *Persuasion strategy.* The EU institution achieves acceptance of its reasons for action which result in changing social norms. Thus, it influences the three streams according to Kingdon's model (1984): the problem, the policy, and the politics streams. Other actors are convinced by the reasons for the actions. Across the three cases (both in their internal and external dimension), this involves the following:
- *Legitimacy build-up.* Norms need to be anchored in pre-existing norms, and normative changes need to be consistent with these pre-existing norms in order to enable the new norms to acquire legitimacy.
- *Expertise and information.* Other actors will only trust the authoritative judgement of an institution if it has sufficient knowledge and has been recognised as an expert.
- *Continued insistence.* The institution has to possess the patience required to bring sometimes tiring negotiations forward (e.g. asylum). This can occasionally be combined with threats of exclusion towards member states which are perceived as obstructive (e.g. the Commission towards Italy regarding the European Arrest Warrant).
- *Negotiation skills.* In order to persuade other political actors, an EU insti-

tution such as the European Commission – in particular, the commissioner responsible (Antonio Vitorino, then Franco Frattini) responsible for the AFSJ, but also his staff – need to possess the social skills required to say the right things to the right people at the right time. A correct political assessment of the situation is crucial.
- *Alliances.* In the bargaining process, it is crucial for the Commission and the Council Secretariat to form initial alliances with powerful actors to create a bandwagon effect, whereby more actors decide to join the 'winning team'. Often, this makes it necessary for the institutions to be closely allied with the Council Presidency of the time (e.g. Belgium in the case of counter-terrorism policy; Ireland in the case of the asylum policy or the Lisbon Treaty).

Overall, the Commission, and to a slightly lesser extent the Council Secretariat, have been successful in all three cases analysed (both in the internal and external dimensions). Indeed, the book has supported and added to other work which has shown that the Commission has an emergent capacity to act as a supranational policy entrepreneur – see, inter alia, telecommunications (Fuchs, 1994, 1995), equal opportunities (Mazey, 1995), research (Peterson, 1995b), and the single market and business affairs (Sandholtz and Zysman, 1989; Sandholtz, 1993a) – and that the Council Secretariat plays a significant role in EU policy-making thanks to its 'power of the pen' (Beach, 2004b). However, while this general conclusion is applicable to all cases, some differences amongst cases have also come to light. They will be analysed in the following section.

What were the differences across the different area of the Area of Freedom, Security and Justice?

As previously suggested, while the effects of the actions of the EU institutions as supranational policy entrepreneurs have been substantiated in all cases, there were differences in the ways in which the Commission, and the Council Secretariat to a lesser extent, achieved these results:

Counter-terrorism and its external dimension

The European Commission, with its ally the Council Secretariat, acted in an alliance of supranational policy entrepreneurs in the area of counter-terrorism, as evidenced by the cases of the European Arrest Warrant (EAW) and the EU–US counter-terrorism co-operation (and to a lesser extent the European Neighbourhood Policy).

The terrorist attacks on 11 September 2001 became a normative defining point – for European integration and for the Commission's role in this process. The Commission has played a significant role in leading the EU into this emerging 'war on terror'. It has managed to construct an important role for the EU in this policy area by being a 'strategic first mover' in order to shape the debate, as indicated above. It also allied with the US to put pressure on reluctant member states – the EAW was the result of a complex process and the political actions of the Commission. However, the European Commission had to use a 'carrot and stick' approach in its relations with the US, symbolised by the fact that the former US Homeland Security Secretary Thomas Ridge stated that his greatest regret was to have not worked more closely with the EU from the start (Lebl, 2006, p. 125).

As will be demonstrated below, this process differed from that characterising the development of the EU asylum and border management policy, including its external dimension, on several counts:

- The internal and external negotiations on counter-terrorism moved comparatively fast (e.g. the EAW), despite significant misgivings amongst member states.
- The Commission managed to contribute to the construction of a role for the EU into the 'war on terror'. Consequently, it used security reasons to move the negotiations faster, in order to secure the adoption of the EAW and an increase in EU–US co-operation.
- At the same time, the Commission continued to push for humanitarian norms in asylum policy. This clearly moved the process along much more slowly, as the Commission avoided drawing upon security arguments on the whole. Ultimately, however, both approaches were successful.

EU asylum and border management policy and its external dimension

A European approach to asylum was established by the end of the Tampere programme, which ran from 1999 to 2004, and has subsequently been consolidated during the Hague Programme, especially in the external dimension, between 2004 and 2009. It has been demonstrated that the Commission acted as an SPE in asylum and border management policy matters. Indeed, there were normative changes throughout the Tampere and the Hague programmes respectively, as well as policy advances.

Yet, as suggested, in that policy area, there were two differences compared to the area of counter-terrorism. Firstly, the success of the four asylum directives was in fact a long and tedious process. It took almost five years to achieve the four directives, whereas the EAW took less than one year of negotiation and two years of preparation. This suggests that it is easier to achieve progress in the area of security than in granting refugee rights.

However, this is not very surprising given that member states were negotiating these legislative proposals during the 'war on terror'. The bulk of the negotiations were conducted after the terrorist attacks of 11 September 2001 in New York and Washington. Madrid (11 March 2004) and London (7 July 2005) soon followed. Why would the Commission push for the rights of refugees in such a difficult political climate? It would have been far easier to link asylum to security and terrorism, as had been done in the case of the

EAW. It worked very well as a strategy in that case – why change?

Actually, the Commission did not pursue this strategy in the area of asylum and border management, and actively resisted it in the external dimension. It continued to push for refugee rights under the Geneva Convention, and opposed the perception of asylum seekers as security threats. It notably managed to divert the British proposal to externalise asylum claims outside the borders of the EU. This is in many ways an even more remarkable success for the Commission than the 'easier' success in counter-terrorism co-operation. All four asylum directives actually increased the legal value of the Geneva Convention, as discussed in chapter five. Moreover, these developments are now reflected in the Hague Programme for the period 2004–2009 (Peers, 5 November 2004). The area has now been communautarised after the first-phase instruments of the Tampere programme. The Commission has therefore become the only actor making legislative proposals; thus, its role has been further strengthened.

The Area of Freedom, Security and Justice and the Lisbon Treaty

Again, in particular the European Commission, with the help of the Council Secretariat (and the European Court of Justice), has acted as a supranational policy entrepreneur regarding the AFSJ dimension of the Lisbon Treaty (LT). During the Tampere programme (1999–2004), norms changed significantly in the policy area. The norm of national sovereignty was reconstructed, resulting in an acceptance of the EU as a legislator. The purpose of the legislation changed from 'a flanking measure of the Single Market' to an AFSJ. Kaunert (2005) has elsewhere named this development a 'European Public Order' in line with the phrase used by the working group in the Convention on the Future of Europe.

The Commission has achieved very significant advances in the institutional architecture of the AFSJ through the Lisbon Treaty:

- The AFSJ has achieved the same legal status as the single market.
- The legal competences of the EU have significantly increased in asylum, migration, border management, counter-terrorism, and crime and police co-operation.
- The application of EU legal instruments and mechanisms has become the norm, and the legislative procedures have become more homogeneous throughout.
- Innovations have included the legal competence to establish a European Public Prosecutor, the transformation of the Charter of Fundamental Rights into a legally binding document, and the so-called solidarity clause.

However, in line with the EU asylum and border management policy, success regarding these institutional matters was more incremental. Yet, the changes to the institutional architecture of the AFSJ are as significant in their scope as the EAW has been for the development of criminal justice co-operation. The innovations regarding the AFSJ were clearly amongst the most significant advances in the LT.

At the same time, the Commission had been pushing for this change from the 1980s onwards, since the construction of the single market. Therefore, this success may not have come as a huge surprise for policy-makers. The Commission acted in the way described by Kingdon: 'policy entrepreneurs lie in wait, in and around the government with their solutions in hand, waiting for problems to float by to which they can attach their solutions, waiting for a development in the politics stream they can use to their advantage' (Kingdon, 1984, p. 165). They are 'advocates willing to invest their resources – time, reputation, money – to promote a position in return for anticipated future gain in the form of material, purposive, or solidary benefits' (ibid., p. 181). The Commission did invest a very significant amount of resources into the future gains – money, expertise, and political credit amongst member states. From a practitioner's point of view, it may come as a logical conclusion that this was finally achieved.

From a theoretical point of view, this has confirmed the importance of the European institutions – in particular the Commission, with the help of the Council Secretariat (and the European Court of Justice) – as SPEs in their various dimensions. Firstly, the Commission, alongside the European Court of Justice, contributed significantly to the changing shifts in norms in the AFSJ during the last decade. However, it is equally important to recognise its contribution to the definition of political problems, the search for policy alternatives and the political bargaining in the politics stream. These aspects are of equal significance. While norms guide the directions of the three other streams, they do not determine them. However, equally, the interpretation of political crises and the problem-solving nature of an EU institution like the Commission facilitated these successes. Finally, while the Commission was significant, one should not underestimate the impact of its allies either, especially the role of the Council Secretariat with its 'power of the pen'.

Such an analysis goes against the beliefs of some scholars, such as Moravcsik (1999a, p. 267) who writes: 'Can faceless bureaucrats, unelected and without power of purse or sword, really influence the decisions of powerful nation-states? Are we seeing the emergence of a "new statecraft" grounded in international networks managed by supranational political entrepreneurs?' This study has demonstrated that, in answer to Moravcsik question, 'faceless bureaucrats' can and indeed do influence policy-making considerably. Antonio Vitorino, as the Justice and Home Affairs Commissioner from 1999 to 2004, and Gilles de Kerchove as the new counter-terrorism co-ordinator, are good examples to illustrate this claim. Of course, it is not just one particular person, but the right person at the right place, at the right time, with the right staff. Thus, the European Commission, and to some extent the Council Secretariat, have evidently demonstrated an emergent capacity to act as SPEs in the AFSJ.

Developments against the global trend?

However, these developments in the AFSJ seem to take place against the backdrop of a global opposite trend. Helen Wallace (2005, p. 56), for example, has argued that, in general, there has been a power shift towards other EU institutions and the member states away from the European Commission. The 'heyday' of success for the Commission is supposed to have been the days of Delors, during which the single market and the economic and monetary union were designed. More recently, scholars (Kurpas et al., 2008) have suggested that the 'heyday' of the Commission in the Delors era is in decline, to which the 2004 'Bing Bang enlargement' was expected to contribute to. 'More would add up to less'; a larger Union would come at the expense of a weaker Commission. Thus, several authors (see Settembri, 2007; Kurpas et al., 2008; Peterson and Birdsall, 2008) have suggested multiple sources of pressure which explain how and why the role, work and status of the European Commission have changed: (1) the rise of new modes of EU governance and (2) administrative reforms in the Commission and changed leadership under President José Manuel Barroso. Indeed, the Commission has had several high points with regard to its political impact – including the 1980s under Commission President Delors with the creation of the single market – but also had several low points. The most infamous of the latter occurred in March 1999, when the College of Commissioners, presided over by President Santer, had to collectively resign. This symbolised very well the new power of the European Parliament, which had threatened to dismiss the Commission on a charge of financial mismanagement against individual commissioners.

Christiansen (2006, p. 113) has argued that this crisis of the European Commission in 1999 could be seen to point in two opposite directions: either the Commission was too unprofessional and so mismanaged that its competences should have been rolled back, or indeed it needed to be fundamentally reformed in order to provide the services it was designed to provide. The predominant view that emerged from these debates was that the Commission President's power had to be strengthened. This was in line with the commonly held view that Delors was a model Commission president, who exerted a significant amount of leadership on the member states and thereby drove European integration forward. Successive treaty revisions agreed in Amsterdam and Nice increased the powers of the Commission president (ibid., p. 114). He/she has to agree to the nominations of the other members of the Commission in the college, who then work under his 'political guidance'. In addition, the president also allocates the portfolios to individual commissioners.

Yet, Commission President Romano Prodi (from 1999 to 2004), his predecessor Jacques Santer (from 1995 to 1999), and his successor José Manuel Barroso (from 2004 to the present) were not perceived to be strong presidents. Quite the opposite – the Commission was perceived to be in deep trouble:

> The European Commission, for many years the driving force of European integration, is in a sorry state. ... These days the Commission seldom sets the EU's agenda ... At the end of October [2004] Romano Prodi will stand down from his five-year term as Commission president ... for Mr Prodi and his predecessor, Jacques Santer, have been weak presidents and a third in a row could prove almost fatal for the Commission. (Grant, 23 February 2004)

This is further confirmed by the strong politicisation of the re-election in 2009 of Commission President Barroso. His nomination by the European Council had been relatively smooth after the European Parliament election in May 2009, where the European People's Party became the largest grouping in the chamber again after 2004. However, Barroso was strongly criticised by the European Socialists, the Greens and the Liberals. He attracted so much negative press that his first attempt at being approved by the European Parliament in July 2009 failed. In fact, the vote looked likely to fail and it was postponed to September 2009. Socialists and Greens accused the Commission president of relying on the 'anti-European votes' of the Tories to secure a second five-year mandate. Martin Schulz, leader of the Parliament's Socialists, even suggested that it was 'Barroso's strategy to go fishing for votes among British Conservatives. He will have a majority, but what a majority! Elected with the votes of anti-Europeans' (*Times*, 16 September 2009).

Nonetheless, Barroso secured a clear mandate in the European Parliament with 382 votes, out of a total 736 MEPs, to seal a second term as European Commission President.

> Having this very clear reaffirmation of support is great. I will use this capital for more energy for Europe. I will use it because I think it is important to fight national egoisms ... as President of the Commission, my party is going to be Europe. Anyone who wants to can come on board in this exciting journey that is the integration of Europe. This is the moment of truth. (*Times*, 16 September 2009)

Thus, despite the strong reliance on UK Conservative support, Barroso suggested that he would push a pro-European agenda, including the implementation of the Lisbon Treaty. However, for the first time, the Commission President had shown to be rather weak on his re-election due to the long uncertainty over his re-election; this had lasted from May until mid-September 2009.

The argument put forward by this book paints a different picture from the Commission as a weak institution. Ever since the resignation of Commission President Santer in 1999, commentators have tended to focus entirely on the leader of the European Commission in order to evaluate whether the Commission as a whole is strong or weak. In the case of Santer, this question received a negative answer, as the College of Commissioners resigned in disgrace. Surprisingly, the same negative answer was also given with regard to the more recent European Commission led by President Romano Prodi. Grant (ibid.) perceived him to have been a weak leader, a poor communicator, a poor manager, who, in addition to everything, picked the wrong fights with member states. We have just exited a period of strong protest against Commission President Barroso, who almost unanimously has been seen as a weak president, certainly by large groupings in the European Parliament.

But what does this global trend really tell us about the power of the Commission? Despite all this negative commentary, this book has generated evidence for the success of the Commission in the AFSJ. Does this indicate that the results disprove the trend explained above? Yes and no; drawing upon the results of this research, it is not possible to completely disprove the suggestion that the Commission led by Barroso was weak. However, the present study has demonstrated that this broad claim has important limitations, as the Commission has played an important role in the development of some policy areas, like the AFSJ, over the last few years.

Therefore, is it really the right level of analysis to focus on the Commission president? In recent years, especially following the eastward enlargement of the EU, the Commission has become more fragmented as an actor. There are twenty-seven commissioners in the Commission led by President Barroso, each with a different portfolio. This will remain to be the case with the ratification of the Lisbon Treaty, despite initial attempts before the first Irish referendum to revise this trend. Despite legal changes in the Lisbon Treaty enhancing the role of the Commission president, it appears that structural changes such as an increasing number of competences for the EU and an increasing number of member states have actually strengthened the leadership of individual commissioners with regard to their portfolio. Consequently, it is possible that one might observe opposing empirical trends at the same time. On the one hand, Barroso (and Prodi before him) may well have been a weak president on the grounds suggested by the European Socialists and the Greens; on the other hand, however, Commissioner Vitorino, later followed Franco Frattini and Jacques Barrot, may – as it has been suggested here – have led its directorate-general in such a way that it considerably influenced the development of the AFSJ. Thus, an analysis that focuses purely on the Commission president is narrow and potentially misleading, as it does not do justice to the specific characteristics of different policy areas.

Future outlook for the Area of Freedom, Security and Justice: a critical reflection on the 'Stockholm programme'

In addition to the points made above, there are a number of other important points raised by this book. The events of 11 September 2001 prompted the proliferation of a new concept –'homeland security' – especially in the US, but also in Europe. Relyea (2002a, p. 397) speculated that 'homeland security' may be '. . . prone to the same use as a justification for the exercise of prerogative powers in ways harmful to constitutional arrangements of government and guaranteed citizens rights.' Yet, the three case studies of this book – EU counter-terrorism (and its external dimension), EU asylum and border policy (and its external dimension), and the Lisbon Treaty and the AFSJ, have not clearly corroborated the idea that there has been a generalised securitisation of a variety of threats, from terrorism to asylum, migration and Europe's borders. Rather, the picture is significantly more nuanced.

Indeed, as argued above, the terrorist attack of 9/11 became a normative defining point. The European Commission played a significant part in the construction of a role for the EU into this emerging 'war on terror' through being a 'strategic first mover' and its alliance with the US. However, the role played by EU institutions differed in the EU asylum and border management policy, in both its internal and external dimensions. In that policy area, the Commission continued to push for humanitarian norms in asylum policy, to the extent that it actively resisted pressure by member states such as Britain to externalise the processing of asylum claims. This made for a relatively slower negotiation process, but this strategy actively prevented a further securitisation that may have occurred in the absence of this strong position taken by the Commission. In the negotiations of the Lisbon Treaty, the Commission managed to achieve significant new competences for the EU in the AFSJ. Nonetheless, it would not be possible to argue that the changes contained in the Lisbon Treaty necessarily open the way to a more repressive AFSJ.

The Commission naturally analysed the achievements of the Tampere and the Hague programmes in a positive light; it is highlighted as an 'ambitious programme with visible achievements' (COM (2009) 263 final). The Commission suggests that in the light of the significant developments within the EU and globally, the implementation of the Hague Programme worked relatively well. It points to EU Enlargement of twelve more member states in 2004 and 2007 which had a strong impact on how the EU functions. It also points out the new character of AFSJ initiatives in comparison with other activities of the EU. 'The Hague programme adopted a long term perspective, but it went further in that its strategic aims were accompanied by a detailed action plan for delivering them. Progress has been mixed, but there have been visible achievements' (ibid., p. 3).

Yet, as ever, the future may manage to contradict history. In the following, this section will refer to the reflection of the so-called 'Council of the European Union's Future Group', which presented its final report at the JHA Council meeting in July 2008 (Future Group, 2008; Bunyan, 2008). The Future Group was set up in January 2007, following a proposal by the German Presidency at the informal JHA meeting in Dresden on 14–16 January 2007 (Bunyan, 2008, p. 2). The meeting of the Future Group was co-chaired by the Interior Minister of the Council Presidency and the vice-chair of the European Commission (first Franco Frattini, and subsequently Jacques Barrot) and attended by the Interior Ministers of Germany, Portugal, Slovenia, France, the Czech Republic, Sweden, as well as Britain as a 'common law observer'. The report of this Future Group has led to a new Justice and Home Affairs programme for 2010–2014, following the Tampere programme (1999–2004) and the Hague programme (2005–2009). The new programme – which is called the 'Stockholm programme' – has been adopted at a special EU Council Summit on 10–11 December 2009.

Bunyan (2008, p. 3) rightly notes that the terminology used in the Future Group report changed considerably from previous EU language. Firstly, for more than a decade (1997–2008) the EU took great care to use the terminology 'Area of Freedom, Security and Justice'. However, the Future Group report seems to depart from that terminology and increasingly talks about 'European home affairs', which is not a million miles away from the term 'European homeland security'. While the report does not merge the concepts of home and security, it is clear in the report that the underlying message is to protect a 'European home' from security threats, which the report aims to combat. Such a move brings this EU policy area considerably closer to what could be described as a 'European homeland security'.

Reflecting further on this report, what does security mean in the AFSJ, or rather 'European home affairs'? Let us reflect on the EU's perception of its own security threats in the AFSJ. Firstly, the report argues that there is an increasing 'blurriness' between internal and external security.

> Protecting the European Union's internal security involves not only measures at and within the Community borders, but also, in particular, engagement abroad. This is the basic idea at the heart of the 2003 European Security Strategy which said that 'In an era of globalisation, distant threats may be as much a concern as those that are near at hand ... the first defence will often be abroad. (Cited in Bunyan, 2008, p. 14)

This implies that the EU's own thinking about security is getting significantly closer to the idea of 'homeland security' in the US with its roots in homeland defence. There are strong indications that the EU sees the emerging 'European home affairs' as a policy area aiming to deal with security threats emanating from abroad as much as those from inside the EU. The Future Group of the EU perceived security threats to emanate both from within and outside the EU.

Secondly, what are the main security threats in the EU? Bunyan suggests that the EU has identified terrorist attacks and migration flows at the two main security threats that it is currently facing (Bunyan, 2008, p. 14). However, an in-depth analysis of the relevant sections of the report leads to more nuanced results. The fight against terrorism is mentioned right at the beginning of the report (Future Group, 2008, pp. 5–6) and includes seven paragraphs. The report states that the EU aims to 'fight terrorism based on a comprehensive global approach' (para. 12). As a consequence, the report suggests the following (para. 13): (1) the different actors involved in the fight against terrorism should be better co-ordinated within the Union, (2) a concept should be developed on the future institutional architecture of the area, and (3) the information flow between the law enforcement authorities of the member states, Eurojust, Europol, and the Joint Situation Centre (SitCen) should be improved. Regarding external relations, the Future Group recommends the achievement of better political, technical, and operational co-operation with third countries, especially the Union's major strategic partners – which are identified as being the US and Russia (para. 15). In addition, the EU should also focus on mid- and long-term prevention of terrorism, especially regarding recruitment and radicalisation (para. 17), but also the possible threat of nuclear, biological or chemical terrorist attacks (para. 18).

Regarding the issue of migration (Future Group, 2008, pp. 6–9), the report states that there is a consensual view in the EU that migration is an inherent phenomenon in globalised societies, with demographics creating more demand for labour migration (para. 23), which needs to be responded to at the European level. Various types of co-operation with partner countries are underlined, to which an integrated approach should be applied, consisting of dialogue, co-operation, and partnership with countries of origin and transit (para. 24). The Group further recommends designing a common immigration policy (para. 26) that excludes general regularisations (para. 27), but includes an effective European returns policy (para. 28). In general, this approach does not depart significantly from previous EU rhetoric on the substance of legal and illegal migration, and thus does not construct migration as a security threat.

Regarding asylum policy, the report (Future Group, 2008, pp. 7–8) notes the existence of continuing divergences between the policies of member states, which is the main reason for which it recommends (para. 31) the development of a Common European Asylum System (CEAS). This was already foreseen by the Hague programme, but has not been fully achieved so far, despite the fact that common minimum standards have already been established as part of the Tampere programme. The main reason for this was a lack of EU competences, as were provided for by the Constitutional Treaty, rejected only a year after the Hague programme had been drawn up. With the ratification of the Lisbon Treaty, this should be much easier to achieve.

However, there are some negative pointers in the Future Group report. The CEAS is bundled together with the notion of 'secure borders' and the prevention of 'illegal migration' (para. 32), as well as the external dimension of asylum policy and the concept of regional protection programmes (para. 33), discussed in Chapter 7. While this does not mean that asylum matters have been unequivocally securitised, it is interesting to note that asylum matters are discussed in conjunction with the idea of 'secure' borders, which suggests the existence of links between asylum and security.

As a result, the section on border management and co-operation with third countries (Future Group, 2008, p. 8) recognises that border controls are only one element of a global policy of security management (para. 36). However, the Future Group recommends a clear strengthening of Frontex to play a central role in threat analysis, the training of the border guards of the member states and the strengthening of links with third countries, as well as the evaluation and inspection of national border forces (para. 37). Reading the section on asylum in conjunction with that on border management conveys the message that 'illegal migrants' are increasingly being perceived as a potential security threat. Moreover, the EU agency Frontex is depicted as having a key role to play by analysing this security threat in order to protect the EU.

Thus, the EU future report further aims at protecting the EU's territory. While the EU does not have a clearly defined territory in principle (due to continuous enlargements and the lack of statehood), its territory is increasingly defended against security threats, both external and internal. The role of Frontex in this context appears to be pivotal. Despite the fact that this agency is not very developed yet, it is being perceived as having accumulated very significant responsibilities – from the analysis of security threats to the training of member states' border guards and the development of links with third countries, as well as the evaluation and inspection of national border forces. It is increasingly looking like a federal border force – albeit more in theory than in practice so far. The report of the Future Group suggests that there is some ambition to move in that direction.

Finally, where does the European political community figure in this reflection? Again, the EU is not yet a full political community in the way we understand the term from its use in the context of nation-states. As explained earlier, the EU is a sui generis form of political organisation, somewhere between an ordinary international organisation and a state, with some characteristics of a confederation (Peterson and Shackleton, 2002, p. 2). Thus, although the EU is not a state, it has made strong inroads into various areas of security – European internal security – which have traditionally been seen as strongholds of national sovereignty. In that sense, the statement by Edwards and Meyer (2008) that '[the] governance of the European Union has been changed through its response to international terrorism' is correct. The actions of Osama Bin Laden and Al Qaeda seem to be achieving a clear response – the increased integration of European nations in response to a security threat.

In the European Parliament, a political community is certainly in the making in response to this security threat, and familiar national fault lines emerge. The Stockholm programme provoked strong criticism from southern Europeans. In their view, the programme does not sufficiently take account of their priorities in the treatment of security and immigration. Maltese centre-right MEP Simon Busuttil commented that 'the axis on security seems to have been watered down in the text', a point which was reinforced by a number of Italian MEPs. British Liberal MEP Diana Wallis countered this: 'We're beginning to see where the fracture lines in the house are ... security is the main sticking point. Do we want to go further in terms of underlining security? Who knows what the final outcome will be in terms of immigration and migration? That could be difficult' (Euractiv, 12 October 2009). The same political faultlines exist at Council level; Sweden, the Council Presidency in the second half of 2009, pushed for as broad a programme as possible in order to achieve consensus in an EU of twenty-seven member states. After the Council approved the Stockholm programme, the real political battles started to emerge. What will the Commission do with this broad and vague programme, which is only a roadmap for proposing specific legislative instruments? As with the Tampere and the Hague programmes, this will make an exciting new research project.

When the Commission outlined its vision for the Stockholm programme on 10 June 2009, this can be seen as a yardstick to measure the future development of the AFSJ. Commission President José Manuel Barroso gives a glimpse into the future:

> In future, EU action must aim above all at delivering the best possible service to the citizen in an area of freedom, security and justice more tangible for the citizens ... we want to promote citizens' rights, make their daily lives easier and provide protection, and this calls for effective and responsible European action in these areas. In this context, I consider immigration policy particularly important. This is the vision the Commission is presenting to the Council and Parliament for debate, with a view to the adoption of the new Stockholm Programme by the European Council in December 2009. (European Commission, 10 June 2009)

Vice-president of the Commission Jacques Barrot continues (ibid.):

> Freedom, security and justice are core values which constitute key components of the European model of society. We have made substantial progress in creating an area of freedom, security and justice in recent years. The priority now must be to put the citizen at the heart of this project in order to demonstrate the added value of the EU in areas that have such a bearing on people's daily lives.

The Commission outlines four major priorities: (1) promoting citizens' rights, (2) making life easier – a Europe of justice, (3) protecting citizens – a Europe that protects, (4) promoting a more integrated society for the citizen – a Europe of solidarity. In addition, it provides ten examples of specific legal measures (European Commission, 10 June 2009):

1. Introduce a comprehensive scheme to ensure better data protection in the European Union.
2. Completely abolish intermediate procedures (exequatur) for enforcing court decisions issued in another Member State.
3. Set up an exchange programme for police officers and improve the scheme that already exists for the judiciary and judicial staff (Erasmus programme for the police and the judiciary).
4. Strengthen procedural guarantees in criminal cases.
5. Develop a domestic security strategy for the European Union.
6. Create an information system architecture that will help to improve the exchange of information between European police forces.
7. Improve the evaluation of European judicial policies and support the efforts of the Member States to improve the quality of their judicial systems.
8. Ensure a flexible immigration policy that is in line with the needs of the job market whilst at the same time support the integration of immigrants and tackle illegal immigration.
9. Enhance solidarity between Member States for hosting refugees and asylum-seekers;
10. Increase the research effort in the area of security technologies.

As indicated in this book, it is important to emphasise that the development of the AFSJ should not only been seen in a negative light. This is despite some similarities with the controversial idea of 'homeland security' that this book has unveiled. However, it is equally important to remain critical and vigilant to ensure that future policy developments in the AFSJ are predominantly positive. Although the existence of a 'European homeland security' may seem unlikely in the near future, we should remember that this is the 'shape of things to come'.[1]

Note

1 With due acknowledgement to Tony Bunyan's report title – a title itself inspired by H. G. Wells's book *The Shape of Things to Come* (1933), which predicted authoritarian tendencies.

Bibliography

Academic sources

Achermann, A. and M. Gattiker (1995), 'Safe Third Countries: European Developments', *International Journal of Refugee Law*, vol. 7, no. 1, pp. 19–38.

Ackers, D. (2005), 'The Negotiations On The Asylum Procedures Directive', *European Journal of Migration and Law*, vol. 7, no. 1, pp. 1–33.

Adler, E. (1997), 'Seizing The Middle Ground', *European Journal of International Relations*, vol. 3, no. 3, pp. 319–363.

Adler, E. (2002), 'Constructivism And International Relations' in Carlsnaes, W., Risse, T. and Simmons, B.A. (eds), *Handbook of International Relations* (London: Sage), pp. 95–118.

Afeef, K.F. (2006), 'The Politics Of Extraterritorial Processing: Offshore Asylum Policies In Europe And The Pacific', Refugee Studies Centre Working Paper no. 36, Oxford: Refugee Studies Centre.

Agier, M. and J. Valluy (2007), 'Le HCR dans la logique des camps', in Le Cour Grandmaison, O., Lhuilier, G. and J. Valluy (eds), *Le Retour des camps? Sangatte, Lampedusa, Guantanamo* (Paris: Autrement), pp. 153–163.

Allen, W. (2003), 'The War Against Terrorist Financing', *Journal of Money Laundering Control*, vol. 6, no. 4, pp. 306–310.

Armstrong, K. and S. Bulmer (1998), *The Governance Of The Single European Market* (Manchester: Manchester University Press).

Aspinwall, M.D. and G. Schneider (2000), 'Same Menu, Separate Tables: The Institutionalist Turn In Political Science And The Study Of European Integration', *European Journal Of Political Research*, vol. 38, pp. 1–36.

Bailer, S. (2004), 'Bargaining Success in the European Union', *European Union Politics*, vol. 5, no. 1, pp. 99–123.

Baldaccini, A. (2003), 'The Recent British Proposals On Asylum Policy: A Critical Evaluation', paper presented at the International Seminar for Experts 'European Migration and Refugee Policy: New Developments', Cicero Foundation, Rome, 13–14 November 2003; on webpage www.cicerofoundation.org.

Baldaccini, A. (2006), 'Introduction', in Baldaccini, A. and E. Guild (eds) (2006), *Terrorism And The Foreigner: A Decade Of Tension Around The Rule Of Law In Europe* (Leiden: Martinus Nijhoff), pp. x–xxii.

Baldaccini, A. and E. Guild (eds) (2006), *Terrorism And The Foreigner: A Decade Of Tension Around The Rule Of Law In Europe* (Leiden: Martinus Nijhoff).

Baldwin-Edwards, M. and M. Schain (eds) (1994), *The Politics Of Immigration In Western Europe* (London: Frank Cass).

Balfour, R. (2007), 'Promoting Human Rights And Democracy In The EU's Neighbourhood: Tools, Strategies And Dilemmas', in Balfour, R. and A. Missiroli (eds), *Reassessing The European Neighbourhood Policy*, EPC Issue Paper no. 54, Brussels: European Policy Centre.

Balfour, R. and A. Missiroli (eds) (2007), *Reassessing The European Neighbourhood Policy*, EPC Issue Paper no. 54, Brussels: European Policy Centre.

Balnaves, M. and P. Caputi (2001), *Introduction To Quantitative Research Methods* (London: Sage).
Balzacq, T. (2005), 'The Three Faces Of Securitization: Political Agency, Audience And Context', *European Journal Of International Relations*, vol. 11, no. 2, pp. 171–201.
Balzacq, T. and S. Carrera (eds) (2005), *Migration, Border And Asylum: Trends And Vulnerabilities In EU Policy* (Brussels: Centre for European Policy Studies).
Balzacq, T. and S. Carrera (eds) (2006), *Security versus Freedom? A Challenge For Europe's Future* (Aldershot: Ashgate).
Balzacq, T. (2008), 'The Policy Tools Of Securitization: Information Exchange, EU Foreign And Interior Policies', *Journal Of Common Market Studies*, vol. 46, no. 1, pp. 75–100.
Barret, G. (ed.) (1997), *Justice Cooperation In The European Union* (Dublin: Institute of European Affairs).
Batjes, H. (2006), *European Asylum Law And Its Relation To International Law*, (Amsterdam: Vrije Universiteit Amsterdam).
Beach, D. (2004a), 'EU Institutions And IGC Negotiations: How The EU Negotiation Process Affects Institutions' Ability To Gain Influence In IGCs', in Meerts, P.W. and F. Cede (eds), *Negotiating European Union* (Basingstoke: Palgrave Macmillan), pp. 71–92.
Beach, D. (2004b), 'The Unseen Hand In Treaty Reform Negotiations: The Role And Impact Of The Council Secretariat', *Journal Of European Public Policy*, vol. 11, no. 3, pp. 1–30.
Beach, D. (2005a), *The Dynamics Of European Integration: Why And When EU institutions Matter* (London: Palgrave Macmillan).
Beach, D. (2005b), 'Why Governments Comply: An Integrative Compliance Model That Bridges The Gap Between Instrumental And Normative Models Of Compliance', *Journal Of European Public Policy*, vol. 12, no. 1, pp. 1–30.
Berthelet, P. (2003), *Le Droit institutionnel de la sécurité intérieure européenne* (Brussels: Presses Interuniversitaires Européennes/Peter Lang).
Betts, A. (2004), 'The International Relations Of The "New" Extraterritorial Approaches To Refugee Protection: Explaining The Policy Initiatives Of The UK Government And UNHCR', *Refuge*, vol. 22, no. 1, pp. 58–70.
Bicchi, F. (2004), 'The European Origins Of Euro-Mediterranean Practices', paper no. 040612, Institute of European Studies, Berkeley, CA: University of California.
Bieber, R. and J. Monar (eds) (1995), *Justice And Home Affairs In The European Union: The Development Of The Third Pillar* (Brussels: Interuniversity Press).
Biersteker, T.J. and S.E. Eckert (eds) (2008), *Countering The Financing Of Terrorism* (London: Routledge).
Bigo, D. (1996), *Polices en réseaux: l'expérience européenne* (Paris: Presses de Sciences Po).
Bigo, D. (1998a), 'L'Europe de la sécurité intérieure: penser autrement la sécurité', in Le Gloannec, A.-M. (ed.), *Entre union et nations: l'état en Europe* (Paris: Presses de Sciences Po), pp. 55–90.
Bigo, D. (1998b), 'Europe passoire et Europe forteresse: la sécurisation/humanitarisation de l'immigration', in Rea, A. (ed.), *Immigration et racisme en Europe* (Brussels: Complexe), pp. 203–241.
Bigo, D. (1998c), 'L'immigration à la croisée des chemins sécuritaires', *Revue européenne des migrations internationales*, vol. 14, no. 1, pp. 25–46.
Bigo, D. (2000), 'When Two Become One: Internal And External Securitizations In Europe' in Kelstrup, M. and M.C. Williams (eds), *International Relations Theory And The Politics Of European Integration: Power, Security And Community* (London: Routledge), pp. 171–204.
Bigo, D. (2001a), 'Migration And Security', in Guiraudon, V. and C. Joppke (eds), *Controlling A New Migration World* (London: Routledge), pp. 121–149.
Bigo, D. (2001b), 'The Möbius Ribbon Of Internal And External Security(ies)', in Albert,

M., Jacobson, D. and Y. Lapid (eds), *Identities, Borders, Orders: Rethinking International Relations Theory* (Minneapolis, MN: University of Minnesota Press), pp. 91–116.

Bigo, D. (2002), 'Security And Immigration: Toward A Critique Of The Governmentality Of Unease', *Alternatives*, no. 27 (special issue), pp. 63–92.

Bigo D. and E. Guild (2003), 'Le visa: instrument de la mise à distance des indésirables', *Cultures et conflits*, nos 49–50, pp. 82–95.

Bigo, D. and E. Guild (2003), *La Mise à l'écart des étrangers: la logique du visa Schengen* (Paris: l'Harmattan).

Bigo, D. (2006), 'Liberty: Whose Liberty? The Hague Programme And The Conception Of Freedom', in Balzacq, T. and S. Carrera (eds), *Security versus Freedom? A Challenge For Europe's Future* (Aldershot: Ashgate).

Blaikie, N. (2000), *Designing Social Research* (Cambridge: Polity Press).

Blitz, J. (2001), 'Berlusconi's Allies Defend Stance On Arrest: Rome Government Says EU Proposal Would Allow Witch-Hunts, But Opponents Claim That Premier Just Wants To Protect Himself', *Financial Times*, 10 December.

Bond, A. (ed.) (2004), *Writing Your Master's Thesis* (Taunton: Studymates).

Bosse, G. (2007), 'Values In The EU's Neighbourhood Policy: Political Rhetoric Or Reflection Of A Coherent Policy?', *European Political Economy Review*, no. 7 (summer), pp. 38–62.

Bossong, R. (2008), 'The Action Plan On Combating Terrorism: A Flawed Instrument Of EU Security Governance', *Journal Of Common Market Studies*, vol. 46, no. 1, pp. 27–48.

Boswell, C. (2003a), 'The "External Dimension" Of EU Immigration And Asylum Policy', *International Affairs*, vol. 79, no. 3, pp. 619–638.

Boswell, C. (2003b), *European Migration Policies In Flux: Changing Patterns Of Inclusion And Exclusion* (London: Royal Institute of International Affairs).

Boswell, C. (2008), 'Evasion, Reinterpretation And Decoupling: European Commission Responses To The "External Dimension" Of Immigration And Asylum', *West European Politics*, vol. 31, no. 3, pp. 491–512.

Boulden, J. and T.G. Weiss (eds) (2004), *Terrorism And The UN: Before And After September 11* (Bloomington, IN: Indiana University Press).

Bouteillet-Paquet, D. (1997), 'European Harmonisation In The Field Of Readmission Agreements', *International Journal Of Human Rights*, vol. 1, no. 3, pp. 31–43.

Bramwell, A.C. (ed.) (1988), *Refugees In The Age Of Total War* (London: Unwin Hyman).

Bretherton, C. and J. Vogler (2006), *The European Union As A Global Actor*, 2nd edn (London: Routledge).

Brochmann, G. (1996), *European Integration And Immigration From Third Countries* (Stockholm: Scandinavian University Press).

Bruter, M. (1999), 'Diplomacy Without A State: The External Delegations Of The European Commission', *Journal Of European Public Policy*, vol. 6, no. 2, pp. 183–205.

Bryman, A. and R.G. Burgess (1994), *Analyzing Qualitative Data* (London: Sage).

Budden, P. (2002), 'Observations On The Single European Act And Relaunch Of Europe: A Less "Intergovernmental" Reading Of The 1985 Intergovernmental Conference', *Journal Of European Public Policy*, vol. 9, no. 1, pp. 76–97.

Bullock, J. *et al.* (2006), *Introduction To Homeland Security* (Burlington, NJ: Elsevier Butterworth-Heinemann).

Bulmer, S. (1994), 'Institutions And Policy Change In The European Communities: The Case Of Merger Control', *Public Administration*, vol. 72, pp. 423–444.

Bulmer, S. (1998), 'New Institutionalism And The Governance Of The Single European Market', *Journal Of European Public Policy*, vol. 5, no. 3, pp. 365–386.

Bunyan, T. (1997), *Key Texts On Justice And Home Affairs In The European Union*, vol. 1, *1976–1993: From Trevi To Maastricht* (London: Statewatch).

Bunyan, T. (2008), *Statewatch: The Shape Of Things To Come: EU Future Report*,

Statewatch Observatory; on website: www.statewatch.org, September.
Bures, O. (2006), 'EU Counter-terrorism: A Paper Tiger', *Terrorism And Political Violence*, vol. 18, no. 1, pp. 57–87.
Burke, P. ed. (1992), *History And Social Theory* (Cambridge: Cambridge University Press).
Burnham, P. (1997), *Surviving The Research Process In Politics* (London: Pinter).
Burns, R. (2000), *Introduction to Research Methods* (London: Sage).
Buzan, B. (1991), *People, States And Fear: An Agenda For International Security Studies In The Post-Cold War Era*, 2nd edn (London: Harvester Wheatsheaf).
Buzan, B., Wæver, O. and J. de Wilde (1998), *Security: A New Framework For Analysis* (London: Lynne Rienner).
Byrne, R., Noll, G., and J. Vedsted-Hansen (eds) (2002), *New Asylum Countries? Migration Control And Refugee Protection In An Enlarged European Union* (Boston, MA: Kluwer Law International).
Cameron, F. (2007), 'Transatlantic Relations And Terrorism', in Spence, D. (ed.), *The European Union And Terrorism* (London: John Harper Publishing).
Carlsnaes, W. (2004), 'Where Is The Analysis Of European Foreign Policy Going?', *European Union Politics*, vol. 5, no. 4, pp. 495–508.
Carrera, S. and F. Geyer (2008), 'The Reform Treaty And Justice And Home Affairs: Implications For The Common Area Of Freedom, Security And Justice', in Guild, E. and F. Geyer, *Security versus Justice? Police and Judicial Cooperation in the European Union* (Aldershot: Ashgate).
Cassese, S. (1987) *The European Administration* (Brussels: IISA).
Castillo Garcia, J.F. (2005), 'The Power Of The European Community To Impose Criminal Penalties', *EIPAscope*, no. 2005/3 (Maastricht: EIPA).
Ceyhan, A. and A. Tsoukala (2002), 'The Securitization Of Migration In Western Societies: Ambivalent Discourses And Policies', *Alternatives*, vol. 27, pp. 21–39.
Checkel, J.T. (1997), 'International Norms And Domestic Politics: Bridging The Rationalist–Constructivist Divide', *European Journal Of International Relations*, vol. 3, no. 4, pp. 473–495.
Checkel, J.T. (1998a), 'Social Construction And Integration', Arena Working Papers, year 1998, no. 14, www.arena.uio.no/publications/wp98_14.htm.
Checkel, J.T. (1998b), 'The Constructivist Turn In International Relations Theory', *World Politics*, vol. 50, no. 2, pp. 324–348.
Checkel, J.T. (1999a), 'Norms, Institutions, And National Identity In Contemporary Europe', *International Studies Quarterly* vol. 43, no. 1, pp. 84–114.
Checkel, J.T. (1999b), 'Social Construction And Integration', *Journal Of European Public Policy*, vol. 6, no. 4, pp. 545–560.
Checkel, J.T. (2001), 'Why Comply? Social Learning And European Identity Change', *International Organization*, vol. 55, no. 1, pp. 553–588.
Christiansen, T. (1997), 'Tensions Of European Governance: Politicized Bureaucracy And Multiple Accountability In The European Commission', *Journal Of European Public Policy*, vol. 4, no. 1, pp. 73–90.
Christiansen, T. and K.E. Jorgensen (1998), 'Negotiating Treaty Reform In The European Union: The Role Of The European Commission', *International Negotiation*, vol. 3, no. 4, pp. 435–552.
Christiansen, T. *et al.* (1999), 'The Social Construction Of Europe', *Journal Of European Public Policy*, vol. 6, no. 4, pp. 528–544.
Christiansen, T. *et al.* (2001), *The Social Construction Of Europe* (London: Sage).
Christiansen, T. (2001), 'Intra-institutional Politics And Inter-institutional Relations In The EU: Towards Coherent Governance?', *Journal Of European Public Policy*, vol. 8, no. 5, pp. 747–769.
Christiansen, T. (2002), 'The Role Of Supranational Actors In EU Treaty Reform', *Journal*

Of European Public Policy, vol. 9, no. 1, pp. 33–53.
Christiansen, T., Falkner, G., and K.E. Jorgensen (2002), 'Social Science Theory And EU Treaty Reform: Beyond Diplomacy And Bargaining', *Journal Of European Public Policy*, vol. 9, no. 1, pp. 12–32.
Christiansen, T. (2006), 'The European Commission', in Richardson, J. (ed.), *European Union: Power And Policy-Making*, 3rd edn (Abingdon: Routledge).
Christiansen, T. and S. Vanhoonacker (2006), *At A Critical Juncture? Present And Future Challenges Facing The Council Secretariat* (London: Connex Thematic Conference).
Christiansen, T. (2008), 'The EU Treaty Reform Since 2000: The Highs And Lows Of Constitutionalising The European Union', *EIPAscope*, no. 1, pp. 39–44.
Christiansen, T. and C. Reh (2009), *Constitutionalizing The European Union* (London: Palgrave Macmillan).
Cini, M. (1996), *The European Commission: Leadership, Organisation And Culture In The EU Administration* (Manchester: Manchester University Press).
Cini, M. (2002), 'The European Commission', in Warleigh, A. (ed.), *Understanding European Union Institutions* (London: Routledge).
Clutterbuck, R. (1990), *Terrorism, Drugs And Crime In Europe After 1992* (London: Routledge).
Coen, D. and A. Héritier (eds) (2005), *Redefining Regulatory Regimes: Utilities In Europe* (Cheltenham: Edward Elgar).
Cohen, M., March, J. And J. Olsen (1972), 'A Garbage Can Model Of Organizational Choice', *Administrative Science Quarterly*, vol. 17, pp. 1–25.
Cohen, S. Humphries, B. and E. Mynott (eds) (2001), *From Immigration Controls To Welfare Controls* (New York: Routledge).
Collinson, S. (1993), *Beyond Borders: West European Migration Policy Towards The Twenty-first Century* (London: Royal Institute of International Affairs/Wyndham Place Trust).
Coombes, D. (1970), *Politics And Bureaucracy In The European Community: A Portrait Of The Commission Of The E.E.C.* (London: Allen & Unwin).
Cortell, A. and J.W. Davis (1996), 'How Do Institutions Matter? The Domestic Impact Of International Rules And Norms', *International Studies Quarterly*, vol. 40, no. 4, pp. 451–478.
Costello, C. (2005), 'The Asylum Procedures Directive And The Proliferation Of Safe Country Practices: Deterrence, Deflection And The Dismantling Of International Protection', *European Journal Of Migration And Law*, vol. 7, no. 1, pp. 35–69.
Cram L. (1994), 'The European Commission As A Multi-organization: Social Policy And IT Policy In The EU', *Journal Of European Public Policy*, vol. 1, no. 2., pp. 195–217.
Cram, L. (2001), 'Whither The Commission? Reform, Renewal And The Issue–Attention Cycle', *Journal Of European Public Policy*, vol. 8, no. 5, pp. 770–786.
Crawford, A. (ed.) (2002), *Crime And Insecurity: The Governance Of Safety In Europe* (Uffculme: Willan Publishing).
Crawley, H. (2005), 'Thematic Paper II. The UK, The EU And Forced Migration', in *Developing DFID's Policy Approach To Refugees And Internally Displaced Persons* (Oxford: Queen Elizabeth House, University of Oxford).
Crombez, C. (2000), 'Policy-Making And Commission Appointment In The European Union' in Moser, P., Schneider, G. and G. Kirchgässner (eds) (2000), *Decision Rules In The European Union: A Rational Choice Perspective* (London: Macmillan).
Dannreuther, R. (2006), 'Developing The Alternative To Enlargement: The European Neighbourhood Policy', *European Foreign Affairs Review*, vol. 11, no. 2, pp. 183–201.
Davis, M.K. (2007), 'An EU Homeland Security? Sovereignty versus Supranational Order', *European Security*, vol. 16, no. 1, pp. 79–97.
Deflem, M. (2006), 'Europol And The Policing Of International Terrorism: Counter-

terrorism In A Global Perspective', *Justice Quarterly*, vol. 23, no. 3, pp. 336–359.

Den Boer, M. (1995), 'Police, Customs And Judicial Cooperation In The Treaty On European Union', in Bieber, R. and J. Monar (eds), *Justice and Home Affairs In The European Union: The Development Of The Third Pillar* (Brussels: Interuniversity Press).

Den Boer, M. and W. Wallace (2000), 'Justice And Home Affairs', in Wallace, H. and W. Wallace (eds), *Policy-Making In The European Union*, 4th edn (Oxford: Oxford University Press).

Den Boer, M. (2001), 'The Incorporation Of Schengen Into The TEU: A bridge Too Far?', in Monar J. and W. Wessels (eds), *The European Union After The Treaty Of Amsterdam* (London: Continuum).

Den Boer, M. (2002), '11 September And Global Terrorism As A Challenge To The EU As A Security Actor', *Journal Of Common Market Studies*, vol. 40, no. 1, pp. 11–28.

Den Boer, M. and J. Monar (2002), 'Keynote Article. 11 September and the Challenge of Global Terrorism to the EU as a Security Actor', *Journal of Common Market Studies*, vol. 40, Annual Review, pp. 11–28.

Den Boer, M., Hillebrand, C. and Nölke, A. (2008), Legitimacy under Pressure: The European Web of Counter-Terrorism Networks', *Journal of Common Market Studies*, 46 (1), 101–124.

De Lobkowicz, W. (2002), *L'Europe et la sécurité intérieure* (Paris: la Documentation française).

De Schoutheete, P (2002), 'The European Council', in J. Peterson and M. Shackleton (eds), *The Institutions Of The European Union* (Oxford: Oxford University Press), pp. 21–46.

Del Sarto, R. A. and T. Schumacher (2005), 'From EMP To ENP: What's At Stake With The European Neighbourhood Policy Towards The Southern Mediterranean', *European Foreign Affairs Review*, vol. 10, no. 1, pp. 17–38.

De Kerchove, G. and A. Weyembergh (eds) (2002), *L'Espace pénal européen: enjeux et perspectives* (Brussels: Editions de l'Université de Bruxelles).

DiMaggio, P. and W. Powell (1991), *The New Institutionalism In Organizational Analysis* (Chicago: University of Chicago Press).

Dinan, D. (1999), *Ever Closer Union*, 2nd edn (London: Lynne Rienner).

Dinan, D. (2000), 'The Commission And The Intergovernmental Conferences', in Nugent, N. (ed.), *At The Heart Of The Union: Studies Of The European Commission*, 2nd edn (London: Macmillan), pp. 250–269.

Donnelly, B. (2008), 'Justice And Home Affairs In The Lisbon Treaty: A Constitutionalising Clarification?', *EIPAscope*, no. 1, pp. 19–23.

Douglas-Scott, S. (2004), 'The Rule Of Law In The European Union: Putting The Security Into The Area Of Freedom, Security And Justice', *European Law Review*, vol. 29, no. 2, pp. 219–242.

Drake, H. (1995), 'Political Leadership And European Integration; The Case Of Jacques Delors', *West European Politics*, vol. 18, no. 1, pp. 140–160.

Drake, H. (2000), 'The European Commission And The Politics Of Legitimacy In The European Union', in Nugent, N. (ed.), *At The Heart Of The Union: Studies Of The European Commission*, 2nd edn (London: Macmillan), pp. 230–249.

Dubois, D. (2002), 'The Attacks Of 11 September: EU–US Cooperation Against Terrorism In The Field Of Justice And Home Affairs', *European Foreign Affairs Review*, vol. 7, no. 3, pp. 317–355.

Duchêne, F. (1973), 'The European Community And The Uncertainties Of Interdependence', in Kohnstamm, M. and W. Hager (eds), *A Nation Writ Large? Foreign Policy Problems Before The European Community* (London: Macmillan).

Edwards, G. and D. Spence (2005), *The European Commission*, 2nd edn (London: Cartermill Publishing).

Edwards, G. and C. Meyer (2008), 'Introduction. Charting A Contested Transformation',

Journal Of Common Market Studies, vol. 46, no. 1, pp. 1–25.
Edwards, G. and Spence, D. (1994), *The European Commission*, 2nd edn (London: Cartermill Publishing).
Eeckhout, P. (2004), *External Relations Of The European Union: Legal And Constitutional Foundations* (Oxford: Oxford University Press).
Eling, K. (2007), 'The EU, Terrorism And Effective Multilateralism' in Spence, D. (ed.), *The European Union And Terrorism* (London: John Harper).
Elgström, O. (2000), 'Norm Negotiations: The Construction Of New Norms Regarding Gender And Development In EU Foreign Aid Policy', *Journal Of European Public Policy*, vol. 7, no. 3, pp. 457–476.
Elgström, O. and C. Jönsson (2000), 'Negotiation In The European Union: Bargaining Or Problem-Solving?', *Journal Of European Public Policy*, vol. 7, no. 5, pp. 684–704.
Elgström, O. and M. Smith (2000), 'Introduction: Negotiation And Policy-Making In The European Union: Processes, System And Order', *Journal Of European Public Policy*, vol. 7, no. 5, pp. 673–683.
Elgström, O. and M. Smith (eds) (2006), *The European Union's Role In International Politics* (London: Routledge).
Eling, K. (2006), 'The EU, Terrorism and Effective Multilateralism', in D. Spence (Ed.) *The European Union and Terrorism* (London: John Harper), pp. 105–123.
Ellermann, A. (2008), 'The Limits of Unilateral Immigration Control: Deportation and Inter-State Cooperation', *Government and Opposition*, 43 (2), pp. 168–189.
Emerson, M., Tessinari, F. and M. Vahl (2006), *A New Agreement Between The EU And Russia: Why, What And When?*, CEPS Policy Brief 103, Brussels: Centre for European Policy Studies.
Endo, K. (1999), *The Presidency of the European Commission under Jacques Delors* (Basingstoke: Macmillan).
Faist, T. (2004), *The Migration–Security Nexus. International Migration And Security Before And After 9/11*, Willy Brandt Series Of Working Papers In International Migration And Ethnic Relations 4/03, Malmö: Malmö University, available at www.bit.mah.se/MUEP.
Falkner, G. (2002), 'Introduction: EU Treaty Reform As A Three-Level Process', *Journal Of European Public Policy*, vol. 9, no. 1, pp. 1–11.
Farage, N. (11 October 2004), *Speech In The European Parliament On The Election Of The President Of The Commission Barroso*, on website: www.ukip.org/abc_news/gen12.php?t=1&id=928.
Faul, J. and L. Soreca (2008), 'EU–US Relations In Justice And Home Affairs', in Martenczuck, B. and S. van Thiel (eds), *Justice, Liberty And Security: New Challenges For EU External Relations* (Brussels: VUB Press/Brussels University Press).
Fierke, K.M. and K.E. Jørgensen (eds) (2001), *Constructing International Relations: The Next Generation* (London: M.E. Sharpe).
Finnemore, M. (1993), 'International Organizations As Teachers Of Norms: The United Nations Educational, Scientific, And Cultural Organization And Science Policy', *International Organization*, vol. 47, no. 4, pp. 565–597.
Finnemore, M. (1996a), *National Interest In International Society* (Ithaca, NY: Cornell University Press).
Finnemore, M. (1996b), 'Norms, Culture And World Politics: Insights From Sociology's Institutionalism', *International Organization*, vol. 50, no. 2, pp. 325–348.
Finnemore, M. and Sikkink, K. (1998), 'International Norm Dynamics And Political Change', *International Organization*, vol. 52, no. 4, pp. 887–917.
Fletcher M., Lööf R. with Gilmore, B. (2008), *EU Criminal Law and Justice* (Cheltenham: Edward Elgar).
Florini, A. (1996), 'The Evolution Of International Norms', *International Studies Quarterly*, vol. 40, pp. 363–389.

Fortescue, A. (1995), 'First Experiences With The Implementation Of The Third Pillar Provisions' in Bieber, R. and J. Monar (eds), *Justice And Home Affairs In The European Union: The Development Of The Third Pillar* (Brussels: Interuniversity Press).

Freeman, G. (1998), 'The Decline Of Sovereignty? Politics And Immigration Restriction In Liberal States', in Joppke, C. (ed.), *Challenge To The Nation State: Immigration In Western Europe And The United States* (Oxford: Oxford University Press), pp. 86–108.

Friedrichs, J. (2005), *Fighting Terrorism And Drugs* (London: Routledge).

Fuchs, G. (1994), 'Policy-Making In A System Of Multi-level Governance: The Commission Of The European Community And The Restructuring Of The Telecommunications Sector', *Journal Of European Public Policy*, vol. 1, no. 2, pp. 176–194.

Fuchs, G. (1995), 'The European Commission As Corporate Actor? European Telecommunications Policy After Maastricht', in Rhodes, C. and S. Mazey (1995), *The State Of The European Union*, vol. 3, *Building A European Polity* (Harlow: Longman), pp. 413–429.

Fullerton, M. (2005), 'Inadmissible In Iberia: The Fate Of Asylum Seekers In Spain And Portugal', *International Journal Of Refugee Law*, vol. 17, no. 4, pp. 659–687.

Gardner, H. (ed.) (2004), *NATO And The European Union: New World, New Europe, New Threats* (Aldershot: Ashgate).

Gardner, K.L. (2007), 'Fighting Terrorism The FATF Way', *Global Governance*, vol. 13, no. 3, pp. 325–345.

Garret, G. and B. Weingast (1993), 'Ideas, Interests, And Institutions: Constructing The European Community's Internal Market', in J. Goldstein and R.O. Keohane (eds), *Ideas And Foreign Policy* (Ithaca, NY: Cornell University Press).

Garret, G. and T. Tsebelis (1996), 'An Institutional Critique Of Intergovernmentalism', *International Organization*, vol. 50, no. 2, pp. 269–299.

Geddes, A. (2000), *Immigration And European Integration. Towards Fortress Europe?* (Manchester: Manchester University Press).

Geddes, A. (2001), 'International Migration And State Sovereignty In An Integrating Europe', *International Migration*, vol. 39, no. 6, pp. 21–39.

George, S. and I. Bache (2001), *Politics In The European Union* (Oxford: Clarendon Press).

Giddens, A. (1979), *Central Problems In Social Theory* (Berkeley, CA: University of California Press).

Giddens, A. (1984), *The Constitution Of Society* (Berkeley, CA: University of California Press).

Ginsberg, R.H. (2001), *The European Union In International Politics: Baptism By Fire* (Lanham, MD: Rowman & Littlefield).

Giraldo, J.K. and H.A. Trinkunas (eds) (2007), *Terrorism Financing And State Responses: A Comparative Perspective* (Stanford, CA: Stanford University Press).

Givens, T. E. *et al.* (eds) (2009), *Immigration Policy And Security: U.S., European And Commonwealth Perspectives* (London: Routledge).

Gottschalk, L. (1969), *Understanding History: A Primer Of Historical Method* (New York: Alfred A. Knopf).

Grabbe, H. (2002), 'Stabilizing The East While Keeping Out The Easterners: Internal And External Security Logics In Conflict', in Lavenex, S. and E. Uçarer (eds), *Migration And The Externalities Of European Integration* (Lanham, MD: Lexington books), pp. 91–104.

Gradin, A. (1999), 'Perspectives Of A European Immigration And Asylum Law', in Hailbronner, K. and P. Weil (eds), *Von Schengen nach Amsterdam. Auf dem Weg zu einem europäischen Einwanderungs- und Asylrecht. From Schengen To Amsterdam: Towards A European Immigration And Asylum Legislation* (Cologne: Bundesanzeiger).

Grant, C. (23. February 2004), 'Top Brussels Appointment Has To Be Right', *Financial Times*, republished on website: www.cer.org.uk/articles/grant_ft_23feb04.html.

Gray, M. (2001), 'Negotiating The Treaty Of Amsterdam: The Role And Influence Of The European Commission', in Laursen, F. (ed.), *The Treaty Of Amsterdam* (Odense: Odense University Press).

Greenwood, J. (2003), *Interest Representation In The European Union* (London: Macmillan).

Gregory, F. (2005), 'The EU's Response To 9/11: A Case Study Of Institutional Roles And Policy Processes, With Special Reference To Issues Of Accountability And Human Rights', *Terrorism And Violence*, vol. 17, pp. 105–123.

Guild, E. and J. Niessen (eds) (1996), *The Developing Immigration And Asylum Policies Of The European Union: Adopted Conventions, Resolutions, Recommendations, Decisions And Conclusions* (The Hague: Kluwer Law International).

Guild, E. (1999), 'The Impetus To Harmonise: Asylum Policy In The European Union', in Nicholson, F. and P. Twomey (1999), *Refugee Rights And Realities. Evolving International Concepts And Regimes* (Cambridge: Cambridge University Press), pp. 313–335.

Guild, E. (2002), 'Between Persecution And Protection: Refugees And The New European Asylum Policy', in *Cambridge Yearbook of European Legal Studies*, vol. 3 (Oxford: Hart Publishing), pp. 169–207.

Guild, E., Brouwer, E. and P. Catz (eds) (2002), *Immigration, Asylum, And Terrorism: A Changing Dynamic In European Law* (Nijmegen: Centrum voor Migratiererechts, Instituut voor Rechtssociologie).

Guild, E. and E. Brouwer (2006), *The Political Life Of Data: The ECJ Decision On The PNR Agreement Between The EU And The US*, CEPS Policy Brief no. 109, Brussels: Centre for European Policy Studies.

Guild, E. (2003a), 'International Terrorism And EU Immigration, Asylum and Borders Policy: The Unexpected Victims Of 11 September 2001', *European Foreign Affairs Review*, vol. 8, no. 3, pp. 331–346.

Guild, E. (2003b), 'Immigration, Asylum, Borders And Terrorism: The Unexpected Victims Of 11 September 2001' in Gökay, B. and R.B.J. Walkers (eds), *11 September 2001: War, Terror And Judgement* (London: Frank Cass), pp. 176–194.

Guild, E. (2003c), 'The Face Of Securitas: Redefining The Relationship Of Security And Foreigners In Europe' in Craig, P. and R. Rawlings (eds), *Law And Administration In Europe: Essays in Honour of Carol Harlow* (Oxford: Oxford University Press), pp. 139–153.

Guild, E. (2004), 'Seeking Asylum: Stormy Clouds Between International Commitments And EU Legislative Measures', *European Law Review*, vol. 29, no. 2, pp. 198–218.

Guild, E., and J. Van Selm (eds) (2005), *International Migration And Security: Opportunities And Challenges* (London: Routledge).

Guild, E. and F. Geyer (2008), *Security versus Justice? Police And Judicial Cooperation In The European Union* (Aldershot: Ashgate).

Guiraudon, V. (2000), 'European Integration And Migration Policy: Vertical Policy-Making As Venue Shopping', *Journal of Common Market Studies*, vol. 38, no. 2, pp. 251–271.

Guiraudon, V., and C. Joppke (eds) (2001), *Controlling A New Migration World* (London: Routledge).

Guiraudon, V. (2003), 'The Constitution Of A European Immigration Policy Domain: A Political Sociology Approach', *Journal of European Public Policy*, vol. 10, no. 2, pp. 263–282.

Gunning, J. (2008), 'Terrorism, Charities And Diasporas: Contrasting The Fundraising Practices Of Hamas And Al Qaeda Among Muslims In Europe', in Biersteker, T.J. and S.E. Eckert (eds), *Countering The Financing Of Terrorism* (London, Routledge).

Guyomarch, A. (1997), 'Cooperation In The Fields Of Policing And Judicial Affairs' in

Stavridis, S. *et al.*, *New Challenges To The European Union: Policy And Policy-Making* (Aldershot: Dartmouth Publishing), pp. 123–150.
Haaland Matlary, J. (1997), 'The Role Of The Commission: A Theoretical Discussion', in Nugent, N. (ed.), *At The Heart Of The Union: Studies Of The European Commission* (London: Macmillan).
Haas, E. (1958), *The Uniting Of Europe: Political, Social, And Economic Forces, 1950–1957* (Stanford, CA: Stanford University Press).
Haas, E. (1964), *Beyond The Nation State: Functionalism And International Organization* (Stanford, CA: Stanford University Press).
Haas, E. (1967), 'The Uniting Of Europe And The Uniting Of Latin America', *Journal Of Common Market Studies*, vol. 5, pp. 315–344.
Haacke, J. (2005), 'The Frankfurt School And International Relations: On The Centrality Of Recognition', *Review Of International Studies*, vol. 31, pp. 181–194.
Habermas, J. (1971), *Theory And Practice*, (London: Heinemann).
Habermas, J. (1990), *Moral Consciousness And Communicative Action* (Cambridge: Polity Press).
Hailbronner, K. and P. Weil (eds) (1999), *Von Schengen nach Amsterdam. Auf dem Weg zu einem europäischen Einwanderungs- und Asylrecht. From Schengen To Amsterdam: Towards A European Immigration And Asylum Legislation* (Cologne: Bundesanzeiger).
Hailbronner, K. (2000), *Immigration And Asylum Law And Policy Of The European Union* (The Hague: Kluwer Law International).
Hailbronner, K. (2004), 'Asylum Law In The Context Of A European Migration Policy', in Walker, N. (ed.), *Europe's Area Of Freedom, Security And Justice* (Oxford: Oxford University Press).
Hailbronner, K., Papakonstantinou, V. and M. Kau (2008), 'The Agreement On Passenger-Data Transfers (PNR) And The EU–US Cooperation In Data Communication', *International Migration*, vol. 46, no. 2, pp. 187–197.
Hall, P. and R. Taylor (1996), 'Political Science And The Three New Institutionalisms', *Political Studies*, no. 44, pp. 936–957.
Hall, R.B. (1997), 'Moral Authority As A Power Resource', *International Organization*, vol. 51, no. 4, pp. 591–622.
Hallstein, W. (1972), *Europe in the Making* (London: Allen & Unwin)
Hathaway, J.C. (1991), *The Law Of Refugee Status* (Toronto and Vancouver: Butterworth).
Hayes, B. (2001), *EU Anti-terrorism Action Plan: Legislative Measures In Justice And Home Affairs Policies*, Statewatch Observatory On Post-11 September 2001 And 11 March 2004 Effects On Civil Liberties And Democratic Standards, no. 6, on webpage www.statewatch.org/observatory2ab.htm.
Hebenton, B. and T. Thomas (1995), *Policing Europe: Co-operation, Conflict And Control* (London: Macmillan).
Heidensohn, F. and M. Farrell (eds) (1993), 2nd ed, *Crime In Europe* (London: Routledge).
Heimans, D. (2008), 'The External Relations Of Europol: Political, Legal And Operational Considerations', in Martenczuck, B. and S. van Thiel (eds), *Justice, Liberty And Security: New Challenges For EU External Relations* (Brussels: VUB Press/Brussels University Press).
Held, D. (1980), *Introduction To Critical Theory: Horkheimer To Habermas* (London: Hutchinson).
Held, D. and J.B. Thompson (eds) (1982), *Habermas: Critical Debates* (Basingstoke: Macmillan).
Helmberg, M. (2007), 'Eurojust And Joint Investigation Teams: How Eurojust Can Support JITs', *ERA Forum*, no. 8, pp. 245–251.
Héritier, A. (1996), 'The Accommodation Of Diversity In European Policy-Making And Its Outcomes: A Regulatory Policy As A Patchwork', *Journal Of European Public Policy*, vol. 3, no. 2, pp. 149–167.

Héritier, A. (2005), 'Managing Regulatory Developments In Rail', in David, C. and A. Héritier (eds), *Redefining Regulatory Regimes: Utilities In Europe* (Cheltenham: Edward Elgar).
Héritier, A. (2007), *Explaining Institutional Change In Europe* (Oxford: Oxford University Press).
Héritier, A., and C. Knill (2008), 'The Shadow Of Hierarchy And New Modes Of Governance', *Journal Of Public Policy*, vol. 28, no. 1, pp. 1–17.
de Hert, P. and B. de Schutter (2008), 'International Transfer Of Data In The Field Of JHA: The Lessons Of Europol, PNR And Swift', in Martenczuck, B. and S. van Thiel (eds), *Justice, Liberty And Security: New Challenges For EU External Relations* (Brussels: VUB Press/Brussels University Press).
Hierlemann, D. (2009), 'Ireland's Second Attempt,' *Spotlight Europe*, no. 2009/09 Gütersloh: Bertelsmann).
Hill, C. (2003), *The Changing Politics Of Foreign Policy* (Basingstoke: Palgrave Macmillan).
Hill, C. and M. Smith (eds) (2005), *International Relations And The European Union* (Oxford: Oxford University Press).
Hix, S. (1994), 'The Study Of The European Community: The Challenge To Comparative Politics', *West European Politics*, vol. 17, no. 1, pp. 1–30.
Hix, S. (1998), 'The Study Of The European Union' II, 'The "New Governance" Agenda And Its Rival', *Journal Of European Public Policy*, vol. 5, pp. 38–65.
Hix, S. (1999), *The Political System Of The European Union* (London: Macmillan).
Hipel, K. von (ed.) (2005), *Europe Confronts Terrorism* (Basingstoke: Palgrave).
Hockett, H. (1979), *The Critical Method In Historical Research And Writing* (Westport, CT: Greenwood Press).
Hoffmann, S. (1982), 'Reflections On The Nation-State In Western Europe Today,' *Journal Of Common Market Studies*, vol. 21, pp. 21–37.
Hoffmann, S. (1966), 'Obstinate Or Obsolete? The Fate Of The Nation-State And The Case Of Western Europe', *Daedalus*, vol. 95, pp. 862–915.
Hoffman, B. (1999), 'Is Europe Soft On Terrorism?', *Foreign Policy*, no. 115, pp. 62–76.
Hoffman, B. (2006), *Inside Terrorism*, 2nd edn (New York: Columbia University Press).
Hoffman, M. (1987), 'Critical Theory And The Inter-paradigm Debate', *Millennium: Journal Of International Studies*, vol. 16, no. 2, pp. 231–246.
Hoffman, M. (1991), 'Restructuring, Reconstruction, Reinscription, Rearticulation: Four Voices In Critical International Theory', *Millennium*, vol. 20, no. 2, pp. 169–185.
Hoffmann, L. (2009), 'Don't Let The Sun Go Down On Me: The German Constitutional Court And Its Lisbon Judgment', *Journal Of Contemporary European Research*, vol. 5, no. 3, pp. 50–68.
Hooghe, L. (2001), 'Top Commission Officials On Capitalism: An Institutionalist Understanding Of Preferences', in G. Schneider and M. Aspinwall (eds), *The Rules Of Integration: Institutionalist Approaches To The Study Of Europe* (Manchester: Manchester University Press).
Hopf, T. (1999), 'The Promise Of Constructivism In International Relations Theory', *International Security*, vol. 23, no. 1, pp. 170–200.
Huysmans, J. (1997), 'Revisiting Copenhagen: About The Development Of A Creative Security Studies Agenda In Europe', *European Journal Of International Relations*, vol. 4, no. 4, pp. 488–506.
Huysmans, J. (2000), 'The European Union And The Securitization Of Migration', *Journal Of Common Market Studies*, vol. 38, pp. 751–777.
Huysmans, J. (2004), 'A Foucaultian View On Spill-over: Freedom And Security In The EU', *Journal Of International Relations And Development*, vol. 7, no. 3, pp. 294–318.
Ibryamova, N. (2002), 'Migration From Central And Eastern Europe And Societal Security In The European Union', *Jean Monnet/Robert Schuman Paper Series*, vol. 1, no. 2, Coral

Gables, FL: Miami European Union Center, University of Miami.
Jay, A. (1999), 'All Bureaucracies Are Bad, But The EC Is A Federalising Behemoth', *Daily Telegraph*, 17 June, on webpage www.euro-sceptic.org/articles/art002.asp (15 March 2004).
Joffé, G. (2008), 'The European Union, Democracy And Counter-terrorism In The Maghreb', *Journal Of Common Market Studies*, vol. 46, no. 1, pp. 147–171.
Johansson-Nogués, E. (2007), 'The EU And Its Neighbourhood: An Overview', in Weber, K., Smith, M.E. and M. Baun (eds) *Governing Europe's Neighbourhood: Partners Or Periphery?* (Manchester: Manchester University Press).
John, P. (1998), *Analysing Public Policy* (London: Continuum).
Joppke, C. (ed.) (1998), *Challenge To The Nation-State: Immigration In Western Europe And The United States* (Oxford: Oxford University Press).
Joppke, C. (2001), 'The Legal-Domestic Sources Of Immigrant Rights: The United States, Germany And The European Union', *Comparative Political Studies*, vol. 34, no. 4, pp. 339–366.
Jørgensen, K.E. (2001), 'Four Levels And A Discipline' in Fierke, K.M. and Jørgensen, K.E. (eds), *Constructing International Relations The Next Generation* (London: M.E. Sharpe), pp. 36–53.
Kaczorowska, A. (2003), *Public International Law* (London: Old Bailey Press).
Karyotis, G. (2003), *European Migration Policy In The Aftermath Of September 11: The Security–Migration Nexus*, paper prepared for presentation at the second workshop of the UACES Study Group 'The Evolving European Migration Law And Policy', Manchester, 11–12 April.
Kaunert, C. (2005), 'The Area Of Freedom, Security And Justice: The Construction Of A "European Public Order"', *European Security*, vol. 14, no. 4, pp. 459–483.
Kaunert, C. (2007), 'Without The Power Of Purse Or Sword: The European Arrest Warrant And The Role Of The Commission', *Journal Of European Integration*, vol. 29, no. 4, pp. 387–404.
Kaunert, C. (2009), 'Liberty Versus Security? EU Asylum Policy and the European Commission', *Journal of Contemporary European Research*, vol. 5, no. 2, pp. 148–170.
Katzenstein, P. (1996), *The Culture Of National Security: Norms And Identity In World Politics* (New York: Columbia University Press).
Keck, M.E., and K. Sikkink (1998), *Activist Beyond Borders. Advocacy Networks In International Politics* (Ithaca, NY, and London: Cornell University Press).
Keleman, D. (2002), 'The Politics Of "Eurocratic" Structure And The New European Agencies', *West European Politics*, vol. 25, no. 4, pp. 93–118.
Keleman, D. (2005), 'The Politics Of Eurocracy: Building A New European State?', in Jabko, N. and C. Parson (eds), *The State Of The European Union*, vol. 7 (Oxford: Oxford University Press).
Kelemen, R.D. (2004), *The Rules Of Federalism* (Cambridge, MA: Harvard University Press).
Kelley, J. (2006), 'New Wine In Old Wineskins: Promoting Political Reforms Through The New European Neighbourhood Policy', *Journal Of Common Market Studies*, vol. 44, no. 1, pp. 29–55.
Keohane, D. (2005), 'The EU And Counter-terrorism', working paper, London: CER.
Keohane, D. (2008), 'The Absent Friend: EU Foreign Policy And Counter-terrorism', *Journal Of Common Market Studies*, vol. 46, no. 1, pp. 125–146.
Kingdon, J.W. (1984), *Agenda, Alternatives, And Public Policies* (Boston, MA: Little Brown).
Kingdon, J.W. (2003), *Agenda, Alternatives, And Public Policies*, 2nd edn (Boston, MA: Little Brown).
Kirchner, E. and J. Sperling (2002), 'The New Security Threats In Europe', *European Foreign Affairs Review*, vol. 7, pp. 423–452.

Kirkhope, T. (2005), *Court Decision A Blow To UK Sovereignty*, on website: www.conservatives.com/tile.do?def=news.story.page&obj_id=124767 (13 September).

Kohler-Koch, B. (1996), 'Catching Up With Change: The Transformation Of Governance In The European Union', *Journal Of European Public Policy*, vol. 3, no. 3, pp. 359–380.

Kohler-Koch, B. and P. Eising (eds) (1999), *The Transformation Of Governance In The European Union* (London: Routledge).

Kostakopolou, T. (2000), 'The Protective Union: Change And Continuity In Migration Law And Policy In Post-Amsterdam Europe', *Journal Of Common Market Studies*, vol. 38, no. 3, pp. 497–518.

Krahnmann, E. (2003), *Multi-level Networks In European Foreign Policy* (Aldershot: Ashgate).

Kratochvil, P. and M. Braun (2009), 'The Lisbon Treaty And The Czech Republic: Past Imperfect, Future Uncertain', *Journal Of Contemporary European Research*, vol. 5, no. 3.

Kratochwil, F. and J.G. Ruggie (1986), 'International Organization: A State Of The Art Or An Art Of The State', *International Organization*, vol. 40, no. 4, pp. 753–775.

Kratochwil, F. (1989), *Rules, Norms And Decisions: On The Conditions Of Practical And Legal Reasoning In International Relations And Domestic Affairs* (Cambridge: Cambridge University Press).

Krause, K. and M.C. Williams (1996), 'Broadening The Agenda Of Security Studies? Politics And Methods', *Mershon International Studies Review*, vol. 40, no. 2, pp. 229–254.

Krueger, R. (1997), *Analysing and Reporting Focus Group Results* (Thousand Oaks, CA: Sage).

Kuijpers, P.J. (2008), 'The Opinion On The Lugano Convention And The Implied External Relations Powers Of The European Community', in Martenczuck, B. and S. van Thiel (eds), *Justice, Liberty And Security: New Challenges For EU External Relations* (Brussels: VUB Press/Brussels University Press).

Kurpas, S. (2005), 'Should Ratification Proceed? An Assessment Of The Different Option After The Failed Referenda', *CEPS Policy Briefs*, no. 75/June, Brussels: CEPS.

Kurpas, S., Grøn, C. and M.P. Kaczynski (2008), 'The European Commission After Enlargement: Does More Add Up To Less?', *CEPS Special Report*, http://shop.ceps.eu/BookDetail.php?item_id=1620 (retrieved 6 March 2009).

Laffan, B. (1997a), 'From Policy Entrepreneur To Policy Manager: The Challenge Facing The European Commission', *Journal Of European Public Policy*, vol. 4, no. 3, pp. 422–438.

Laffan, B. (1997b), *The Finances Of The European Union* (London: Macmillan).

Laffan, B. (2001), 'The European Union Polity: A Union Of Regulative, Normative And Cognitive Pillars', *Journal Of European Public Policy*, vol. 8, no. 5, pp. 709–727.

Lambert, H. (2004), 'A Missed Opportunity? EU Law and Asylum in the Twenty-first Century', in T. Tridimas and P. Nebbia (eds), *European Law for the Twenty-first Century: Rethinking the New Legal Order* (Oxford: Hart Publishing), pp. 361–375.

Latter, R. (1991), *Crime And The European Community After 1992* (London: HMSO).

Laqueur, W. (2004), *No End To War: Terrorism In The Twenty-first Century* (London: Continuum).

Lavenex, S. (1998), 'Transgressing Borders: The Emergent European Refugee Regime And "Safe Third Countries"', in Cafruny, A. and P. Peters (eds) (1998), *The Union And The World. The Political Economy Of A Common European Foreign Policy* (The Hague: Kluwer Law International), pp. 113–132.

Lavenex, S. (1999), *Safe Third Countries. Extending The EU Asylum And Immigration Policies To Central And Eastern Europe* (Budapest and New York: Central European University Press).

Lavenex, S. (2001a), 'The Europeanization Of Refugee Policies: Normative Challenges And Institutional Legacies', *Journal Of Common Market Studies*, vol. 39, no. 5, pp. 851–74.
Lavenex, S. (2001b), *The Europeanisation Of Refugee Policies. Between Human Rights And Internal Security* (Aldershot: Ashgate).
Lavenex, S. (2004), 'EU External Governance In "Wider Europe"', *Journal Of European Public Policy*, vol. 11, no. 4, pp. 680–700.
Lavenex, S. (2006), 'Shifting Up And Out: The Foreign Policy Of European Immigration Control', *West European Politics*, vol. 29, no. 2, pp. 329–50.
Lavenex, S. and E. Uçarer (eds) (2002), *Migration And The Externalities Of European Integration* (Lanham, MD: Lexington Books).
Lawrence Neuman, W. (1999), *Social Research Methods: Qualitative And Quantitative Approaches*, 4th edn (Boston, MA: Allyn & Bacon).
Lawton, T.C. (2000), 'Uniting European Industrial Policy: A Commission Agenda For Integration', in Nugent, N. (ed.) (2000), *At The Heart Of The Union: Studies Of The European Commission*, 2nd edn (London: Macmillan), pp. 131–146.
Lebl, L.S. (2006), 'Working With The European Union', *Orbis*, vol. 50, no. 1, pp. 117–132.
Leeuwen, van M. (ed.) (2003), *Confronting Terrorism* (Leiden: Martinus Nijhoff).
Legro, J.W. (1997), 'Which Norms Matter? Revisiting The Failure Of Internationalism', *International Organization*, vol. 51, no. 1, pp. 31–63.
Léonard, S. (2007), 'The European Union And The "Securitization" Of Asylum And Migration: Beyond The Copenhagen School's Framework', PhD thesis, Aberystwyth: University of Wales.
Lewis, J. (2005), 'The Janus Face of Brussels: Socialization and Everyday Decision Making in the European Union', *International Organization*, vol. 59, no. 4, pp. 937–971.
Levy, C. (2005), 'The European Union after 9/11: the Demise of a Liberal Democratic Asylum Regime?', *Government and Opposition*, vol. 40, no. 1, pp. 26–59.
Lindberg, L. (1963), *The Political Dynamics Of European Economic Integration* (Stanford, CA: Stanford University Press).
Lindberg, L.N. and S.A. Scheingold (1970), *Europe's Would-be Polity. Patterns Of Change In The European Community* (Englewood Cliffs, NJ: Prentice-Hall).
Lindberg, L.N. and S.A. Scheingold (eds) (1971), *Regional Integration. Theory And Research* (Cambridge, MA: Harvard University Press).
Lindstrom, C. (2003), *Addressing The Root Causes Of Forced Migration: A European Union Policy Of Containment?* RSC Working Paper no. 11, Oxford: International Development Centre, University of Oxford.
Linklater, A. (1990), *Men And Citizens In The Theory Of International Relations* (London: Macmillan).
Linklater, A. (1992), 'The Question Of The Next Stage In International Relations Theory: A Critical-Theoretical Point Of View', *Millennium: Journal Of International Studies*, vol. 21, no. 1, pp. 77–98.
Linklater, A. (1998), *The Transformation Of Political Community: Ethical Foundations Of The Post-Westphalian Era* (Cambridge: Polity Press).
Linklater, A. (2001), *Beyond Realism And Marxism* (Basingstoke: Macmillan).
Linklater, A. (2007), *Critical Theory And World Politics* (Abingdon: Routledge).
Lodge, J. (2004), 'EU Homeland Security: Citizens Or Suspects?', *Journal of European Integration*, vol. 26, no. 3, pp. 253–279.
Lodge, J. (ed.) (2007), *Are You Who You Say You Are? The EU and Biometric Borders* (Nijmegen: Wolf).
Louis, J.-V. and D. Waelbroeck (1989), *La Commission Au coeur du système institutionnel des Communautés européennes* (Brussels: Editions de l'Université de Bruxelles).
Ludlow, P. (1991), 'The European Commission', in Keohane, R. and Hoffmann, S. (eds),

The New European Community: Decision-Making And Institutional Change (Oxford: Westview Press).

Ludlow, P. (2002a), *The Laeken Council* (Brussels: EuroComment).

Ludlow, P. (2002b), *The Seville Council* (Brussels: EuroComment).

Lugna, L. (2006), 'Institutional Framework Of The European Union Counter-terrorism Policy Setting', *Baltic Security and Defence Review*, no. 8, pp. 101–127.

Lutz J. and B. (2004), *Global Terrorism* (London: Routledge).

Loescher, G. (1989), 'The European Community And Refugees', *International Affairs*, vol. 65, no. 4, pp. 617–636.

Loescher, G. (1992), *Refugee Movements And International Security*, Adelphi Paper no. 268 (London: International Institute of Strategic Studies).

Loescher, G. (1993), *Beyond Charity: International Cooperation And The Global Refugee Crisis* (Oxford: Oxford University Press).

Loescher, G. (1995), 'International Security And Population Movements' in Cohen, R. (ed.), *The Cambridge Survey Of World Migration* (Cambridge: Cambridge University Press), pp. 557–560.

Loescher, G. (2004), 'Refugee Protection And State Security: Towards A Greater Convergence', in Price, R.M. and M.W. Zacher (eds), *The United Nations And Global Security* (Basingstoke: Palgrave Macmillan), pp. 161–176.

MacNamara, K. (2002), 'Rational Fictions: Central Bank Independence And The Social Logic Of Integration', *West European Politics*, no. 25, pp. 47–76.

Mahncke, D., Wyn Rees and W.C. Thompson (2004), *Redefining Transatlantic Security Relations: The Challenge Of Change* (Manchester: Manchester University Press).

Majone, G. (1991), 'Cross-national Sources Of Regulatory Policy-Making In Europe And The United States', *Journal Of Public Policy*, vol. 11, no. 1, pp. 79–106.

Majone, G. (1993), 'The European Community Between Social Policy And Social Regulation', *Journal Of Common Market Studies*, vol. 31, no. 2, pp. 153–170.

Majone, G. (1994), 'The Rise Of The Regulator State In Europe', *West European Politics*, vol. 17, no. 3, pp. 77–101.

Majone, G. (1996), *Regulating Europe* (London and New York: Routledge).

Majone, G. (1997), 'The New European Agencies: Regulation By Information', *Journal Of European Public Policy*, vol. 4, no. 2, pp. 262–275.

Majone, G. (2005), *Dilemmas Of European Integration: The Ambiguities And Pitfalls Of Integration By Stealth* (Oxford: Oxford University Press).

Manners, I. (2002), 'Normative Power Europe: A Contradiction In Terms?', *Journal Of Common Market Studies*, vol. 40, no. 2, pp. 235–258.

March, J. and Olsen, J. (1984), 'The New Institutionalism: Organizational Factors In Political Life', *American Political Science Review*, vol. 78, no. 3, pp. 734–749.

March, J. and J. Olsen (1989), *Rediscovering Institutions: The Organisational Bias Of Politics* (New York: Free Press).

March, J. and J. Olsen (1996), 'Institutional Perspectives On Political Institutions', *Governance: An International Journal Of Policy And Administration*', vol. 9, no. 3, pp. 247–264.

March, J.G. and J.P. Olsen (1998), 'The Institutional Dynamics Of International Political Orders', *International Organization*, vol. 52, no. 4, pp. 943–969.

Marks, G. (1993), 'Structural Policy And Multi-level Governance In The EC', in A. Cafruny and G. Rosenthal (eds), *The State Of The European Community*, vol. 2, *The Maastricht Debates and Beyond* (Boulder, CO: Lynne Rienner).

Marrus, M.R. (1985), *The Unwanted. European Refugees In The Twentieth Century* (Oxford: Oxford University Press).

Marrus, M.R. (1988), 'Introduction', in Bramwell, A.C. (ed.), *Refugees In The Age Of Total War* (London: Unwin Hyman), pp. 1–6.

Marsh, D. and G. Stoker (ed.) (2002), *Theory And Methods In Political Science*, 2nd edn (Basingstoke: Palgrave Macmillan).

Martenczuck, B. and S. van Thiel (eds) (2008), *Justice, Liberty And Security: New Challenges For EU External Relations* (Brussels: VUB Press/Brussels University Press).

Martin, G. (2006), *Understanding Terrorism: Challenges, Perspectives, And Issues* (Thousand Oaks, CA: Sage).

Mason, J. (1996), *Qualitative Researching* (London: Sage).

Matláry, J.H. (1997), *Energy Policy In The European Union* (Basingstoke: Macmillan).

Matláry, J.H. (2000), 'The Role Of The Commission: A Theoretical Discussion', in Nugent, N. (ed.) (2000), *At The Heart Of The Union: Studies Of The European Commission*, 2nd edn (London: Macmillan), pp. 270–287.

Mattli, W. (1999), *The Logic Of Regional Integration: Europe And Beyond* (Cambridge: Cambridge University Press).

Mazey, S. (1995), 'The Development Of EU Equality Policies: Bureaucratic Expansion On Behalf Of Women?', *Public Administration*, vol. 73, no. 4, pp. 591–609.

Mazey, S. and J. Richardson (2001), 'Institutionalising Promiscuity: Commission: Interest Group Relations In The European Union' in Stone Sweet, A., W. Sandholtz and N. Fligstein (2001), *The Institutionalization Of Europe* (Oxford: Oxford University Press).

McGowan, L. and Wilks, S. (1995), 'The First Supranational Policy In The European Union: Competition Policy', *European Journal Of Political Research*, vol. 28, no. 2, pp. 141–169.

Meunier, S. (2005), *Trading Voices: The European Union In International Commercial Negotiations* (Princeton, NJ: Princeton University Press).

Meyer, C.O. (2006), *The Quest For A European Strategic Culture: A Comparative Study Of Strategic Norms And Ideas In The European Union* (Basingstoke: Palgrave).

Milliken, J. (2001), 'Discourse Study: Bringing Rigor To Critical Theory' in Fierke, K.M. and K.E. Jørgensen (eds), *Constructing International Relations The Next Generation* (London: M.E. Sharpe), pp. 136–159.

Mitrany D. (1966), *A Working Peace* (Chicago: Quadrangle Books).

Mitsilegas, V., Monar, J. and W. Rees (2003), *The European Union And Internal Security: Guardian Of The People* (London: Macmillan).

Mitsilegas, V. (2003), 'The New EU–USA Cooperation On extradition, Mutual Legal Assistance And The Exchange Of Police Data', *European Foreign Affairs Review*, no. 8, pp. 515–536.

Mitsilegas, V. (2009), 'Borders, Security, And Transatlantic Cooperation In The Twenty-first Century: Identity And Privacy In An Era Of Globalized Surveillance' in Givens, T. E. *et al.* (eds), *Immigration Policy And Security: U.S., European And Commonwealth Perspectives* (London: Routledge).

Mitsilegas, V. and B. Gilmore (2007), 'The EU Legislative Framework Against Money Laundering and Terrorist Finance: A Critical Analysis in the Light of Evolving Global Standards', *International and Comparative Law Quarterly*, vol. 56, no. 1, pp. 119–141.

Monar, J. (1999a), 'An Emerging Regime Of European Governance For Freedom, Security And Justice', *ESRC One Europe Of Several?* Programme Briefing Note 2/99 (Swindon: ESCRC).

Monar, J. (1999b), 'Justice And Home Affairs In A Wider Europe: The Dynamics Of Inclusion And Exclusion', *ESRC One Europe Of Several?* Working Paper 07/00 (Swindon: ESCRC)

Monar, J. (2000), 'Justice And Home Affairs', *Journal Of Common Market Studies*, vol. 38, Annual Review, pp. 125–142.

Monar, J. (2001a), 'Justice And Home Affairs', *Journal Of Common Market Studies*, vol. 39, Annual Review, pp. 121–37.

Monar, J. (2001b), 'The Dynamics Of Justice And Home Affairs: Laboratories, Driving Factors And Costs', *Journal Of Common Market Studies*, vol. 39, no. 4, pp. 747–764.

Monar, J. (2004), 'The EU As An International Actor In The Domain Of Justice And Home Affairs', *European Foreign Affairs Review*, no. 9, pp. 395–415.

Monar, J. (2005), 'A New Area Of Freedom, Security And Justice For The Enlarged EU? The results Of The European Convention' in Henderson, K. (ed.), *The Area Of Freedom, Security And Justice In The Enlarged Europe* (Basingstoke: Palgrave Macmillan), pp. 110–134.

Monar, J. (2007), 'The EU's Approach Post-September 11: Global Terrorism As A Multidimensional Law Enforcement Challenge', *Cambridge Review of International Affairs*, vol. 20, no. 2, pp. 267–283.

Monnet, J. (1978), *Memoirs* (London: Collins).

de Moraes Ruehsen, M. (2007), 'Arab Government Responses To The Threat Of Terrorist Financing', in Giraldo, J.K. and H.A. Trinkunas (eds), *Terrorism Financing And State Responses: A Comparative Perspective* (Stanford, CA: Stanford University Press).

Moravcsik, A. (1991), 'Negotiating The Single European Act: National Interests And Conventional Statecraft In the European Community', *International Organization*, vol. 45, no. 1, pp. 19–56.

Moravcsik, A. (1993), 'Preferences And Power In The European Community: A Liberal Intergovernmentalist Approach', *Journal Of Common Market Studies*, vol. 33, no. 4, pp. 611–628.

Moravcsik, A. (1995), 'Liberal Intergovernmentalism And Integration: A Rejoinder', *Journal Of Common Market Studies*, vol. 33, no. 4, pp. 611–628.

Moravcsik, A. (1997), 'Taking Preferences Seriously: A Liberal Theory Of International Politics', *International Organization*, vol. 51, no. 4, pp. 513–553.

Moravcsik, A. (1998), *The Choice For Europe: Social Purpose and State Power, From Messina To Maastricht* (Ithaca, NY: Cornell University Press).

Moravcsik, A. (1999a), 'A New Statecraft? Supranational Entrepreneurs And International Cooperation', *International Organization*, vol. 53, no. 2, pp. 267–306.

Moravcsik, A. (1999b), 'Theory And Method In The Study Of International Negotiation: A Rejoinder To Oran Young', *International Organization*, vol. 53, no. 4, pp. 811–814.

Moravcsik, A. (1999c), 'Is Something Rotten In The State Of Denmark? Constructivism And European Integration', *Journal Of European Public Policy*, vol. 6, no. 5, pp. 669–681.

Moravcsik, A. and K. Nicolaïdes (1999d), 'Explaining The Treaty Of Amsterdam: Interests, Influence, Institutions', *Journal of Common Market Studies*, vol. 37, no. 1, pp. 59–86.

Moravcsik, A. (2001), 'Constructivism And European Integration: A Critique', in Christiansen, T. *et al.* (2001), *The Social Construction Of Europe* (London: Sage).

Morgan, D. (1998), *Focus Groups As Qualitative Research* (Thousand Oaks, CA: Sage).

Moser, P., Schneider, G. and G. Kirchgässner (eds) (2000), *Decision Rules In The European Union: A Rational Choice Perspective* (London: Macmillan).

Mueller, R. (2005), 'Gericht. Rahmenbeschluesse der EU haben unmittelbare Wirkung', *Franfurter Allgemeine Zeitung* (*FAZ.net*), 16 June, on webpage www.faz.net /s/Rub812F1B901A514F208C613F6B1B336BCC/Doc~ED3119B.

Müller-Wille, B. (2008), 'The Effect of International Terrorism on EU Intelligence Co-operation', *Journal of Common Market Studies*, vol. 46, no. 1, pp. 49–73.

Mutimer, D. (1999), 'Beyond Strategy: Critical Thinking And The New Security Studies' in Snyder, C.A. (ed.), *Contemporary Security And Strategy* (Basingstoke: Macmillan), pp. 77–101.

Myers, P. (1995), 'The Commission's Approach To The Third Pillar: Political And Organizational Elements' in Bieber, R. and J. Monar (eds), *Justice And Home Affairs In The European Union: The Development Of The Third Pillar* (Brussels: Interuniversity Press).

Nicolaïdis, C. and R. Howse (2003), 'This Is My EUtopia ... : Narrative As Power', in Weiler, J.H.H., Begg, I. and J. Peterson (eds), *Integration In An Expanding European Union* (Oxford: Blackwell), pp. 341–366.

Noll, G. (2000), *Negotiating Asylum: The EU Acquis, Extraterritorial Protection And The Common Market Of Deflection* (The Hague: Martinus Nijhoff).

Norman, P. (2001), 'Common Criminals', *Financial Times*, 6 December.

Norman, P. (2003), *The Accidental Constitution* (Brussels: EuroComment).

Nugent, N. (1995), 'The Leadership Capacity Of The European Commission', *Journal Of European Public Policy*, vol. 2, no. 4, pp. 603–623.

Nugent, N. (1999), *The Government And Politics Of The European Union*, 4th edn (Basingstoke: Macmillan).

Nugent, N. (ed.) (1997), *At The Heart Of The Union: Studies Of The European Commission*, 1st edn (London: Macmillan).

Nugent, N. (ed.) (2000), *At The Heart Of The Union: Studies Of The European Commission*, 2nd edn (London: Macmillan).

Nugent, N. (2001), *The European Commission* (Basingstoke: Palgrave).

Nugent, N. (2006), *The Government And Politics Of The European Union*, 6th edn (Basingstoke: Palgrave).

Occhipinti, J. (2003), *The Politics Of EU Police Cooperation: Towards A European FBI?* (Boulder, CO: Lynne Rienner).

Occhipinti, J. (2008), 'Progress Amid Difference: The EU And US Counter-terrorism', paper presented at the annual conference of the International Studies Association, San Francisco, 29 March.

Onuf, N. (1989), *World Of Our Making: Rules And Rules In Social Theory And International Relations* (Columbus, SC: University of South Carolina Press).

Papademetriou, D.G. and K.A. Hamilton (1996), '*Converging Paths To Restriction: French, Italian And British Responses To Immigration*, International Migration Policy Program 3 (Washington, DC: Carnegie Endowment for International Peace).

Pardo, S. and L. Zemer (2005), 'Towards A New Euro-Mediterranean Neighbourhood Space', *European Foreign Affairs Review*, vol. 10, no. 1, pp. 39–77.

Park, P. (2001), 'Knowledge And Participatory Research' in Reason, P. and H. Bradbury (eds), *Handbook of Action Research* (London: Sage).

Pastore, F. (2002) 'Aeneas's Route: Euro-Mediterranean Relations And International Migration', in Lavenex, S. and E. Uçarer (eds), *Migration And The Externalities Of European Integration* (Lanham, MD: Lexington Books), pp. 105–123.

Payne, R.A. (2001), 'Persuasion, Frames And Norm Construction', *European Journal Of International Relations*, vol. 7, no. 1, pp. 37–61.

Peers, S. (2000), *EU Justice And Home Affairs Law* (London: Longman).

Peers, S. (2001), 'Proposed Framework Decision On European Arrest Warrants', *Statewatch Post-11 September 2001 Analyses*, no. 3, on webpage www.statewatch.org.

Peers, S. (2002), 'Key Legislative Developments On Migration In The European Union', *European Journal Of Migration And Law*, vol. 4, no. 1, pp. 85–126.

Peers, S. (2004), 'Irregular Immigration And EU External Relations', in Bogusz, B. *et al.* (eds), *Irregular Migration And Human Rights: Theoretical, European And International Perspectives* (Leiden and Boston, MA: Martinus Nijhoff), pp. 193–219.

Peers, S. (2004), 'The Hague Programme: Annotation Of Final Version', approved 5 November, on website: www.statewatch.org/news/2004/nov.

Peers, S. (2005), 'Statewatch Briefing: Vetoes, Opt-outs, And EU Immigration And Asylum Law', 8 November, on website: www.statewatch.org/news/2004/nov.

Peers, S. (2006), *EU Justice And Home Affairs Law*, 2nd edn (Oxford: Clarendon Press).

Peers, S. and N. Rogers (eds) (2006), *EU Asylum And Migration Law: Text And Commentary* (Leiden: Martinus Nijhoff).

Peters, G. (1994), 'Agenda-Setting In The European Community', *Journal Of European Public Policy*, vol. 1, no. 1, pp. 9–26.
Peters, G. (2001), 'Agenda Setting In The European Union', in Richardson, J. (ed.), *European Union: Power And Policy-Making*, 2nd edn (London: Routledge).
Peterson, J. (1995a), 'EU Research Policy: The Politics Of Expertise' in Rhodes, C. and S. Mazey (eds), *The State Of The European Union*, vol. 3, *Building A European Polity* (Harlow: Longman), pp. 391–412.
Peterson, J. (1995b), 'Playing The Transparency Game: Consultation And Policy-Making In The European Commission', *Public Administration*, vol. 73, no. 3, pp. 474–92.
Peterson, J. (1999), 'The Santer Era: The European Commission In Normative, Historical And Theoretical Perspective', *Journal Of European Public Policy*, vol. 6, no. 1, pp. 46–65.
Peterson, J. and E. Bomberg (1999b), *Decision-Making In The European Union* (London: Macmillan).
Peterson, J. and A. Birdsall (2008), 'The European Commission: Enlargement As Reinvention?', in E. Best, Christiansen, T. and P. Settembri (eds), *The Governance Of The Wider Europe: EU Enlargement And Institutional Change* (Aldershot and Northampton, MA: Edward Elgar), pp. 54–81.
Peterson, J. (2001), 'The Choice For EU Theorists: Establishing A Common Framework For Analysis', *Europ Research*, vol. 39, no. 3, pp. 289–318.
Peterson, J. and M. Shackleton (eds) (2002), *The Institutions Of The European Union* (Oxford: Oxford University Press).
Pierson, P. (1996), 'The Path To European Integration: A Historical Institutionalist Analysis', *Comparative Political Studies*, vol. 29, no. 2, pp. 123–163.
Pollack, M.A. (1996), 'The New Institutionalism And EC Governance: The Promise And Limits Of Institutional Analysis', *Governance: An International Journal Of Policy And Administration*; vol. 9, no. 4, pp. 429–458.
Pollack, M.A. (1997a), 'Delegation, Agency And Agenda-Setting In The European Community', *International Organization*, vol. 51, no. 1, pp. 99–134.
Pollack, M.A. (1997b), 'Representing Diffuse Interests In The EC Policy-Making Process', *Journal Of European Public Policy*, vol. 4, no. 4, pp. 572–590.
Pollack, M.A. (2000), 'The Commission As An Agent', in Nugent, N. (ed.), *At The Heart Of The Union: Studies Of The European Commission*, 2nd edn (London: Macmillan), pp. 111–129.
Pollack, M.A. (2003), *The Engines Of European Integration* (Oxford: Clarendon Press).
Puchala, D. (1971), 'Of Blind Men, Elephants And International Integration', *Journal Of Common Market Studies*, vol. 10, no. 2, pp. 267–284.
Puchala, D. (1984), *Fiscal Harmonization In The European Communities. National Politics And International Cooperation* (London and Dover: Pinter).
Price, R. (1998), 'Reversing The Gun Sights: Transnational Civil Society Targets Land Mines', *International Organization*, vol. 52, pp. 613–644.
Quine, W. (1961), *From A Logical Point Of View* (New York: Harper & Row).
Raz, J. (1975), *Practical Reason And Norms* (London: Hutchinson).
Reason, P. and H. Bradbury (eds) (2001), *Handbook Of Action Research* (London: Sage).
Rees, W. (2006), *Transatlantic Counter-terrorism Cooperation: The New Imperative* (London: Routledge).
Rees, W. and R. Aldrich (2005), 'Contending Cultures Of Counter-terrorism: Trans-atlantic Divergence Or Convergence, *International Affairs*, vol. 81, no. 5, pp. 905–923.
Reinares, F. (ed.) (2000), *European Democracies against Terrorrism: Government Policies And Intergovernmental Cooperation* (Aldershot: Ashgate).
Relyea, H. (2002a), 'The Law: Homeland Security: The Concept And The Presidential Coordination Office: First Assessment,' *Presidential Studies Quarterly*, vol. 32, no. 2 (June), pp. 397–411.

Relyea, H. (2002b), 'Homeland Security And information', *Government Information Quarterly*, vol. 19, pp. 213–223.

Reus-Smit, C. (2001), 'Constructivism', in Burchill, S. *et al.*, *Theories Of International Relations*, 2nd edn (Basingstoke, Palgrave), pp. 209–230.

Richardson, J. (ed.) (2001), *European Union: Power And Policy-Making*, 2nd edn (London: Routledge).

Rijken, C. and G. Vermeulen (2006), *Joint Investigation Teams In The European Union: From Theory To Practice* (The Hague: Asser Press).

Rosamond, B. (2000), *Theories Of European Integration* (London: Macmillan).

Rosecrance, R. (1998), 'The European Union: A new Type Of International Actor', in Zielonka, J. (ed.), *Paradoxes Of European Foreign Policy* (The Hague: Kluwer Law International), pp. 15–23.

Ross, G. (1993), 'Sidling Into Industrial Policy: Inside The European Commission', *French Politics And Society*, vol. 11, no. 1, pp. 20–43.

Ross, G. (1994), 'Inside The Delors Cabinet', *Journal Of Common Market Studies*, vol. 32, no. 4, pp. 499–523.

Ross, G. (1995), *Jacques Delors And European Integration* (Cambridge: Polity Press).

Ruggie, J.G. (1998a), 'What Makes The World Hang Together? Neo-utilitarianism And The Social Constructivist Challenge', *International Organization*, vol. 52, no. 4, pp. 855–885.

Ruggie, J.G. (1998b), *Constructing The World Polity: Essays On International Institutionalization* (New York: Routledge).

Ruggie, J.G. (1998c), *Building The World Polity* (London: Routledge).

Sandholtz, W. and J. Zysman (1989), '1992: Recasting The European Bargain', *World Politics*, vol. 42, no. 1, pp. 95–128.

Sandholtz, W. (1993a), 'Institutions And Collective Action: The New Telecommunications In Western Europe', *World Politics*, vol. 45, no. 2, pp. 242–270.

Sandholtz, W. (1993b), 'Choosing Union: Monetary Politics And Maastricht', *International Organization*, vol. 47, no. 1, pp. 1–39.

Schieffer, M. (2003), 'Community Readmission Agreements With Third Countries: Objectives, Substance, And Current State Of Negotiations', *European Journal Of Migration And Law*, vol. 5, no. 3, pp. 343–357.

Schmidt, S. (1998), 'Commission Activism: Subsuming Telecommunications And Electricity Under Competition Law', *Journal Of European Public Policy*, vol. 5, no. 1, pp. 169–184.

Schneider, M. and P. Teske (1992), 'Toward A Theory Of The Political Entrepreneur: Evidence From Local Government', *American Political Science Review*, vol. 86, no. 3, pp. 737–747.

Schneider, G. and M. Aspinwall (eds) (2001), *The Rules Of Integration: Institutionalist approaches To The Study Of Europe* (Manchester: Manchester University Press).

Schoppa, L.J. (1999), 'The Social Context In Coercive International Bargaining', *International Organization*, vol. 53, no. 2, pp. 307–342.

Schuster, L. (2003b), 'Asylum Seekers: Sangatte And The Tunnel', *Parliamentary Affairs*, vol. 5, no. 3, pp. 206–522.

Schwellnus, G. (2001), 'Minority Protection And The EU Charter Of Fundamental Rights: Much Ado About Nothing?', *Constitutionalism Web Papers*, ConWEB no. 5/2001, http://les1.man.ac.uk/conweb/.

Seiple, C. (2002), 'The New Protracted Conflict: Homeland Security Concepts And Strategy', *Orbis*, vol. 46, no. 2, pp. 259–273.

Settembri, P. (2007), 'The Surgery Succeeded. Has The Patient Died? The Impact Of Enlargement On The European Union', Jean Monnet Working Paper no. 4, retrieved 28 September 2009, from www.jeanmonnetprogram.org/papers/07/070401.html.

Shaw, J. (2000), *Law Of The European Union*, 3rd edn (London: Palgrave).

Silverman, D. (2001), *Interpreting Qualitative Data* (London: Sage).
Simpson, G. (1999), 'Asylum And Immigration In The European Union After The Treaty Of Amsterdam', *European Public Law*, vol. 5, no. 1, pp. 91–124.
Smith, H. (2002), *European Union Foreign Policy: What It Is And What It Does* (London: Pluto Press).
Smith, K.E. (2003), *European Union Foreign Policy In A Changing World* (Cambridge: Polity Press).
Smith, M. (1998), *Social Science In Question* (London: Sage).
Smith, M.E. (1984), *Western Europe And The United States: The Uncertain Alliance* (London: Allen & Unwin).
Smith, M.E. (1998), 'Competitive Cooperation And EU–US Relations: Can The EU Be A Strategic Partner For The US In The World Economy?', *Journal Of European Public Policy*, vol. 5, no. 4, pp. 561–577.
Smith, M.E. (2004), 'Towards A Theory Of EU Foreign Policy-Making: Multi-level Governance, Domestic Politics, And National Adaptations To Europe's Common Foreign And Security Policy', *Journal Of European Public Policy*, vol. 11, no. 4, pp. 740–58.
Smith, M.S. (2004), 'Institutionalization, Policy Adaptation And European Foreign Policy Cooperation', *European Journal Of International Relations*, vol. 10, no. 1, pp. 95–136.
Smith, S. (1999), 'Social Constructivism And European Studies', in Christiansen, T. *et al.* (eds), 'The Social Construction Of Europe', *Journal Of European Public Policy*, vol. 6, no. 4, pp. 682–691.
Snyder, C.A. (ed.) (1999), *Contemporary Security And Strategy* (Basingstoke: Macmillan).
Spence, D. (ed.) (2007), *The European Union And Terrorism* (London: John Harper Publishing).
Spencer, S. (1996), 'Tackling The Root Causes Of Forced Migration: The Role Of The European Union', paper presented to the ECSA World Conference 'The European Union in a Changing World', Brussels, 19–20 September, on webpage www.ecsanet.org/conferences/ecsaworld3/spencer.htm.
Stedward, G. (1997), 'On The Record: An Introduction To Interviewing' in P. Burnham (1997), *Surviving the Research Process in Politics* (London: Pinter).
Stessens, G. (2002), 'The Principle Of Mutual Confidence Between The Judicial Authorities In The Area Of Freedom, Security And Justice', in De Kerchove, G. and A. Weyembergh (eds), *L'Espace pénal européen: enjeux et perspectives* (Brussels: Editions de l'Université de Bruxelles).
Stessens, G. (2008), 'The EU–US Agreements On Extradition And On Mutual Legal Assistance', in Martenczuck, B. and S. van Thiel (eds), *Justice, Liberty And Security: New Challenges For EU External Relations* (Brussels: VUB Press/Brussels University Press).
Stetter, S. (2000), 'Regulating Migration: Authority Delegation In Justice And Home Affairs', *Journal Of European Public Policy*, vol. 7, no. 1, pp. 80–103.
Stetter, S. (2007), *EU Foreign And Interior Policies: Cross-pillar Politics And The Social Construction Of Sovereignty* (New York: Routledge).
Steuneberg, B., Koboldt, C. and D. Schmidtchen (2000), 'Beyond Comitology: A Comparative Analysis Of Implementation Procedures With Parliamentary Involvement' in Moser, P., Schneider, G. and G. Kirchgässner (eds), *Decision Rules In The European Union: A Rational Choice Perspective* (London: Macmillan).
Stone Sweet, A. and W. Sandholtz (1997), 'European Integration And Supranational Governance', *Journal Of European Public Policy*, vol. 4, no. 3, pp. 297–317.
Stone Sweet, A. and W. Sandholtz (1998), 'Integration, Supranational Governance, and the Institutionalization of the European Polity', in W. Sandholtz and A. Stone Sweet (eds), *European Integration and Supranational Governance* (Oxford: Oxford University Press), pp. 1–26.

Stone Sweet, A., Sandholtz, W. and N. Fligstein (2001), *The Institutionalization Of Europe* (Oxford: Oxford University Press).
Tallberg, J. (2002), 'Delegation to Supranational Institutions: Why, How, and with What Consequences?', *West European Politics*, vol. 25, no. 1, pp. 23–46.
Tallberg, J. (2003), *European Governance And Supranational Institutions* (London: Routledge).
Tallberg, J. (2006), *Leadership And Negotiation In The European Union* (Cambridge: Cambridge University Press).
Tallberg, J. (2008), 'Bargaining Power in the European Council', *Journal of Common Market Studies*, vol. 46, no. 3, pp. 685–708.
Thelen, K. and S. Steinmo (eds) (1992), 'Historical Institutionalism In Comparative Politics', in Thelen, K. and S. Steinmo (eds), *Structuring Politics: Historical Institutionalism In Comparative Analysis* (Cambridge: Cambridge University Press).
Thielemann, E. (2001a), 'The Soft Europeanisation Of Migration Policy: European Integration And Domestic Policy Change', paper prepared for the ECSA seventh Biennial International Conference, 31 May–2 June, Madison, WI.
Thielemann, E. (2001b), 'The Evolution Of A European Asylum Policy: Escaping International And Domestic Constraints', in Oppermann, S. (ed.), *Magnet Societies: Immigration in Deutschland und in den USA* (Rehburg-Loccum: Evangelische Adademie), pp. 49–80.
Thielemann E. (2004), 'Why European Policy Harmonization Undermines Refugee Burden-Sharing', *European Journal of Migration and Law*, vol. 6, no. 1, pp. 43–61.
Thielemann E. and T. Dewan (2006), 'The Myth of Free-Riding: Refugee Protection and Implicit Burden-Sharing', *West European Politics*, vol. 29, no. 1, pp. 351–369.
Tsebelis, G. and G. Garret (2001), 'The Institutional Foundations Of Intergovernmentalism And Supranationalism In The European Union', *International Organization*, vol. 55, no. 2, pp. 357–390.
van Thiel, S. (2008), 'UN Anti-Terrorism Sanctions And EU Human Rights: The Lessons Of European integration', in Martenczuck, B. and S. van Thiel (eds), *Justice, Liberty And Security: New Challenges For EU External Relations* (Brussels: VUB Press/Brussels University Press).
Thony, J.-F. and C.-A. Png (2007), 'FATF Special Recommendations And UN Resolutions On The Financing Of Terrorism', *Journal Of Financial Crime*, vol. 14, no. 2, pp. 150–169.
Tonra, B. (2000), 'Mapping EU Foreign Policy Studies', *Journal Of European Public Policy*, vol. 7, no. 1, pp. 163–209.
Tonra, B. and T. Christiansen (eds) (2004), *Rethinking European Union Foreign Policy* (Manchester: Manchester University Press).
Trauner, F. and I. Kruse (2008), 'EC Visa Facilitation And Readmission Agreements: Implementing A New EU Security Approach In The Neighbourhood', CEPS Working Document no. 290 (Brussels: Centre for European Political Studies).
Tsebelis, G. (1994), 'The Power Of The European Parliament As A Conditional Agenda Setter', *American Political Science Review*, vol. 88, no. 1, pp. 128–142.
Tsoukalis, L. (2005), *What Kind Of Europe?* 2nd edn (Oxford: Oxford University Press).
Uçarer, E. (2001a), 'From The Sidelines To Center Stage: Sidekicks No More? The European Commission In Justice And Home Affairs', *European Integration Online Papers (EioP)*, vol. 5, no. 5, http://eiop.or.at/eiop/texte/2001–005a.htm.
Uçarer, E. (2001b), 'Managing Asylum And European Integration: Expanding Spheres Of Exclusion?', *International Studies Perspectives*, vol. 2, no. 3, pp. 288–304.
UNHCR (2006), *The State Of The World's Refugees. Human Displacement In The New Millennium* (Oxford: Oxford University Press).
Van der Linde, E., O'Brien, K., G. Lindstrom, S. de Spielgeleire, M. Varynen and H. de Vries (2002), *Quick Scan Of Post-9/11 National Counterterrorism Policymaking And*

Implementation In Selected European Countries (The Hague: Rand Europe).
van Selm, J. (2002), 'Immigration And Asylum Or Foreign Policy: The EU's Approach To Migrants And Their Countries Of Origin', in Lavenex, S. and E. Uçarer (eds), *Migration And The Externalities Of European Integration* (Lanham, MD: Lexington Books), pp. 143–156.
van Selm, J. (2003), 'Refugee Protection In Europe And The US After 9/11', in Steiner, N., Gibney, M. and G. Loescher (eds), *Problems Of Protection: The UNHCR, Refugees And Human Rights* (New York and London: Routledge), pp. 237–261.
van Selm, J. (2005), 'Where Migration Policy Is Made: Starting To Expose The Labyrinth Of National Institutional Settings For Migration Policy-Making And Implementation', *Global Migration Perspectives* no. 37 (Geneva: Global Commission on International Migration), on webpage www.gcim.org/attachements/GMP%20No%2037.pdf.
van Selm, J. and B. Cooper (2005), 'The New "Boat People": Ensuring Safety And Determining Status' (Washington, DC: Migration Policy Institute), on webpage www.migrationinformation.org.
Vitorino, A. (4 October 2004), 'The Future Of The European Union Agenda On Asylum, Migration And Borders', conference of the European Policy Center and King Baudouin Foundation, Brussels, 4 October, SPEECH/04/435, on webpage www.europa.eu.int.
Vogel, J. (2001), 'Abschaffung der Auslieferung? Kritische Anmerkungen zur Reform des Auslieferungsrechts in der Europäischen Union', *Juristenzeitung*, vol. 56, no. 19, pp. 937–943.
Von Hippel, K. (2004), 'Improving the International Response to the Transnational Terrorist Threat', in Boulden, J. and T.G. Weiss (eds), *Terrorism And The UN: Before And After September 11* (Bloomington, IN: Indiana University Press).
Waever, O. *et al.* (1993), *Identity, Migration And The New Security Agenda In Europe* (London: Pinter).
Waever, O. (1995), 'Securitization And Desecuritization', in Lipschutz, R.D. (ed.), *On Security* (New York: Columbia University Press), pp. 46–86.
Wagner, W. (2003a), 'Building an Internal Security Community: The Democratic Peace and the Politics of Extradition in Western Europe', *Journal of Peace Research*, vol. 40, no. 6, pp. 695–712.
Wagner, W. (2003b), 'Analysing the European Politics of Internal Security', *Journal of European Public Policy*, vol. 10, no. 6, pp. 1033–1039.
Walker, N. (ed.) (2004), *Europe's Area Of Freedom, Security And Justice* (Oxford: Oxford University Press).
Wallace, H. and W. Wallace (eds) (2000), *Policy-Making In The European Union*, 4th edn (Oxford: Oxford University Press).
Wallace, H. (2005), 'An Institutional Anatomy And Five Policy Modes', in Wallace, H., W. Wallace and M.A. Pollack (2005), *Policy-Making In The European Union*, 5th edn (Oxford: Oxford University Press).
Wallace, H., Wallace, W. and M.A. Pollack (eds) (2005), *Policy-Making In The European Union*, 5th edn (Oxford: Oxford University Press).
Warleigh, A. (ed.) (2002), *Understanding European Union Institutions* (London: Routledge).
Weiler, J. (1991), 'The Transformation Of Europe', *Yale Law Journal*, vol. 100, no. 8, pp. 2405–2483.
Weiler, J. (1999), 'The Constitution Of Europe: "Do The New Clothes Have An Emperor?"', in *Other Essays On European Integration* (Cambridge: Cambridge University Press).
Wendt, A. (1987), 'The Agent–Structure Problem In International Relations Theory', *International Organization*, vol. 41, no. 3, pp. 335–370.
Wendt, A. (1992), 'Anarchy Is What States Make Of It: The Social Construction Of Power Politics', *International Organization*, vol. 46, no. 2, pp. 391–426.

Wendt, A. (1995), 'Constructing International Politics', *International Security*, vol. 20, no. 1, pp. 71–81.

Wendt, A. (1999), *Social Theory Of International Politics* (Cambridge: Cambridge University Press).

Westlake, M. (1994), *The Commission And The Parliament: Partners And Rivals In The European Policy-making Process* (London: Butterworth).

Westlake, M. (1995), *The Council Of The European Union* (London: Cartermill International).

Wiener, A. (2001), 'Social Facts In World Politics: The Value-added Of Constructivism', paper prepared for presentation to the forty-second annual convention of the International Studies Association, Chicago, 20–25 February.

Williams, M.C. (2003), 'Words, Images, Enemies: Securitization And International Politics', *International Studies Quarterly*, vol. 47, no. 4, pp. 517–531.

Wincott, D. (1995), 'Institutional Interaction And European Integration: Towards An Everyday Critique Of Liberal Intergovernmentalism', *Journal Of Common Market Studies*, vol. 33, no. 4, pp. 597–609.

Wilkinson, P. (2006), *Terrorism versus Democracy: The Liberal State Response* (London: Routledge).

Wilkinson, P. (2007), 'The Threat From The Al-Qaeda Network', in Wilkinson, P. (ed.), *Homeland Security In The UK: Future Preparedness For Terrorist Attack Since 9/11* (London: Routledge).

Wilkinson, P. (ed.) (2007), *Homeland Security In The UK; Future Preparedness For Terrorist Attack Since 9/11* (London: Routledge).

Whittaker, D. (2003), *The Terrorism Reader* (London: Routledge).

White, B. (1999), 'The European Challenge To Foreign Policy Analysis', *European Journal Of International Relations*, vol. 5, no. 1, pp. 37–66.

White, B. (2004), 'Foreign Policy Analysis And European Foreign Policy', in B. Tonra and T. Christiansen (eds), *Rethinking European Union Foreign Policy* (Manchester: Manchester University Press).

Wolff, S. (2006), 'The Externalisation Of Justice And Home Affairs To The Southern Neighbours: The EU's Dilemmas In The Fight Against Terrorism', paper presented at the EuroMeSCo annual conference.

Wolff, S. (2009), 'The Mediterranean Dimension Of EU's Internal Security', in Balzacq, T. (ed.), *The External Dimension Of EU Justice And Home Affairs: Neighbours, Governance, Security* (Basingstoke: Palgrave Macmillan).

Wyn Rees, G. and M. Webber (2002), 'Fighting Organised Crime: The European Union And Internal Security', in Crawford, A. (ed.), *Crime And Insecurity: The Governance Of Safety In Europe* (Uffculme: Willan Publishing).

Wyn Rees, G. (2006), *Transatlantic Counter-terrorism Cooperation* (London: Routledge).

Yin, R (1994), *Case Study Research: Design And Methods*, Applied Social Research Methods Series, vol. 5 (London: Sage).

Young, O.R. (1989), 'The Politics Of International Regime Formation: Managing Natural Resources And The Environment', *International Organization*; vol. 43, no. 3, pp. 349–375.

Young, O.R. (1991), 'Political Leadership In Regime Formation: On The Development Of Institutions In International Society', *International Organization*, vol. 45, no. 3, pp. 281–308.

Young, O. and G. Osherenko (1993), *Polar Politics: Creating International Environmental Regimes* (Ithaca, NY: Cornell University Press).

Young, O.R. (1999), 'Comment On Andrew Moravcsik, *A New Statecraft? Supranational Entrepreneurs And International Cooperation*', *International Organization*, vol. 53, no. 4, pp. 805–809.

Youngs, R. (2006), *Europe And The Middle East: In the Shadow Of September 11* (Boulder, CO: Lynne Rienner).
Zehfuss, M. (2002), *Constructivism In International Relations: The Politics Of Reality* (Cambridge: Cambridge University Press).
Zimmermann, D. (2006), 'The European Union And Post-9/11 Counterterrorism: A Reappraisal', *Studies In Conflict And Terrorism*, vol. 29, no. 1, pp. 123–145.
Zwaan, J.W. and F. Goudappel (2006), *Freedom, Security And Justice In The European Union: Implementation Of The Hague Programme* (The Hague: Asser Press).
Zwolski, K. (2009), 'Euthanasia, Gay Marriages And Sovereignty: Polish Ratification Of The Lisbon Treaty', *Journal Of Contemporary European Research*, vol. 5, no. 3.

Primary documents

Austrian Ministry of Justice and Interior (2007), 'Twinning Fiche Strengthening Data Protection In Israel'.
Ad Hoc Committee for Institutional Affairs (March 1985), 'Report To The European Council (Dooge Report)', Bull.EC 3–1985, point 3.5.1.
Amnesty International (2003), 'UK/EU/UNHCR. Unlawful And Unworkable: Amnesty International's Views On Proposals For Extra-territorial Processing Of Asylum Claims', 18 June 2003, on webpage http://web.amnesty.org.
Amnesty International EU Office (2003), 'Strengthening Fortress Europe In Times Of War', 27 March 2003.
BBC News (16 October 1999), 'UK Hails Crime Summit Success' on webpage http://news.bbc.co.uk/1/hi/uk_politics/476666.stm.
BBC News (12 September 2001), 'Text Of Bush's Act Of War Statement' on webpage http://news.bbc.co.uk/1/hi/world/americas/1540544.stm.
BBC News (16 September 2001), 'Britain 'At War With Terrorism' on webpage http://news.bbc.co.uk/1/hi/uk_politics/1545411.stm.
BBC News (19 September 2001), 'Terrorism War Unites Bush And Jiang' on webpage http://news.bbc.co.uk/1/hi/world/asia-pacific/1606986.stm.
BBC News (19 September 2001), 'Immigration Controls Tightened' on webpage www.bbc.co.uk.
BBC News (20 September 2001), 'EU Must Act Fast On Terror – Blunkett' on webpage http://news.bbc.co.uk/1/hi/uk_politics/1553851.stm.
BBC News (21 September 2001), 'EU Leaders Open Emergency Summit' on webpage http://news.bbc.co.uk/1/hi/world/europe/1556397.stm.
BBC News (22 September 2001), 'Leaders Back Bush War Plans' on webpage http://news.bbc.co.uk/1/hi/world/europe/1557499.stm.
BBC News (3 October 2001), 'Russia Stands By West In War On Terror' on webpage http://news.bbc.co.uk/1/hi/world/europe/1573318.stm.
BBC News (11 October 2001), 'Bush Pledges "Every Weapon" For War' on webpage http://news.bbc.co.uk/1/hi/world/americas/1594059.stm.
BBC News (18 October 2001), 'Schroeder Issues EU Rallying Cry' on webpage http://news.bbc.co.uk/1/hi/world/europe/1606438.stm.
BBC News (19 October 2001), 'Terrorism War Unites Bush And Jiang' on webpage http://news.bbc.co.uk/1/hi/world/asia-pacific/1606986.stm.
BBC News (22 October 2001), 'Washington Presses EU In Terror War' on webpage http://news.bbc.co.uk/1/hi/world/europe/1614139.stm.
BBC News (1 December 2001), 'Straw Backs Euro War On Terrorism' on webpage http://news.bbc.co.uk/1/hi/uk_politics/1049822.stm.

BBC News (14 December 2001), 'Laeken's Anti-terror Agenda' on webpage http://news.bbc.co.uk/hi/english/world/europe/newsid_1704000/1704502.stm.

BBC News (28 December 2001), ' EU Arrest Warrant To Help Spain' on webpage http://news.bbc.co.uk/1/hi/world/europe/1731737.stm.

BBC News (22 May 2002), 'Prodi Pushes For More Power' on webpage http://news.bbc.co.uk/1/hi/world/europe/2002213.stm.

BBC News (5 December 2002), 'Prodi Seeks Strong Powers For Brussels' on webpage http://news.bbc.co.uk/1/hi/world/europe/2545331.stm.

BBC News (5 February 2003), 'UK Discussing Asylum Obligation' on webpage http://news.bbc.co.uk/1/hi/uk_politics/2723345.stm.

BBC News (19 February 2003), 'Asylum "Havens" Considered By UK' on webpage www.bbc.co.uk.

BBC News (19 February 2003), '"We Must Deal With AsyluM", Says P.M.' on webpage www.bbc.co.uk.

BBC News (15 June 2003), 'Croatia Asylum Camp For "UK Refugees"' on webpage www.bbc.co.uk.

BBC News (19 June 2003), 'Setback For UK At EU Summit' on webpage www.bbc.co.uk.

BBC News (22 September 2004), 'Howard Calls For Immigrant Quotas' on webpage www.bbc.co.uk.

BBC News (15 October 2004), 'EU Plan Risks UK Asylum Powers' on webpage http://news.bbc.co.uk/1/hi/uk_politics/3741870.stm.

BBC News (22 April 2005), 'Howard Gets Tough On Immigration' on webpage http://news.bbc.co.uk/1/hi/uk_politics/vote_2005/frontpage/4473417.stm.

BBC News (18 July 2005), 'Al Quaeda Man Win German Appeal' on webpage http://newsvote.bbc.co.uk/mpapps/pagetools/print/news.bbc.co.uk/1/hi/world/europe/...

BBC News (22 November 2006), 'EU And AU Tackle Migration Crisis' on webpage www.bbc.co.uk.

BBC News (23 November 2006), 'Gaddafi: Migration "Inevitable"' on webpage www.bbc.co.uk.

BBC News (15 October 2009), 'Havel Attacks Klaus On EU Treaty' on webpage www.bbc.co.uk.

Bundesministerium des Innern (2005), 'Effektiver Schutz für flüchtlinge, wirkungsvolle Bekämpfung illegaler Migration. Überlegungen des Bundesministers des Innern zur Errichtung einer EU-Aufnahmeeinrichtung in Nordafrika', on webpage www.bmi.bund.de.

Bulletin EU (December 1998), 'Justice And home Affairs Cooperation 5/18'.

Bulletin Quotidien Europe (29 September 2004), 'Débat Et Explications Sur Les Camps De Réfugiés Et La Politique Européenne D'Asile Au Conseil Informel Jeudi Et Vendredi' .

Bulletin Quotidien Europe (2 October 2004), 'Accord Sur Le Principe De Développer Une Politique D'Asile À L'Étranger, Mais Flou Et Problèmes Pour La Mise En OEuvre: Projets Pilotes De La Commission Européenne'.

BVG (18 July 2005), 'Urteil des zweiten Senats vom 18. Juli 2005 – 2 BvR 2236/04' on webpage www.bunderverfassungsgericht.de/entscheidungen/frames/rs20050718_2 BvR 2236/04.

BVG (30 June 2009), 'Federal Constitutional Court Press Release no. 72/2009 Of 30 June 2009, Judgment of 30 June 2009 – 2 BvE 2/08, 2 BvE 5/08, 2 BvR 1010/08, 2 BvR 1022/08, 2 BvR 1259/08 und 2 BvR 182/09' on webpage www.bverfg.de /entscheidungen/es20090630_2bve000208en.html.

Commission Of The European Communities (1985), 'Completing The Internal Market,' Brussels, 14 June 1984, COM (85) 310 final.

Commission Of The European Communities (1990), 'One Market, One Money: An

Evaluation Of The Potential Benefits And Costs Of Forming An Economic And Monetary Union', European Economy, no. 44 (Brussels).
Commission Of The European Communities (1991), 'Communication De La Commission Au Conseil Et Au Parlement Europeen Sur Le Droit D'Asile', Brussels, 11 October 1991, SEC(91) 1857 final.
Commission Of The European Communities (1994), 'Communication From The Commission To The Council And The European Parliament: On Immigration And Asylum Policies', Brussels, 23 February 1994, COM (94) 23 final.
Commission Of The European Communities (2001), 'Increasing The Capacity Of The EU To Fight International Terrorism', Brussels 19/09/01, SEC (2001) 1429/3.
Commission of the European Communities (2001), 'Proposal For A Council Framework Decision On Combating Terrorism' Brussels, 19.9.2001, COM (2001) 521 final.
Commission of the European Communities (2001), 'Proposal For A Council Framework Decision On The European Arrest Warrant And The Surrender Procedures Between The Member States', Brussels, 19 September 2001, COM (2001) 522 final.
Commission of the European Communities (2001), 'Overview Of EU Action In Response To The Events Of The 11 September And Assessment Of Their Likely Economic Impact', Brussels, 17 October 2001, COM (2001) 611.
Commission of the European Communities (2001), 'Commission Working Document: The Relationship Between Safeguarding Internal Security And Complying With International Protection Obligations And Instruments', Brussels, 5 December 2001, COM (2001) 743 final.
Commission of the European Communities (2004), 'Communication From The Commission To The Council And The European Parliament: Area Of Freedom, Security And Justice: Assessment Of The Tampere Programme And Future Orientations', Brussels, 2 June 2004, COM (2004) 401 final.
Commission of the European Communities (2004), 'Commission Decision 2004/535/EC On The Adequate Protection Of Personal Data Contained In The Passenger Name Record Of Air Passengers Transferred To The United States' Bureau of Customs and Border Protection, OJ L 235, 6 July 2004.
Commission of the European Communities (2005), 'Commission Welcomes Court Of Justice Judgment Recognising The Exclusive Competence Of The Community To Adopt Criminal Law Measures To Ensure The Effectiveness Of Community Law', 23 November 2005, MEMO/05/437.
Commission of the European Communities (2005), 'Report From The Commission: Based On Article 34 Of The Council Framework Decision On The European Arrest Warrant And The Surrender Procedures Between The Member States', Brussels, 23 February 2005, COM (2005) 63 final.
Commission of the European Communities (2007), 'Commission Activities In The Fight Against Terrorism', Brussels, 12 March 2007, MEMO/07/08.
Commission of the European Communities (2009), 'Communication From The Commission To The Council And The European Parliament: Justice, Freedom, And Security In Europe Since 2005: An Evaluation Of The Hague Prorgamme And Action Plan', Brussels, 10 June 2009, COM (2009) 263 final.
Conference of the Representatives of the Governments of the Member States (2004), CIG 87/04, 'Treaty Establishing A Constitution For Europe'.
Convention (2002), Final Report of the Working Group X 'Freedom, Security And Justice',2 December 2002, Conv426/02 (Brussels).
Convention (2002), Calendar of meetings of the Working Group X 'Freedom, Security And Justice', 6 September 2002, Conv256/02 (Brussels).
Convention (2002), Paper by Mr Antonio Vitorino, Working Group X, Document 14, 15 November 2002, WGX-WD14.

Convention (2002), 'A European Public Prosecutor', Working Group X, Document 27, 25 November 2002, WGX-WD27.
Convention (2002), 'Changes To The Draft Final Report By Mr Antonio Vitorino', Working Group X, Document 30, 26 November 2002, WGX-WD30.
Convention (2002), Franco-German Proposals By Mr Fischer And Mr De Villepin', Working Group X, Document 32, 27 November 2002, WGX-WD32.
Council Directive (20 July 2001; 2001/55/EC), 'On Minimum Standards For Giving Temporary Protection In The Event Of A Mass Influx Of Displaced Persons And On Measures Promoting A Balance Of Efforts Between Member States In Receiving Such Persons And Bearing The Consequences Thereof', OJ L212/12, 7 August 2001.
Council Directive (27 January 2003; 2003/9/EC), 'Laying Down Minimum Standards For The Reception Of Asylum Seekers', OJ L31/18, 6 February 2003.
Council Directive (29 April 2004; 2004/83/EC), 'On Minimum Standards For The Qualification And Status Of Third-Country Nationals And Stateless Persons As Refugees Or As Persons Who Otherwise Need International Protection', OJ L304/12, 30 September 2004.
Council Framework Decision (13 June 2002), 'On The European Arrest Warrant And The Surrender Procedures Between Member States' (2002/584/JHA).
Council of the European Union (1998a), 'Strategy Paper On Immigration And Asylum Policy', Doc. 9809/98 LIMITE CK4 27 ASIM 170, 1 July 1998.
Council of the European Union (1998b), 'Council Act Laying Down Rules Governing Europol's External Relations With Third States And Non-European Union Related Bodies', 3 November 1998.
Council of the European Union (2000), 'Council Decision Of 27 March 2000 Authorising The Director Of Europol To Enter Into Negotiations On Agreements With Third States And Non-EU Related Bodies', OJ C106, 13 April 2000, pp. 0001–0002.
Council of the European Union (2001), 'Conclusions Adopted By The Council (Justice And Home Affairs)', Doc. SN 3926/6/01, 20 September 2001.
Council of the European Union (2002), 'Council Decision Of 28 February Setting Up Eurojust With A View To Reinforcing The Fight Against Serious Crime', 2002/187/JHA.
Council of the European Union (2003a), 'Presidency Conclusions Of The Brussels European Council, 20–21 March 2003', Doc. 8410/3 POLGEN 29, 5 May 2003.
Council of the European Union (2003b), 'Presidency Conclusions Of The Thessaloniki European Council, 19–20 June 2003', Doc. 11638/03 POLGEN 55, 1 October 2003.
Council of the European Union (2005a), 'Press Release October 2005'.
Council of the European Union (2005b), 'Draft Council Conclusions On Migration And External Relations', DOC. 14310/05 LIMITE ASIM 50, DEVGEN 210, RELEX 623, 11 November 2005.
Council of the European Union (2006a), 'Press Release, 2728th Council Meeting, General Affairs And External Relations', 15 May 2006, Doc. 9001/06 (Presse 126).
Council of the European Union (2006b), 'Fight Against Terrorism: Six-Monthly Report', Doc, 16370/06, 6 December 2006.
Council of the European Union (2006c), 'Note From The EU Counter-terrorism Coordinator To COREPER: Working Structures Of The Council In Terrorism Matters: Options Paper', Doc. 9791/04, 25 May 2004.
Council of the European Union (2007a), 'Combating Terrorist Financing: Fair And Clear Procedures In Targeted Sanctions', Doc. 11355/07 (Presse 159), 29 June 2007.
Council of the European Union (2007b), 'Fight Against Terrorism: Six-Monthly Report', Doc. 11948/2/07, 5 October 2007.
Council of the European Union and European Commission (1998), 'Action Plan Of The Council And The Commission On How Best To Implement The Provisions Of The

Treaty Of Amsterdam On An Area Of Freedom, Security And Justice', Doc. 1999/C 10/01, 3 December 1998.

Deutsche Welle (7 October 2005), 'Spain Starts Deporting Immigrants', on webpage www.deutschewelle.de.

Die Presse (10/09/08), 'Irland, die Zweite. Aus nein werde Ja', www.diepresse.at, accessed on 12/09/08.

Die Zeit (9 July 2009), 'Fischer–Lissabon Vertrag. Ein nationaler Riegel', No. 29-09, July 2009 on webpage www.zeit.de/2009/29/Lissabon.

Dietrich, H. (2005), 'The Desert Front: EU Refugee Camps In North Africa?' (URL: www.statewatch.org/news/2005/mar/12eu-refugee-camps.htm. Accessed on 28 March 2005).

Economist (11 December 2003), 'Might It All Tumble Down' on webpage www.economist.com/PrinterFriendly.cfm?Story_ID=2291407.

Economist (16 December 2003), 'A Constitution In Tatters' on webpage www.economist .com/agenda/PrinterFriendly.cfm?Story_ID=2295754.

Economist (5 February 2004), 'Back From The Dead' on webpage www.economist .com/PrinterFriendly.cfm?Story_ID=2410025.

Economist (26 March 2004), 'Revived To Die Another Day?' on webpage www.economist.com/agenda/PrinterFriendly.cfm?Story_ID=2550082.

Economist (10 June 2004), 'Try, Try, Try Again' on webpage www.economist .com/PrinterFriendly.cfm?Story_ID=2747818.

Economist (18 June 2004), 'The Summit Of All Fears' on webpage www.economist.com/agenda/PrinterFriendly.cfm?Story_ID=2765199.

Economist (22 June 2004), 'Finally, A Constitution. Now The Hard Part' on webpage www.economist.com/agenda/PrinterFriendly.cfm?Story_ID=2783543.

Economist (24 June 2004), 'A Difficult Birth' on webpage www.economist .com/PrinterFriendly.cfm?Story_ID=2792646.

ECRE (European Council on Refugees and Exiles) (1995), '"Safe Third Countries": Myths And Realities'.

El Mundo (3 May 2000), 'Canarias: 800 pateristas' on webpage www.elmundo.es.

El Mundo (14 July 2000), 'Un "muro electrónico" detectará la ilegada de Pateras a Andalucía' on webpage www.elmundo.es.

El Mundo (11 December 2001), 'Aznar dara prioridad a la lucha contra el terrorismo durante la presidencia de la UE', on webpage www.elmundo.es.

El Mundo (12 August 2002), 'El gobierno active el sistema ee vigilancia del estrecho'.

El Mundo (1 August 2004), 'Avalancha de inmigrantes en las Costas Canaria y Andaluza' on webpage www.elmundo.es.

El Mundo (7 November 2004), 'Destino: Canarias' on webpage www.elmundo.es.

El Mundo (31 August 2005), 'Marruecos investiga la muerte de al menos un subsahariano que intentaba entrar en Melilla' on webpage www.elmundo.es.

El Mundo (9 September 2005),'Más metros de protección' on webpage www.elmundo.es.

El Mundo (28 June 2005), 'Canarias ya cuenta con su plan de inmigración' on webpage www.elmundo.es.

El Mundo (21 September 2005), 'Doce inmigrantes heridos en una nueva avalancha para llegar a Melilla' on webpage www.elmundo.es.

El Mundo (29 September 2005), 'Cinco muertos en un asalto en la frontera de Ceuta; Zapatero moviliza a 480 soldados' on webpage www.elmundo.es.

El Mundo (30 September 2005), 'Rajoy acusa a Zapatero de dejar a su suerte a Ceuta y Melilla pese a las advertencias del efecto ilamada' on webpage www.elmundo.es.

El Mundo (6 October 2005), 'Zapatero: la Españolidad de Ceuta y Melilla ni está ni estará en discusión' on webpage www.elmundo.es.

El Mundo (17 May 2006), 'El sistema integrado de vigilancia en Almería' on webpage

www.elmundo.es.
El Mundo (23 May 2006), 'El parlamento canario exige que la armada blinde las costas ante la oleada de inmigrantes' on webpage www.elmundo.es.
El Mundo (23 May 2006), 'Canarias pide que la armada blinde las costas y solicita a la UE un fondo para abordar la inmigración' on webpage www.elmundo.es.
El Mundo (29 August 2006), 'La CE podría pedir a los países más colaboracíon con España en las patrullas en Canarías' on webpage www.elmundo.es.
El Mundo (29 August 2006), 'De La Vega viaja hoy a Finlandia para pedir que la UE se implique más en materia de inmigración' on webpage www.elmundo.es.
El Mundo (6 October 2006), 'Un informe de SOS racismo documenta 376 devolucioned ilegales en 2005' on webpage www.elmundo.es.
El País (5 July 2002), 'La solucíon es que el gobierno no nos envíe ni un inmigrante más' on webpage www.elpais.es.
El País (29 May 2006), 'Nueve países de la UE patrullarán con España las zonas de origen de los Cayucos' on webpage www.elpais.es.
El País (3 June 2006), 'El mayo más africano de las islas Canarias' on webpage www.elpais.es.
El País (1 August 2006), 'La UE retrasa el plan para frenar la afluencia de sin papeles' on webpage www.elpais.es.
El País (2 August 2006), 'Las costas españolas reciben al menos 360 inmigrantes a lo largo del día' on webpage www.elpais.es.
Encyclopaedia Britannica (1992), 'Macropaedia'.
EUbusiness (18 October 2004), 'G5 Ministers Fail To Agree On "Transit Tamps"', on www.eubusiness.com.
EUobserver (28 March 2003), 'UK Minister Proposes Refugee "Camp" Plan', on www.euobserver.com.
EUobserver (31 March 2003), 'Germany Attacks UK's Refugee "Camp" Plan', on www.euobserver.com.
EUobserver (6 June 2003), 'Asylum Centres Plan Gains EU Support', on www.euobserver.com.
EUobserver (16 June 2003), 'Asylum Seekers To Wait In Croatia', on www.euobserver.com.
EUobserver (4 October 2004), 'Commission Says Funds Not Linked To North African Asylum Camps', on www.euobserver.com.
EUobserver (28 August 2006), 'Spain Seeks More EU Help On Immigration' on www.euobserver.com.
EUobserver (28 July 2008), 'Ireland Strongly Opposed To Lisbon Revote', on www.euobserver.com.
EUobserver (31 July 2008), 'Ireland Mulls Autumn Lisbon Revote', on www.euobserver.com.
EUobserver (8 August 2008), 'EU Keeps Ticking Without The Lisbon Treaty', on www.euobserver.com.
EUobserver (4 September 2008), 'Ireland Shoots Down Idea Of Swift Lisbon Revote', on www.euobserver.com.
EUobserver (17 September 2008), 'Juncker Rules Out Lisbon Treaty Before 2010', on www.euobserver.com.
EUobserver (15 July 2009), 'Brussels Expresses Concern At Germany's Court Judgement', on www.euobserver.com.
EUobserver (3 October 2009), 'Irish Vote Unleashes Flurry Of EU Activity', on www.euobserver.com.
EUpolitix (30 August 2006), 'EU Calls For More Cash To Fight Illegal Migration' on www.eupolitix.com.

Eurasylum (27 January 2005), 'Eurasylum's Monthly Policy Interviews: Robert Visser' on webpage www.eurasylum.org/Portal/DesktopDefault.aspx?tabindex=2&tabid=19.

Eurasylum (10 May 2005), Interview With Franco Frattini On 'Recent And Unfolding Developments On EU Asylum And Immigration Policy' (URL: www.eurasylum.org).

Euroactiv (18 June 2005), 'EU Law Supremacy Even In Criminal Matters' on webpage www.euractiv.com/Article?tcmuri=tcm:29–141124–16&type=News.

Euroactiv (5 October 2009), 'EU Leaders Face Difficult Task Naming New Commission' on webpage www.euractiv.com/en/future-eu/eu-leaders-face-difficult-task-naming-new-commission/article-186074.

Euractiv (3 October 2009), 'Resounding Irish "Yes" To EU's Lisbon Treaty' on webpage www.euractiv.com/en/future-eu/resounding-irish-eu-lisbon-treaty/article-186051.

Euractiv (12 October 2009), 'Parliament Split On "Progressive" Swedish Immigration Programme' on webpage www.euractiv.com/en/mobility/parliament-split-progressive-swedish-immigration-programme/article-186266.

Euro-Mediterranean Partnership (2005), '10th Anniversary Euro-Mediterranean Summit' (Barcelona, 27–28 November 2005): Annexes. Doc. EURO-MED 2/05, November 2005.

Euro-Mediterranean Partnership (2007), 'First Euro-Mediterranean Ministerial Meeting On Migration' (Algarve, 18–19 November 2007): Agreed Ministerial Conclusions, November 2007.

European Commission (1993), *Eurobarometer*, vol. 43, December 1993 (Brussels: European Commission).

European Commission (1996), *Eurobarometer*, vol. 46, autumn 1996 (Brussels: European Commission).

European Commission (1997), *Eurobarometer*, vol. 47, autumn 1997 (Brussels: European Commission).

European Commission (1998), *Eurobarometer*, vol. 48, autumn 1998 (Brussels: European Commission).

European Commission (1999), *Eurobarometer*, vol. 49, autumn 1996 (Brussels: European Commission).

European Commission (2000), *Eurobarometer*, vol. 50, autumn 2000 (Brussels: European Commission).

European Commission (1991), 'Commission Communication To The European Council And The Parliament On Immigration', SEC(1991) 1855 final, 11 October 1991.

European Commission (1994), 'Communication From The Commission To The Council And The European Parliament On Immigration And Asylum Policies', COM (94) 23 final, 23 February 1994.

European Commission (1998), 'Communication From The Commission On The Abolition Of Controls Of Persons At Intra-Community Border', COM (1988) 640/final.

European Commission (2000), 'Communication From The Commission To The Council And The European Parliament. Towards A Common Asylum Procedure And A Uniform Status, Valid Throughout The Union, For Persons Granted Asylum', COM (2000) 755, 22 November 2000.

European Commission (2001a), 'Communication From The Commission To The Council And The European Parliament. On The Common Asylum Policy, Introducing An Open Coordination Method', COM (2001) 710, 28 November 2001.

European Commission (2001b), 'Communication From The Commission To The Council And The European Parliament On A Common Policy On Illegal Immigration', COM (2001) 672, 15 November 2001.

European Commission (2002), 'Communication From The Commission To The Council And The European Parliament. Integrating Migration Issues In The EU's Relations

With Third Countries', COM (2002) 703 final, 3 December 2002.
European Commission (2003a), 'Communication From The Commission To The Council And The European Parliament 'Towards More Accessible, Equitable And Managed Asylum Systems', COM (2003) 315 final, 3 June 2003.
European Commission (2003b), 'Commission Staff Working Paper. Intensified Cooperation On The Management Of Migration Flows With Third Countries', Report by the Commission's Services on the implementation of the Council conclusions on intensified cooperation on the management of migration flows with third countries of 18 November 2002, SEC(2003) 815, 9 July 2003.
European Commission (2003c), 'Communication From The Commission To The Council And The European Parliament 'Wider Europe – Neighbourhood: A New Framework For Relations With Our Eastern And Southern Neighbours', COM (2003) 104, 11 March 2003.
European Commission/Danish Centre for Human Rights (2003), 'Study On The Feasibility Of Processing Asylum Claims Outside The EU Against The Background Of The Common European Asylum System And The Goal Of A Common Asylum Procedure', Luxembourg: Office for Official Publications of the European Communities.
European Commission (2005a), 'Communication From The Commission To The Council And The European Parliament On Regional Protection Programmes', 1 September 2005.
European Commission (2005b), 'Communication From The Commission To The Council And The European Parliament. Priority Actions For Responding To The Challenges Of Migration: First Follow-up To Hampton Court', COM (2005) 621 final, 30 November 2005.
European Commission (2005c), 'Communication From The Commission To The Council, The European Parliament, The Economic and Social Committee And The Committee Of The Regions. Migration And Development: Some Concrete Orientations', COM (2005) 390 final.
European Commission (2006a), 'Communication From The Commission To The Council And The European Parliament: The Global Approach To Migration One Year On: Towards A Comprehensive European Migration Policy', COM (2006) 735, 30 November 2006.
European Commission (2006b), 'Commission Simplifies External Cooperation Programmes', IP/06/82, 25/01/2006.
European Commission (2006c), 'Communication From The Commission To The Council And The European Parliament On Strengthening The European Neighbourhood Policy', COM (2006) 726, 4 December 2006.
European Commission (2007a), 'Global Approach To Migration', MEMO/07/549, 5 December 2007.
European Commission (2007b), 'Commission Staff Working Document Accompanying The Communication From The Commission To The European Parliament, The Council, The European Economic And Social Committee And The Committee Of The Regions Towards A Common Immigration Policy: Interim Report On The Global Approach To Migration', SEC(2007) 1632, 5 December 2007.
European Commission (10 June 2009), 'European Commission Outlines Its Vision For The Area Of Freedom, Security And Justice In The Next Five Years', Press release on webpage http://europa.eu/rapid/pressReleasesAction.do?reference=IP/09/894&format=HTML&aged=0&language=EN&guiLanguage=en.
European Commission and Danish Centre for Human Rights (2003), 'Study On The Feasibility Of Processing Asylum Claims Outside The EU Against The Background Of The Vommon European Asylum System And The Goal Of A Common Asylum

Procedure'. Luxembourg: Office for Official Publications of the European Communities.
European Council (1992), 'Conclusions Of The Presidency', European Council in Edinburgh, SN456/92, 11–12 December 1992.
European Council (October 1999), 'Presidency Conclusions Of The Tampere European Council (1999)', 15–16 October 1999, SN 200/99 (Brussels: General Secretariat of the Council).
European Council (March 2000), 'Presidency Conclusions Of The Lisbon European Council (2000)', 23–24 March 2000 (Brussels: General Secretariat of the Council).
European Council (September 2001), 'Conclusions And Plan Of Action Of The Extraordinary Meeting On 21 September', SN140/01 (Brussels: General Secretariat of the Council).
European Council (December 2001), 'Presidency Conclusions Of The Laeken European Council', 14–15 December 2001, SN 00300/01 (Brussels: General Secretariat of the Council).
European Council (June 2002), 'Presidency Conclusions Of The Seville European Council', 21–22 June 2002, SN 13463/02 (Brussels: General Secretariat of the Council).
European Council (June 2003), 'Presidency Conclusions Of The Thessaloniki European Council', 19–20 June 2003, SN 11638/03 (Brussels: General Secretariat of the Council).
European Council (December 2003), 'A Secure Europe In A Better World? European Security Strategy', 12 December 2003 (Brussels: General Secretariat of the Council).
European Council (March 2004), 'Declaration On Combating Terrorism', 25 March 4 (Brussels: General Secretariat of the Council), http://ue.eu.int/uedocs/cmsUpload /DECL-25.3.pdf.
European Council (2004), 'Integrating The Fight Against Terrorism Into EU External Relations Policy' (Brussels: General Secretariat of the Council).
European Council (2004), 'Presidency Conclusions For The Euro-Mediterranean Meeting Of Ministers Of Foreign Affairs' (Brussels: General Secretariat of the Council).
European Council (December 2004), 'Presidency Conclusions Of The Brussels European Council', 8 December 2004, Annex 1: The Hague Programme: strengthening freedom, security and justice in the European Union, 4–05 November 2004, SN 14292/04 (Brussels: General Secretariat of the Council).
European Council (2005), 'The European Union Counter-terrorism Strategy' (Brussels: General Secretariat of the Council).
European Council (May 2007), 'Implementation Of The Strategy And Action Plan To Combat Terrorism', 20 May 2007 (Brussels: General Secretariat of the Council).
European Council for Refugees and Exiles (ECRE), Amnesty International and Human Rights Watch (28 April 2004), 'Refugee And Human Rights Organisations Across Europe Axpress Their Deep Concern At The Expected Agreement On Asylum Measures In Breach Of International Law' (Brussels: press release).
European Court of Justice (16 June 2005), 'Judgment Of The Court Of Justice In Case C-105/03', Press Release no. 59/05 (Luxembourg: European Court of Justice).
European Court of Justice (13 September 2005), 'Judgment Of The Court Of Justice In Case C-176/03', Press Release no. 75/05 (Luxembourg: European Court of Justice).
European Parliament (1993), 'Report On Cooperation In The Field Of Justice And Internal Affairs Under The Treaty Of The European Union (Robles Piquer Report)', Committee on Civil Liberties and Internal affairs, EP Documents 1993/0215 A3, Luxembourg.
European Parliament (2006), 'Report: With A Proposal For A European Parliament Recommendation To The Council On Evaluations Of The European Arrest Warrant', Committee on Civil Liberties, Justice and Home Affairs, Brussels, 27 February 2006, A6–0049/2006 final.

European Union (2004), 'European Union Factsheet: EU And The Fight Against Terrorism' (Council Secretariat: Brussels).
European Union Presidency (2006), 'Interior Minister Liese Prokop Opens CoMMA Conference', Press Release, 21 April 2006, (www.eu2006.at/en/News/Press_Releases /April/2104prokop.html).
Europol (2003), *Annual Report 2003* (The Hague: European Police Office).
Europol (2006), *External Strategy Of Europol 2006–2008: Explanatory note*, File 3710–242r4, 25 October 2006.
Europol (2006), *Annual Report 2006* (The Hague: European Police Office).
Europol (2007), *Annual Report 2007* (The Hague: European Police Office).
European Voice (27 September 2001), 'Justice Chief Warns Against Rushing EU Arrest Warrant', *European Voice*, vol. 7, no. 35, p. 1–3.
Financial Times, FT (16 October 99), 'German Court Rules EU Arrest Warrant Invalid' on webpage http://financialtimes.printthis.clickability.com/pt/cpt?action=cpt&title=FT .com%2F.
Financial Times, FT (28 March 2003), 'UK Asylum Proposals Draw Mixed Response', on www.ft.com
Financial Times, FTFT (16 June 2003), 'UK moots 'zones of protection' for refugees' on webpage www.ft.com.
Financial Times, FT (1 October 2004), 'EU Aims To Turn Back Would-be Migrants' on webpage www.ft.com.
Frankfurter Allgemeine Zeitung (23 July 2004), 'Afrikas Probleme In Afrika Lösen'; F.A.Z.-Gastbeitrag von Otto Schily on webpage www.faz.de.
Future Group (June 2008), *Freedom, Security, Privacy: European Home Affairs In An Open World. Report Of The Informal High Level Advisory Group On The Future Of European Home Affairs Policy (The Future Group)*, on website: www.statewatch.org /news/2008/jul/eu-futures-jha-report.pdf.
Guardian (8 June 2000), 'Straw Aims To Rewrite Treaty On Refugees', on www.guardian.co.uk.
Guardian (5 February 2003a), 'Shifting A Problem Back To Its Source', on www.guardian.co.uk.
Guardian (5 February 2003b), 'Safe Havens Plan To Slash Asylum Numbers', on www.guardian.co.uk
Guardian (6 February 2003), 'You Can't Quit Treaties, Blair Warned', on www.guardian.co.uk.
Guardian (10 February 2003), 'Refugee Camps Don't Work', on www.guardian.co.uk.
Guardian (1 March 2003), 'Blunkett Pushes For Refugee Safe Havens', on www.guardian.co.uk.
Guardian (11 March 2003), 'Welcome To Camp Tirana', on www.guardian.co.uk.
Guardian (8 May 2003), 'Non-EU Asylum Centres "Within Months"', on www.guardian.co.uk.
Guardian (9 May 2003), 'New Asylum Centres Open By End Of Year: UK-bound Refugees To Be Processed Outside The EU', on www.guardian.co.uk.
Guardian (9 May 2003), 'Nowhere To Go', on www.guardian.co.uk.
Guardian (16 June 2003a), 'Britain Wavers On Asylum Plans', on www.guardian.co.uk.
Guardian (16 June 2003b), '"No plans" For Asylum Camps Outside EU', on www.guardian.co.uk.
Guardian (19 June 2003), 'Fortress Europe Set To Keep Up Barricades', on www.guardian.co.uk.
Guardian (20 June 2003a), 'EU Rejects Asylum Camps Plan', on www.guardian.co.uk.
Guardian (20 June 2003b), 'Put An End To Their Wandering', on www.guardian.co.uk.
Guardian (19 October 2004), 'France And Spain Object To Plan For EU Transit Camp', on

www.guardian.co.uk.
Guardian (30 March 2005), 'Just Another Day In The 2005 Elections', on www.guardian.co.uk.
Guardian (23 December 2005), 'French Celebrities Desert Sarkozy In Wake Of Attack On Urban Poor', on www.guardian.co.uk.
House of Commons Home Affairs Committee (2003), 'Asylum Removals', *Fourth Report of Session 2002–03*, HC 654–I. London: The Stationery Office Limited.
House of Lords European Union Committee (2004), 'Handling EU Asylum Claims: New Approaches Examined', *HL Paper 74*, Report with Evidence. London: The Stationery Office Limited.
Human Rights Watch (2003), *An Unjust "Vision" For Europe's* Refugees. *Human Rights Watch Commentary On The U.K.'s "New Vision" Proposal For The Establishment Of Refugee Processing Centers Abroad*, 17 June 2003.
Immigration Law Practitioners' Association (ILPA) (2003), 'Memorandum By The ILPA Submitted To The House Of Lords Select Committee On The European Union On New Approaches To Asylum Processing', in House of Lords European Union Committee, Handling EU Asylum Claims: New Approaches Examined, *HL Paper 74*, Report with Evidence.
Independent (29 March 2003), 'Europe Lukewarm On Asylum Centre Plans', on webpage www.independent.co.uk.
Independent (20 June 2003a), 'Blair Loses Fight For "Refugee Protection" Zones', on webpage www.independent.co.uk.
Independent (20 June 2003b), 'Human Rights Groups Say Scheme May Be Unlawful', on webpage www.independent.co.uk.
Independent (20 June 2003c), 'Blair Loses Fight For "Refugee Protection" Zones', on webpage www.independent.co.uk.
Intergovernmental Consultations on Asylum, Refugee and Migration Policies in Europe, North America and Australia (IGC) (1994), 'Working Paper On Reception In The Region Of Origin', Geneva: IGC.
Intergovernmental Consultations on Asylum, Refugee and Migration Policies in Europe, North America and Australia (IGC) (1994), 'Reception In The Region Of Origin: Draft Follow-up To The 1994 Working', Geneva: IGC.
International Herald Tribune (30 August 2006), 'EU Is Urged To Help Spain'.
IPSterraviva (29 September 2005), 'Rights: EU Plans To Keep Asylum Seekers At Bay'.
Irish Times (7 December 2001), 'EU Justice Ministers Agree Terror Definition', on webpage www.ireland.com/newspaper/ireland/2001/1207/hom6.hmt.
Irish Times (12 December 2001), 'Italy Accepts European Arrest Warrant', on webpage www.ireland.com/newspaper/world/2001/1212/wor2.htm.
Irish Times (5 October 2009), 'High Calibre Commissioner Is Key To Restoring Our Goodwill In EU', on webpage www.irishtimes.com/newspaper/ireland/2009/1005/1224255888412.html.
ISN Security Watch (28 July 2004), 'Germany Considers Setting Up Asylum Camps In Africa'.
Justice (2003), 'In The Matter Of The Proposal By The United Kingdom To Establish Transit Processing Centres In Third Countries And The Compatibility Of This Proposal With The United Kingdom's Obligations Under The 1951 Refugee Convention And The European Convention On Human Rights', 22 June 2003 (available at www.justice.org.uk).
Le Monde (30 September 2004), 'En Allemagne, le projet du Ministre de l'intérieur est critiqué', on webpage www.lemonde.fr.
Le Monde (1 October 2004), 'Débat confus sur la politique d'asile européenne', on webpage: www.lemonde.fr.

Le Monde (27 July 2006), 'Controverse politique sur le nombre d'étrangers sans papiers en Espagne', on webpage www.lemonde.fr.

Le Monde (16 August 2006), 'Edito: equilibre rompu', on webpage: www.lemonde.fr.

Le Monde (21 August 2006), 'Madrid désemparé face à l'affluence de clandestins sur ses côtes', on webpage: www.lemonde.fr.

Le Monde (23 November 2006), 'Tripoli accueille une cinquantaine de pays pour une conférence Afrique-Europe sur les migrations', on webpage www.lemonde.fr.

Libération (3 September 2005), 'Mort suspecte dans l'enclave espagnole', on webpage www.liberation.fr.

Libération (7 October 2005), 'L'Europe, Eldorado communautaire', on webpage www.liberation.fr.

Libération (11 October 2005), 'Inquiétudes sur le drame des déportés de Ceuta-Melilla', on webpage www.liberation.fr.

Libération (10 March 2006), 'Une funeste nouvelle voie d'immigration en Afrique', on webpage www.liberation.fr.

Luxembourg Presidency (18 June 2005), 'Declaration By The Heads Of State Or Governments Of The Member States Of The European Union On The Ratification Of The Treaty Establishing A Constitution For Europe – European Council, 16 and 17 June 2005', on webpage www.eu2005.lu/en/actualites/conseil/2005/06/17conseurdecl/index.html.

Middle East and North Africa Financial Action Task Force (2007a), *Mutual Evaluation Report Of The Republic Of Tunisia On anti-Money Laundering And Combating Financing Of Terrorism.*

Middle East and North Africa Financial Action Task Force (2007b), *Mutual Evaluation Report Of The Kingdom Of Morocco On anti-Money Laundering And Combating Financing Of Terrorism.*

Migration News Sheet (February 2003), 'Persons Arrested In Connection With A Terrorist Plot Using A Highly Dangerous And Toxic Chemical Include Three Asylum-Seekers', p. 19.

Migration News Sheet (March 2003), 'All-time Record Of Asylum Applications Recorded Last Year', pp. 17–18.

Migration News Sheet (March 2003), 'Prime Minister Holds Firm On His Promise To Reduce The Number Of Asylum-Seekers By Half Even Though His Home Secretary Described The Target As "Undeliverable"', p. 19.

Migration News Sheet (July 2003), 'UK Is Forced To Withdraw Proposal To Set Up "Transit Processing Centres"', p. 14.

Migration News Sheet (August 2004), 'Germany Now Supports UK Idea Of Asylum Processing Centres Outside The EU', p. 10.

Migration News Sheet (August 2004), 'African Asylum-Seekers Finally Authorised To Land, But Almost All Are Denied Asylum For Falsely Claiming To Be Sudanese: Refugee Determination Process Strongly Criticised By The UNHCR', pp. 12–13.

Migration News Sheet (November 2005), 'Another 30,000 Sub-Saharan Migrants Are Waiting In North Africa For An Opportunity To Reach Europe', p. 5.

Migration News Sheet (November 2005), 'Migrants Who Stormed The Border Of Ceuta Were Encouraged To Do So By Events In Melilla', pp. 11–12.

Migration News Sheet (January 2006), 'Sub-Saharans Continue To Try To Enter Melilla', p. 9.

Migration News Sheet (April 2006), 'Opposition Partido Popular Blames Upsurge Of Irregular Migration On Last Year's Amnesty', pp. 8–9.

Migration News Sheet (June 2006), 'Opinion Poll Suggests That Large Majority Of Spanish People Have Had Enough Of Immigration', p. 9.

Migration News Sheet (July 2006), 'A Number Of Member States Provide Material

Assistance To Spain To Combat Illegal Migration To The Canary Islands', p. 5.
Migration News Sheet (September 2006), 'First EU Naval Operation To Combat Illegal Migration', p. 4.
Migration News Sheet (September 2006), 'Madrid Is Informed That It Can Expect No More EU Financial Assistance Until 2007', p. 5.
Migration News Sheet (September 2006), 'Italian Coast Guard Ship Involved In The HERA II Operation Broke Down For 10 Days Before Even Coming Into Action', p. 5.
Migration News Sheet (October 2006), 'Madrid Obtains Nothing From Informal Justice And Home Affairs Meeting, Only Advice To Solve Its Own Problem', p. 4.
Migration News Sheet (October 2006), 'Director Of FRONTEX Shifts The Blame For The Late Deployment Of Naval And Aerial Vessels On Spain', p. 7.
NATO Statement (12 September 2001), 'Statement By The North Atlantic Council' on webpage www.nato.int/docu/pr/2001/p01–124e.htm.
Observer (15 June 2003), 'Secret Balkan Camp Built To Hold UK Asylum Seekers'.
Observer (2 October 2005), 'Under Fire At Europe's Border'.
Refugee Council (2003), 'Refugee Council Briefing. Unsafe Havens, Unworkable Solutions', May 2003.
Reuters (6 October 2005), 'Spain Says Police Did Not Shoot Migrants'.
Reuters (25 August 2006), 'Spain To Call For More Help With Migrants'.
Reuters (21 November 2006), 'Europe, Africa Seek Joint Effort On Migrant Surge', Russian Embassy Statement (12 September 2001), by President Putin of Russia, on the Terrorist Acts in the US, Moscow, 12 September 2001, on webpage www.russianembassy.org/NEWS/VZRYV/001.htm.
Spiegel (14 March 2005), 'Why The EU Is Unconstitutional', *Der Spiegel*, no. 11/2005, on website www.spiegel.de/international/spiegel/0,1518,347059,00.html.
Standing Committee of Experts on International Immigration, Refugee and Criminal Law (2006), 'Comment On Proposal For A Regulation Establishing A Mechanism For The Creation Of Rapid Border Intervention Teams And Amending Council Regulation (EC) No. 2007/2004 As Regards That Mechanism (COM (2006) 401 final)', Utrecht: Standing Committee of Experts on International Immigration, Refugee and Criminal Law, on webpage www.commissie-meijers.nl.
Statewatch (2004), '"Killing Me Softly"? Improving Access To Durable Solutions: Doublespeak And The Dismantling Of Refugee Protection In The EU', July.
Sunday Times, Malta (19 November 2006), 'Euro-African Partnership On Migration In Sight'.
Tagesschau (17 October 2009), 'Klaus: Lissabon Kann Nicht Mehr Gestoppt Werden', on webpage www.tagesschau.de.
Telegraph (9 September 2003), 'Blunkett Plans To Send Asylum Seekers To Albania' on webpage www.telegraph.co.uk.
Telegraph (29 September 2009), 'EU Intervention In Irish Referendum "Unlawful"' on webpage www.telegraph.co.uk.
Ten Downing Street News (12 October 2001), 'The Prime Minister Tony Blair Has Made The Following Statement In Response To Terrorist Attacks In The United States,' on webpage www.number-10.gov.uk/output/page3420.asp.
Terra Actualidad (26 August 2006), 'F. Vega viaja martes Helsinki y Bruselas para pedir más medios UE'.
The Times (7 December 2001), 'Italy Blocks Agreement On Europe Warrant', on webpage www.thetimes.co.uk/article/0,,2001560011-2001564475,00.html.
The Times (16 September 2009), 'José Manuel Barroso Reelected European Commission President', on webpage www.telegraph.co.uk/news/worldnews/europe/eu/6198292/Jos-Manuel-Barroso-reelected-European-Commission-president.html.
UNHCR (1999), *Revised Guidelines In Applicable Criteria And Standards Relating To The*

Detention Of Asylum Seekers.
UNHCR (2001), *Asylum Applications In Industrialized Countries, 1980–1999* (UNHCR: Geneva).
UNHCR (2002), *Agenda For Protection*, A/AC/96/965/Add. 1, 26 June.
UNHCR (2003a), 'Summary Of UNHCR Proposals To Complement National Asylum Systems Through New Multilateral Approaches', UNHCR Working Paper, on webpage www.statewatch.org.
UNHCR (2003b), 'A Revised "EU Prong" Proposal', *UNHCR Working Paper*, on webpage www.statewatch.org.
UNHCR (2007), *Rescue At Sea: A Guide To Principles And Practice As Applied To Migrants And Refugees.* Geneva: UNHCR.
UN Press Release GA/9903 (12 September 2001), 'Opening Its Fifty-sixth Session, General Assembly Condemns Heinous Acts Of Terrorism Perpetrated In Host City And Washington', on webpage www.un.org/News/Press/docs/2001/ga9903.doc.htm.
United Nations Security Council (28 September 2001), *Resolution 1373.*
United Nations Security Council (2004), *Report By The Chair Of The Counter-terrorism Committee On The Problems Encountered In The Implementation Of Security Council Resolution 1373 (2001)*, S/2004/70, 26 January 2004.
UK Government (2003), *New International Approaches To Asylum Processing And Protection*, on webpage www.statewatch.org.
UK Cabinet Office and Home Office (2003), *A New Vision For Refugees*, on webpage www.proasyl.de/texte/Europe/union/2003/UK_NewVision.pdf.

Elite interviews, identity coded

A list with the names and the functions of the interviewees is available upon request.

European Commission

Date of interview	*Identity code*
14 July, 4:30 p.m.	COM1
25 May, 4:00 p.m.	COM2
27 May, 11:00 a.m.	COM3
1 June, 8.30 a.m.	COM4
16 June, 2:30 p.m.	COM5
23 June, 11:00 a.m.	COM6
23 June, 5:30 p.m.	COM7
26 May, 9:00 a.m.	COM8
26 April, 7:15 p.m.	COM9
19 May, 3:30 p.m.	COM10
4 June, 3:00 p.m.	COM11
4 June, 3:00 p.m.	COM12
3 June, 11:00 a.m.	COM13
15 July, 3:00 p.m.	COM14
28 June, 11:00 a.m.	COM15
5 July, 10:00 a.m.	COM16
26 July, 10:30 a.m.	COM17
26 July, 3:00 p.m.	COM18
15 July, 10:00 a.m.	COM19
5 May, 3:00 p.m.	COM20
24 June, 2:30 p.m.	COM21

24 June, 5:30 p.m.	COM22
10 June, 0:00	COM23
22 July, 6:00 p.m.	COM24
1 July, 7:00 p.m.	COM25

European Council

Date of interview	*Identity code*
24 May, 3:00 p.m.	CON1
14 June, 10:00 a.m.	CON2
28 June, 3:00 p.m.	CON3
7 June, 11:00 a.m.	CON4
7 June, 3:00 p.m.	CON5
3 June, 5:00 p.m.	CON6
26 May, 4:00 p.m.	CON7
30 June, 9:30 a.m.	CON8
30 June, 11:00 a.m.	CON9

European Parliament

Date of interview	*Identity code*
14 April, 1:00 a.m.	EP1
27 April, 4:00 p.m.	EP2
27 April, 6:00 p.m.	EP3
28 April, 4:00 p.m.	EP4
6 October, 8:30 p.m.	EP5

Permanent representations of the member states to the European Union

Date of interview	*Identity code*
28 June, 5:00 p.m.	PR1
17 June, 10:00 a.m.	PR2
1 June, 4:00 p.m., 2 June, 11:30 a.m.	PR3
25 May, 6:30 p.m., 24 June, 10:30 a.m.	PR4
18 June, 10:00 a.m., 18 June, 10:00 a.m.	PR5
30 June, 3:00 p.m.	PR6
4 May, 4:30 p.m.	PR7
1 June, 2:00 p.m.	PR8
18 May, 12:00 a.m., 2 June, 5:00 p.m.	PR9
4 June, 10:00 a.m.	PR10
21 June, 5:00 p.m.	PR11
24 May, 9:00 a.m.	PR12
17 June, 3:00 p.m., 15 June, 10:00 a.m.	PR13
21 June, 2:30 p.m.	PR14
16 June, 12:00 a.m.	PR15
30 June, 5:00 p.m.	PR16
23 June, 3:00 p.m.	PR17
25 June, 2:30 p.m.	PR18
17 June, 5:00 p.m.	PR19
29 June, 10:00 a.m.	PR20
21 June, 10:00 a.m.	PR21
14 June, 1:00 p.m.	PR22
15 July, 5:00 p.m.	PR23
25 June, 5:00 p.m.	PR24

18 June, 2:00 p.m.	PR25
14 June, 4:00 p.m.	PR26

NGOs and lobbying

Date of interview	*Identity code*
14 April, 3:00 p.m., 22 June, 3:00 p.m., 24 May, 11:00 a.m.	NGO1
23 April, 2:00 p.m.	NGO2
26 April, 2:00 p.m.	NGO3
30 April, 10:00 a.m.	NGO4
3 May, 9:00 a.m.	NGO5
18 May, 10:00 a.m.	NGO6
18 May, 6:00 p.m.	NGO7
21 May, 11:00 a.m.	NGO8
25 May, 9.30 a.m.	NGO9
5 July, 8:00 a.m.	NGO10
20 July, 2:00 p.m.	NGO11

IGOs

Date of interview	*Identity code*
21 May, 2:00 p.m., 11 June, Paris	IGO1
28 May, 5:00 p.m.	IGO2

Academics

Date of interview	*Identity code*
24 May, 6:00 p.m., 10 June, Paris	AC1
1 June, 10:00 a.m.	AC2

INDEX